An Analysis of Content of Student-Teaching Courses for Education of Elementary Teachers in State Teachers Colleges

ESTHER MARION NELSON, Ph.D.

TEACHERS COLLEGE, COLUMBIA UNIVERSITY

CONTRIBUTIONS TO EDUCATION, NO. 723

Bureau of Publications

TEACHERS COLLEGE, COLUMBIA UNIVERSITY

NEW YORK CITY   1939

Printed and Bound in the U. S. A. by
KINGSPORT PRESS, Inc., KINGSPORT, TENNESSEE

ACKNOWLEDGMENTS

ACKNOWLEDGMENT is made to Professor Thomas Alexander, chairman of my dissertation committee, who first suggested this study and whose constructive guidance, helpful counsel, and professional inspiration throughout the entirety of my graduate work have been invaluable in carrying this study to completion; and to Professors William C. Bagley and Florence B. Stratemeyer, members of my committee, whose valuable suggestions, kindly criticisms, and active encouragement have contributed so largely to the growth and development of this thesis.

Further expression of appreciation is due the administrators, faculty members, and student-teachers in state teachers colleges, and to all others in the teacher-education field who co-operated so willingly and freely in furnishing the data on which this study is based.

Special recognition is given to the faithful assistance rendered by Mary C. Olsen in preparing this material for publication, and to all others who have assisted in any way with the preliminary tabulation and typing.

E. M. N.

CONTENTS

*An Analysis
of Content of Student-Teaching Courses
for Education of Elementary Teachers
in State Teachers Colleges*

CHAPTER ONE

THE PROBLEM OF THIS STUDY

INTRODUCTION

VITAL and thought-provoking problems constantly confront those who are actively engaged in the education of teachers. New and changing conceptions of subject-matter, recent experiments in individual and group instruction, modern ideas of child growth and development, and progressive theories and principles of education have prompted much research in the field of elementary education. These research studies have brought to light a great need for more efficient teachers in our elementary schools. Our leading educators contend that the future success and effectiveness of our elementary schools will depend largely upon the nature and the quality of the preparation of each teacher. Bagley has stated that

The surest index to a nation's future is the degree in which its elementary schools touch and quicken the great masses of the people, and this depends not only upon the school building and school equipment that are provided, but also and far more fundamentally upon the competence of the teachers and the quality of the teaching. Among the first and foremost problems of a modern democracy, therefore, is the selection and training of its elementary school teachers.[1]

During recent years scientific investigations and experiments have been carried out in certain states, and extensive studies have been made in the hope that more effective teacher-education programs might be initiated and carried out. Our best teachers colleges and normal schools are searching and working continuously for more effective teacher-education—curricula that will develop and promote high academic and professional standards and that will prepare for the most successful teaching in the field.

Many of our professional schools for teachers are undergoing important and radical stages of transition induced by the application

[1] W. C. Bagley, "The Selection and Training of the Teacher." *New York State Education,* XIV:219–223, December 1926.

of progressive educational ideals, principles, and theories. Some are rapidly changing from two-year and three-year normal schools to four-year teachers colleges that offer prospective teachers opportunity to obtain richer academic backgrounds and more adequate professional preparation. Distinct changes and marked progress have been made during the past few decades, but as yet there are innumerable unsolved problems which must be dealt with in a serious and an intelligent manner before the most effective preparation of teachers can be brought about.

Reasons for Making This Study

This study has grown out of a specific and felt need on the part of some individuals who are genuinely concerned with one of the most important phases of the professional education of teachers for the elementary schools—that of student-teaching. There is a general agreement among educators today that student-teaching is of major importance in the education of elementary teachers. Some of the leading educators have expressed the conviction that supervised student-teaching is an almost indispensable factor in the professional preparation of undergraduate students. Mead has specified that initiating students into the teaching profession without supervised student-teaching is a wasteful process.[2]

If student-teaching is to serve most effectively in the preparation for efficient teaching in the field, there must be developed on the part of those who are responsible for the success of this work (1) consistently resourceful planning so as to secure the best results in the preparation of teachers; (2) highly intelligent understanding of the objectives to be attained in student-teaching, and of the means by which these can be accomplished; and (3) truly open-minded attitudes toward improvement.

In many cases both the scope and the richness of the content of student-teaching courses have been far too limited to prepare for effective teaching in the field. In different schools such deficiencies have been produced by one or more of the following causal factors: limited laboratory-school facilities and short periods of time for student-teaching; poor academic and cultural backgrounds on the part of student-teachers; low academic and professional standards on the part of some faculty members; inadequate backgrounds and

[2] A. R. Mead, *Supervised Student-Teaching*, p. 156. Johnson Publishing Company, 1930.

no special training for the job on the part of some critic teachers in the affiliated laboratory schools; biased viewpoints or lack of intelligent vision of the whole teaching situation on the part of administrators in charge of student-teaching; and lack of usable and worthy standards by which to compare and to evaluate. In the teacher-education field at the present time there are few scientific investigations and studies that can be used as a sound basis for determining and for enriching the content of student-teaching in elementary teacher-education curricula. In the absence of scientific knowledge many supervisors and critic teachers have based their standards and requirements for the conduct of student-teaching courses on those experiences that they as individuals considered essential to the preparation of elementary teachers, or on those activities that needed to be performed in a particular situation. Failure of the administrative, instructional, and supervisory staff members to establish a sound basis for determining the content of student-teaching has often produced confusion, misunderstanding, and neglect in the preparation of elementary teachers.

The large majority of critic teachers and supervisors are extremely conscientious in their efforts to give student-teachers the best preparation possible, but many are handicapped because they do not have a clear conception of (1) what should be included in the content of student-teaching courses; (2) the objectives and principles of student-teaching and how to carry these into effect; and (3) how to take advantage of opportunities for making the work more purposeful and valuable. Many have not had adequate professional preparation for critic work or for supervision of student-teaching in the elementary grades.

Statement of the Problem

This study attempts to discover and to analyze the experiences and contacts of student-teachers in connection with student-teaching courses in elementary teacher-education curricula of state teachers colleges; and, in the light of these findings, to draw such inferences as will help to answer the following questions:

1. What is the content of student-teaching in the primary and intermediate curricula of state teachers colleges?

2. How can the content of student-teaching be made to serve more effectively in the preparation of teachers for the elementary grades?

Determining Method of Approach

This study is based on the assumption that only through careful analysis, thorough knowledge, and clear understanding of existing conditions in the field of teacher-education can intelligent plans be made to bring about more effective preparation of teachers in the future.

The solution of the problem has, therefore, necessitated the setting up of techniques and procedures whereby we may secure a true picture of present practices in the content of student-teaching courses in elementary curricula of state teachers colleges.

With reference to the determination of the content of student-teaching, Charters has stated,

The content of student-teaching courses can be determined with considerable definiteness by the use of job-analysis techniques.[3]

This process would involve an analysis of the student-teacher's job, including the listing of student-teaching activities and procedures. Charters has further pointed out that

Equally important in determining the content of student-teaching courses is an analysis of the activities of teachers. For in developing a good teacher we are concerned not only with the kind of teacher that is to be graduated, but with the skill with which he carries on the duties of teachers.[4]

Mossman has enlarged upon the job-analysis techniques in her statement,

A job-analysis of the work of the teacher does not necessarily give enough attention to the vital thing a teacher does, e.g., guiding the process of learning as it takes place in varying children under varying conditions.[5]

According to this viewpoint, complicating factors that may influence the nature of the content of student-teaching would also have to be considered.

A combination of the two above procedures and suggestions has been used in this study. To simplify matters, the problem has been divided into the following working units:

1. Some administrative phases of teacher-education affecting the nature and scope of the content of student-teaching.

[3] W. W. Charters, "Techniques of Determining Content of Student-Teaching Courses." *Educational Administration and Supervision*, 15:343, May 1929.
[4] *Ibid.*, p. 346.
[5] Lois Coffey Mossman, "Introduction to Teaching." *Educational Administration and Supervision*, 16:503, October 1930.

2. Evaluation of student-teaching activities, procedures, and contacts contained in inquiry sheets and *Master Activity Check List*.

3. Student-teaching activities, difficulties, and problems reported as outstanding by student-teachers and laboratory-school faculty members.

4. Ways in which content of student-teaching courses could be enriched to help student-teachers more effectively, according to reports from student-teachers and laboratory-school faculty members.

5. Suggestions and recommendations proposed for enriching the content of student-teaching courses in state teachers colleges.

PROCEDURES AND SOURCES USED IN SECURING DATA

Numerous types of procedures and different sources of information were used in securing the data for this study.

1. *Personal Visits to Representative State Teachers Colleges*

Data for this study were secured partly by personal visits to state teachers colleges. During the years 1930 and 1931, ten months were devoted by the writer to making personal visits to state teachers colleges for the purpose of securing information relative to the content of student-teaching. Fifty-seven institutions offering four-year teacher-education curricula were visited. These schools were located in twenty-seven different states and represented a coast-to-coast geographical distribution. Some were selected because of their superior work in the field of teacher-education, but the majority were selected because of their accessibility to the itineraries decided upon.

The teacher-preparing institutions visited from which data were secured are listed below. (For brevity of terms in this study, these have all been referred to as "state teachers colleges.")

1. Alabama State Teachers College, Florence, Alabama
2. Arizona State Teachers College, Flagstaff, Arizona
3. Teachers College Department, University of Southern California, Los Angeles, California
4. Santa Barbara State College, Santa Barbara, California
5. San Diego State College, San Diego, California
6. San Francisco State College, San Francisco, California
7. San Jose State College, San Jose, California
8. Colorado State College of Education, Greeley, Colorado
9. Southern Illinois State Normal University, Carbondale, Illinois
10. Northern Illinois State Teachers College, De Kalb, Illinois

11. Ball State Teachers College, Muncie, Indiana
12. Indiana State Teachers College, Terre Haute, Indiana
13. Iowa State Teachers College, Cedar Falls, Iowa
14. Kansas State Teachers College, Pittsburg, Kansas
15. Western Kentucky State Teachers College, Bowling Green, Kentucky
16. Western Michigan State Teachers College, Kalamazoo, Michigan
17. Michigan State Normal College, Ypsilanti, Michigan
18. Minnesota State Teachers College, Duluth, Minnesota
19. Minnesota State Teachers College, Moorhead, Minnesota
20. Minnesota State Teachers College, St. Cloud, Minnesota
21. Minnesota State Teachers College, Winona, Minnesota
22. Southeast Missouri State Teachers College, Cape Girardeau, Missouri
23. Southwest Missouri State Teachers College, Springfield, Missouri
24. Nebraska State Teachers College, Kearney, Nebraska
25. New Jersey State Teachers College, Trenton, New Jersey
26. New Mexico Normal University, Las Vegas, New Mexico
27. New York State Teachers College, Buffalo, New York
28. East Carolina Teachers College, Greenville, North Carolina
29. North Dakota State Teachers College, Valley City, North Dakota
30. Bowling Green State University, Bowling Green, Ohio
31. East Central State Teachers College, Ada, Oklahoma
32. Southeastern State Teachers College, Durant, Oklahoma
33. Central State Teachers College, Edmond, Oklahoma
34. Southwestern State Teachers College, Weatherford, Oklahoma
35. Pennsylvania State Teachers College, Millersville, Pennsylvania
36. Pennsylvania State Teachers College, Shippensburg, Pennsylvania
37. Pennsylvania State Teachers College, West Chester, Pennsylvania
38. Tennessee State Teachers College, Johnson City, Tennessee
39. Tennessee State Teachers College, Memphis, Tennessee
40. Tennessee State Teachers College, Murfreesboro, Tennessee
41. West Texas State Teachers College, Canyon, Texas
42. East Texas State Teachers College, Commerce, Texas
43. North Texas State Teachers College, Denton, Texas
44. School of Education, University of Utah, Salt Lake City, Utah
45. Virginia State Teachers College, East Radford, Virginia
46. Virginia State Teachers College, Farmville, Virginia
47. Virginia State Teachers College, Fredericksburg, Virginia
48. Western Washington College of Education, Bellingham, Washington
49. Eastern Washington College of Education, Cheney, Washington
50. Central Washington College of Education, Ellensburg, Washington
51. Wisconsin State Teachers College, Eau Claire, Wisconsin
52. Wisconsin State Teachers College, La Crosse, Wisconsin
53. Wisconsin State Teachers College, Milwaukee, Wisconsin

54. Wisconsin State Teachers College, Oshkosh, Wisconsin
55. Wisconsin State Teachers College, River Falls, Wisconsin
56. Wisconsin State Teachers College, Superior, Wisconsin
57. James Ormond Wilson Teachers College, Washington, D. C.

2. *Personal Interviews with Student-Teachers and Laboratory-School Faculty Members in These State Teachers Colleges*

Many valuable data relative to the content of student-teaching in the different elementary curricula were secured by means of personal interviews. Student-teachers as well as laboratory-school staff members were interviewed for the purpose of obtaining a more accurate interpretation of the student-teaching situation. The student-teachers were frequently met in group conferences in order to conserve time; but the critic teachers, the supervisors of student-teaching, the principals of laboratory schools, and the directors of training were usually interviewed in private.

3. *Observation of Student-Teachers in Actual Classroom Situations in State Teachers Colleges*

Observations of more than five hundred student-teachers at work with children in actual classroom situations were made by the writer. Detailed records of these observations were kept on previously prepared blanks. Exact diaries were kept in a large number of cases for the purposes of diagnosing and discovering (1) the degree of difficulty encountered by student-teachers in certain activities and procedures, (2) the chief underlying causes of the difficulties encountered by student-teachers, (3) the amount of emphasis placed upon various types of activities and procedures, and (4) how the amount and kind of experiences that student-teachers obtained in each activity were affected by the organization and administration of the student-teaching. These records were especially helpful in the interpretation of data obtained from the student-teachers.

4. *Formulation and Checking of a Master List of Student-Teaching Activities*

One of the initial steps in the solution of the problem was to formulate a comprehensive student-teaching activity check list that might be used as a definite guide in securing data through interviews and observations. These data included activities and procedures designed to enrich the experiences of student-teachers in the elementary grades. In making the activity check lists the major activities were first determined. The specific activities and procedures through which each of these large major activities was carried out by student-teachers were then listed. It was decided that each activity should be listed but once, being placed under the most appropriate heading. This was a simple task during the early part of the investigation, but as the activities accumulated, considerable difficulty was encountered because of overlapping. These activities were carefully selected with reference to both difficulty and importance. The activities that were ranked low in both difficulty and value in the *Commonwealth Teacher-Training Study* by W. W. Charters and Douglas Waples were not included in this study.

The *Master Activity Check List,* the master list of student-teaching activities, was submitted personally to 450 laboratory-school faculty members, who evaluated most of the instructional and extra-class activities according to three definite criteria. The three criteria used in evaluating these activities and procedures are as follows:

1. What degree of difficulty is encountered by student-teachers in carrying out skillfully each activity and procedure?

2. How valuable is the activity or procedure in the preparation of teachers for the elementary grades, that is, how essential is it that student-teachers obtain institutional training in each activity?

3. How many contacts and how much experience do student-teachers obtain in connection with each activity, that is, to which of the activities or procedures do student-teachers devote most of their time, effort, and thought?

Each activity classified under the following major headings in the *Master Activity Check List* was evaluated according to the above three criteria:

A. Securing perspective and understanding of the elementary school curricula.

B. Acquiring adequate command of subject-matter in order to direct effectively the learning activities of the children.

C. Obtaining an understanding of individual differences of children by studying and analyzing factors that condition their learning.

D. Planning, studying, experimenting with, and using different types of educational procedures in directing the learning activities of children. (Applying methods of instruction.)

E. Helping children to build up and develop desirable personal and social habits, interests, appreciations, ideals, and attitudes.

F. Taking charge of activities in connection with school and class-room routine.

G. Planning, participating in, and directing children's extra-class activities.

H. Developing desirable teaching personality.

I. Making contacts with the staff-personnel and with the administrative phases of elementary schools.

J. Making contacts with community activities.

K. Making professional contacts outside the teachers colleges.

The approximate per cent of student-teachers who obtained actual experience in the activities listed under each of the following major headings has been computed in this study:

Activities in connection with directed observation.

Activities involved in lesson planning.

Activities involved in finding and assembling materials and information.

Activities pertaining to teaching a variety of subjects.

Activities in connection with school and classroom routine.

Contacts with the staff-personnel and with the administrative phases of elementary schools.

Contacts of student-teachers with community activities.

Professional contacts outside the teachers colleges.

5. *Formulation and Compilation of Inquiry Sheets Relative to Student-Teaching.*

Five inquiry sheets—designated as Forms A, B, C, D, and E—were used to secure further data essential to the solution of the problem.*

Form A pertained to some phases of administration that might to some degree influence the content of student-teaching, namely, (1) purposes and objectives of the student-teaching courses, (2) length of each elementary teacher-education curriculum, (3) college years in which student-teachers usually were scheduled for major student-teaching courses, (4) the amount and distribution of time provided for the various phases of student-teaching, (5) amount and types of laboratory-school facilities, (6) personnel responsible for student-

* These forms are contained in Appendix C in Volume II which is on file in manuscript form in the Library at Teachers College, Columbia University.

teaching courses, (7) supervisory loads of the critic teachers, (8) use made of laboratory-school facilities for directed observation, (9) use made of laboratory-school facilities for directed teaching, and (10) the general plan of inducting student-teachers into teaching.

As a first step in the procedure of securing data from each school, this form was filled out by the person in charge of student-teaching during a personal conference with the author. This practice was found necessary because student-teaching is conducted under varied and complicated conditions in many state teachers colleges.

Form B called for information regarding administrative phases of student-teaching which affected each student-teacher. Most of the questions were the same in content as those in *Form A,* but they were directed to and filled out by student-teachers in the elementary teacher-education curricula at the close of their student-teaching experiences.

Forms C and D were directed to both student-teachers and laboratory-school faculty members. These forms requested information relative to different types of activities and contacts involved in the content of student-teaching. They also called for personal reactions toward certain practices in connection with student-teaching.

Form E was so constructed as to secure from both student-teachers and laboratory-school faculty members their understanding and interpretation of student-teachers' difficulties and problems, and their suggestions and recommendations for enriching the content of student-teaching so as to help student-teachers more effectively.

Inquiry sheets directed to faculty members were submitted by the author in person, and filled out during personal interviews. Those directed to student-teachers were submitted by the author or by the person in charge of student-teaching in each school, and filled out at the close of final student-teaching courses.

There were 2,550 student-teachers and 475 laboratory-school faculty members who answered questions in the inquiry sheets pertaining to the administration and organization of student-teaching; and 2,550 student-teachers and 480 laboratory-school faculty members —423 critic teachers [6] and supervisors of student-teaching, and 57 directors of training [7]—who answered questions relative to the ac-

---

[6] The term "critic teacher" refers to persons performing the double function of teaching children and supervising student-teachers.

[7] The term "director of training" refers to the person at the head of the laboratory-school department in each state teachers college.

tivities, contacts, and problems involved in the content of student-teaching.

6. *Correspondence with Student-Teachers and Faculty Members in State Teachers Colleges*

Following the personal visits to the different teacher-preparing institutions, some additional materials were obtained by correspondence with faculty members and student-teachers.

Data secured from reports filled out by student-teachers were often clarified and interpreted by means of correspondence with the director of training or with some other person in charge of student-teaching.

7. *Study of Catalogs, Manuals, and Reports from State Teachers Colleges*

Bulletins, manuals, reports, and college catalogs were obtained from the schools visited and were consulted as sources for comparison of data secured on the administrative phases of the elementary teacher-education curricula.

8. *Investigation of Literature in the Field of Teacher-Education*

Books, surveys, research studies, articles, and reports dealing with student-teaching in the elementary grades were also examined in order to secure further data in verification of certain statements and conclusions.

9. *First-hand Experiences of the Writer as a Supervisor of Student-Teachers*

Experiences of the writer as a supervisor of student-teachers in the Idaho State Normal School at Lewiston, Michigan State Normal College at Ypsilanti, and the New York State Normal School at Oneonta have been helpful in the organization and interpretation of data used in this study.

JUSTIFICATION OF PROCEDURES USED IN SECURING DATA

The personal visits, the private interviews and conferences, and the direct observations were invaluable aids in this study because through these procedures, in comparison with the questionnaire method or other forms of correspondence, it was possible to secure from each school visited data which were (1) more nearly uniform in interpretation, (2) fuller in content, and (3) more reliable than those which might have been obtained by other methods because each item could be checked and rechecked from several sources. Errors and discrepancies in the reports were checked and corrected through personal conferences during visitations and by correspondence. Many of the conclusions and statements were further verified by means of college catalogs, reports, manuals, and bulletins.

SUMMARY

This study is based on the assumptions that (1) the future success and effectiveness of our elementary schools depend largely upon the nature and quality of the preparation of the teachers; (2) student-teaching is of major importance in the education of elementary teachers; (3) the degree of real value to be derived from student-teaching is in direct ratio to the quantity and quality of its content; and (4) only through careful study and thorough understanding of existing conditions in teacher-education can intelligent plans be made to bring about more effective preparation of teachers.

The major problem of this study was to make an analysis of the content of student-teaching in elementary teacher-education curricula in state teachers colleges; and, in light of these findings, to suggest ways in which it could be made to function more effectively in the preparation of teachers for the elementary grades. The great influence of certain conditioning factors upon the effectiveness of student-teaching made imperative an investigation of these factors, as a basis for recommendations of means by which the content of student-teaching may be enriched.

Data for this study were obtained partly by means of personal visits to fifty-seven teacher-preparing institutions, located in twenty-seven different states and representing a coast-to-coast geographical distribution. From these institutions there were 2,550 student-teachers and 480 laboratory-school faculty members who filled out inquiry sheets pertaining to the content of student-teaching; and 450 laboratory-school faculty members who evaluated the student-teaching activities contained in the *Master Activity Check List*.

Discrepancies in the data obtained were checked and corrected through such means as personal interviews during visitations, correspondence, and teachers college catalogs. Observation of student-teachers at work in actual classroom situations, investigation of the literature in the teacher-education field, and first-hand experience as a supervisor of student-teachers furnished additional data for the conclusions and recommendations made in this study.

CHAPTER TWO

SOME ADMINISTRATIVE PHASES OF TEACHER-EDUCATION
AFFECTING THE NATURE AND SCOPE OF THE CONTENT
OF STUDENT-TEACHING

WHY is the content of student-teaching so rich and extensive in some state teachers colleges and so meager and limited in others? The answer to this question requires intelligent understanding of all the factors that influence the content of student-teaching. It necessitates thorough investigation of the whole organization of teacher-education in the different state teachers colleges.

Some of the vital administrative problems that confront administrators and faculty members in connection with the content of student-teaching courses have been taken into consideration in this study. How does the length of the teacher-education curriculum affect the content of student-teaching? How does the time element in student-teaching courses affect the content? How is the content of student-teaching affected by the amount, type, and use made of laboratory-school facilities? How is the content of student-teaching affected by the personnel of the laboratory schools? In order to answer these problems one must have a knowledge of the organization of student-teaching in each state teachers college.

LENGTHS OF PRIMARY AND INTERMEDIATE TEACHER-EDUCATION CURRICULA

The fifty-seven teacher-preparing institutions that participated in this study offered advanced four-year teacher-education curricula, but as late as 1932 approximately 80% of these institutions required a minimum of only two years or less of academic and professional preparation above the high school level for certification to teach in the elementary grades. Table I presents the minimum number of years of college preparation which these different state teachers colleges required for certification to teach in the elementary grades in 1932.

TABLE I

Minimum Number of Years of College Preparation Required by 57 State
Teachers Colleges for Certification to Teach in the Elementary Grades

Minimum Number of Years	Number of State Teachers Colleges
Two years (or less).............................	46
Three years.....................................	6
Four years......................................	5

College Years in Which Student-Teachers Were Scheduled for Major Student-Teaching Courses

In forty-six state teachers colleges the students who desired teaching certificates at the completion of two-year elementary teacher-education programs were required to take student-teaching courses during the second year. Eighteen of these schools offered observation and participation courses during the first college year or during the early part of the second year, and twenty-eight required additional student-teaching courses during the fourth year for the completion of the four-year curricula in elementary education. The students who enrolled for the regular three-year and four-year curricula from the beginning of the teacher-preparatory work, however, postponed the major student-teaching courses to the third and fourth years.

Major student-teaching courses were usually completed during the fourth year in teachers colleges requiring a minimum of four years of college preparation, and during the third year in schools requiring a minimum of three years.

Number of Hours of Student-Teaching Required in State Teachers Colleges

There was a wide range of practice in the number of hours[1] of student-teaching required in the different state teachers colleges that participated in this study. The median teachers college required approximately 180 hours of student-teaching in the two-year programs, and a total of about 240 hours for the completion of four-year elementary curricula.[2] There were extreme variations from these medians in both directions, the range being from 60 to 432 hours in two-year programs and from 120 to above 500 hours in four-year

---

[1] The term "hour" is equivalent to one clock hour consisting of sixty minutes.

[2] The term "elementary curricula" in this study refers to the primary and intermediate teacher-education programs.

elementary curricula. These figures include the total number of hours required for all courses in directed observation, participation, and teaching under the direction of regular critic teachers or supervisors of student-teaching.

In the two-year programs in forty-six state teachers colleges, approximately 35% of the primary and 39% of the intermediate departments required 120 hours or less of student-teaching; about 22% of the primary and 20% of the intermediate required about 180 hours of student-teaching; and approximately 33% of the primary and 30% of the intermediate required more than 180 hours of student-teaching.

The median teachers college required sixty hours of advanced student-teaching during the fourth year of the four-year elementary

TABLE II

Number of Hours of Student-Teaching Observation, Participation, and Teaching—Required in Two-Year Programs and in Four-Year Curricula

Number of Hours	Number of State Teachers Colleges			
	Two-Year Elementary Programs		Four-Year Elementary Curricula	
	Primary	Intermediate	Primary	Intermediate
490– up............	....	....	1	1
470–489............	....	....	1	1
450–469............	....	....	....	....
430–449............	1	1	1	1
410–429............	....	....	1	1
390–409............	....	....	1	1
370 389............	....	....	....	....
350–369............	3	2	5	3
330–349............	1	1	2	1
310–329............	....	....	3	3
290–309............	2	2	3	3
270–289............	....	....	2	3
250 269............	....	1	1	1
230–249............	7	6	7	7
210–229............	....	....	1	1
190–209............	1	1	1	1
170–189............	10	9	12	14
150–169............	2	2	2	2
130–149............	3	3	2	2
110–129............	11	13	6	6
90–109............	4	4	....	....
70 –89............	....	....	....	....
50– 69............	1	1	....	....
Total..............	46	46	52	52

curricula for students who had completed major student-teaching courses in the two-year programs. In the four-year curricula in fifty-two state teachers colleges, approximately 10% of both the primary and the intermediate departments required about 120 hours of student-teaching; approximately 23% of the primary and 27% of the intermediate required about 180 hours; and approximately 54% of the primary and 50% of the intermediate required from 240 to over 500 hours of student-teaching. There was a tendency in most state teachers colleges to require a greater number of hours of student-teaching in the four-year elementary curricula than in the two-year programs. Table II presents the number of hours of student-teaching—observation, participation, and teaching—required in the two-year elementary programs of forty-six state teachers colleges and in the four-year elementary curricula of fifty-two state teachers colleges in 1932.

Five state teachers colleges required from 60 to 180 hours of additional student-teaching when the student-teachers were assigned to the off-campus laboratory schools or to the co-operative schools of urban and rural communities.

The state teachers colleges that had the most nearly adequate [3] laboratory-school facilities required the greatest number of hours of directed observation, participation, and responsible teaching on the part of the student-teachers, and those with the least adequate facilities required the smallest number of hours. In some institutions where the laboratory-school facilities were very limited, the student-teachers of necessity devoted a large proportion of their student-teaching time to the observation of one another's work.

LENGTH OF TIME PROVIDED EACH DAY FOR MAJOR STUDENT-TEACHING COURSES

There was considerable variation of practice among the different state teachers colleges as to the number of hours assigned to student-teaching each day. In some schools all student-teaching courses were scheduled for one or two hours a day; in other schools courses in observation and participation were scheduled for one hour a day, while major student-teaching or responsible teaching

---

[3] The term "adequate laboratory-school facilities" indicates that the teachers college has expanded its practice facilities to such an extent as to provide ample opportunities for all its students to observe master teachers at work with children, to participate in teaching situations, and to do responsible teaching.

was scheduled for half day or whole day; and in still other schools all student-teaching courses were scheduled for half day or whole day. Some of the teachers colleges that allotted one hour a day to student-teaching in the campus laboratory schools provided for half-day teaching in the off-campus and affiliated schools; other institutions that conducted student-teaching courses on the one-hour-a-day or half-day basis in the campus laboratory schools conducted them on the whole-day basis in the co-operative laboratory schools of urban and/or rural communities.

The teachers colleges that provided the most nearly adequate laboratory-school facilities tended to devote longer periods of time each day to major student-teaching courses than did those with limited facilities.

Table III summarizes, for forty-six state teachers colleges that offered two-year elementary programs and eleven state teachers colleges that offered three-year and four-year curricula as minimum requirements for elementary teachers, the average lengths of time a day for which major student-teaching courses were scheduled in 1932.

TABLE III

Average Lengths of Time a Day for Which Major Student-Teaching Courses Were Scheduled in Different Types of Laboratory Schools in Various Elementary Curricula of 57 State Teachers Colleges

Average Length of Time a Day for Which Major Student-Teaching Courses Were Scheduled	Number of State Teachers Colleges							
	Campus Laboratory Schools				Off-Campus and Affiliated*			
	Teachers Colleges That Offered Two-Year Elementary Programs		Teachers Colleges That Required Minimum of Three or Four Years		Teachers Colleges That Offered Two-Year Elementary Programs		Teachers Colleges That Required Minimum of Three or Four Years	
	P**	I**	P	I	P	I	P	I
1 to 2 hours	27	28	6	6	6	7	5	5
½ day (2½ to 4 hours daily)....	16	15	3	3	12	12	3	3
All day or whole day	3	3	2	2	5	4	2	2
Total....	46	46	11	11	23	23	10	10

* Affiliated = Co-operative schools of urban and/or rural communities which are used for student-teaching purposes.
** P = Primary; I = Intermediate.

Major student-teaching courses conducted in the campus laboratory schools were usually scheduled for the following lengths of time a day:

(1) One to two hours a day in 57.9% of the primary and 59.6% of the intermediate departments of the state teachers colleges.

(2) Half day (2½ to 4 hours a day) in 33.3% of the primary and 31.6% of the intermediate departments of the state teachers colleges.

(3) Whole day in 8.8% of the teacher-preparing institutions.

Major student-teaching courses conducted in the off-campus laboratory schools and in the affiliated schools of urban and/or rural communities, by the state teachers colleges that utilized cooperative laboratory schools for student-teaching purposes, were usually scheduled for the following lengths of time a day:

(1) One to two hours a day in 33.3% of the primary and 36.3% of the intermediate departments of these state teachers colleges.

(2) Half day to four hours a day in 45.5% of both the primary and the intermediate departments.

(3) Whole day in 21.2% of the primary and 18.2% of the intermediate departments.

NUMBER OF HOURS OF STUDENT-TEACHING REQUIRED UNDER DIFFERENT TYPES OF ORGANIZATION IN FIFTY-SEVEN STATE TEACHERS COLLEGES

The amount of student-teaching required in any of the state teachers colleges was largely determined by the type of organization under which student-teaching was conducted. In the state teachers colleges that conducted student-teaching on the one-hour- and two-hours-a-day plans, the range was from 60 to 180 hours in the two-year elementary programs; and approximately 59% of the primary and 64% of the intermediate departments required a total of only 120 hours or less of student-teaching in the two-year programs. For the completion of four-year curricula most of these teachers colleges required an additional 60 to 90 hours of student-teaching, the exact amount being determined by each institution. Such a policy usually placed the range in requirements for the four-year curricula between 120 and 270 hours, with the median of these teachers colleges requiring 180 hours of student-teaching.

In state teachers colleges that conducted student-teaching on the half-day plan the range in requirements was from 135 to 432 hours of student-teaching in the two-year programs, and in many cases with an addition of 60 to 90 hours in the four-year curricula. The median of these teachers colleges required about 234 hours of student-teaching in the two-year elementary programs and more than 300 hours in the four-year elementary curricula.

In state teachers colleges that offered whole-day student-teaching, the range in the two-year elementary programs was from 300 to 336 hours in the campus laboratory schools and up to 450 hours in

TABLE IV

Number of Hours of Student-Teaching Required under Different Types of Organization in 57 State Teachers Colleges

Number of Hours of Student-Teaching	Number of Teachers Colleges That Offered Two-Year Elementary Programs						Number of Teachers Colleges That Required a Minimum of Three or Four Years for Elementary Curricula							
	1-2 Hours*		½ Day*		All Day*		1-2 Hours		½ Day		All Day		Total	
	P	I	P	I	P	I	P	I	P	I	P	I	P	I
490- up..	..	..	..	..	..	..	..	..	..	..	1	1	1	1
470-489..	..	..	..	..	..	..	..	..	1	1	..	..	1	1
450-469..	..	..	..	..	..	..	..	..	..	..	..	..	..	..
430-449..	..	..	1	1	..	..	..	..	..	..	..	..	1	1
410-429..	..	..	..	..	..	..	..	..	..	..	..	..	..	..
390-409..	..	..	..	..	..	..	..	..	1	1	..	..	1	1
370-389..	..	..	..	..	..	..	..	..	..	..	..	..	..	..
350-369..	..	..	3	2	..	..	..	..	..	..	1	1	4	3
330-349..	..	..	..	..	1	1	..	..	..	..	..	..	1	1
310-329..	..	..	..	..	..	..	..	..	..	..	..	..	..	..
290-309..	..	..	..	..	2	2	..	..	1	1	..	..	3	3
270-289..	..	..	..	..	..	..	2	2	..	..	..	..	2	2
250-269..	..	..	..	1	..	..	..	..	..	..	..	..	..	1
230-249..	..	..	7	6	..	..	1	..	..	..	..	..	8	6
210-229..	..	..	..	..	..	..	..	..	..	..	..	..	..	..
190-209..	..	..	1	1	..	..	..	..	..	..	..	..	1	1
170-189..	7	6	3	3	..	..	2	3	..	..	..	..	12	12
150-169..	2	2	..	..	..	..	..	..	..	..	..	..	2	2
130-149..	2	2	1	1	..	..	..	..	..	..	..	..	3	3
110-129..	11	13	..	..	..	..	1	1	..	..	..	..	12	14
90-109..	4	4	..	..	..	..	..	..	..	..	..	..	4	4
70- 89..	..	..	..	..	..	..	..	..	..	..	..	..	..	..
50- 69..	1	1	..	..	..	..	..	..	..	..	..	..	1	1
Total..	27	28	16	15	3	3	6	6	3	3	2	2	57	57

* 1-2 Hours = All student-teaching courses scheduled for one or two hours a day.
* ½ Day = Major student-teaching courses scheduled for half day.
* All Day = All major student-teaching courses scheduled for whole day. (Average: 5 hours a day.)

the affiliated urban and rural schools; and from 336 to more than 500 hours in the four-year elementary curricula. The median of these teachers colleges required more than 300 hours in the two-year programs and more than 360 hours in the four-year curricula.

The teachers colleges that organized the major student-teaching courses in units of half days and whole days usually required the greatest number of hours of student-teaching.

Table IV presents the number of hours of student-teaching required, under the different types of student-teaching organization in the two-year programs of forty-six state teachers colleges and in the three-year and four-year curricula offered by eleven state teachers colleges, as minimum requirements for elementary teachers in 1932.

AMOUNT OF CREDIT ALLOWED FOR STUDENT-TEACHING COURSES

The amount of credit required for student-teaching varied widely in the different state teachers colleges. Table V presents the total number of term-hours of credit allowed for all scheduled courses in directed observation, participation, and teaching in the two-year programs of forty-six state teachers colleges and in the four-year curricula of fifty-two state teachers colleges in 1932.

TABLE V

Number of Term-Hours of Credit Allowed for Student-Teaching Courses— Directed Observation, Participation, and Teaching—in Two-Year Programs and in Four-Year Elementary Curricula

Number of Term-Hours * of Credit	Number of State Teachers Colleges			
	TWO-YEAR ELEMENTARY PROGRAMS		FOUR-YEAR ELEMENTARY CURRICULA	
	Primary	Intermediate	Primary	Intermediate
28–30.................	....	....	1	1
25–27.................	....	....	....	....
22–24.................	....	....	3	3
19–21.................	....	....	5	3
16–18.................	4	3	9	10
13–15.................	11	10	9	9
10–12.................	10	10	17	18
7– 9.................	15	17	5	5
4– 6.................	5	5	3	3
1– 3.................	1	1	....	....
Total..............	46	46	52	52

* 3 term-hours are equivalent to 2 semester-hours of credit.

The median teachers college required about ten term-hours of credit in student-teaching in the two-year programs, and approximately thirteen term-hours in the four-year elementary curricula. There were wide variations from these medians, the range being from three to eighteen term-hours in two-year programs, and from five to thirty term-hours in four-year elementary curricula.

AMOUNT OF TIME DEVOTED TO ATTENDANCE AT STUDENT-TEACHING CONFERENCES

Provision was usually made for both group and individual conferences. In most of the state teachers colleges, the time devoted to these conferences was supplementary to the prescribed number of hours for student-teaching and carried no additional credit.

Group Conferences

The number of group conferences and the time devoted to each varied greatly in the different state teachers colleges. Table VI

TABLE VI

Approximate Amounts of Time That Student-Teachers, under Various Types of Student-Teaching Organization, Devoted to Attendance at Group Conferences Conducted by Different Faculty Members or by Student-Teachers

Length or Frequency of Group Conferences	Number of State Teachers Colleges																	
	1–2 Hours						½ Day						All Day					
	DT*	DS*	SS*	CI*	CT*	ST*	DT	DS	SS	CI	CT	ST	DT	DS	SS	CI	CT	ST
Daily	..	..	..	..	1	..	..	..	..	..	1	..	..	..	..	..	1	..
Four hours a week	..	..	..	..	..	..	..	..	..	..	1	..	..	..	..	..	..	..
Three hours a week	..	..	..	..	1	..	..	..	1	..	2	1	..	..	..	..	..	..
Two hours a week	..	2	1	..	9	..	2	1	..	..	5	..	..	1	1	..	1	..
One hour a week	8	5	6	1	18	4	5	2	5	..	9	3	..	1	2	..	4	..
Thirty minutes a week	..	..	1	..	1	1	..	..	..	..	..	..	..	..	..	..	..	..
Two hours a month	2	2	..	..	1	2	2	..	..	..	..	..	..	..	..	..	..	..
One hour a month	1	..	1	..	..	..	2	..	..	..	..	..	1	1	..	..	..	..
Four hours a semester	..	1	..	..	..	..	..	..	..	..	..	..	..	..	..	..	..	..
Three hours a semester	1	..	..	..	..	..	..	..	..	..	..	..	..	..	..	..	..	..
Two hours a term	4	..	..	..	..	..	..	..	..	..	..	..	..	..	..	..	..	..
Two hours a semester	1	1	..	..	..	..	1	1	..	..	..	..	1	..	..	..	..	..
One hour a term	4	..	..	..	..	..	1	1	..	..	..	..	2	..	..	..	..	..
One hour a semester	2	..	..	..	..	..	1	..	..	..	..	..	..	..	..	..	..	..
When needed or as occasion arises	8	..	5	4	2	2	4	..	..	3	1	4	2	1	..	2	..	3
Upon request	2	..	..	7	..	..	..	..	..	4	..	..	..	..	..	2	..	..

* DT = Directors of training or principals of laboratory schools; DS = Department supervisors; SS = Supervisors of special subjects; CI = College instructors; CT = Critic teachers; ST = Student-teachers.

shows the approximate amount of time that student-teachers, working under the different student-teaching plans, devoted to attendance at group conferences.

The median teachers college required student-teachers to attend group conferences for approximately two hours each week—one hour under the direction of regular critic teachers and another hour conducted by the director of training, supervisors of student-teaching, college instructors, or supervisors of special subjects. The median director of training held group conferences with the student-teachers for approximately two hours each semester. In 10.7% of the state teachers colleges the critic teachers held group conferences with student-teachers from three to five hours a week; in 26.8%, about two hours a week; in 55.4%, about one hour a week; and in 7.1%, thirty minutes or less each week.

Individual Conferences

Individual conferences between laboratory-school faculty members and student-teachers were held in the fifty-seven teacher-

TABLE VII

Frequency of Individual Conferences Held between the Various Faculty Members and Student-Teachers under Different Forms of Student-Teaching Organization

Frequency of Individual Conferences	Number of State Teachers Colleges														
	1–2 HOURS					½ DAY					ALL DAY				
	DT*	DS*	SS*	CI*	CT*	DT	DS	SS	CI	CT	DT	DS	SS	CI	CT
Daily	..	..	..	..	7	..	..	..	..	8	..	..	..	..	3
Three a week	..	..	..	..	1	..	..	..	..	2	..	..	..	..	1
Two a week	..	2	..	..	3	..	..	..	..	2	..	..	..	..	1
One hour a week	..	1	..	1	5	..	..	..	..	1	..	..	..	..	..
Thirty minutes a week	..	1	3	..	3	..	..	2	..	1	..	..	..	..	..
Four a semester	..	..	..	..	..	..	1	1	..	..	..	..	..	..	..
Three a semester	1	..	..	..	..	..	..	..	..	..	1	..	..	..	..
Two a term	3	..	..	..	4	1	..	..	..	..	1	..	..	..	..
One a term	2	..	..	..	..	..	..	..	3	..	..	..	..	..	..
One a semester	1	..	..	..	..	..	..	..	..	..	..	..	..	..	..
Both prior to and subsequent to assignments of student-teachers to any grade, subject, or special work	6	2	3	6	..	4	1	3	..	..	1	..	1	..	..
When necessary to preparation for teaching; and after observing the student-teachers teach	6	4	6	5	9	5	3	4	4	3	1	4	2	2	1
When needed or as occasion arises	12	1	..	9	1	8	..	..	6	1	2	..	..	2	3
Upon request	2	..	2	8	..	..	..	..	3	..	..	..	..	1	..
Occasionally	..	..	..	3	..	..	..	..	1	..	..	..	..	..	..

* DT = Directors of training or principals of laboratory schools; DS = Department supervisors; SS = Supervisors of special subjects; CI = College instructors; CT = Critic teachers.

preparing institutions that participated in this study. In approximately 32% of the schools, the critic teachers held daily conferences with their student-teachers. It was usually possible for student-teachers to secure individual conferences with college instructors and with supervisors of special subjects, if help was required in connection with some particular phase of subject-matter or specialized instruction. The type of individual conferences held most frequently were those in which faculty members approached student-teachers after having observed their work in regular teaching situations in the laboratory schools. A greater amount of time was devoted to individual conferences between critic teachers and student-teachers in schools that organized student-teaching in units of half days and whole days, than in those that organized student-teaching on the one-hour- or two-hours-a-day basis.

Table VII presents the frequency of individual conferences held between faculty members and student-teachers under one hour and two-hours-a-day, half-day, and all-day student-teaching plans.

LABORATORY-SCHOOL FACILITIES

There was a consensus of opinion among teachers college administrators that sufficient laboratory facilities for observation, participation, and teaching are highly essential in working out an effective program of student-teaching for the elementary grades. The data in this study revealed that a large proportion of the teachers colleges had very limited laboratory facilities.

Of the fifty-seven state teachers colleges studied, approximately 42.0% conducted all the student-teaching for the elementary grades in campus laboratory schools or in local schools so closely connected with the colleges as to constitute an equivalent situation; and about 58.0% utilized, in addition to the campus laboratory schools, urban and/or rural schools not under the direct control of the colleges. Three of these institutions used the campus laboratory schools almost exclusively for observation and participation, while the actual teaching by students was done in urban and rural schools of local and neighboring communities. Five institutions used off-campus laboratory schools in addition to the campus and affiliated schools. In these off-campus schools the critic teachers were employed by the college and were regular members of the teachers college faculty, but the actual buildings and equipment were largely financed and controlled by local communities.

Table VIII shows the per cent of forty-six teachers colleges offering two-year programs and of fifty-two teachers colleges providing four-year elementary curricula that utilized each of the different types of laboratory-school facilities in 1932.

TABLE VIII

Per Cent of 52 State Teachers Colleges That Utilized the Different Types of Laboratory-School Facilities in Two-Year Programs and in Four-Year Elementary Teacher-Education Curricula

Type of Facilities	Per Cent of State Teachers Colleges	
	TWO-YEAR PROGRAMS	FOUR-YEAR CURRICULA
Campus (only)....................................	50.0	40.4
Campus and affiliated* schools of local, neighboring, and distant communities.............................	43.5	50.0
Campus, off-campus, and affiliated* schools of local and other communities................................	6.5	9.6

* Affiliated = Co-operative schools of urban and/or rural communities.

In some of the state teachers colleges where all the student-teaching was carried out in the campus schools, there were more students who should have been scheduled in student-teaching courses than there were children in the laboratory schools. In many schools the ratio of pupils to student-teachers fell far below the standards set up by the American Association of Teachers Colleges, and in some of the schools it was so low that a question arose regarding the effectiveness of the student-teaching.

The state teachers colleges that utilized effectively the urban and rural schools of local and neighboring communities, in addition to the campus laboratory schools, had the most nearly adequate practice facilities for the preparation of teachers for the elementary schools. These institutions offered the greatest amount of directed observation, participation, and teaching, and required the largest number of hours of credit in student-teaching.

THE PERSONNEL RESPONSIBLE FOR STUDENT-TEACHING COURSES

The directors of training or the directors of student-teaching were largely responsible for assigning student-teachers to departments or grades in the laboratory schools. (In some schools the deans or the heads of the departments of education acted as directors of student-teaching.) Assistant directors or department supervisors of student-teaching, principals of laboratory schools, and critic teachers assisted in making these assignments in some teachers colleges.

In each teachers college, the director of training or the director of student-teaching assumed certain supervisory responsibilities. The critic teachers and supervisors of student-teaching, however, assumed most of the responsibility for the work of the student-teachers in the primary and intermediate grades after assignments had been made. Instructors in special subjects—for example, art, music, and physical education—assisted with the supervision of special subjects in many of the laboratory schools. Table IX summarizes the data relative to which persons supervise the work of the student-teachers in the elementary grades during student-teaching courses in fifty-seven state teachers colleges.

TABLE IX

Persons, Besides the Directors of Training, Responsible for the Student-Teachers' Work after They Have Been Assigned to Student-Teaching

Persons Responsible	Number of Schools
Critic teachers (including those classified as training teachers, supervising teachers, room supervisors, and critics)	20
Departmental supervisors or assistant directors of student-teaching and critic teachers in the campus laboratory schools; and supervisors of student-teaching, principals, and either critic teachers or regular grade teachers in co-operative schools of urban and/or rural communities	14
Departmental supervisors or assistant directors of training or principals of laboratory schools and critic teachers	10
Critic teachers in the campus laboratory schools; and supervisors of student-teaching, principals, and either critic teachers or regular grade teachers in the co-operative schools of urban and/or rural communities	7
Grade supervisors and assistant room teachers	3
Critic teachers in the campus laboratory schools; and superintendents of schools and grade teachers in the co-operative schools	2
Critic teachers in the campus laboratory schools; and supervisors of student-teaching and principals of public schools in the field	1
Total number of state teachers colleges	57

According to findings in this study, the laboratory-school staff is largely responsible for the student-teaching work in elementary teacher-education curricula of state teachers colleges. These data show a lack of integration between the subject-matter and the laboratory-school departments.

The Supervisory Load of the Campus-School Critic Teacher

There were wide variations in the number of student-teachers assigned to critic teachers in the campus laboratory-schools of different state teachers colleges. In some schools the supervisory loads were extremely heavy, while in others they were comparatively light. These loads were largely determined by the facilities available for student-teaching. They were heaviest in schools having limited facilities and lightest in schools providing ample facilities.

Since student-teachers were scheduled in student-teaching from one hour a day in some schools to all day in others, a unit had to be employed in this study which would make the supervisory loads comparable. The unit adopted was one student-teacher assigned to do student-teaching under the direction of a critic teacher for 180 clock hours a year or for one hour a day for one school year.

To the median critic teacher was assigned the equivalent of twelve student-teachers a year, each doing 180 hours of student-teaching under the critic's direction. There were extreme variations from this median: to one-fourth of the critics were assigned from nineteen to forty such student-teachers a year; to one-half, from eight to eighteen such student-teachers; and to one-fourth, from two to seven such student-teachers. To critic teachers in a few teachers colleges were assigned as many as thirty to forty such student-teachers a year, while to some critics in other teachers colleges were assigned as few as two, three, and four student-teachers. In addition to the above numbers of regular student-teachers, some critics were responsible for from one to thirty-seven scheduled observers.

The findings in this study show that, in comparison with the standards of the American Association of Teachers Colleges, more than one-half of the campus-school critic teachers had supervisory loads far greater than one individual could effectively handle when also assuming responsibility for a classroom of children.

Use Made of Laboratory-School Facilities for Directed Observation

The median student-teacher scheduled for one or two hours a day in the required student-teaching courses had observed the work of four different critic teachers and supervisors in one school and in three grades. The median student-teacher scheduled for half day in major teaching courses had observed the work of five different critic teachers and supervisors in two schools and in four grades.

The median student-teacher scheduled for all-day teaching had observed the work of six different critic teachers and supervisors in two schools and in five grades. Tables X, XI, and XII show the wide range of variation from these medians.

Table X summarizes the replies from 2,311 student-teachers who answered the question, "In how many different schools have you observed during student-teaching courses, including directed observation, participation, and teaching?"

TABLE X

Per Cent of Student-Teachers under Different Administrative Organizations Who Had Observed in Each of the Specified Numbers of Schools

Number of Schools	Per Cent of Student-Teachers						Total
	1–2 Hours		½ Day		All Day		
	P	I	P	I	P	I	
7 and up..........	1.9	1.5	....	.3	1.3	3.4	1.3
6...............	1.3	2.2	2.7	2.6	2.6	2.3	2.0
5...............	.8	.4	2.4	2.3	1.3	2.3	1.2
4...............	2.1	2.4	4.1	5.2	15.4	8.0	3.6
3...............	7.9	7.7	16.8	18.4	23.1	23.8	11.8
2...............	30.9	27.4	38.6	32.2	29.5	34.1	31.2
1...............	55.1	58.5	35.4	39.0	26.8	26.1	48.8

TABLE XI

Per Cent of Student-Teachers under Different Administrative Organizations Who Had Observed in Each of the Specified Total Numbers of Grades

Total Number of Grades	Per Cent of Student-Teachers						Total
	1–2 Hours		½ Day		All Day		
	P	I	P	I	P	I	
12...............	.7	.9	....	....	....	2.4	.6
11...............	....	....	....	.9	....	....	.1
10...............	.3	.3	.3	1.1	....	....	.4
9...............	.9	1.4	1.5	2.3	1.2	....	1.3
8...............	4.9	5.4	8.8	10.0	2.5	7.1	6.4
7...............	3.9	3.8	3.2	5.0	5.0	3.5	4.0
6...............	9.7	11.3	12.6	12.0	31.3	33.3	12.6
5...............	5.1	6.2	11.9	12.6	11.3	8.3	7.9
4...............	14.7	11.3	20.5	17.5	7.5	4.8	14.3
3...............	29.2	24.3	18.4	16.9	38.7	40.7	24.9
2...............	18.7	22.0	13.4	14.9	2.5	....	17.1
1...............	11.9	13.1	9.4	6.9	....	....	10.3

The reports from 2,302 student-teachers relative to the number of grades in which they had observed during directed observation, participation, and teaching courses are summed up in Table XI.

Table XII shows the distribution of replies from 2,289 student-teachers who answered the question, "How many different demonstration teachers, supervisors, and critic teachers have you observed?"

TABLE XII

Per Cent of Student-Teachers under Different Administrative Organizations Who Had Observed the Work of Each of the Specified Numbers of Supervisors, Critics, and Demonstration Teachers

Number of Supervisors, Critics, and Demonstration Teachers	Per Cent of Student-Teachers						Total
	1–2 Hours		½ Day		All Day		
	P	I	P	I	P	I	
12 and up........	3.5	3.0	4.1	4.6	....	....	3.4
11..............	.3	.6	1.2	....	....	....	.4
10..............	2.8	2.3	1.8	2.6	11.7	11.9	3.0
9..............	2.9	2.3	6.9	7.8	....	4.8	4.0
8..............	4.7	4.3	8.8	7.5	12.9	13.1	6.2
7..............	4.5	5.2	7.4	6.0	2.6	2.4	5.2
6..............	13.1	12.5	10.7	8.6	23.4	19.0	12.5
5..............	8.5	6.6	10.9	12.9	12.9	14.3	9.3
4..............	15.3	15.9	16.6	18.1	15.6	10.7	15.9
3..............	21.5	20.5	10.7	12.9	6.5	14.3	17.6
2..............	13.5	17.5	12.7	12.1	9.1	9.5	14.1
1..............	8.5	8.7	8.0	6.0	5.2	....	7.7
0..............	.9	.7	.3	.8	....	....	.7

Use Made of Laboratory-School Facilities for Directed Teaching

The median student-teacher scheduled for one or two hours a day in major teaching courses had done responsible teaching in one school, in two different grades, under the direction of two different regular critic teachers, and had taught classes of twenty-four pupils. The median student-teacher scheduled for half day in major teaching courses had done responsible teaching in one school, in two grades, under the direction of two different regular critic teachers, and had taught classes of twenty-seven pupils. The median student-teacher scheduled for all day had done responsible teaching in two different schools, in two different grades, under the direction of two different critic teachers, and had taught classes of thirty-two pupils.

There were wide variations from these medians, as indicated in Tables XIII, XIV, XV, XVI, and XVII. Some of these student-teachers had also done responsible teaching under the direction of a departmental supervisor of student-teaching, and many had done so under the direction of one or more supervisors of special subjects, for example, music, art, and physical education.

Table XIII summarizes the reports from 2,338 student-teachers relative to the question, "In how many different schools have you done actual teaching during your student-teaching courses?"

TABLE XIII

Per Cent of Student-Teachers under Different Administrative Organizations Who Had Done Directed Teaching in Each of the Specified Numbers of Schools

Number of Schools	Per Cent of Student-Teachers						
	1–2 Hours		½ Day		All Day		Total
	P	I	P	I	P	I	
4	.5	.4	....	.6	....	....	.4
3	2.5	1.9	3.4	4.5	12.5	13.3	3.5
2	32.4	28.8	38.6	35.6	56.3	55.6	34.4
1	64.6	68.9	58.0	59.3	31.2	31.1	61.7

Table XIV presents the distribution of answers that were given by 2,352 student-teachers to the question, "In how many different grades did you obtain actual teaching experience during your student-teaching courses?"

TABLE XIV

Per Cent of Student-Teachers under Different Administrative Organizations Who Had Obtained Actual Teaching Experience in Each of the Specified Numbers of Grades

Number of Grades	Per Cent of Student-Teachers						
	1–2 Hours		½ Day		All Day		Total
	P	I	P	I	P	I	
8	....	.4	....	.3	....	2.2	.3
7	....	.3	....	.3	....	....	.1
6	.9	2.3	.3	.6	3.7	3.3	1.4
5	.3	.3	.6	2.3	....	2.2	.7
4	5.3	3.8	6.9	8.9	7.4	5.6	5.7
3	24.0	22.3	25.9	19.5	37.0	30.0	23.8
2	38.8	39.3	36.5	39.6	39.5	43.3	38.9
1	30.7	31.3	29.8	28.5	12.4	13.3	29.1

The student-teachers who had taught in five or more different grades had usually done so under the direction of critic teachers who had charge of two or more grades.

The student-teachers were also asked to give the number of regular critic teachers and supervisors who had directed their work in teaching. They were requested to count only those to whom they had been responsible for definite work in a grade. This did not include supervisors of special subjects. Table XV presents the distribution of answers that were given by 2,336 student-teachers to

TABLE XV

Per Cent of Student-Teachers under Different Administrative Organizations Who Had Done Actual Teaching under the Direction of Each of the Specified Numbers of Critic Teachers and Supervisors

Number of Critic Teachers and Supervisors	Per Cent of Student-Teachers						Total
	1–2 Hours		½ Day		All Day		
	P	I	P	I	P	I	
7.................	....	.1	....	....	....	....	.04
6.................	.1	.1	....	....	....	....	.1
5.	.5	.5	....	....	....	....	.3
4.................	4.9	4.8	7.2	10.3	4.9	1.1	5.9
3.................	18.4	19.8	22.1	21.0	18.5	23.3	19.9
2.................	44.3	42.5	40.2	40.2	56.9	55.6	43.4
1.................	31.8	32.2	30.5	28.5	19.7	20.0	30.3

TABLE XVI

Per Cent of Student-Teachers under Different Administrative Organizations Who Had Taught Each of the Specified Average Numbers of Pupils during the Early Part of Student-Teaching

Average Number of Pupils	Per Cent of Student-Teachers						Total
	1–2 Hours		½ Day		All Day		
	P	I	P	I	P	I	
40 and up........	1.4	2.9	1.4	2.8	3.7	6.6	2.3
35–39............	1.1	.7	3.4	3.9	5.0	7.7	2.1
30–34............	2.2	2.9	5.1	5.7	12.5	15.4	4.2
25–29............	11.1	9.9	9.3	12.8	17.5	15.4	11.1
20–24............	16.3	20.8	8.8	9.1	6.3	9.9	14.9
15–19............	21.6	18.7	19.8	18.8	18.8	15.4	19.7
10–14............	26.0	23.4	29.5	28.4	22.5	19.7	25.7
5– 9............	16.7	18.7	20.4	15.6	11.3	7.7	17.2
0– 4............	3.6	2.0	2.3	2.9	2.5	2.2	2.8

the question, "Under the direction of how many regular critic teachers and supervisors of student-teaching, not including supervisors of special subjects, have you done actual teaching during student-teaching courses?"

Table XVI summarizes the distribution of answers that were given by 2,345 student-teachers to the question, "How many pupils did you have in your classes or in your group when you first began to teach during the early part of student-teaching?"

The student-teachers were also requested to answer the question, "Of how many pupils did the largest class that you taught during student-teaching consist?" Table XVII presents the distribution of replies that were given by 2,343 student-teachers.

TABLE XVII

Per Cent of Student-Teachers under Different Administrative Organizations Whose Largest Class during Student-Teaching Courses Consisted of Each of the Specified Numbers of Pupils

Number of Pupils	Per Cent of Student-Teachers						Total
	1–2 Hours		½ Day		All Day		
	P	I	P	I	P	I	
50 and up	.3	.7	.6	.6	....	....	.5
45–49	.7	1.8	2.0	2.2	1.3	2.2	1.6
40–44	4.1	5.3	4.1	5.0	11.3	17.8	5.4
35–39	9.3	8.4	12.8	12.6	21.5	13.3	10.6
30–34	11.2	13.2	22.9	24.0	31.6	31.1	16.9
25–29	19.7	17.7	15.9	17.3	17.8	28.9	18.4
20–24	24.7	22.1	11.3	17.6	15.2	6.7	19.8
15–19	10.0	12.6	12.8	9.5	....	....	10.4
10–14	15.1	14.3	13.3	8.4	1.3	....	12.5
5–9	4.6	3.8	4.1	2.8	....	....	3.7
0–4	.3	.1	.3	....	....	....	.2

SUMMARY

An investigation of certain administrative phases as conditioning factors influencing the content of student-teaching was made imperative in this study. The many complexities of teacher-education presupposed the interrelation of a variety of factors, each of which was conditioned upon the others; but so involved a process rendered analysis difficult. In many institutions the administrative phases obviously constituted causal factors of great significance to the quality and quantity of the content of student-teaching. While all observations made throughout this survey must include others, certain conclusions regarding the extent of these administrative influences were inescapable. Although practices and opinions relative to the administration of student-teaching varied greatly among the different teacher-preparing institutions, some conditions were found to be prevailing.

1. In 1932 approximately 80% of the fifty-seven state teachers colleges participating in this study required a minimum of two years or less of academic and professional preparation beyond the high school level for certification of elementary teachers.

2. There was a direct relation between the types of student-teaching organization and the total number of hours of scheduled student-teaching. A larger number of hours was usually devoted to supervised student-teaching—directed observation, participation, and teaching—when conducted on the half-day and whole-day basis than on the one-hour-a-day plan. There were also larger total requirements in the number of clock hours of student-teaching for those enrolled in the four-year curricula than for those in the two-year programs.

3. Laboratory facilities for student-teaching were inadequate in most state teachers colleges. This lack of technical equipment amounted in many instances to extremely overcrowded conditions. The teachers colleges that furnished the most nearly adequate laboratory facilities tended to devote longer periods of time each day to major student-teaching courses; required a larger number of clock hours of student-teaching; and provided for greater amounts of well-directed observation and responsible teaching than did those with limited laboratory facilities. In the schools that offered the most nearly complete facilities, the major student-teaching courses were conducted on the half-day and whole-day plans rather than on the one-hour-a-day basis.

4. In the median teachers college, the amount of time devoted to attendance at conferences was in addition to that allotted to student-teaching courses in the teachers college curriculum and was divided rather uniformly between individual and group conferences. The tendency was to require attendance at group conferences and to allow individual conferences great latitude in matters of length, frequency, and purpose.

5. The major responsibility for the direction of student-teaching in elementary teacher-education curricula was assumed by the

laboratory-school staff members. In consequence of deficient integration between the laboratory-school and the college departments in
many teacher-preparing institutions, the student-teaching contacts
were greatly limited.

6. In comparison with the standards of the American Association
of Teachers Colleges, excessive supervisory loads were carried by
a majority of the critic teachers in the campus laboratory schools.

7. An investigation was also conducted to discover how extensively the laboratory-school facilities were used for directed observation and directed teaching. In the institutions that were most
completely equipped with laboratory facilities and that required the
greatest amounts of student-teaching, student-teachers were offered
the greatest variety of opportunities for directed observation and
responsible teaching in different schools and in different grades, and
were afforded contacts with the greatest number of critic teachers,
supervisors, and children.

CHAPTER THREE

EVALUATION OF STUDENT-TEACHING ACTIVITIES, PROCEDURES,
AND CONTACTS CONTAINED IN INQUIRY SHEETS AND
MASTER ACTIVITY CHECK LIST

INTRODUCTION

THE synthesis of effective teacher-education should be preceded by an intelligent analysis of teaching into its component parts, so that due emphasis may be placed upon the most important and the most difficult phases thereof. Such an analysis must necessarily reveal that a major part of teaching consists of activities and procedures which vary widely as to nature, purpose, difficulty, and significance. The most effective teacher-education program must therefore make ample provision for the acquisition of a thorough background preparation and the development of technical skill in all the contacts, activities, and procedures which are fundamental to the success of a teacher—educationally, socially, and in all other capacities.

Of the many activities and procedures that have been compiled in various studies for teachers in the elementary field, only those should be included in the content of student-teaching that are sufficiently difficult and important to warrant consideration. Great care should be exercised in the selection and elimination of activities to permit the devotion of the greatest amounts of time and energy to the most essential ones. Hence it became a major purpose of this study to determine which activities were the most important and the most difficult, so that these might be assured inclusion in the content of student-teaching.

Questions comprised in the inquiry sheets elicited a great deal of valuable information and a wide variety of personal reactions. Answers to these questions were obtained from a total of 2,550 student-teachers and 480 laboratory-school faculty members, although there were very few individual questions to which all of these students and faculty members made reply. In order that comparisons of the trends of thought discussed in the following chapters may be properly weighted, statistical tables have been prepared. These tables show the number of student-teachers and laboratory-school faculty members, within each administrative group, who participated in this study by filling out inquiry sheets relative to student-teaching. Table XVIII-A presents the number of participants among primary and intermediate student-teachers in the two-year, three-year, and four-year curricula under each of the different forms of student-teaching organization—one-hour- or two-hours-a-day, half-day, and whole-day. The number of participants among laboratory-school faculty members, under each of the specified forms of student-teaching organization, are presented in Table XVIII-B.

TABLE XVIII–A

Number of Student-Teachers under Each of the Specified Forms of Student-Teaching Organization Who Participated in This Study

Forms of Student-Teaching Organization	Number of Student-Teachers				
	Two-Year Programs		Three-Year and Four-Year Curricula		Total
	Primary	Intermediate	Primary	Intermediate	
1–2 Hours..........	490	492	301	306	1589
½–Day............	241	252	136	132	761
All-Day............	51	51	50	48	200
Total...........	782	795	487	486	2550

TABLE XVIII–B

Number of Laboratory-School Faculty Members under Each of the Specified Forms of Student-Teaching Organization Who Participated in This Study

Forms of Student-Teaching Organization	Number of Laboratory-School Faculty Members			
	Critic Teachers and Supervisors		Directors of Training	Total
	Primary	Inter-mediate		
1–2 Hours.................	122	132	33	287
½–Day..................	64	61	18	143
All-Day..................	23	21	6	50
Total.................	209	214	57	480

ACTIVITIES IN CONNECTION WITH DIRECTED OBSERVATION

Carefully directed observation of expert teaching is an important phase of student-teaching courses. Activities in connection with directed observation, therefore, should be classified as an essential part of the content of student-teaching for the elementary grades.

Some of the activities listed in this study in connection with directed observation have been classified under the following headings:

A. Making definite preparation for observation.

B. Using manuals and guides during observation periods.

C. Writing up the results of observations.

There were 2,383 student-teachers, including 1,190 from the primary and 1,193 from the intermediate and upper grades, who answered questions pertaining definitely to directed observation. The distribution of these replies is presented in Table XIX.

A. *Making Definite Preparation for Observation*

During the early part of student-teaching, approximately 72% of the primary and 78% of the intermediate student-teachers prepared work for some observation periods; about 55% of the primary and 62% of the intermediate student-teachers made some definite preparation for most of the class periods in which they observed critic teachers and supervisors at work with children. During the latter part of student-teaching, approximately 59% of the primary and 66% of the intermediate student-teachers prepared work for some observation periods; about 43% of the primary and 52% of the intermediate student-teachers made some definite preparation for most of the class periods in which they observed critic teachers and supervisors teach children. Approximately 25% of the student-teachers had never made any definite preparation for observation periods during student-teaching courses. Table XIX shows the per cent of student-teachers, under the different forms of student-teaching organization, who made definite preparation for observation work.

A larger per cent of the student-teachers majoring in intermediate grades than of those majoring in primary grades made definite preparation for observation work. This was partly due to the fact that many of the student-teachers in the intermediate grades did not have the necessary background in subject-matter to enable them to observe intelligently the class work without definite preparation preceding the observation period.

A variety of activities served as preliminary approaches to the work of observation. Of these preparatory activities, those that were most widely used—either singly or in combination with others—are listed below according to the frequency with which they were mentioned by both student-teachers and critic teachers:

1. Interviewing critic teachers relative to the specific subject-matter and educational procedures to be observed.
2. Studying both subject-matter and educational procedures to be observed.
3. Becoming familiar with materials of instruction to be used in connection with demonstration lessons.
4. Reading professional books and articles that relate to the points to be observed in connection with child study and teaching.
5. Planning and studying techniques that might be used in connection with specific teaching situations.
6. Writing plans for the lessons, activities, and units to be taught by critic teachers or supervisors.
7. Studying lesson plans prepared by critic teachers for the specific demonstration work.
8. Studying outlines in student-teaching manuals or in directed observation guides.
9. Preparing definite outlines to be used as guides while observing.
10. Formulating questions relative to the different teaching situations to be observed.

B. *Using Manuals and Guides during Observation Periods*

Many different types of manuals, check lists, and guides were used by student-teachers in connection with directed observation in the different state teachers colleges. Standard observation guides or check lists were used by all the student-teachers in a few institutions. In some laboratory schools the student-teachers were encouraged to adapt observation guides to specific situations, for example, to particular groupings of children, to materials and methods of instruction, to teaching and learning environment, and to their own individual needs. A large proportion of the student-teachers reported, however, that they had never used any definite observation guides in connection with student-teaching courses.

Approximately 38% of the primary and 34% of the intermediate student-teachers used student-teaching manuals, directed observation sheets, check lists, or other definite observation guides when they observed classwork during the early part of student-teaching. About 34% of the primary and 29% of the intermediate student-teachers continued to use observation guides during the more advanced or latter part of student-teaching. Such helps were used more extensively by those majoring in the primary departments than by those in the intermediate departments; a situation which resulted partly from the fact that in the primary grades greater emphasis was

TABLE

Per Cent of Student-Teachers under Different Administrative Organizations
if They Obtained Actual Practice in Each of

Activities in Connection with Observation	1–2 Hours			
	Yes		No	
	P	I	P	I
A. *Making definite preparation for observation*				
1. Making some definite preparation for most of the class periods in which they observed supervisors, critics, and demonstration teachers teach children during:				
a. Early part of student-teaching, under the direction of a regular supervisor or critic teacher...	53.3	63.0	37.9	34.0
b. Latter part of student-teaching..............	40.9	50.7	51.1	43.2
2. Making careful preparation for some lessons, units, or activities which they observed during:				
a. Early part of student-teaching, under the direction of a regular supervisor or critic teacher...................................	69.4	77.0	28.3	20.3
b. Latter part of student-teaching.............	54.1	61.3	38.6	34.6
B. *Using manuals and guides during observation periods*				
1. Following manuals or directed observation sheets when they observed during:				
a. Early part of student-teaching, under the direction of a regular critic teacher..............	37.9	33.3	55.5	63.8
b. Latter part of student-teaching.............	34.7	28.9	58.0	64.3
2. Observing daily class work for specific techniques.	87.6	88.1	9.2	9.4
3. Having definite things to look for during most of the class periods in which they observed critic teachers or supervisors teach children....................	82.9	84.6	12.8	12.1
C. *Writing up the results of observations*				
1. Writing up the results of their observations after they observed critic teachers, supervisors, and demonstration teachers teach children during:				
a. Early part of student-teaching..............	57.1	58.4	35.2	36.0
b. Latter part of student-teaching.............	44.0	43.0	47.1	49.5
2. Writing up the results of their observations after they observed student-teachers..............	42.1	43.2	49.5	50.7

placed upon child study and teaching environment, while in the intermediate and upper grades more time was devoted to materials of instruction. The per cents of student-teachers under different forms of student-teaching organization who used definite observation guides are presented in Table XIX.

A large proportion of the student-teachers who never used regular or definite observation guides, nevertheless, observed classwork for

XIX

Who Answered "Yes" or "No," or Who Failed to Answer at All When Asked the Activities in Connection with Observation

Per Cent of Student-Teachers										
½ Day				All Day				Total		
Yes		No		Yes		No		Yes	No	Blank
P	I	P	I	P	I	P	I			
56.2	61.7	40.1	34.1	62.5	61.1	33.8	27.7	58.7	35.8	5.5
46.4	54.8	50.4	40.0	43.8	48.9	48.8	36.7	47.3	46.2	6.5
75.4	80.0	20.9	16.5	77.5	80.0	18.8	15.5	75.0	22.0	3.0
63.3	71.3	33.5	23.5	75.0	76.7	21.3	20.0	62.0	33.0	5.0
38.4	33.5	57.9	62.3	43.8	34.4	50.0	55.5	35.9	59.3	4.8
33.8	29.3	61.6	65.6	33.8	25.6	60.0	66.7	31.5	62.1	6.4
92.3	91.3	5.7	5.9	96.3	96.7	2.5	1.1	89.6	7.7	2.7
89.1	88.3	7.7	8.9	85.0	87.0	11.5	10.0	85.4	11.1	3.5
68.5	68.7	29.7	27.7	67.5	73.3	28.8	23.3	61.9	32.9	5.2
40.7	38.5	55.0	57.5	50.0	46.7	40.0	47.8	42.7	50.4	6.9
42.1	38.5	53.6	56.1	43.8	43.3	46.2	44.4	42.0	51.2	6.8

specific techniques and definite points. Approximately 90% of the student-teachers indicated that they had observed some classwork for specific techniques, and about 85% specified that they usually watched for some definite points when they observed critic teachers or supervisors teach children.

The points or the things to be observed by student-teachers were most frequently determined by critic teachers or through the cooperative efforts of both critic teachers and student-teachers. In a few laboratory schools, however, they were largely determined by directors of training or by departmental supervisors; and in these schools most of the student-teachers were required to follow definitely prepared observation outlines. Table XX summarizes the distribution of replies that were given by 2,383 student-teachers to whom the following question was submitted: "Who usually determined what you should look for and observe in the classroom during directed observation periods?"

TABLE XX

Per Cent of Student-Teachers under Different Administrative Organizations Who Indicated Each of the Persons or Groups Responsible for Determining the Points that Student-Teachers Should Look for and Observe during Directed Observation Periods

Persons or Groups Responsible for Determining the Points that Student-Teachers Should Look for and Observe during Directed Observation Periods	Per Cent of Student-Teachers								Sum Total
	1–2 Hours		½ Day		All Day		Total		
	P	I	P	I	P	I	P	I	
1. Critic teachers or supervisors and student-teachers (jointly).....	33.6	30.6	37.6	35.2	43.8	47.8	35.5	33.3	34.4
2. Critic teachers.......	32.3	35.4	31.2	33.8	30.0	28.9	31.7	34.5	33.1
3. Student-teachers.....	10.8	12.9	12.0	12.9	12.5	8.9	11.3	12.6	11.9
4. Directors of training..	4.7	4.8	6.0	5.0	....	....	4.8	4.5	4.7
5. Department supervisors and principals....	4.0	3.1	3.4	3.3	12.5	10.0	4.4	3.6	4.0
6. No definite person was designated..........	14.6	13.2	9.8	9.8	1.2	4.4	12.3	11.5	11.9

C. *Writing up the Results of Observations*

The median student-teacher obtained some experience in writing reports subsequent to observing critic teachers and supervisors at work with children. Approximately 61.9% of the student-teachers wrote reports for some lessons, units, or activities which they observed during the early part of student-teaching; and 42.7% did so for some class periods during the latter part of student-teaching. (See Table XIX, item C.)

In the inquiry sheets was included a list of procedures that might be used by student-teachers in writing up or in recording the classroom activities observed. The student-teachers were requested first to mark the procedures which they had used in recording their observations during the early part of student-teaching; and then to check the ones which they had employed during the more advanced work. They were also asked to add procedures not listed. The reports are summarized in Tables XXI and XXII.

The procedures for recording observations during the early part of student-teaching were sometimes quite different from those of the

TABLE XXI

Per Cent of Student-Teachers Who Had Used Each of the Specified Procedures In Writing up Their Observations of Teaching and Learning Situations during Early Part of Student-Teaching

Procedures	Per Cent of Student-Teachers		
	Primary	Intermediate	Total
1. Outlining procedures used in the teaching and learning situations observed................	36.6	38.1	37.4
2. Writing summaries of the work observed.....	31.6	35.1	33.4
3. Following directed observation guides, check lists, and manuals in writing up the work observed, i.e.:			
a. Special or general outlines or observation guides..................................	31.8	28.8	30.3
b. Directed observation sheets or student-teaching manuals......................	22.8	18.8	20.8
c. Check lists...........................	20.3	18.1	19.2
4. Listing or stating outcomes.................	32.5	28.0	30.3
5. Writing observation reports in the form of diaries, narratives, or essays...............	32.2	28.2	30.2
6. Writing lesson plans, i.e.:			
a. Brief plans of the work observed.........	22.5	27.6	25.1
b. Detailed or partly detailed.............	15.4	18.8	17.1
c. Follow-up lessons......................	15.1	11.7	13.4
d. Similar lesson plans...................	11.6	12.9	12.3
7. Outlining subject-matter...................	16.0	34.0	25.0
8. Writing personal reactions to the teaching and learning situations observed................	25.7	18.5	22.1
9. Writing constructive criticisms on the teaching and learning situations observed............	20.9	18.5	19.7
10. Writing informal notes....................	10.7	7.9	9.3

more advanced stages. *Outlining activities* and *writing summaries of work observed* were used most frequently in recording observations during the early part of student-teaching, while *writing constructive criticisms* and *personal reactions* were used most frequently during the more advanced observation work. Observation aids, such as check lists, directed observation guides, outlines, and student-teaching manuals were used most frequently during the early part of student-teaching.

A larger per cent of the student-teachers majoring in the intermediate departments than of those in the primary departments outlined subject-matter and methods of instruction. A larger per cent of those majoring in the primary departments wrote constructive criticisms and personal reactions, used directed observation guides and manuals, and listed outcomes.

TABLE XXII

Per Cent of Primary and Intermediate Student-Teachers Who Had Used Each of the Specified Procedures in Recording Class Work Observed during Latter Part of Student-Teaching

Procedures	Per Cent of Student-Teachers		
	Primary	Intermediate	Total
1. Writing constructive criticisms on the teaching and learning situations observed; suggesting possible improvements......................	42.2	41.0	41.6
2. Writing personal reactions to the teaching and learning situations observed................	41.0	39.2	40.1
3. Listing or stating outcomes.................	36.8	34.0	35 4
4. Outlining or writing up procedures and techniques observed.......................	30.4	34.1	32.2
5. Outlining subject-matter observed...........	16.2	34.4	25.3
6. Writing summaries of the work observed.....	22.3	25.7	24.0
7. Following directed observation guides, check lists, and manuals in writing up the work observed, i.e.:			
a. Special or general outlines..............	18.9	15.8	17.4
b. Directed observation sheets or manuals...	17.1	13.5	15.3
c. Check lists...........................	15.1	11.9	13.5
8. Writing lesson plans, i.e.:			
a. Brief plans of the work observed.........	16.3	18.1	17.2
b. Follow-up lessons....................	11.8	11.2	11.5
c. Similar lesson plans....................	9.5	8.8	9.2
d. Detailed or partly detailed plans.........	7.5	10.6	9.1
9. Writing observation reports in form of diaries, narratives, or essays......................	15.8	14.0	14.9
10. Writing informal notes....................	5.9	2.9	4.4

PART II

STUDENT-TEACHING ACTIVITIES CONTAINED IN THE MASTER ACTIVITY CHECK LIST

The *Master Activity Check List* comprises a large and representative group of student-teaching activities, which 450 faculty members rated according to the three criteria listed on page 8. Table XXIII presents the mean of the ratings for each of these activities.

KEY AND DIRECTIONS FOR READING TABLE XXIII

Difficulty   indicates *degree of difficulty* encountered by student-teachers in carrying out skillfully each activity and procedure.

Symbols used in evaluating each activity.
1   indicates high degree of difficulty.
2   indicates medium degree of difficulty.
3   indicates low degree of difficulty.

Value   indicates *degree of need for institutional training* in each activity or procedure on the part of student-teachers preparing to teach in the elementary grades.

Symbols used in evaluating each activity.
1   indicates that institutional training is highly essential.
2   indicates that institutional training is reasonably essential.
3   indicates that institutional training is slightly essential.
4   indicates that institutional training is not essential.

Experience   indicates the *number of contacts and amount of experience* that student-teachers obtain in each activity during student-teaching courses in the elementary grades.

Symbols used in evaluating each activity.
1   indicates that the largest number of contacts and the greatest amount of experience are obtained in this activity.
2   indicates that an average number of contacts and a medium amount of experience are obtained in this activity.
3   indicates that few contacts and very little experience are obtained in this activity.
4   indicates that no contacts and no experience are obtained in this activity during student-teaching.

1–2 Hours   indicates that student-teachers obtain their major student-teaching work in units of one hour or two hours a day.

½ Day   indicates that student-teachers obtain their major student-teaching work in units of half days.

All Day   indicates that student-teachers obtain their major student-teaching work in units of whole days.

P   indicates primary student-teachers (Grades 1, 2, 3).

I   indicates intermediate student-teachers (Grades 4, 5, 6, sometimes 7, 8).

Student-Teaching Activities

A. *Securing perspective and understanding of elementary school curricula*
   1. Examining and studying existing courses of study, subject-matter outlines, texts, reference books, and supplementary materials, for the purpose of determining essentials that should be studied by the children in a grade . . . .
   2. Making general outlines of subjects as a whole for a grade . . . .
   3. Planning and working out developmental units of instruction . . . .
   4. Thinking out each day's work in terms of large units of instruction . . . .
   5. Building up the curriculum from day to day through the combined initiative and co-operation of pupils and teacher . . . .
B. *Acquiring adequate command of subject-matter in order to direct effectively the learning activities of the children*
   1. Planning the selection and organization of subject-matter . . . .
   2. Arranging sequence of topics and units of subject-matter to be studied by the children . . . .
   3. Finding and assembling materials and information
      a. Reading as a means of securing information . . . .
      b. Making efficient use of sources of supply, e.g., libraries, publishing houses, business and industrial concerns, transportation companies, geographical and historical societies, social and civic organizations, museums and art galleries
      c. Interviewing people for the purpose of securing information relative to problems in connection with student-teaching . . . .
      d. Visiting places of interest for the purpose of securing information relative to the work in student-teaching (Visiting places of industrial, commercial, scientific, geographical, historical, educational, civic, social, recreational, and scenic interest) . . . .
      e. Collecting and assembling appropriate specimens and suitable materials needed for activities . . . .
   4. Making annotated bibliographies for subjects, units of work, problems or projects, and activities . . . .
   5. Selecting and adapting subject-matter and activities
      a. Selecting particular bodies of facts which might be used in connection with units of instruction under different conditions of pupil groupings . . . .
      b. Selecting the most educative activities . . . .
      c. Selecting and adapting subject-matter in daily work with reference to:
         (1) Children's abilities (Recognizing individual differences in chronological and mental ages, achievements, and special talents) . . . .
         (2) Children's interests (Taking into consideration their experiences, environments, seasons of the year, etc.) . . . .
         (3) Children's needs (Taking into account their emotional, ethical, intellectual, physical, and social needs) . . . .
         (4) Objectives set up . . . .

XXIII

Check List

| DIFFICULTY | | | | | | VALUE | | | | | | EXPERIENCE | | | | | |
| 1–2 Hours | | ½ Day | | All Day | | 1–2 Hours | | ½ Day | | All Day | | 1–2 Hours | | ½ Day | | All Day | |
P	I	P	I	P	I	P	I	P	I	P	I	P	I	P	I	P	I
2.2	2.1	2.3	2.1	2.2	2.3	2.3	2.1	2.1	2.0	2.2	2.0	2.6	2.8	2.6	2.5	2.5	2.1
..	..	..	..	..	..	..	..	..	..	..	..	3.5	3.3	3.4	3.7	3.3	3.3
1.0	1.0	1.1	1.0	1.1	1.1	1.1	1.1	1.0	1.1	1.0	1.0	1.8	2.1	1.4	1.6	1.3	1.4
1.2	1.1	1.2	1.2	1.4	1.2	1.1	1.1	1.1	1.1	1.0	1.0	1.8	2.0	1.4	1.5	1.3	1.4
1.0	1.0	1.0	1.0	1.0	1.0	1.6	1.7	1.3	1.4	1.3	1.4	2.8	3.0	2.3	2.7	2.2	2.5
1.3	1.1	1.4	1.2	1.4	1.2	1.1	1.0	1.1	1.0	1.0	1.0	1.4	1.2	1.3	1.2	1.3	1.2
1.6	1.7	1.8	1.7	1.7	1.9	1.7	1.9	1.7	1.6	1.5	1.6	2.3	2.4	2.2	2.1	1.8	2.0
1.5	1.4	1.6	1.5	1.6	1.5	1.2	1.0	1.1	1.0	1.0	1.0	1.2	1.1	1.2	1.2	1.3	1.1
1.3	1.2	1.4	1.3	1.5	1.4	1.1	1.0	1.0	1.0	1.0	1.0	1.6	1.4	1.3	1.2	1.3	1.2
1.9	1.8	2.0	1.9	2.1	1.9	1.8	2.0	1.8	1.6	1.7	1.6	2.6	2.9	2.5	2.7	2.0	2.2
2.1	2.0	2.2	2.0	2.2	2.1	1.8	2.0	1.6	1.8	1.6	1.8	2.5	2.6	2.3	2.4	2.0	2.2
2.1	2.0	2.1	2.2	2.1	2.3	1.7	1.9	1.6	1.8	1.5	1.8	1.7	1.8	1.5	1.6	1.5	1.6
1.5	1.6	1.7	1.5	1.9	1.7	2.0	1.8	1.9	1.8	2.0	1.7	2.8	2.7	2.9	2.6	2.8	2.5
1.8	1.6	2.0	1.7	1.9	1.9	2.1	1.9	2.0	1.8	1.8	1.7	2.3	2.1	2.0	1.8	2.0	1.9
1.7	1.9	2.0	1.9	1.8	2.0	1.8	2.1	1.6	2.0	1.8	2.0	1.8	2.0	1.0	1.9	1.5	1.7
1.1	1.1	1.2	1.1	1.1	1.0	1.1	1.0	1.1	1.0	1.0	1.0	1.4	1.3	1.2	1.2	1.1	1.1
1.4	1.6	1.5	1.8	1.6	1.9	1.3	1.5	1.2	1.4	1.2	1.3	1.2	1.4	1.2	1.3	1.1	1.1
1.4	1.2	1.5	1.3	1.5	1.3	1.1	1.2	1.1	1.0	1.0	1.0	1.4	1.6	1.3	1.4	1.2	1.4
1.5	1.4	1.5	1.6	1.6	1.4	1.3	1.2	1.1	1.1	1.1	1.1	1.6	1.5	1.4	1.5	1.3	1.3

Mean of the Ratings Given by Laboratory-School Faculty Members to Each Activity Listed Below

TABLE XXIII

Master Activity

Student-Teaching Activities

      (5) Probable outcomes sought...................................

      (6) Environment in which the teaching and learning activities take place.

6. Evaluating subject-matter in the light of criteria set up for that purpose......

7. Organizing subject-matter and activities

    a. Organizing subject-matter and materials.............................

    b. Developing and organizing series of activities which could be used appropriately in connection with units of instruction, projects, or daily work.........

    c. Reorganizing subject-matter around some elements of the children's experiences arising during the progress of the work, in order to make these experiences more meaningful to them.....................................

8. Mastering subject-matter to be used in daily work (Securing sufficient mastery of subject-matter to stimulate, guide, and direct children properly).............

9. Arranging, recording, and filing data and materials

    a. Keeping illustrative materials and supplies in order and available for use when needed.....................................

    b. Arranging reference materials for special problems that they may be found with minimum time and effort.....................................

    c. Recording important elements of data for future use...................

    d. Filing important data and materials topically with minor classifications under each major topic...

    e. Cross-indexing data and materials that they may be easily referred to at any time...

C. *Obtaining an understanding of individual differences of children by studying and analyzing factors that condition their learning*

  1. Studying and analyzing personality traits of individual children

    a. Making quiet and unobserved studies of individual children's personality traits relative to: (1) mental attitudes, characteristics, and capacities; (2) physical features, traits, and habits; (3) emotional reactions and impulses; (4) will-profile and temperamental attitudes; (5) social and moral-ethical attitudes, tendencies, and characteristics; (6) aesthetic talents and interests..

    b. Giving tests designed to reveal character traits, attitudes, and co-ordination. (Giving behavioristic tests, affectivity tests, and motor co-ordination tests)..

  2. Studying experiences, backgrounds, and environments of pupils

    a. Studying and analyzing the children's social and experiential backgrounds...

    b. Investigating and studying the children's home, neighborhood, and community environments.....................................

    c. Investigating the family history and the heredity of individual children......

    d. Visiting the homes of the children in the laboratory schools..............

  3. Measuring the level of mental development that each child has reached by

    a. Giving intelligence tests.....................................

    b. Studying results of intelligence tests.................................

(Continued)

Check List

Mean of the Ratings Given by Laboratory-School Faculty Members to Each Activity Listed Below																	
DIFFICULTY						VALUE						EXPERIENCE					
1–2 Hours		½ Day		All Day		1–2 Hours		½ Day		All Day		1–2 Hours		½ Day		All Day	
P	I	P	I	P	I	P	I	P	I	P	I	P	I	P	I	P	I
1.5	1.4	1.5	1.6	1.6	1.4	1.3	1.2	1.1	1.1	1.1	1.1	1.6	1.5	1.4	1.5	1.3	1.3
1.5	1.6	1.7	2.0	1.8	2.1	1.5	1.8	1.4	1.6	1.3	1.5	1.7	2.0	1.5	1.8	1.4	1.5
1.4	1.3	1.5	1.3	1.5	1.5	1.6	1.4	1.5	1.3	1.5	1.5	2.3	2.1	2.2	2.0	2.2	1.9
1.4	1.2	1.5	1.3	1.5	1.3	1.6	1.4	1.5	1.3	1.5	1.3	1.6	1.3	1.5	1.2	1.4	1.2
1.8	1.6	2.0	1.7	2.0	1.8	1.8	2.1	1.6	2.0	1.7	2.0	2.1	2.5	2.0	2.2	1.8	2.1
1.3	1.2	1.5	1.4	1.4	1.5	1.5	1.7	1.4	1.6	1.4	1.5	1.7	2.1	1.5	1.7	1.4	1.5
1.4	1.2	1.6	1.4	1.6	1.4	1.0	1.0	1.0	1.0	1.0	1.0	1.4	1.2	1.5	1.2	1.4	1.2
2.1	2.2	2.2	2.3	2.1	2.3	2.0	2.1	2.1	2.3	2.0	2.1	1.8	2.0	1.9	2.1	1.8	2.0
2.2	2.1	2.3	2.1	2.3	2.2	2.4	2.1	2.2	2.1	2.3	2.2	2.4	2.3	2.3	2.3	2.2	2.4
2.2	2.0	2.1	2.0	2.2	2.1	2.0	1.8	2.1	2.0	2.1	1.9	2.4	2.3	2.6	2.5	2.3	2.3
2.1	2.0	2.0	2.1	2.0	2.0	2.4	2.1	2.3	2.2	2.4	2.2	3.1	3.3	3.2	3.2	3.0	2.8
2.1	2.0	2.0	2.1	2.2	2.1	3.0	2.7	2.8	2.5	3.0	2.6	3.8	3.8	3.7	3.6	3.8	3.7
1.2	1.2	1.3	1.2	1.3	1.4	1.1	1.2	1.0	1.1	1.0	1.1	1.6	2.0	1.5	1.6	1.2	1.4
..	..	..	..	..	..	..	..	..	..	..	..	4.0	3.9	4.0	4.0	3.8	3.9
1.2	1.2	1.4	1.4	1.2	1.4	1.3	1.4	1.2	1.3	1.2	1.3	3.0	3.2	2.6	2.7	2.2	2.5
1.1	1.1	1.1	1.0	1.1	1.1	1.6	1.8	1.5	1.7	1.5	1.5	3.7	3.8	3.5	3.6	3.1	3.1
..	..	..	..	..	..	..	..	..	..	..	..	3.8	3.7	3.4	3.5	3.3	3.2
..	..	..	..	..	..	..	..	..	..	..	..	3.7	3.8	3.6	3.7	3.2	3.5
..	..	..	..	..	..	..	..	..	..	..	..	3.8	3.9	3.8	3.7	3.7	3.5
..	..	..	..	..	..	..	..	..	..	..	..	3.2	3.0	3.1	3.0	3.1	2.9

TABLE XXIII

Master Activity

Student-Teaching Activities

4. Examining and observing the conditions of health and physical equipment of individual children
   a. Testing and examining children for physical defects (Testing for defects in hearing, vision, speech, posture, and teeth)...........................
   b. Watching for symptoms of poor health and physical ailments of children.....
   c. Making surveys to find the number of children below or above normal weight (Weighing and measuring children, and keeping charts or records showing necessary data)...
   d. Making out disease survey charts to find out what diseases the children have had...
   e. Studying results of medical examinations of individual children............
5. Investigating reasons for deficiencies in school education of individual children
   a. Investigating past attendance records of individual children..............
   b. Finding out what types of schools these children have attended and the quality of work done there...
6. Reading books and articles dealing with problems of maladjustment in children..
7. Securing better understanding of children through personal interviews and conferences
   a. Holding individual conferences with the children to be taught by the student-teacher..
   b. Interviewing the parents of the children.................................
   c. Interviewing social workers, physicians, school nurses, and other interested people, relative to a pupil's welfare..................................
8. Discovering individual interests of the children through a wide variety of illustrative materials and reference books....................................
D. *Planning, studying, experimenting with, and using different types of procedures in directing the learning activities of the children*
   1. Planning, selecting, and adapting methods of instruction
      a. Planning methods that will provide sufficient opportunities for pupils' activities...
      b. Planning methods of instruction.....................................
      c. Selecting and adapting methods of instruction with reference to
         (1) The abilities, interests, and needs of the children..................
         (2) The environment in which the teaching and learning activities take place
   2. Utilizing effective methods of instruction
      a. Applying the following different types of procedures:
         (1) Activity units or projects..
         (2) Appreciation method (Stimulating appreciation, admiration, and enjoyment of things of aesthetic, intellectual, and social value)...........
         (3) Creative work...
         (4) Dramatic play or dramatic expression.............................

(Continued)

Check List

Mean of the Ratings Given by Laboratory-School Faculty Members to Each Activity Listed Below

DIFFICULTY						VALUE						EXPERIENCE					
1–2 Hours		½ Day		All Day		1–2 Hours		½ Day		All Day		1–2 Hours		½ Day		All Day	
P	I	P	I	P	I	P	I	P	I	P	I	P	I	P	I	P	I
..	..	..	..	..	..	..	..	..	..	..	..	3.5	3.7	3.4	3.5	3.1	3.3
1.9	2.0	1.8	2.1	2.0	2.1	1.4	1.7	1.4	1.5	1.3	1.5	2.3	2.6	2.1	2.4	2.0	2.3
2.6	2.5	2.7	2.8	2.9	3.0	2.7	2.9	2.5	2.8	2.7	2.9	3.4	3.5	3.2	3.3	2.9	3.1
3.0	3.0	3.0	3.0	3.0	3.0	3.3	3.6	3.2	3.4	3.1	3.3	3.8	3.9	3.7	3.6	3.8	3.8
..	..	..	..	..	..	3.0	3.3	3.0	3.2	3.0	3.3	3.8	3.9	3.7	3.6	3.8	3.8
3.0	3.0	3.0	3.0	3.0	3.0	3.2	3.3	3.2	3.0	3.1	3.0	3.7	3.6	3.7	3.2	3.5	3.2
3.0	2.9	3.0	3.0	3.0	3.0	3.2	3.0	3.0	3.0	3.1	3.0	3.7	3.6	3.7	3.2	3.5	3.2
2.1	2.0	2.2	2.0	2.2	2.1	2.3	2.1	2.2	2.0	2.2	2.0	3.0	2.9	3.0	2.8	3.0	2.8
1.5	1.5	1.7	1.6	1.9	1.6	1.4	1.5	1.4	1.3	1.3	1.3	1.9	2.2	1.9	1.8	1.4	1.5
..	..	..	..	..	..	..	..	..	..	..	..	3.7	3.8	3.6	3.8	3.4	3.5
..	..	..	..	..	..	3.5	3.7	3.3	3.5	3.0	3.3	3.8	3.9	3.8	3.9	3.8	3.8
1.8	1.6	1.9	1.8	2.0	2.0	1.2	1.4	1.1	1.3	1.1	1.2	1.7	1.9	1.5	1.5	1.3	1.4
1.2	1.2	1.3	1.2	1.3	1.3	1.1	1.2	1.1	1.1	1.0	1.0	1.4	1.5	1.2	1.2	1.1	1.2
1.5	1.4	1.5	1.6	1.5	1.6	1.2	1.2	1.1	1.1	1.0	1.0	1.3	1.3	1.2	1.2	1.2	1.2
1.2	1.2	1.3	1.2	1.3	1.3	1.1	1.2	1.1	1.0	1.0	1.0	1.3	1.4	1.1	1.1	1.1	1.1
1.7	1.8	1.9	1.8	1.8	2.0	1.5	1.8	1.5	1.7	1.5	1.6	2.0	2.0	1.6	1.8	1.5	1.7
1.3	1.2	1.4	1.3	1.5	1.3	1.2	1.3	1.1	1.2	1.1	1.1	2.0	2.3	1.6	1.8	1.4	1.5
1.3	1.2	1.4	1.3	1.4	1.3	1.1	1.2	1.0	1.1	1.0	1.0	1.7	2.0	1.5	1.6	1.4	1.5
1.3	1.2	1.4	1.3	1.4	1.2	1.3	1.5	1.2	1.3	1.2	1.3	2.0	2.3	1.7	2.0	1.6	1.8
1.5	1.4	1.6	1.5	1.5	1.5	1.5	1.7	1.4	1.6	1.4	1.6	1.8	2.3	1.6	1.9	1.5	2.0

TABLE XXIII

Master Activity

Student-Teaching Activities

    (5) Dramatizations in regular school subjects...........................
    (6) Drill lessons and exercises......................................
    (7) Exposition methods (Telling or lecturing).........................
    (8) School journeys, excursions, and field trips......................
    (9) Individualized instruction
        (a) Using contract plan.......................................
        (b) Individualizing the learning activities to meet the needs, interests, and capacities of the children.............................
   (10) Inductive-deductive types of procedures...........................
   (11) Laboratory types (Trying out new experiments)....................
   (12) Organized question and answer methods...........................
   (13) Organized topical recitations....................................
   (14) Problem-solving..
   (15) Review work and reorganization of old knowledge.................
   (16) Socialized recitations or socialized discussions....................
   (17) Study-test plan of procedure....................................
   (18) Supervised or directed study....................................
   (19) Textbook recitations (Reciting from one basic textbook)............
   (20) Visualized instruction...
   (21) Testing
        (a) Giving exploratory tests to determine children's needs...........
        (b) Giving diagnostic tests to locate specific errors, difficulties, and lack of progress in each child's learning...........................
        (c) Giving standard achievement tests..........................
        (d) Making and giving attainment tests in regular class work........

3. Helping children to develop adeptness in the basic skill subjects
   a. Teaching the basic skill subjects
     (1) Directing the learning of new materials, fundamental processes, skills, and habits by:
        (a) Guiding children in developing situations and conditions from which will emerge the needs for habits, skills, and more formal learning...
        (b) Stimulating a desire or a motive on the part of the children to learn or to master new materials, fundamental processes, or specific skills and habits..
        (c) Giving pupils a clear conception or idea of what is to be learned (Demonstrating and illustrating each new process or each new step in the process, and giving explanations and specific directions as to the best methods to be used).................................
        (d) Giving separate training on difficult points.....................

(Continued)

Check List

Mean of the Ratings Given by Laboratory-School Faculty Members to Each Activity Listed Below

DIFFICULTY						VALUE						EXPERIENCE					
1–2 Hours		½ Day		All Day		1–2 Hours		½ Day		All Day		1–2 Hours		½ Day		All Day	
P	I	P	I	P	I	P	I	P	I	P	I	P	I	P	I	P	I
1.6	1.5	1.6	1.5	1.7	1.6	1.6	1.8	1.5	1.7	1.5	1.6	1.8	2.2	1.6	2.0	1.5	2.0
1.7	1.9	2.1	1.9	1.8	1.9	1.5	1.6	1.6	1.8	1.6	1.7	1.4	1.5	1.5	1.6	1.5	1.7
2.0	2.1	2.1	2.2	2.0	2.3	1.9	2.1	2.0	2.2	2.0	2.3	1.6	1.8	1.8	2.0	1.9	2.0
1.2	1.2	1.3	1.2	1.4	1.3	1.5	1.7	1.4	1.6	1.4	1.5	3.0	3.3	2.6	3.0	2.5	2.7
..	..	..	..	..	..	..	..	..	..	..	..	3.9	3.8	3.9	3.7	4.0	3.8
1.2	1.1	1.3	1.2	1.4	1.3	1.2	1.3	1.1	1.2	1.1	1.1	1.7	1.9	1.4	1.6	1.4	1.4
1.9	1.7	2.0	1.9	2.2	2.0	1.9	1.8	2.1	2.0	2.1	1.8	2.2	2.0	2.3	2.1	2.3	2.0
..	..	..	..	..	..	..	..	..	..	..	..	2.8	2.6	2.5	2.3	2.4	2.4
2.2	2.1	2.4	2.2	2.3	2.2	2.4	2.0	2.5	2.3	2.5	2.3	2.6	2.2	2.9	2.4	3.0	2.4
2.1	2.0	2.2	2.0	2.3	2.1	2.3	2.1	2.4	2.2	2.5	2.3	2.4	2.2	2.5	2.2	2.6	2.3
1.2	1.3	1.2	1.4	1.4	1.3	1.5	1.3	1.3	1.2	1.4	1.3	2.0	1.7	1.6	1.3	1.5	1.4
1.8	1.6	1.8	1.7	2.0	1.8	1.8	1.4	1.8	1.5	1.9	1.5	1.8	1.4	1.8	1.5	1.9	1.5
1.3	1.2	1.4	1.3	1.5	1.3	1.3	1.4	1.2	1.3	1.2	1.3	1.7	2.1	1.4	1.6	1.4	1.5
2.2	2.1	2.3	2.1	2.3	2.2	2.3	2.2	2.5	2.1	2.5	2.2	2.6	2.2	2.7	2.3	2.8	2.3
1.7	1.8	1.6	1.5	1.6	1.5	2.1	1.9	2.0	1.7	1.8	1.6	2.0	1.8	1.8	1.5	1.7	1.4
2.2	2.1	2.3	2.2	2.3	2.2	2.2	2.1	2.3	2.2	2.3	2.1	2.2	2.0	2.4	2.2	2.3	2.1
1.7	1.9	1.9	1.8	2.0	1.8	1.5	1.7	1.4	1.5	1.3	1.3	2.0	2.2	1.8	1.9	1.8	1.7
2.2	2.1	2.3	2.1	2.3	2.2	2.3	2.1	2.2	2.0	2.1	2.0	2.8	2.5	2.6	2.4	2.9	2.3
2.2	2.1	2.3	2.1	2.3	2.2	2.2	2.1	2.1	2.0	2.1	2.0	2.7	2.4	2.5	2.3	2.5	2.3
2.2	2.1	2.3	2.2	2.3	2.2	2.5	2.3	2.4	2.3	2.5	2.4	3.5	3.3	3.4	3.2	3.4	3.2
1.6	1.4	1.7	1.5	1.7	1.6	1.6	1.4	1.7	1.4	1.7	1.5	2.1	1.5	2.0	1.7	2.0	1.7
1.3	1.4	1.4	1.4	1.4	1.3	1.3	1.4	1.4	1.4	1.3	1.4	1.6	1.8	1.5	1.6	1.3	1.4
1.2	1.3	1.5	1.4	1.5	1.4	1.2	1.3	1.3	1.4	1.2	1.3	1.3	1.4	1.2	1.4	1.2	1.3
1.4	1.3	1.4	1.5	1.3	1.4	1.3	1.2	1.3	1.4	1.3	1.4	1.4	1.3	1.3	1.5	1.3	1.4
1.8	2.0	2.2	2.0	2.3	2.0	1.7	1.8	2.0	1.8	2.0	2.0	1.7	1.9	1.5	1.6	1.5	1.7

TABLE XXIII

Master Activity

Student-Teaching Activities

(e) Guiding children in making associations (Leading children to observe points of similarity in materials to be learned, or relations
between one experience and another)..........................

(f) Providing incentives for sustained effort on the part of each child
(Relating materials to the child's experiences and interests; employing mental or physical devices, i.e., independent work sheets, charts,
flash cards, picture diagrams, graphs, games, contests, exhibitions; encouraging each child to work against his own previous record)

(2) Directing learning of the fundamental processes and helping pupils to
increase comprehension, accuracy, and speed in:

(a) Reading

  1′ Oral...
  2′ Silent..

(b) Spelling..

(c) Fundamentals of language...............................

(d) Number work and arithmetic............................

(e) Writing...

b. Handling remedial work

(1) Diagnosing and analyzing causes of errors of:

(a) Individual children...................................

(b) A group or a whole class of children......................

(2) Applying proper remedial instruction at the point of error and difficulty
in any work..

4. Guiding children in utilizing skills and subject-matter

a. Helping children to develop appropriate mental set for purposeful learning
activities to be undertaken...................................

b. Helping the children to understand objectives and purposes of work to be
accomplished...

c. Inducing children to formulate and to set up standards to be attained in a
stated piece of work.......................................

d. Initiating and carrying to completion, with the co-operation of the pupils,
large units of instruction which include the integration and drawing together
of various phases of subject-matter, different types of activities, and many
experiences within the comprehension of the children

(1) Guiding children in initiating and carrying into effect such purposeful
learning activities as:

(a) Centers of interest, vital problems, and developmental units of
work which will draw upon many phases of experience within the
comprehension of the children.............................

(b) Appropriate and constructive activity units or projects..........

(Continued)

Check List

Mean of the Ratings Given by Laboratory-School Faculty Members to Each Activity Listed Below																	
DIFFICULTY						VALUE						EXPERIENCE					
1–2 Hours		½ Day		All Day		1–2 Hours		½ Day		All Day		1–2 Hours		½ Day		All Day	
P	I	P	I	P	I	P	I	P	I	P	I	P	I	P	I	P	I
1.8	1.9	1.9	2.0	2.0	2.1	1.7	1.8	1.6	1.8	1.7	1.9	1.8	2.0	1.6	1.8	1.6	1.7
1.3	1.6	1.5	1.8	1.5	1.8	1.3	1.6	1.5	1.7	1.3	1.6	1.5	1.8	1.4	1.7	1.4	1.7
1.5	2.0	1.6	1.8	1.6	2.0	1.4	1.6	1.3	1.7	1.3	1.8	1.6	2.0	1.5	2.0	1.5	2.0
1.3	1.6	1.4	1.6	1.5	1.7	1.3	1.4	1.3	1.5	1.2	1.5	1.4	1.7	1.3	1.6	1.3	1.5
2.1	2.2	2.2	2.3	2.1	2.3	2.2	2.0	2.2	2.1	2.2	2.1	2.4	2.3	2.3	2.2	2.2	2.0
2.0	1.8	2.0	1.8	2.1	2.0	2.0	2.0	2.0	2.0	1.8	1.7	2.2	2.1	2.1	2.0	1.8	1.7
2.1	1.7	2.1	2.0	2.3	2.0	1.8	1.7	1.9	1.6	1.7	1.6	2.1	2.0	2.0	1.7	1.8	1.6
1.9	2.2	2.0	2.2	2.1	2.2	2.0	2.2	2.0	2.2	2.0	2.2	2.2	2.4	2.1	2.3	2.0	2.2
1.3	1.2	1.4	1.3	1.3	1.4	1.3	1.2	1.2	1.2	1.1	1.1	1.7	1.6	1.5	1.5	1.3	1.5
1.3	1.2	1.3	1.3	1.3	1.4	1.3	1.2	1.2	1.2	1.1	1.1	1.8	1.7	1.6	1.5	1.4	1.5
1.3	1.2	1.4	1.3	1.3	1.5	1.3	1.3	1.4	1.2	1.3	1.3	1.7	1.6	1.6	1.5	1.4	1.5
1.4	1.2	1.5	1.4	1.5	1.4	1.2	1.3	1.2	1.3	1.2	1.2	1.3	1.5	1.2	1.4	1.2	1.3
1.4	1.3	1.4	1.5	1.5	1.4	1.6	1.4	1.5	1.4	1.5	1.3	2.1	1.8	1.9	1.7	1.8	1.6
1.4	1.2	1.4	1.3	1.5	1.4	1.6	1.4	1.4	1.4	1.5	1.3	2.2	2.1	1.8	1.6	1.6	1.5
1.0	1.0	1.1	1.0	1.1	1.1	1.2	1.3	1.1	1.1	1.1	1.1	2.2	2.5	1.8	2.1	1.4	1.5
1.1	1.1	1.2	1.1	1.2	1.2	1.2	1.3	1.1	1.2	1.1	1.1	2.2	2.4	1.8	2.1	1.4	1.5

TABLE XXIII

Master Activity

Student-Teaching Activities

(2) Recognizing and making effective use of children's leads, questions, and contributions...

(3) Directing children in making surveys of what they should do or accomplish during stated periods of time (Planning what should be accomplished but taking into consideration the present environment, common experiences of the children, accomplishments by previous groups of children in the same grade, the current interests of the community, and the events of the world at large).........................

(4) Leading the children to suggest, to choose, and to plan effective methods for solving problems and for working out units of work or projects....

(5) Guiding children in the execution and progress of learning activities that a high purpose may be maintained consistently under changing conditions...

e. Teaching children to study

  (1) Utilizing assignments as effective guides for study

    (a) Adapting assignments to abilities, interests, and needs of:

      1' Individual children.......................................

      2' The class...

    (b) Guiding children in initiating their own assignments...........

  (2) Providing for purposeful pupil activity during independent study periods as well as for class work...............................

  (3) Helping children to develop proper techniques for reference work

    (a) Guiding children in making surveys of suitable materials and available equipment to be used in carrying out activities.........

    (b) Guiding the children in finding, collecting, assembling and selecting materials.......................................

    (c) Directing learning in the use of the library

      1' Explaining to children how to use card indexes, card slips, *The Readers' Guide*, encyclopedias, etc...........................

      2' Showing children how to find reference books, current magazines, and bound volumes of periodicals.....................

    (d) Directing learning in the economical and effective use of books

      1' Teaching children how to take care of books...............

      2' Guiding children in finding and using the essential parts of a book, i.e., title, author, illustrator, publisher, date of publication, pages, index, table of contents, chapter headings, glossary, footnotes, and marginal notes.................................

      3' Guiding children in making effective use of different types of books and recorded matter................................

      4' Leading children to form the habit of searching in various sources for related materials................................

(Continued)

Check List

Mean of the Ratings Given by Laboratory-School Faculty Members to Each Activity Listed Below																	
DIFFICULTY						VALUE						EXPERIENCE					
1–2 Hours		½ Day		All Day		1–2 Hours		½ Day		All Day		1–2 Hours		½ Day		All Day	
P	I	P	I	P	I	P	I	P	I	P	I	P	I	P	I	P	I
1.1	1.1	1.2	1.1	1.2	1.1	1.2	1.3	1.1	1.2	1.1	1.1	2.2	2.3	1.8	2.0	1.4	1.5
1.3	1.3	1.4	1.5	1.5	1.4	1.6	1.4	1.4	1.5	1.4	1.3	2.2	2.3	2.2	2.1	1.8	1.6
1.1	1.1	1.1	1.1	1.2	1.2	1.1	1.2	1.1	1.1	1.0	1.0	2.2	2.3	1.8	2.0	1.5	1.6
1.1	1.1	1.2	1.1	1.2	1.1	1.1	1.0	1.0	1.0	1.0	1.0	2.0	2.0	1.6	1.8	1.4	1.4
1.2	1.1	1.2	1.1	1.2	1.1	1.3	1.2	1.2	1.1	1.1	1.1	1.8	1.6	1.6	1.5	1.4	1.4
1.2	1.2	1.4	1.3	1.4	1.3	1.2	1.2	1.3	1.2	1.3	1.1	1.6	1.5	1.6	1.4	1.5	1.3
1.1	1.1	1.2	1.2	1.3	1.2	1.5	1.4	1.3	1.2	1.2	1.2	2.4	2.3	2.1	2.0	1.8	1.7
1.2	1.2	1.3	1.3	1.3	1.3	1.5	1.3	1.3	1.2	1.3	1.1	2.1	1.8	1.8	1.5	1.6	1.3
1.5	1.6	1.8	1.7	1.8	2.0	1.7	1.8	1.5	1.6	1.5	1.5	2.4	2.6	2.3	2.2	1.8	1.8
1.5	1.6	1.8	1.7	1.8	2.0	1.6	1.7	1.4	1.6	1.5	1.4	2.1	2.0	1.8	1.6	1.8	1.8
..	2.0	..	2.2	..	2.1	..	2.3	..	2.1	..	2.0	3.8	2.8	3.4	2.4	3.1	2.4
..	2.0	..	2.1	..	2.1	..	2.4	..	2.1	..	2.0	3.5	2.8	3.5	2.5	3.1	2.5
2.1	2.3	2.1	2.3	2.3	2.7	2.1	2.4	2.2	2.5	2.1	2.4	2.8	2.9	2.5	2.0	2.4	2.8
1.6	1.6	1.8	1.6	1.8	1.5	1.6	1.3	1.5	1.4	1.5	1.4	2.5	2.2	2.4	2.0	2.2	1.8
1.2	1.2	1.3	1.2	1.3	1.3	1.4	1.2	1.3	1.1	1.3	1.1	1.9	1.7	1.7	1.5	1.6	1.4
1.2	1.2	1.3	1.2	1.3	1.2	1.5	1.2	1.4	1.1	1.3	1.1	2.3	1.9	2.1	1.5	2.0	1.6

TABLE XXIII

Master Activity

Student-Teaching Activities

5′ Guiding the children in judging the validity and reliability of materials and information...................................

(e) Directing learning in the economical and effective use of the dictionary...

(4) Helping the children to develop skill in the following specific study habits:

(a) Deciding what is to be done................................

(b) Studying with some definite aim in view.....................

(c) Concentrating on the work at hand and keeping the thinking systematically organized..................................

(d) Searching for information through thoughtful and reflective reading

(e) Analyzing data into their elements..........................

(f) Organizing subject-matter and materials......................

(g) Discriminating between essentials and nonessentials in subject-matter...

(h) Connecting ideas in their proper relationships.................

(i) Assimilating the ideas of an author...........................

(j) Memorizing subject-matter and materials.....................

(k) Formulating conclusions and summaries.....................

(l) Verifying conclusions formed...............................

(m) Making economical and practical use of materials.............

(n) Outlining and recording useful materials and information........

(o) Comparing work with standards in order to check errors.........

(p) Correcting errors...

(q) Maintaining critical attitudes toward materials studied..........

(r) Making economical use of time.............................

5. Teaching a variety of subjects....................................

6. Setting up criteria and making effective use of these for determining value of:

a. Subject-matter to be used...................................

b. Units of work or units of instruction.........................

c. Teaching procedures and learning activities....................

7. Evaluating different types of methods of instruction in light of criteria set up for that purpose...

E. *Helping children to build up and develop desirable personal and social habits, interests, appreciations, ideals, and attitudes*

1. Defining, explaining, and discussing with the children, as occasion arises, underlying principles of:

a. Good social standards......................................

b. Good moral-ethical standards...............................

2. Setting up situations which provide opportunities and utilizing those which present themselves for helping children to develop the highest types of:

(Continued)

Check List

Mean of the Ratings Given by Laboratory-School Faculty Members to Each Activity Listed Below

DIFFICULTY						VALUE						EXPERIENCE					
1–2 Hours		½ Day		All Day		1–2 Hours		½ Day		All Day		1–2 Hours		½ Day		All Day	
P	I	P	I	P	I	P	I	P	I	P	I	P	I	P	I	P	I
1.2	1.2	1.4	1.2	1.4	1.2	1.8	1.4	1.6	1.4	1.6	1.3	3.0	2.2	2.7	1.8	2.5	1.8
..	1.7	..	1.5	..	1.8	..	1.8	..	1.8	..	2.0	3.9	2.6	3.8	2.2	3.8	2.4
1.2	1.3	1.3	1.4	1.4	1.4	1.4	1.3	1.3	1.2	1.4	1.2	1.4	1.2	1.3	1.2	1.3	1.2
1.3	1.3	1.4	1.5	1.4	1.5	1.4	1.3	1.3	1.2	1.3	1.2	1.4	1.3	1.3	1.3	1.3	1.2
1.2	1.2	1.2	1.3	1.2	1.4	1.4	1.2	1.3	1.2	1.3	1.1	1.5	1.3	1.4	1.2	1.3	1.1
1.4	1.5	1.5	1.7	1.5	1.7	1.7	1.3	1.5	1.2	1.5	1.2	1.8	1.4	1.6	1.2	1.5	1.2
1.0	1.1	1.0	1.1	1.0	1.0	3.0	2.5	2.9	2.5	3.1	2.6	3.4	3.0	3.2	2.5	3.3	2.6
1.2	1.2	1.2	1.3	1.3	1.3	1.5	1.2	1.5	1.1	1.4	1.1	2.0	1.5	1.8	1.4	1.8	1.3
1.2	1.2	1.2	1.3	1.3	1.4	1.4	1.2	1.3	1.1	1.3	1.1	2.0	1.5	1.8	1.4	1.8	1.4
1.2	1.2	1.2	1.3	1.3	1.4	1.8	1.2	1.8	1.2	1.5	1.2	2.0	1.6	1.8	1.5	1.8	1.4
1.3	1.4	1.4	1.5	1.5	1.5	1.6	1.2	1.5	1.2	1.5	1.2	2.0	1.5	1.6	1.3	1.6	1.3
1.7	1.8	1.8	2.0	1.8	2.0	1.7	1.8	2.0	1.9	1.8	2.0	1.7	1.8	2.0	1.9	1.8	2.0
1.4	1.5	1.3	1.5	1.3	1.6	2.0	1.3	1.8	1.2	1.8	1.2	2.4	2.0	2.3	1.9	2.2	1.8
1.2	1.2	1.4	1.2	1.4	1.2	2.2	1.4	2.1	1.4	2.2	1.3	3.0	2.2	2.8	2.0	2.8	2.0
1.5	1.4	1.7	1.5	1.6	1.6	1.5	1.4	1.6	1.5	1.6	1.6	1.5	2.0	1.4	1.7	1.4	1.6
1.2	1.2	1.2	1.3	1.3	1.4	2.0	1.3	1.8	1.2	2.0	1.2	2.7	2.1	2.5	2.0	2.1	1.6
2.2	2.1	2.3	2.2	2.3	2.2	2.2	2.1	2.3	2.2	2.2	2.2	2.3	2.1	2.4	2.2	2.3	2.0
2.2	2.0	2.3	2.2	2.3	2.2	2.2	2.0	2.3	2.2	2.2	2.2	2.0	1.8	1.8	1.9	1.8	1.6
1.0	1.0	1.0	1.1	1.0	1.2	2.2	1.5	2.0	1.3	1.8	1.3	2.6	2.1	2.4	1.9	2.5	1.7
1.8	1.6	1.8	1.8	1.9	2.0	1.7	1.6	1.8	1.8	1.9	1.8	1.8	1.6	1.6	1.5	1.8	1.5

(See Tables XXVIII, XXIX, and XXX for details.)

DIFFICULTY						VALUE						EXPERIENCE					
1.4	1.3	1.4	1.3	1.5	1.5	2.0	1.7	2.0	1.8	2.0	1.8	3.5	3.1	3.2	3.0	3.2	3.1
1.3	1.3	1.4	1.3	1.5	1.5	2.0	1.7	1.8	1.8	2.0	1.8	3.4	3.2	3.2	3.0	3.0	2.8
1.3	1.4	1.4	1.5	1.5	1.5	1.8	1.6	1.7	1.8	1.6	1.8	3.3	3.0	3.0	3.1	2.8	3.1
1.5	1.6	1.4	1.6	1.4	1.7	1.5	1.6	1.4	1.6	1.4	1.7	1.9	2.1	1.8	2.0	1.7	1.8
1.6	1.6	1.7	1.8	1.6	1.8	1.6	1.6	1.7	1.8	1.6	1.8	2.2	2.5	1.7	2.0	1.6	1.8
1.6	1.5	1.7	1.8	1.6	1.8	1.8	1.6	2.0	1.8	2.0	1.8	2.3	2.2	2.0	2.0	2.0	2.0

TABLE XXIII

Master Activity

Student-Teaching Activities

    a. Co-operative living (Providing opportunity for team work, and for group co-operation through committee work, reports, debates, experiments, class discussion, and extra-class activities)...................................

    b. Social responsibility (Stimulating a sense of responsibility to the group rather than to the individual teacher; developing in each member of the class a sense of responsibility for the success or failure of the work)............

    c. Initiative (Leading children to initiate purposeful activities)............

    d. Self-expression (Drawing out each child's inner capacities for self-expression by creating a desire to make personal contributions to group enterprises)..

    e. Self-confidence and self-reliance (Finding out the timid child's special interests and encouraging him to share these with the group)............

    f. Aggressiveness (Helping the children to develop capacity for becoming interested in what other people have to say and to become interested in any purposeful activity)..

    g. Constructive leadership (Helping the children to satisfy their desire for power, influence, and popular favor through group organizations in which they may exercise constructive leadership)...........................

    h. Ethical conduct...

  3. Dealing with problems of child behavior; and handling discipline of children....

F. *Taking charge of activities in connection with school and classroom routine*

  1. Regulating physical factors of the room................................

  2. Tending to schoolroom housekeeping....................................

  3. Arranging work on blackboards and bulletin boards........................

  4. Selecting and displaying children's work................................

  5. Keeping records and making reports of a routine nature...................

  6. Selecting and ordering materials and equipment.........................

  7. Making programs and schedules..

G. *Planning, participating in, and directing children's extra-class activities*

  1. Planning and directing programs and festivals

    a. Planning, directing, and staging assembly presentations and programs (Directing regular school assemblies; staging special day, week, or holiday programs)..

    b. Planning and coaching pageants (Coaching historical, geographical, civic, patriotic, health, and safety first pageants)...........................

    c. Planning and directing festivals (Directing amusement, seasonal, and holiday festivals)...

  2. Participating in children's school parties, picnics, and other similar activities..

  3. Planning and conducting excursions and field trips........................

  4. Directing and participating in children's organizations

    a. Planning, directing, or participating in children's social organizations......

(Continued)

Check List

Mean of the Ratings Given by Laboratory-School Faculty Members to Each Activity Listed Below																	
DIFFICULTY						VALUE						EXPERIENCE					
1–2 Hours		½ Day		All Day		1–2 Hours		½ Day		All Day		1–2 Hours		½ Day		All Day	
P	I	P	I	P	I	P	I	P	I	P	I	P	I	P	I	P	I
1.2	1.2	1.3	1.2	1.4	1.3	1.2	1.3	1.2	1.2	1.1	1.1	2.2	2.5	1.8	2.1	1.6	1.7
1.2	1.1	1.3	1.2	1.3	1.3	1.3	1.3	1.2	1.1	1.1	1.1	2.0	2.2	1.6	1.8	1.5	1.5
1.2	1.1	1.3	1.2	1.4	1.2	1.4	1.4	1.2	1.2	1.1	1.1	2.2	2.4	1.8	2.0	1.5	1.6
1.2	1.2	1.3	1.2	1.4	1.3	1.2	1.3	1.2	1.2	1.1	1.1	2.0	2.2	1.6	1.8	1.5	1.6
1.2	1.2	1.3	1.3	1.3	1.4	1.2	1.3	1.1	1.2	1.1	1.2	1.8	2.0	1.5	1.6	1.4	1.4
1.2	1.2	1.4	1.3	1.3	1.4	1.2	1.4	1.2	1.2	1.2	1.2	1.8	2.1	1.7	1.6	1.5	1.5
1.2	1.2	1.3	1.4	1.4	1.3	1.5	1.4	1.3	1.4	1.4	1.3	2.2	2.5	1.8	2.1	1.5	1.7
1.2	1.1	1.4	1.3	1.5	1.4	1.1	1.0	1.1	1.1	1.2	1.1	..	..	..	..	..	..
1.2	1.0	1.4	1.2	1.5	1.4	1.1	1.0	1.1	1.1	1.2	1.1	1.6	1.4	1.7	1.6	1.7	1.5
2.5	2.7	2.6	2.8	2.5	2.7												
2.3	2.7	2.6	2.8	2.3	2.7												
2.4	2.5	2.5	2.5	2.6	2.7												
2.4	2.6	2.6	2.8	2.5	2.7												
2.5	2.7	2.6	2.7	2.7	2.7												
2.5	2.5	2.6	2.5	2.5	2.7												
2.5	2.8	2.7	2.6	2.5	2.8												

Table XXXI presents the per cent of student-teachers, under different types of student teaching organization, who obtained considerable practice in each of these activities.

DIFFICULTY						VALUE						EXPERIENCE					
P	I	P	I	P	I	P	I	P	I	P	I	P	I	P	I	P	I
1.3	1.3	1.4	1.3	1.4	1.4	1.4	1.3	1.3	1.4	1.3	1.4	2.8	3.0	2.3	2.7	2.2	2.3
1.1	1.2	1.2	1.3	1.1	1.2	2.3	2.4	2.1	2.2	2.1	2.1	3.3	3.5	3.1	3.3	3.0	3.1
1.2	1.3	1.3	1.4	1.2	1.5	2.0	2.3	2.0	2.1	2.0	2.1	3.4	3.5	3.1	3.3	3.0	3.1
1.8	1.9	2.0	2.0	1.9	2.0	2.0	2.0	2.0	2.1	1.9	2.0	3.0	3.2	2.5	2.6	2.5	2.7
1.2	1.2	1.3	1.2	1.4	1.3	1.5	1.7	1.4	1.6	1.4	1.5	3.0	3.3	2.6	3.0	2.5	2.7
1.7	1.8	1.9	1.8	1.8	1.9	2.0	2.0	2.0	1.9	1.9	1.8	3.1	3.3	2.7	2.5	2.7	2.4

TABLE XXIII

Master Activity

Student-Teaching Activities

      b. Directing or participating in pupils' civic organizations (Taking part in room organizations, elementary councils, school banking, and traffic committees).
      c. Directing or participating in international and national organizations (Participating in Boy Scout, Girl Scout, and Junior Red Cross organizations)
      d. Guiding, managing, or participating in children's club work (Participating in children's book clubs, citizenship clubs, literary clubs, and various types of hobby clubs)..
   5. Supervising the children in various phases of physical education work (Supervising playground, group and team games, dancing, posture work, and relaxation exercises)...
   6. Assisting with children's school publications...........................
H. *Developing desirable teaching personality*
   1. Attending and participating in conferences (Interviewing critic teachers and other faculty members for purposes of securing criticisms and help in diagnosing personality traits, and of obtaining suggestions and aids for overcoming weak points and for building up on strong points)..............................
   2. Making personality studies
      a. Approaching personality study through analysis of the traits of others.....
      b. Studying, analyzing, and diagnosing their own personalities in light of the objectives and principles of modern education.........................
      c. Evaluating their own personality traits by use of rating devices.........
   3. Obtaining and applying suggestions and special instruction for the improvement of personality..
I. *Making contacts with the staff-personnel and with the administrative phases of elementary schools*
   1. Attending and participating in conferences............................
   2. Working on committees with other student-teachers.....................
   3. Working on committees with laboratory-school staff members..............
   4. Participating in educational research..................................
J. *Making contacts with community activities*
   1. Attending community functions and activities..........................
   2. Participating in the established social, civic, and welfare organizations of the community..
K. *Making professional contacts outside the teachers colleges*
   1. Attending sectional, city, state, or national educational meetings...........
   2. Joining professional organizations....................................
   3. Contributing to professional meetings or programs......................
   4. Preparing educational articles for publication..........................

(Continued)

Check List

Mean of the Ratings Given by Laboratory-School Faculty Members to Each Activity Listed Below																	
DIFFICULTY						VALUE						EXPERIENCE					
1–2 Hours		½ Day		All Day		1–2 Hours		½ Day		All Day		1–2 Hours		½ Day		All Day	
P	I	P	I	P	I	P	I	P	I	P	I	P	I	P	I	P	I
1.6	1.8	1.7	1.9	2.0	2.0	2.3	2.2	2.2	2.0	2.0	2.0	3.1	3.0	2.9	2.7	3.0	2.5
..	..	..	..	..	..	..	..	..	..	..	..	3.9	3.8	3.9	3.7	3.9	3.7
1.6	1.7	1.7	1.4	1.6	1.8	2.3	2.2	2.2	2.0	2.1	2.0	3.5	3.2	3.0	2.7	2.8	2.5
1.8	1.6	2.0	1.8	1.9	2.0	1.5	2.0	1.4	1.8	1.5	1.7	2.1	2.9	2.0	2.3	1.8	2.2
1.9	1.8	2.0	2.0	2.0	2.0	2.3	2.2	2.1	2.1	2.0	2.0	3.3	3.5	3.1	3.2	2.7	3.0
2.2	2.2	2.2	2.3	2.2	2.4	1.1	1.1	1.1	1.1	1.1	1.1	2.3	2.5	2.0	2.2	1.8	2.0
2.5	2.7	2.4	2.5	2.5	2.7	2.5	2.7	2.4	2.5	2.5	2.8	2.7	2.8	2.5	2.7	2.5	2.8
1.3	1.3	1.5	1.5	1.5	1.6	1.1	1.2	1.1	1.1	1.0	1.0	2.2	2.4	2.0	2.1	1.7	1.8
2.4	2.2	2.3	2.5	2.5	2.4	2.2	2.3	2.4	2.2	2.7	2.4	2.5	2.7	2.8	3.1	3.0	3.2
1.5	1.5	1.6	1.6	1.7	1.8	1.1	1.2	1.0	1.1	1.1	1.1	2.4	2.5	2.0	2.1	1.7	2.0
2.2	2.2	2.3	2.4	2.3	2.5	1.2	1.2	1.1	1.2	1.1	1.1	2.2	2.4	2.0	2.1	1.8	2.0
..	..	..	..	..	..	See pages 116–117 for details.											
..	..	..	..	..	..	See pages 117–118 for details.											
..	..	..	..	..	..	..	..	..	..	..	..	3.6	3.5	3.3	3.4	3.2	3.2
..	..	..	..	..	..	See page 119 for details.											
..	..	..	..	..	..	See page 119 for details.											
..	..	..	..	..	..	..	..	..	..	..	..	3.7	3.8	3.6	3.7	3.5	3.5
..	..	..	..	..	..	..	..	..	..	..	..	3.8	3.8	3.6	3.7	3.8	3.8
..	..	..	..	..	..	..	..	..	..	..	..	3.8	3.9	3.8	3.8	3.6	3.5
..	..	..	..	..	..	..	..	..	..	..	..	3.9	3.9	3.7	3.8	3.6	3.5

For the sake of convenience to the reader, the key and directions for reading the complicated statistical tables are repeated below.

KEY AND DIRECTIONS FOR READING TABLES

CONTENT OF STUDENT-TEACHING

The term "Content of Student-Teaching," as used in this study, includes all the contacts and experiences that student-teachers obtain in connection with student-teaching courses—directed observation, participation, and teaching.

MASTER ACTIVITY CHECK LIST

The "Master Activity Check List" includes a large number of representative student-teaching activities.

Difficulty indicates *degree of difficulty* encountered by student-teachers in carrying out skillfully each activity and procedure.

Symbols used in evaluating each activity.
1 indicates high degree of difficulty.
2 indicates medium degree of difficulty.
3 indicates low degree of difficulty.

Value indicates *degree of need for institutional training* in each activity or procedure on the part of student-teachers preparing to teach in the elementary grades.

Symbols used in evaluating each activity.
1 indicates that institutional training is highly essential.
2 indicates that institutional training is reasonably essential.
3 indicates that institutional training is slightly essential.
4 indicates that institutional training is not essential.

Experience indicates the *number of contacts and amount of experience* that student-teachers obtain in each activity during student-teaching courses in the elementary grades.

Symbols used in evaluating each activity.
1 indicates that the largest number of contacts and the greatest amount of experience are obtained in this activity.
2 indicates that an average number of contacts and a medium amount of experience are obtained in this activity.
3 indicates that few contacts and very little experience are obtained in this activity.
4 indicates that no contacts and no experience are obtained in this activity during student-teaching.

1–2 Hours indicates that student-teachers obtained their major student-teaching work in units of one hour or two hours a day.

½ Day indicates that student-teachers obtained their major student-teaching work in units of half days.

All Day indicates that student-teachers obtained their major student-teaching work in units of whole days.

P indicates primary student-teachers (Grades 1, 2, 3).

I indicates intermediate student-teachers (Grades 4, 5, 6, sometimes 7, 8).

Activities Pertaining to the Instructional Phases
of Student-Teaching

A. *Securing Perspective and Understanding of Elementary School Curricula*

Laboratory-school faculty members conceded that students preparing to teach in the elementary grades should obtain broad perspective and clear understanding of elementary school curricula, and recommended that the evolvement of the background for this work should be the joint responsibility of both the laboratory-school and the college departments. Suggestions implied that the approach to curriculum studies should be made through a variety of activities designed to accelerate the acquisition of essential information, the formation of fundamental concepts, and the development of proper perspective. Some of these activities are evaluated in the *Master Activity Check List.* (See Table XXIII.)

It is interesting to note that the student-teachers who completed their major student-teaching work under the half-day and whole-day student-teaching plans obtained a greater amount of practice in each of these activities than did those who completed all student-teaching under the one-hour-a-day plan. The student-teachers in the four-year elementary curricula obtained much wider and richer experiences than did those in the two-year programs.

1. *Examining and studying existing courses of study, subject-matter outlines, texts, reference books, and supplementary materials, for the purpose of determining essentials that should be studied by the children in a grade*

While most of the student-teachers obtained some experience in connection with these activities, the nature and extent of such contacts varied in the different teachers colleges. In some schools the student-teachers were required to become familiar with several courses of study and to apply the ideas and suggestions derived therefrom to their own teaching situations as occasion arose; while in other schools they were required to study and to use only the local courses of study. Many student-teachers were encouraged to examine outlines of subject-matter and to study records of the work that had been carried out in a grade during previous years; some were required to examine the outlines and written records of former student-teachers in order that they might know what had already been accomplished by a grade; and still others were given definite outlines or mimeographed sheets of the work to be covered for a designated period of time. Many student-teachers searched for suitable materials and purposeful activities to meet the needs of particular groups of children, while some adhered closely to a definitely prescribed syllabus. Some student-teachers examined and used a large number of textbooks and supplementary materials for several grades during their student-teaching; some did so for one grade; and a few used only the textbooks within one grade.

Some definite training in the use of courses of study, syllabi, and other written records was considered reasonably essential for elementary teachers. Inasmuch as adherence to prescribed courses of study and syllabi was in many instances required by state or local administrators of education, it was deemed wise for students to become familiar with curriculum materials and with the effective application of the content of such materials to actual teaching situations. Some of the more progressive critic teachers and supervisors, however, implied that it cramps the style of teachers to use predetermined courses of study and suggested that student-teachers be prepared to design independently such course outlines as would fit the particular group of children to be taught. Such a procedure would require the selection and adaptation of materials of instruction with reference to (*a*) individual abilities, aptitudes, interests, and needs of the pupils; (*b*) purposeful activities suitable to the group of children under consideration; and (*c*) environment of the teaching and learning situation.

2. *Making general outlines of subjects as a whole for a grade*

The fact that only a very small proportion of the student-teachers outlined subjects as a whole for a grade is explained by the following circumstances: (*a*) the discontinuity of student-teaching assignments, which permitted only fragmentary contacts with subjects as a whole; (*b*) the brevity of student-teaching periods, which made impossible the undertaking of projects of such wide scope; (*c*) the nature of certain subjects which rendered them ill-adapted to this sort of treatment; and (*d*) the lack of the necessary background preparation on the part of student-teachers. Many faculty members further maintained that the only courses, if any, in which there was time enough for this activity were professionalized subject-matter courses; and that practice should, therefore, be confined to such courses.

3. *Planning and working out developmental units of instruction*

Although faculty members specified that it was highly essential for student-teachers to obtain practice in planning and working out developmental units of instruction during both student-teaching and other professionalized college courses, less than two-thirds of the student-teachers who participated in this study had done so. Some of these student-teachers obtained rich experiences in planning and working out developmental units, while many had very limited experiences. Table XXIV, item A, 1, *d,* shows the per cent of student-teachers under different forms of administrative organization who answered "yes" or "no," or who failed to answer the question, "Have you obtained practice in planning and writing units of instruction or units of work?"

A larger per cent of the student-teachers who taught under the half-day and whole-day student-teaching plans than of those under the one-hour-a-day plan obtained experience in long-range planning and in working out whole units of instruction. The student-teachers who majored in the primary departments had more experience in developing whole units of work than did those in the intermediate grades. The student-teachers who taught in the intermediate grades, on the other hand, had more practice in writing detailed daily lesson plans and in making daily outlines for the work to be covered. (See Table XXIV, item A, 1.)

There was almost unanimous agreement among critic teachers that most of the beginning student-teachers encountered great difficulties in planning and working out large developmental units of work. Some of the chief underlying causes of these difficulties were: limited cultural backgrounds; inadequate working knowledge of materials of instruction, of modern educational procedures, and of progressive education; lack of time and opportunity to see a teaching situation as a whole; undeveloped teaching personality on the part of the student-teachers; insufficient understanding of children; and lack of knowledge of standards and requirements for the elementary grades.

4. *Thinking out each day's work in terms of large units of instruction*

Although this activity was unanimously rated high in both difficulty and value, the amount of experience which student-teachers

Per Cent of Student-Teachers under Different Administrative Organizations
if They Obtained Actual Practice in Each of the

Activities in Connection with Lesson Planning	1–2 Hours			
	Yes		No	
	P	I	P	I
A. *Planning and writing different types of plans previous to teaching*				
1. Writing lesson plans in the form of:				
a. Partly detailed lesson plans.................	84.5	87.7	8.9	8.0
b. Detailed daily lesson plans.................	74.9	80.1	16.3	12.9
c. Daily outlines............................	68.2	71.1	22.0	20.3
d. Units of instruction........................	64.1	60.4	29.1	30.1
e. Weekly outlines...........................	30.8	25.8	54.7	59.2
f. Term or semester outlines.................	24.4	20.3	59.8	64.4
2. Making brief memoranda of important points to be taught......................................	81.3	86.2	13.2	8.4
3. Writing lesson plans according to definite forms...	82.9	84.2	13.2	12.1
B. *Writing different types of records and plans subsequent to their teaching activities in student-teaching*				
1. Writing the outcomes or results after the completion of:				
a. Daily lessons.............................	57.4	52.6	29.4	32.9
b. Whole units of work........................	41.0	38.5	46.3	48.7
c. Activity units.............................	36.9	32.3	46.0	51.4
d. Sub-units.................................	34.2	31.4	49.7	52.6
e. Term's or semester's work.................	22.7	25.4	59.1	55.6
2. Writing summaries of work after completion of:				
a. Units of instruction.......................	45.3	44.7	46.6	50.6
b. Term's or semester's work.................	26.7	29.1	54.5	56.8
3. Outlining and recording units of work as they were actually carried out with the pupils..............	35.5	31.5	52.9	56.6
4. Keeping records of the work as it was actually covered by the class from day to day...............	34.7	31.8	57.0	61.7
5. Writing up a daily lesson in the form of a definite plan subsequent to the teaching of it...........	32.8	29.5	57.5	60.5
6. Writing post-plans subsequent to most of the class periods in which they taught..................	9.7	8.3	77.3	79.2

obtained in thinking out each day's work in terms of large units of
instruction varied greatly in the different institutions.

    5. *Building up the curriculum from day to day through the combined initiative and co-operation of pupils and teacher*

Student-teachers, for the most part, obtained very limited experiences in helping to build up the curriculum from day to day

XXIV

Who Answered "Yes" or "No," or Who Failed to Answer at All When Asked
Activities in Connection with Lesson Planning

	½ Day			All Day				Total		
	Yes		No		Yes		No		Yes	No	Blank
	P	I	P	I	P	I	P	I			
	88.3	88.0	8.0	8.7	85.0	81.1	10.0	14.4	86.5	8.7	4.8
	70.5	76.3	24.1	18.4	77.5	76.7	18.8	17.8	76.3	16.8	6.9
	72.2	78.2	21.0	17.3	75.0	80.0	17.5	13.3	72.0	20.1	7.9
	72.5	68.7	22.6	24.6	82.5	80.0	12.5	15.6	66.1	26.7	7.2
	39.5	36.0	51.9	57.8	37.5	41.1	50.0	50.0	31.9	55.8	12.3
	28.1	24.3	65.9	68.7	31.3	22.2	50.0	52.2	23.8	62.9	13.3
	84.0	90.2	12.0	6.7	85.0	91.1	13.8	4.4	85.1	10.2	4.7
	80.5	80.2	16.3	17.3	73.8	73.3	18.8	20.0	81.8	14.4	3.8
	65.3	61.7	30.1	32.1	82.5	80.0	13.8	15.6	59.8	30.0	10.2
	47.9	45.0	44.7	46.1	60.0	50.0	25.0	32.2	42.8	45.5	11.7
	48.2	36.6	40.1	54.2	67.5	54.4	30.0	34.4	38.8	47.1	14.1
	43.8	37.4	47.8	52.2	52.5	41.1	32.5	25.5	36.1	49.2	14.7
	25.2	27.7	56.7	47.5	42.5	38.9	52.5	51.1	26.0	55.3	18.7
	56.7	55.3	30.9	36.0	71.3	67.8	25.0	24.4	50.1	42.4	7.5
	26.6	26.5	65.0	61.7	35.0	38.9	51.3	36.7	28.2	57.1	14.7
	44.7	41.1	45.8	48.0	60.0	46.7	26.3	36.7	37.7	50.8	11.5
	44.4	40.5	49.3	52.5	60.0	57.8	38.8	38.9	37.8	55.4	6.8
	32.7	33.8	65.3	62.8	45.0	38.9	40.0	47.7	32.5	59.4	8.1
	9.5	7.8	82.0	82.4	7.5	8.9	40.0	63.3	8.8	77.6	13.6

through the combined initiative and co-operation of the pupils.
Many reasons were given to explain why they obtained such limited
practice in this activity, the chief reasons being inexperience and
lack of readiness for the work. Many student-teachers were unable
to build up a curriculum because of the same deficiencies in their
teaching equipment as hindered them in working out comprehen-

sive units of instruction. They had not developed the ability to use discrimination in their evaluations, to take initiative, to work out relationships, and to assume responsibility for this type of work.

Some faculty members suggested that student-teachers should learn, first, how to use the regular courses of study and how to make effective use of the available references and sources of supply suggested in these, and then gradually build up a background for more truly creative work. Some added that it takes a master mind to build up a curriculum and that student-teachers should be inducted into this work very gradually.

The more conservative critic teachers stated that student-teachers should not attempt to build up the curriculum but should adhere closely to courses of study already prepared by experts. They suggested that student-teachers needed something definite to follow during their student-teaching and that they should be trained to use the state or local courses of study. Some of the faculty members indicated that it was not necessary for the average teacher to attempt to construct a curriculum, but that he or she should know how to analyze and to use a functioning course of study.

The critic teachers in some of the more progressive schools stated that every teacher should be a curriculum builder; that the detail of the curriculum should be determined by the actual classroom situation; and that the combination of teacher- and pupil-effort in the continuous and co-operative reconstruction of the curriculum constituted the ideal situation. These critic teachers implied that it was essential for prospective teachers to be properly oriented to this phase of the teacher's work, and thus carefully guided their student-teachers in curriculum construction and adjustment. They first helped them to record suggestions, leads, contributions, interests, difficulties, needs, personality and character traits, and problems of the children from day to day; and then led them to select and to adapt subject-matter and activities to meet these interests, needs, difficulties, traits, and problems. The student-teachers kept cumulative records and outlines of the work as it was covered from day to day, thus helping to build up the curriculum. Most of these critic teachers dealt with student-teachers who were completing four-year teacher-education curricula. Table XXIV, item B, presents the per cent of student-teachers under different administrative organizations who answered "yes" or "no," or who failed to answer at all, when asked if they obtained practice in writing each of the specified types of records and plans subsequent to their teaching activities in student-teaching.

In some schools the student-teachers in the primary grades secured a greater amount of practice in helping to build up the curriculum from day to day than did those in the intermediate or upper elementary grades, because the work in the primary grades, more often than in the upper grades, was centered about large child activities which were determined through the co-operative efforts of teacher and pupils.

B. *Acquiring Adequate Command of Subject-Matter in Order to Direct Effectively the Learning Activities of Children*

According to reports from educators in the teacher-education field, a fund of general information and a broad knowledge of subject-matter to be taught, together with an intelligent working organization of materials of instruction, are essential for the most effective teaching in the elementary grades. In order that student-teachers might attain to a high level of accomplishment during their student-teaching courses, the valuable activities involved in *acquiring adequate command of content subject-matter and other materials of instruction* should have a large place in their institutional experience. Emphasis should, therefore, be placed upon the acquisition of subject-matter and the organization of materials of instruction during college courses sufficient to insure a satisfactory carry-over of these activities into student-teaching.

1. *Planning the selection and organization of subject-matter*

Most of the student-teachers obtained considerable practice in planning the selection and the organization of subject-matter, an activity which was rated comparatively high in both difficulty and value. Because of the difference in the nature of the work in the various elementary grades, student-teachers in the intermediate or upper elementary departments obtained somewhat greater amounts of experience in selecting and organizing subject-matter than did those in the primary grades.

2. *Arranging sequence of topics and units of subject-matter to be studied by the children*

There was great variation in the ratings of this activity. Some stated that in order for it to be of real educative value to prospective teachers, it should be constructively guided.

3. *Finding and assembling materials and information*

Student-teachers encountered many difficulties in finding and assembling suitable materials and pertinent information. These difficulties were often the result of inadequate working knowledge of subject-matter, of libraries, and of other sources of supply; narrow experiences in searching for reference materials; lack of standards and criteria by which to evaluate materials and subject-matter; tendency to read every word on a page rather than to assimilate the main ideas; inability to discriminate between essentials and nonessentials; limited amounts of time and opportunity for this type of work; and lack of confidence, foresight, and initiative in doing independent work.

The median student-teacher consulted numerous sources for the necessary information for daily plans and units of instruction. Some of these sources may be classified as reading materials, interviews, visits, and observation.

a. *Reading as a means of securing information*

In order to obtain essential preparation for teaching activities, most of the student-teachers devoted considerable time during student-teaching courses to reading for information. A great deal of extra time had to be devoted to this activity because student-

TABLE XXV

Per Cent of Student-Teachers Who Used Each of the Types of Reading Materials as Principal Sources of Information in Addition to Their Regular Textbooks and Classroom Materials

Types of Reading Materials	Per Cent of Student-Teachers		
	Primary	Intermediate	Total
1. Supplementary books, reference materials, and other resources of the library	94.0	95.9	95.0
2. Current publications			
a. Magazines, reports, and bulletins	85.7	89.5	87.6
b. Newspapers, leaflets, etc.	69.0	81.0	75.0
3. Advertising materials from business houses and industrial concerns	35.4	44.9	40.2
4. Pamphlets and other reading materials from railroad, steamship, bus, aviation, and other transportation companies	23.9	32.0	28.0
5. Literature from civic, historical, and geographical societies	8.3	15.3	11.8

teachers lacked the sound working knowledge of subject-matter which they should have acquired prior to the period of responsible student-teaching.

Table XXV shows the per cent of student-teachers, out of a total of 2,383, who used each of the types of reading materials specified as sources of information supplementary to their regular textbooks and classroom materials.

Because of the nature of the subject-matter prescribed for the different grades, a larger per cent of the student-teachers in the intermediate departments than of those in the primary departments utilized the various types of reading materials in connection with their teaching activities.

b. Making efficient use of sources of supply

It was considered essential for prospective teachers to be trained to utilize various sources of supply in obtaining instructional materials. Some teachers colleges provided valuable guidance in the use of such sources as libraries, publishing houses, business and industrial concerns, transportation companies, geographical and historical societies, social and civic organizations, and museums and art galleries.

c. Interviewing people for the purpose of securing information relative to problems in connection with student-teaching

In the preparation of certain daily plans and units of instruction, most of the student-teachers obtained some specific information by means of personal interviews with faculty members or with students in the teachers colleges. The median student-teacher also secured some information through interviews with people outside the teachers colleges.

Table XXVI summarizes the reports from 2,242 student-teachers who answered the question, "Have you interviewed people outside the teachers college faculty and students for the purpose of securing information relative to problems and units of work that you have taught during student-teaching courses?" Approximately 50% of the student-teachers definitely stated that they had interviewed people other than those in the teachers colleges for the purpose of obtaining information that would apply to their own teaching problems; about 25% designated that they had done so incidentally; and about 25% reported that they had not done so at all.

TABLE XXVI

Per Cent of Student-Teachers Who Answered "Yes," "Incidentally," or "No"
When Asked if They Had Interviewed People Outside the Teachers
Colleges for the Purpose of Securing Information Applicable
to Their Student-Teaching Work

Answer	Per Cent of Student-Teachers								Sum Total
	1–2 Hours*		½ Day*		All Day*		Total		
	P	I	P	I	P	I	P	I	
Yes...................	48.1	47.2	54.3	51.9	58.1	57.2	50.6	49.3	50.0
Incidentally...........	28.0	23.5	22.6	24.3	21.6	22.6	26.0	23.7	24.8
No...................	23.9	29.3	23.1	23.8	20.3	20.2	23.4	27.0	25.2

* 1–2 Hours = All student-teaching courses scheduled for one hour or two hours a day.
* ½ Day = Major student-teaching courses scheduled for half day.
* All Day = Major student-teaching courses scheduled for whole day.

The persons, other than faculty members and students in the teachers colleges, who were interviewed by student-teachers are grouped in the following list according to frequency of mention:

1. Teachers in and administrators of public and private schools.
2. Friends not connected with the teachers colleges.
3. Relatives.
4. Librarians.
5. Business men and women (merchants, bankers, heads of business houses, managers of industrial concerns, real estate dealers).
6. Skilled workmen (clerks, printers, skilled labor in mills and factories, electricians, mechanics, plumbers, carpenters).
7. Farmers and dairymen (farmers, nurserymen, florists, dairymen).
8. Professional men and women outside the educational field (doctors, dentists, ministers, lawyers, judges, musicians, artists, architects, writers, actors).
9. State, city, and community officials and employees (state or city administrators and office holders, policemen, firemen).
10. Civil service and government employees (postmasters, forest rangers, revenue officers).
11. Social welfare workers.

A large proportion of the student-teachers reported that they had interviewed teachers, librarians, friends, and relatives outside the teachers colleges; but only a relatively small proportion had actually gone into the industrial, business, and civic fields for first-hand information on specific problems. The following approximate per cents of student-teachers reported that they had obtained definite help in connection with their teaching problems through interviews with the various occupational groups given below: approximately 12%, with business men and women; 10%, with skilled workmen; 9%, with farmers and dairymen; 5%, with professional people outside of the teaching field; 3%, with state, city, and community officials and employees; and 3%, with civil service and government employees.

d. Visiting places of interest for the purpose of securing information relative to the work in student-teaching

The following question was submitted to 2,383 student-teachers at the close of their final student-teaching work: "Have you visited places of interest relative to some problem or unit of work that you have taught during student-teaching courses?" The answers from 2,244 of these student-teachers are summarized in Table XXVII.

TABLE XXVII

Per Cent of Student-Teachers Who Answered "Yes" or "No" When Asked if They Had Visited Places of Interest for the Purpose of Securing Information Relative to Their Work in Student-Teaching Courses

Answer	Per Cent of Student-Teachers								
	1–2 Hours		½ Day		All Day		Total		Sum Total
	P	I	P	I	P	I	P	I	
Yes	59.5	54.9	64.3	60.8	72.0	70.3	61.8	57.7	59.8
No	40.5	45.1	35.7	39.2	28.0	29.7	38.2	42.3	40.2

Approximately 62% of the primary and 58% of the intermediate student-teachers reported that they had visited places of interest relative to some problem or unit of work which they had taught during student-teaching courses. Some had visited numerous places of interest, while others had visited only one. Many of the student-teachers had limited their visits to schools, libraries, and other educational centers.

A larger per cent of the student-teachers had obtained specific information by means of personal visits than through personal interviews with people other than teachers and relatives. Less than one-half of the student-teachers had obtained experience in securing information for specific problems by visiting places of interest, outside schools and libraries; but less than one-fourth had done so by interviewing people outside the teachers colleges other than teachers, librarians, personal friends, and relatives.

Places of interest, besides schools and libraries, that student-teachers had visited to secure information are listed below according to the frequency with which they were mentioned.

1. Scenic spots (parks, woods, forests, valleys, rivers, streams, waterfalls and rapids, lakes, oceans, mountains, caves, deserts).
2. Business concerns (markets, stores, banks, printing and newspaper offices, real estate offices, insurance companies).
3. Industrial concerns (factories, mills, canneries, bakeries, electric light and power plants, gas plants, warehouses, mines, foundries, fisheries).
4. Agricultural industries (farms, orchards, nurseries, greenhouses, dairies).
5. Transportation facilities (highways, railroads, airports, harbors, lighthouses).
6. Recreational facilities (sports—athletic fields, swimming pools, public and private playgrounds, race tracks, gymnasiums; amusements— theaters, social halls).
7. Museums, zoos, and aquariums.
8. Places of historical interest.
9. Civic departments (post offices, police departments, fire departments, city water departments, chambers of commerce, courthouses).
10. Government, state, and municipal buildings.
11. Monuments, statues, and memorials.
12. Building constructions.
13. Churches, cathedrals, and missions.
14. Irrigation projects, dams, and canals.

e. Collecting and assembling appropriate specimens and suitable materials needed for activities

The student-teachers' experiences, in many cases, were too meager to enable them to think through and to foresee the materials that were necessary for the completion of large developmental units. Many lacked knowledge of suitable materials for the different grade levels and had not built up standards by which to select the most valuable ones.

In some schools the student-teachers obtained considerable practice in collecting and assembling materials, while in others the critic teachers assumed the greatest share of the responsibility for this work. Reports indicated, however, that student-teachers should have some definite and carefully directed training in these activities.

4. *Making annotated bibliographies*

Bibliographies previously compiled by faculty members or other interested groups were frequently provided; the median student-teacher thus had very little practice in making annotated bibliographies for specific problems, units, or subjects. The reports indicated that it was desirable for student-teachers to know how to make annotated bibliographies, but that the background preparation for this activity should be obtained in other college courses.

5. *Selecting and adapting subject-matter and activities*

More than 95% of the student-teachers reported practice in selecting and adapting materials of instruction during student-teaching. Many encountered difficulties in providing subject-matter and educative child activities which were best adapted to the abilities, experiences, interests, special aptitudes, and needs of individual children, as well as to the objectives and purposes to be attained. An inventory revealed that many student-teachers were lacking in background preparation essential to intelligent selection and adaptation of subject-matter, such as, clear conception of purposes and objectives, broad knowledge of materials of instruction and informational resources, sympathetic understanding of the children to be taught, and proper sense of responsibility.

6. *Evaluating subject-matter in light of criteria set up for that purpose*

Although the evaluation of subject-matter by definite criteria was rated comparatively high in both difficulty and value, the median student-teacher had too limited experience in this activity. Many student-teachers depended too much upon the judgment of critic teachers and other faculty members, thus obtaining little practice in determining the relative worth of the subject-matter presented in textbooks and supplementary sources. The reports indicated that this condition resulted from insufficient emphasis being placed on such essential activities as, acquisition of wide informational resources, cultivation of habits of clear and reflective thinking, and development of attitudes of critical discrimination.

7. *Organizing subject-matter and activities*

Organizing materials of instruction was rated above average in degree of difficulty, in need for special training, and in the amount of actual practice which the student-teachers obtained during student-teaching. A common difficulty among student-teachers was the organization of units of work where the subject-matter had to be secured from numerous sources.

Student-teachers met many trying situations in organizing and carrying out series of activities which could be used appropriately from day to day in building up large developmental units of instruction. They were also confronted with many involved and thought-provoking problems in reorganizing subject-matter around definite phases of the children's activities and experiences which arose during the progress of the work.

Difficulties encountered were frequently caused by a tendency on the part of different student-teachers to copy words rather than ideas; to memorize facts rather than do reflective thinking on a problem; to think in terms of isolated experiences rather than in terms of larger activities; and to follow previously prepared plans too closely rather than to take advantage of the experiences, contributions, and leads of the children which develop during the progress of class or extra-class activities.

The summarized reports showed that student-teachers should secure careful training in these activities, and that they should especially be led to see how the reorganization of subject-matter around children's activities and experiences can help to vitalize the whole teaching situation.

8. *Mastering subject-matter to be used in daily work*

Faculty members unanimously agreed that it was highly essential for student-teachers to secure sufficient command of subject-matter to stimulate, guide, and direct children properly. According to reports from both student-teachers and faculty members, the student-teachers devoted a large proportion of the student-teaching time to the acquisition and mastery of subject-matter. This was especially true in the two-year programs, because of the student-teachers' limited academic and cultural backgrounds. Poor study habits and indifference to high scholastic attainments also increased the amount of time necessary for sufficient mastery of subject-matter.

9. *Arranging, recording, and filing data and materials*

The amount and type of practice which student-teachers obtained in arranging, recording, and filing materials varied greatly in the different schools. Some student-teachers were held responsible for adding to the permanent files in the schools; some were required to make large folders or individual filing cases in which to place materials for their own future use; some were expected to add to the files in the school as well as to make their own individual filing cases; and others had no practice in these activities during student-teaching. (See Table XXIII.)

Some student-teachers were trained to index materials in systematic alphabetical order; some to arrange important subject-matter topically with minor classifications under each major topic; and a few to cross-index materials. Some were taught various other devices for keeping together and classifying papers, articles, and other types of supplementary and reference materials.

C. Obtaining an Understanding of Individual Differences of Children by Studying and Analyzing Factors That Condition Their Learning

There was general agreement among educators that successful teaching requires intelligent understanding of the children to be taught; and that it was highly essential for student-teachers to secure a broad working knowledge of child development through varied contacts with children in real life, as well as through theoretical instruction. The reports indicated that prospective teachers should be provided adequate opportunities to study the abilities, attitudes, interests, traits, habits, problems, and needs of children; and that they should be trained to understand individual differences by studying and analyzing factors that condition child learning and behavior.

The amount, type, and richness of the experiences that student-teachers secured in connection with child study varied widely in the different state teachers colleges. In some schools the student-teachers obtained wide contacts with children and had rich experiences in connection with child study, while in others they secured very limited contacts and experiences. The primary student-teachers obtained slightly more practice in studying problems dealing with child development than did those in the intermediate departments. Greater amounts of practice and richer experiences, in studying factors which produce individual differences of children and which condition child learning, were obtained (1) by student-teachers in four-year curricula than by those in two-year and three-year programs; and (2) by those under half-day and whole-day student-teaching plans than by those under the one-hour-a-day plan.

Table XXIII lists and evaluates the principal activities that help student-teachers to secure an understanding of factors which condition child learning and development.

1. *Studying and analyzing personality traits of individual children*

This activity is very much involved and requires careful analysis of the following factors pertaining to personality: (1) mental attitudes, characteristics, and capacities; (2) physical features, traits, and habits; (3) emotional reactions and impulses; (4) will-profile and temperamental attitudes; (5) social and moral-ethical attitudes, tendencies, and characteristics; and (6) aesthetic talents and interests. Analyzing personality traits in children was rated high in difficulty, very high in value, and above average in the amount of experience which student-teachers obtained during student-teaching courses. The student-teachers obtained practically no experience, however, in giving standard tests to reveal character traits.

Owing to limited experience with children and to inadequate working knowledge of child psychology, many student-teachers encountered difficulties in analyzing personality traits of individual children. Many of the faculty members suggested that the theory and underlying principles of child study taught in connection with professional courses should be made sufficiently practical to function in actual teaching situations.

Numerous procedures were used in studying personality traits of children in different laboratory schools. The following were mentioned most frequently: (1) determining attitudes, traits, and habits that needed particular attention in the class as a whole; (2) observing the whole group and writing case reports on certain individuals; (3) observing and studying one or more children who had been selected for special reasons, and writing up the findings; (4) making personality studies of two or more different types of children for comparative purposes; (5) making careful diagnoses of one or more problem children; (6) filling out extensive questionnaires concerning one or more children during a designated period of time; (7) keeping diaries and records for each child in the class; (8) checking and grading the children on definite lists of habits, traits, interests, and attitudes; (9) keeping diagrams and charts of individual progress; and (10) utilizing the diagnoses made by the psychology, the physical education, and the health departments. The personality traits of the children were discussed during conferences between critic teachers and student-teachers.

2. *Studying experiences, backgrounds, and environments of the pupils*

Numerous means were used by the student-teachers in obtaining information about the experiences, backgrounds, and environments of their pupils, chief among which were: observation and study of the pupils in class and extra-class activities; conferences in which pertinent facts relative to the children were discussed by student-teachers and critics or other faculty members; conferences between student-teachers and children; special case studies made by individual student-teachers; group studies made by student-teachers; study of permanent office files, temporary school records, report cards, and charts concerning the children; and contacts with parents at social or school functions.

Only a very small per cent of the student-teachers had direct contact with the homes of the pupils in the laboratory schools. Some of the student-teachers who were scheduled for whole-day teaching in the co-operative schools devoted considerable time to visiting the homes of their pupils, while those assigned to less than half-day student-teaching in the campus laboratory schools devoted practically no time to this activity. Some of the student-teachers in the campus laboratory schools were encouraged to make social contacts with the parents, but only a small proportion were permitted to visit the homes for the purpose of counseling the parents relative to the children.

Numerous reasons were given why only such a small proportion of the student-teachers in the campus laboratory schools made close contacts with the homes. Many of the laboratory-school faculty members indicated that it was a very delicate matter to send student-teachers to interview parents regarding their children. For the following reasons they advised that student-teachers should not visit the homes of the campus laboratory-school pupils for the purpose of counseling the parents, unless accompanied by a faculty member: some student-teachers were so immature, inexperienced, curious, and tactless as to constitute potential causes of trouble; some had difficulty in being truthful and tactful at the same time and, through their inability to discriminate between actual child diagnosis and flattery, gave parents wrong notions which were difficult to rectify;

and some did not know how to give helpful suggestions and constructive criticisms, or were too timid and self-conscious to express themselves. Some faculty members reported that it would be unwise for every student-teacher to visit the homes of the pupils because the parents would resent it, and that it would lower the reputation of the school to have such large numbers of student-teachers go out into the homes to secure data relative to the children. Some indicated that student-teachers too often did not have a complete understanding of the whole situation and, consequently, misrepresented cases; that the student-teaching periods were too short and piecemeal for this type of work; and that the supervisory loads of the critic teachers were too heavy to permit proper guidance of this activity.

Reports indicated that it was very essential for student-teachers to obtain a thorough background for studying the experiences and environment of children, but that the basic foundation for this work should be so well mastered in other professional courses that it will function in student-teaching and later in the field.

3. *Giving intelligence tests and studying the results of these tests*

Many critic teachers questioned the advisability of permitting all the student-teachers to give intelligence tests to their pupils. Some indicated that prospective teachers should develop right mental attitudes toward intelligence testing; that they should learn how to administer such tests, and how to check and interpret the results; but that they should be technically trained before they give intelligence tests to children and attempt to use the results of these for diagnostic purposes. They suggested that this training should be secured in professional courses other than student-teaching.

Many student-teachers observed experts give intelligence tests; some assisted in administering these tests, and helped in checking the answers and in tabulating the results; but only a few assumed responsibility for giving such tests to children. Most of those who obtained actual practice in administering intelligence tests to groups of children were advanced students in the four-year curricula. Critic teachers, for the most part, did not consider it wise for student-teachers, who were not technically and scientifically trained for this work, to know the I. Q.'s of individual children in the laboratory schools. In some schools the I. Q.'s were never shown to the student-teachers, except in rare cases, because the faculty members considered it a dangerous practice.

Faculty members implied that the whole testing program depended upon training, accuracy, and diagnosis and that standard intelligence tests should therefore be given only by experts.

4. *Examining and observing the conditions of health and physical equipment of individual children*

The median student-teacher obtained very little actual practice in examining the conditions of health and physical equipment of the children. Some of the student-teachers observed and participated in health examinations, but did not assume responsibility for conducting them. These examinations were usually given by the physical education department, the health department, the school nurse, the school doctor, or other experts in the field of health. Some student-teachers, however, examined one or more children for physical defects in connection with special case studies; some examined the hair, the skin, and the nails of children during regular health inspections; some weighed and measured children; some assisted in giving tests; and some made charts and kept records.

Many of the critic teachers suggested that student-teachers should obtain more actual practice in these health activities in order to promote the health work in the field, but they implied that the students should secure the background for this work in the health and physical education departments.

5. *Investigating reasons for deficiencies in school education of individual children*

Background preparation for this activity should be obtained in connection with child study and other professionalized courses, and then applied to individual case studies as need arises during student-teaching.

6. *Reading books and articles dealing with problems of maladjustment in children*

Reports indicated that this reading should be done largely in connection with other professional courses and then applied during student-teaching.

7. *Securing better understanding of children through personal interviews and conferences*

Both faculty members and student-teachers pointed out that well-planned and purposeful conferences are valuable means through which friendly relations and willing co-operation can be established between student-teachers and their pupils. Many stated that through constructive personal interviews the student-teacher became better acquainted with the children and secured better understanding of their interests, attitudes, traits, habits, difficulties, problems, and needs.

The median student-teacher held individual conferences with children as need arose or when there was a special purpose for doing so; some had much practice in this activity at the beginning of each term; others frequently held personal interviews with special case studies or with problem children; and still others did so only occasionally. Owing to lack of time and opportunity, some never held personal interviews with individual children.

8. *Discovering individual interests of the children through a wide variety of illustrative materials and reference books*

Inasmuch as there is so great a variety of interests represented in a group of children, teachers are obliged to employ many different agencies in discovering the individual interests of all the pupils. The use of a wide variety of visual aids, books, and other instructional materials was given as one of the valid means of discovering these interests of the children. Many teachers specified that training in this activity was, therefore, highly essential.

D. *Planning, Studying, Experimenting with, and Using the Different Types of Educational Procedures in Directing the Learning Activities of Children (Applying Methods of Instruction)*

In the different state teachers colleges numerous types of techniques were used in directing the learning activities of the children. There was a consensus of opinion that student-teachers should secure rich contacts and broad experiences with a wide variety of teaching techniques and educational procedures, together with an intelligent understanding of the philosophy, theory, and principles underlying the most important ones.

Table XXIII shows that the student-teachers scheduled for half-day and whole-day student-teaching had considerably more practice in guiding children in activity units, creative work, and socialized activities than did those scheduled for one-hour-a-day student-teaching. Those who did their student-teaching during the third and fourth years of the elementary teacher-education curricula usually had a great deal more practice in handling developmental units of instruction and creative activities than did those in the two-year programs. The student-teachers in the two-year programs who had been assigned to student-teaching for one hour a day, on the other hand, had more practice in drill work, exposition methods, and the typical textbook recitations. These conditions were partly due to the fact that those student-teachers who came in contact with the laboratory school for only one hour a day had very little opportunity to become acquainted with the children in all types of activities or to see the teaching situation as a whole.

1. *Planning, selecting, and adapting methods of instruction*

Many new and thought-provoking problems presented themselves to the student-teachers in planning methods of instruction that would provide sufficient opportunities for pupils' activities. The student-teachers were also faced with many vital and involved problems in selecting and adapting the methods of instruction with reference to the children's abilities, interests, and needs as well as to the environments in which the teaching and learning activities took place. In most of the teachers colleges the student-teachers fortunately devoted a large proportion of their student-teaching time to the planning, selection, and adaptation of different methods of instruction.

2. *Utilizing effective methods of instruction*

The techniques and procedures in which student-teachers obtained the greatest amount of practice are enumerated alphabetically in the *Master Activity Check List,* item D. In Table XXIII these activities are evaluated by faculty members according to the three criteria listed on page 8. Their chief comments and suggestions, relative to the nature of the difficulties and to the need for definite training in each of these techniques, will here be briefly set forth.

(1) *Activity units or projects*

The reports indicated that most of the beginning student-teachers encountered many difficulties and problems which challenged their powers of adjustment in adapting themselves to an activity program. A somewhat detailed treatment of the underlying causes of these difficulties is to be found on pages 181 to 196.

Most of the laboratory-school faculty members stated that it was highly essential for student-teachers to secure proper preparation for carrying out activity work, if this type of teaching was to be carried on effectively in the field. Some of the more progressive critics rec-ommended that the whole school life be organized around construc-tive activity work, a set-up which would require the highest type of education on the part of the teachers.

The interpretation and use of the term "Activity Unit" varies among teachers colleges. The term may be applied to units which are conducted as separate and distinct problems of instruction in a single subject and/or to units which complement the integration of a variety of subjects in forming large units of instruction, designed for use over a prolonged period of time. An activity unit might in-clude many types of specific activities, such as collecting, construct-ing, creating, dancing, directing, dramatizing, drawing, exercising, figuring, listening, observing, playing, questioning, reading, reciting, singing, spelling, studying, and writing.

Critic teachers in progressive schools pointed out that compre-hensive activity units furnished splendid opportunities for the inte-gration of various types of subject-matter and instructional mate-rials; for creative and socialized work; and for the development of such traits as alertness, co-operativeness, imaginativeness, initiative, leadership, originality, resourcefulness, self-control, and sociability.

(2) *Appreciation method*

Student-teachers usually needed definite guidance in learning how to stimulate in the pupils a genuine appreciation of, and sincere ad-miration for, things of aesthetic value. Many also needed careful direction in recognizing true worth in things of intellectual value, and in creating real enjoyment for these in others. They found diffi-culty in stimulating real appreciation in others because they them-selves had not developed broad perception and intelligent compre-hension, and lacked attitudes of sympathetic understanding. They had not lived fully enough nor obtained sufficiently rich cultural backgrounds by which to inspire others.

(3) *Creative work*

Constructive creative activities represented many intricate prob-lems for the student-teachers. Many were thwarted in the successful handling of these activities because of their own limited creative abilities, narrow backgrounds, and meager experiences, together with their lack of understanding of the philosophy behind it all.

In many of the laboratory schools a large proportion of the

student-teachers had very limited experiences in guiding children in various types of purposeful creative activities, although faculty members contended that it was highly essential for them to obtain definite preparation for this very important phase of the elementary teacher's work.

Progressive critic teachers implied that creative work should not be taught as an isolated type of procedure, but as an integral part of every class period; and that it should play an especially important part in the development of activity units in all the grades.

(4) *Dramatic play and dramatic expression*

Work, if of the right type, in connection with creative plays and dramatic expression was considered very valuable. Although the median student-teacher obtained an average amount of practice in directing dramatic play, a faulty conception of truly creative dramatic expression unfortunately diminished the real value of these experiences for many of the student-teachers. Progressive critic teachers suggested that student-teachers should be (*a*) led to realize the importance of creative activities in developing self-expression in the pupils; (*b*) taught how to build dramatic plays around both class work and extra-class activities; and (*c*) constructively guided in the art of directing the children in creative dramatizations.

(5) *Dramatization work in regular school subjects*

Regular school subjects can often be made very real, interesting, and meaningful through dramatizations. Many critic teachers recommended that student-teachers should be taught (*a*) where to find and how to select appropriate subject-matter and suitable materials for dramatizations; (*b*) when and how to direct children in carrying these out effectively; and (*c*) how to make dramatizations simultaneously purposeful, stimulating, valuable to all the members in a class, and economical of time and expense.

(6) *Drill lessons and exercises*

The acquisition of skill in applying drill techniques was rated about average in the degree of difficulty encountered by beginning student-teachers. They had considerably less difficulty in acquiring skill in conducting drill exercises than they had in guiding activity units or creative work. Some of the outstanding problems which they met in connection with drill work were as follows: (*a*) making drill functional and meaningful for the children; (*b*) providing for economical and effective practice drill; and (*c*) keeping the children attentive and interested.

Drill work of the right type is exceedingly important and must have a very definite place in the curriculum. The critic teachers, therefore, urged that every student-teacher develop wholesome attitudes toward drill work, together with the ability to apply the most effective drill techniques. Some stated that student-teachers should be made to realize that certain fundamentals must be made automatic; that intensive and thorough drill is necessary for the mastery of essentials; and that drill is the mother of efficiency in later work. The student-teachers for the most part secured considerable practice in conducting drill exercises.

(7) *Exposition methods*

According to reports from both faculty members and student-teachers, most of the student-teachers had a natural inclination toward the exposition methods of teaching; and they often devoted too much time to it. It was usually easier for them to tell facts in subject-matter than to lead the children to discover these through developmental procedures.

(8) *School journeys, excursions, and field trips*

The suggestions which were offered relative to planning and conducting excursions and field trips are given on page 107 under the major heading "Contacts with Children's Extra-Class Activities."

(9) *Individualized instruction*

(*a*) *The contract plan*

A very small per cent of the student-teachers obtained any definite experience in connection with the contract plan of teaching. Training in this activity, however, was not considered essential because the contract plan of teaching is usually too highly mechanical and too teacher-imposed.

(*b*) *Individualizing instruction to meet the needs, interests, and capacities of each child in the class*

Both bright and slow children have a right to achieve at a rate commensurate with their respective capacities and to receive the encouragement and help that will stimulate them to progress at their maximum speed. Careful preparation is necessary, however, to enable the teacher to individualize instruction effectively and at the same time to safeguard the rights of all. The many complex situations that resulted from the efforts of student-teachers to recognize and provide for individual differences served to convince both student-teachers and laboratory-school faculty members that efficient guidance and adequate practice must precede such efforts.

(10–13) *Inductive-deductive types of procedure, organized question-answer methods, and organized topical recitations*

These techniques were all rated about average in the difficulties which they presented to the student-teachers and in the need for specific training to carry them out effectively. The value of training in these more formal types of teaching techniques was rated higher for teachers in the intermediate grades than for those in the primary grades; and the majority of the student-teachers in the intermediate departments likewise obtained greater amounts of practice in them than did those in the primary departments.

(14) *Problem-solving*

The student-teachers in the intermediate departments who had the richest experiences in planning, organizing, and carrying out large units of instruction also had the greatest amount of practice in connection with problem-solving. Progressive critic teachers pointed out that problem-solving is an important factor in carrying out activity units or large units of instruction, and that it was highly essential for students to obtain practice in working out many types of thought-provoking and vital problems with children.

(15) *Review work and reorganization of old knowledge*

Critic teachers in the primary departments rated review work about average in difficulty and value. Many of those in the intermediate departments, however, contended that constructive reviews presented many involved problems and perplexing difficulties for a large number of the student-teachers in the intermediate and upper grades; and suggested that those preparing to teach in the intermediate grades should especially have definite training in these procedures.

(16) *Socialized discussions*

Progressive methods of teaching encourage the use of a large variety of educational procedures for the purpose of developing the child as a whole. Socialized discussion was rated as one of the most valuable types of procedure in which student-teachers should obtain practice, because socialized discussion of an instructional nature requires the highest type of constructive leadership and co-operative guidance; it helps to develop, in both student-teachers and children, such important personality traits as adaptability, co-operation, initiative, leadership, poise, self-confidence, self-control, self-expression, sociability, tact, and unselfishness.

Whereas the intermediate student-teachers obtained slightly more practice in connection with problem-solving, those in the primary grades had more experience in guiding socialized discussions.

(17) *Study-test plan of procedure*

Reports indicated that student-teachers had but little practice in the study-test plan of procedure in the lower grades, and that it was only slightly essential for them to do so.

(18) *Supervised or directed study*

Critic teachers pointed out that it was reasonably essential for student-teachers to obtain definite training in directing children's study periods. See pages 94–96 for more detailed information.

(19) *Textbook recitations*

Many of the critic teachers contended (*a*) that textbooks were valuable if rightly used; (*b*) that since teachers were required to have textbooks in the field, they should be trained to use them effectively; (*c*) that student-teachers should be taught to use textbooks as guides and to guard against the slavish or formal adherence to them; and (*d*) that a variety of methods of book study were difficult because the student-teachers were not familiar with the textbooks in the different subjects and grades.

(20) *Visualized instruction*

The difficulties encountered by student-teachers in connection with visualized instruction were usually due to inability to find and collect appropriate illustrative materials; inadequate working knowledge of how to use available materials; and lack of equipment in the schools.

Although most of the critic teachers indicated that it was very essential for student-teachers to obtain definite training in assembling and using different types of visual materials in connection with the various subjects in the elementary grades, the median student-teacher had but limited experience in working with such materials. Increased amounts of time and effort should, therefore, be expended on visualized instruction.

(21) *Testing*

The construction of thought-provoking tests and the utilization of the results of different types of standard tests, rather than the actual giving of these to the children, produced trying problems for the student-teachers. Difficulties encountered in giving tests were usually due to insufficient knowledge of the scientific procedures involved.

Some student-teachers had considerable practice in *giving exploratory and diagnostic tests,* while others had but little. Reports indicated that student-teachers should have some responsibility in giving and in analyzing the results of these types of tests, in order to obtain a better understanding of the progress and the needs of the children.

Except for a small per cent of the advanced students in the three-year and four-year curricula, the student-teachers had practically no experience in *giving standard achievement tests* to children, although many spent considerable time checking answers and tabulating scores. A few schools reported that student-teaching time devoted to correcting standard tests was often at the expense of the more essential teaching activities. In the schools where the results of these tests were filed for future use, the testing program was usually administered by experts.

Most of the student-teachers in the intermediate grades had considerable experience in *making and giving attainment tests* in regular class work. Many critics pointed out that this type of testing stimulates present work and directs future teaching; that it helps teachers to know the difficulties, weaknesses, and progress of each child and thus enables them to adjust their work according to both individual and group needs; that testing is an important phase of the regular teaching program when rightly handled; and that student-teachers should, therefore, secure definite training in these activities.

3. *Helping children to develop adeptness in the basic skill subjects*

a. *Teaching the basic skill subjects*

The ratings of the specific activities involved in teaching some of the basic skill subjects are summarized, in accordance with reports from laboratory-school faculty members, in Table XXIII. Activities that were rated high or above average both in difficulty and in the need for definite training are as follows: (*a*) guiding children in developing situations and conditions from which will emerge the need for habits, skills, and more formal learning; (*b*) stimulating desire or motive on the part of children to learn or to master new materials; (*c*) giving children a clear conception of what is to be learned; (*d*) providing incentives for sustained effort on the part of each child; and (*e*) utilizing progressive methods to attain the most desirable results.

The median student-teacher devoted a large part of the student-teaching time to directing children's learning of new materials, fundamental processes, skills, and habits. In the primary and intermediate grades, the majority of the student-teachers obtained some practice in teaching one or more of the basic skill subjects, such as reading and arithmetic. (See Table XXIX.)

Reports indicated that student-teachers preparing to teach in the primary grades should secure special training in teaching the language arts—reading, language, writing—and the number concepts. Those preparing to teach in the intermediate grades should have definite training in helping children to increase comprehension, accuracy, and speed in the following basic skill subjects: reading, arithmetic, spelling, and language.

b. Handling remedial work

Discovering and diagnosing causes of deficiencies and difficulties of children, and then applying proper remedial instruction, were rated high in both difficulty and value. Some of the principal difficulties encountered by student-teachers in dealing with remedial work were often due to one or more of the following causes: lack of proper analysis of subject-matter; insufficient understanding of psychology involved; inadequate working knowledge of underlying principles and specific skills needed; inexperience with children; and too little foresight, insight, initiative, resourcefulness, thoroughness, and persistence on the part of the student-teachers.

In view of the fact that much of the practice secured by the median student-teacher was gained through contacts with problem children and small isolated groups, critic teachers recommended a greater amount of practice and with more representative groups. Remedial work involves problems that require a great degree of practical skill and experiential knowledge, which only expanded contacts will produce.

4. *Guiding children in utilizing skills and subject-matter*

Table XXIII enumerates and summarizes the ratings of some of the important specific activities involved in guiding the children in utilizing skills and subject-matter.

a. *Helping children to develop appropriate mental set*

The vital importance of an appropriate mental set to any effective learning situation makes it most advisable for student-teachers to obtain all possible experiences in stimulating proper mental attitudes on the part of the children. Numerous contacts with a variety of procedures for attracting and holding the attention of the children were recommended as essential in this regard.

b. *Helping children to understand objectives and purposes of work to be accomplished*

The chief difficulties encountered in this activity were usually due to the student-teachers' own limited knowledge of the objectives and purposes to be attained. It is obvious, however, that a great deal of skill is required to convey to the pupils, uninformed and immature as they are, conceptions which can be fully grasped only after the work has been completed—if then. A broad working knowledge of materials of instruction suitable to children at a given age level, as well as intelligent understanding of the needs of the children to be taught, would considerably minimize the student-teachers' difficulties in carrying out this activity.

c. *Inducing children to formulate and to set up standards to be attained in a stated piece of work*

It was natural that student-teachers should find it difficult to induce children to set up criteria by which to guide their efforts and measure their accomplishments, inasmuch as the children's opportunities for evaluation and for establishment of standards are limited by their age and inexperience with the more abstract phases of learning. Most of the faculty members, however, considered that the resultant clarification of the student-teachers' own conceptions of standards more than justified participation in this activity, and for this reason advised that considerable practice be secured.

d. Initiating and carrying to completion, with the co-operation of the pupils, large units of instruction which include the integration and drawing together of various phases of subject-matter, different types of activities, and many human experiences within the comprehension of the children

Although the activities listed under this heading were rated very high in both difficulty and value, the median student-teacher obtained limited experiences in this phase of the teacher's work.

The student-teachers encountered many challenging problems and trying situations in connection with the following types of activities:

(1) Guiding the pupils in initiating and carrying into effect such purposeful learning activities as:
   (a) Centers of interest, vital problems, and developmental units of work which will draw upon many phases of human experience within the comprehension of the children.
   (b) Appropriate, constructive, and comprehensive activity units or projects.

(2) Recognizing and making effective use of children's leads, questions, and contributions.

(3) Directing children in making surveys of what they should do or accomplish during stated periods of time. (Planning what should be accomplished but taking into consideration the present environment, common experiences of the children, accomplishments by previous groups of children in the same grade, the current interests of the community life, and the events of the world at large).

(4) Leading children to suggest, to choose, and to plan effective methods for solving problems and for carrying out large developmental units of work.

(5) Guiding children in the execution and progress of learning activities that a high purpose may be maintained consistently under changing conditions.

The failure of student-teachers to secure the amount of experience commensurate with the difficulty and value of these activities may be explained from a dual standpoint: lack of the necessary equipment on the part of many student-teachers, and absence of progressive attitudes on the part of administrators and supervisors of student-teaching.

It was stated that these activities were far beyond the reach of many of the student-teachers, especially those in the two-year and three-year programs. They were so occupied by the mechanics of teaching that their minds were not alert to constructive leads of the children. Many student-teachers were unable to adjust to new situations and to make effective use of children's questions and contributions, because they lacked the necessary initiative, sense of responsibility, resourcefulness, vivid imagination, creative ability, fund of ideas, breadth of vision, foresight, and sound judgment. Slack habits of reasoning handicapped them in their attempts to think through whole problems and to grasp different points of view. Fragmentary knowledge of subject-matter, meager cultural backgrounds, and inaccurate concepts of child life and interests hindered them in discriminating properly between essentials and nonessentials of subject-matter and in drawing out of the children the maximum of expression and activity. Some of the advanced student-teachers in the four-year curricula, however, displayed amazing dexterity in directing these activities.

In many cases the inexperience of student-teachers in initiating and carrying to completion, with the co-operation of the children, a variety of activity units was largely the fault of the particular teacher-education set-up. Some student-teachers were provided opportunity for observation of activity units during student-teaching, but were hampered in putting them into practice because no contacts with these had been afforded in any of their previous educational experiences. Some critic teachers provided few opportunities for their student-teachers to obtain experience in such activities as *guiding pupils in initiating activities* and *leading children to choose methods of working out units or projects,* on the grounds that such procedures were adapted only to creative subjects; that student-teachers tended to do too much of the work for the children; that many were inclined to entertain the children, rather than to stimulate substantial accomplishment; and that the value derived did not justify the risk involved for the children at the hands of inexperienced teachers.

In order, however, that such valuable activities might be properly developed, it was recommended that:

1. Frequent opportunity be provided for the evaluation, development, and organization of subject-matter into whole units in connection with college courses, so that student-teachers may become adept at gaining an overview of whole topics and in thinking through whole problems.
2. Thorough background in subject-matter and educational procedures be acquired so that the use of the teaching tools may be automatized,

leaving the teacher's mind alert to the potentialities of the teaching and learning situations.

3. More practical knowledge of children be secured so that each child may be given maximum opportunity for participation and development in these activities.

4. Induction into these activities be begun early in student-teaching courses, and great emphasis be laid upon the development and exercise of the necessary traits of mind and action.

5. Practice in such procedures be long and consecutive, and under the sympathetic guidance of well-prepared and progressive supervisors or critic teachers.

The chief causes underlying the difficulties encountered in these activities are presented in Table XLIV, and discussed in more detail under the heading, *Chief Underlying Causes of Difficulties Encountered by Student-Teachers during Student-Teaching,* in Chapter V.

e. Teaching children to study

(1) Utilizing assignments as effective guides for study

This activity was rated one of the most difficult and valuable activities in which student-teachers in the intermediate and upper grades should obtain experience. Special attention should be given to (*a*) adapting assignments to the abilities, interests, and needs of both individual children and the class; and (*b*) guiding children in initiating their own assignments.

(2) Providing for purposeful pupil activity during independent study periods as well as for class work

Inasmuch as this procedure presents considerable difficulty and is so vital a part of the teacher's work, it was advised that it be given emphasis in the preparation of teachers. Ratings in value were slightly higher for student-teachers in the intermediate grades than for those in the primary grades, and the intermediate student-teachers likewise obtained a greater amount of experience in this activity.

(3) Helping children to develop proper techniques for reference work

(a) Guiding children in making surveys of suitable materials and available equipment to be used in carrying out activities

It was considered essential for student-teachers to obtain practice in this activity because it helps the student-teachers to see possibilities in many types of crude materials as well as in the regular school equipment; aids them in acquiring better understanding of the different types of materials needed in teaching and learning situations; teaches them how to utilize environments and available materials; and helps them to obtain better working knowledge of how to lead children in working with different types of materials, as well as to acquire broader conception of the whole teaching situation.

(b) *Guiding the children in finding, collecting, assembling, and selecting materials*

(c) *Directing learning in the use of the library*

Some recommended that prospective teachers for the intermediate grades were particularly in need of special practice in the following activities in connection with the use of the library:

1. Explaining to children how to use card indexes, card slips, *The Readers' Guide,* and encyclopedias.
2. Showing children how to find reference books, current magazines, and bound volumes of periodicals.
3. Directing learning in the economical and effective use of the dictionary.

(d) *Directing learning in the economical and effective use of books*

Types of activities in which both primary and intermediate student-teachers should obtain practice are listed according to their value in the preparation of teachers, on the basis of ratings given in the *Master Activity Check List:*

1. Guiding children in making effective use of different types of books and recorded matter.
2. Leading children to form habit of searching in various sources for related materials.
3. Guiding children in finding and using the essential parts of a book, i.e., title, author, illustrator, publisher, date of publication, pages, table of contents, index, chapter headings, glossary, footnotes, and marginal notes.
4. Guiding the children in judging the validity and reliability of materials and information.
5. Teaching children how to take care of books.

(4) *Helping children to develop skill in specific study habits*

Laboratory-school faculty members recommended that student-teachers in the intermediate and upper elementary grades should obtain adequate practice in helping children to develop skill in each of the following activities: (*a*) deciding what is to be done; (*b*) studying with some definite aim in view; (*c*) concentrating on the work at hand and keeping the thinking systematically organized; (*d*) organizing subject-matter and materials; (*e*) discriminating between essentials and nonessentials in subject-matter; (*f*) connecting ideas in their proper relationships; (*g*) searching for information through thoughtful and reflective reading; (*h*) outlining and recording useful materials and information; (*i*) assimilating the ideas of an author; (*j*) memorizing essentials in subject-matter; (*k*) formulating conclusions and summaries; (*l*) verifying conclusions formed; (*m*) maintaining critical attitudes toward materials studied; (*n*) comparing work with standards in order to check errors; (*o*) correcting errors; (*p*) making economical and effective use of time and materials.

5. *Teaching a variety of subjects*

There was a wide range in both the type and the number of subjects in which the different student-teachers obtained actual teaching experience during student-teaching courses. Table XXVIII summarizes the reports from 2,345 student-teachers under different administrative organizations who answered the question, "How many different subjects did you teach in connection with your student-teaching courses?"

TABLE XXVIII

Per Cent of Student-Teachers under Different Administrative Organizations Who Obtained Actual Practice in Teaching Each of the Indicated Number of Subjects during Their Student-Teaching Courses

Number of Subjects	Per Cent of Student-Teachers								Sum Total
	1–2 Hours		½ Day		All Day		Total		
	P	I	P	I	P	I	P	I	
8 and up	10.2	8.7	17.6	17.7	57.0	50.0	15.6	14.5	15.1
7	3.4	5.3	6.4	7.6	11.4	2.2	4.8	5.8	5.3
6	8.6	8.1	15.6	14.3	7.6	16.7	10.6	10.6	10.6
5	13.5	10.7	18.5	14.9	7.6	7.8	14.6	11.7	13.2
4	25.7	20.4	24.0	22.8	12.6	16.7	24.3	20.8	22.6
3	18.1	19.9	10.4	12.9	3.8	6.7	14.8	16.8	15.8
2	16.3	18.5	5.2	6.4	...	...	11.9	13.5	12.7
1	4.1	8.3	2.3	3.3	...	...	3.3	6.2	4.7

Approximately 20.4% of these student-teachers obtained practice in teaching seven or more different subjects during student-teaching courses; this total per cent included about 13.8% of those scheduled in major student-teaching courses for one and two hours a day, 24.7% of those scheduled for half day, and 60.3% of those scheduled for all day.

About 23.6% of those scheduled for one-hour- and two-hours-a-day, 8.6% of those scheduled for half-day, and none of those scheduled for whole-day student-teaching taught less than three subjects.

The median student-teacher under each of the specified student-teaching plans obtained actual practice in teaching the following number of elementary school subjects: one-hour-a-day plan, four subjects; half-day plan, five subjects; and whole-day plan, eight subjects. The median student-teacher who participated in this study obtained actual practice in teaching reading, arithmetic, one of the social sciences, and one other subject.

A larger proportion of the student-teachers who majored in the primary grades than of those who majored in the intermediate grades obtained practice in teaching four or more different subjects. Some of the chief reasons are:

1. A greater number of term- or semester-hours of student-teaching was required in some teachers colleges for the completion of the primary curriculum than for the intermediate curriculum.

2. The children's class periods in the primary grades were sometimes shorter than those in the intermediate grades, thus making it possible for a primary student-teacher to teach two, three, or more different subjects during a sixty-minute student-teaching period.

3. The children were sometimes divided into smaller groups for some subjects, thus providing opportunity for several student-teachers to teach under the direction of the same critic teacher during a class period. This situation was more common in the primary than in the intermediate grades.

4. There was more integration of subjects, on the whole, in the primary grades than in the intermediate grades.

5. In the intermediate grades more frequently than in the primary grades, such subjects as music, art, and physical education were taught by special supervisors, thus providing more opportunity for student-teachers to teach these subjects in the primary grades.

Table XXIX shows the per cent of student-teachers, under various administrative organizations, who obtained practice in teaching the different subjects.

TABLE XXIX

Per Cent of Student-Teachers under Different Administrative Organizations Who Reported That They Obtained Actual Practice in Teaching Each of the Following Subjects during Student-Teaching Courses

Subjects Taught by Student-Teachers	Per Cent of Student-Teachers								Sum Total
	1-2 Hours		½ Day		All Day		Total		
	P	I	P	I	P	I	P	I	
1. Reading									
a. Reading..........	68.0	45.0	79.5	51.4	86.1	60.0	72.6	48.1	60.4
b. Literature........	7.1	9.9	9.8	14.3	17.7	16.7	8.6	11.7	10.2
c. Phonics..........	7.2	.4	10.7	.3	22.9	1.1	9.3	.4	4.8
2. Arithmetic—Numbers	51.1	55.9	52.6	61.2	74.5	80.0	53.1	59.4	56.3
3. Social and Natural Sciences									
a. Social Studies.... (Designated)	30.7	24.1	47.7	28.4	68.4	37.8	38.3	26.4	32.3
b. Geography......	17.3	33.5	22.2	43.3	34.2	63.3	20.0	38.7	29.4
c. History.........	3.0	24.7	4.6	41.3	11.4	60.0	4.1	32.7	18.4
d. Health..........	17.2	14.4	20.3	18.5	40.5	37.8	19.6	17.4	18.5
e. Science and Nature Study....	15.8	14.1	20.3	20.5	35.4	33.3	18.5	17.5	18.0
f. Citizenship......	2.0	2.3	3.5	5.9	6.3	10.0	2.8	4.0	3.4
4. Language—English..	35.6	38.0	42.2	44.9	59.5	67.8	39.2	42.3	40.8
5. Spelling...........	34.3	38.5	34.1	43.5	57.0	67.8	35.8	42.2	39.0
6. Physical Education (Games—Playground)..........	37.8	22.6	57.0	38.5	81.0	60.2	46.4	30.3	38.3
7. Arts and Handicrafts									
a. Art—Drawing...	24.9	21.4	29.8	25.6	69.6	51.1	29.4	24.8	27.1
b. Industrial Arts...	4.9	5.3	6.1	6.5	12.6	8.9	5.9	5.9	5.9
8. Penmanship—Writing...............	26.3	21.4	30.9	28.1	54.4	53.3	29.6	25.8	27.7
9. Activity Work......	24.5	13.8	33.2	16.6	60.8	33.3	29.6	16.1	22.8
10. Music and Rhythms.	17.6	11.6	24.3	16.9	45.5	33.3	21.5	15.0	18.2

Reasons for Which Student-Teachers Should Obtain Practice in Teaching a Variety of Subjects

More than 98% of the laboratory-school faculty members stated that student-teachers preparing to teach in the elementary grades should teach a variety of subjects during student-teaching courses. The per cents of these faculty members who gave each of the specified reasons for which student-teachers should obtain practice in teaching a variety of subjects are presented in Table XXX.

More than 98% of the student-teachers indicated a felt need for practice in teaching a variety of subjects during student-teaching

TABLE XXX

Per Cent of Faculty Members Who Gave Each of the Specified Reasons for Which Student-Teachers Should Obtain Practice in Teaching a Variety of Subjects

Reasons for Which Student-Teachers Should Obtain Practice in Teaching a Variety of Subjects during Student-Teaching Courses	Per Cent of Faculty Members		
	Critic Teachers and Supervisors		Directors of Training
	P	I	
1. Provides opportunity for wider range of experiences and for broader view of the work, problems, and responsibilities of teachers in the elementary grades........................	24.1	30.5	22.1
2. Prepares the student-teachers more definitely to meet real situations in the field, where they must teach several or all the subjects in one or more grades.............................	24.1	20.9	25.9
3. Provides opportunity for student-teachers to obtain experience in integrating subjects and in carrying out activity units which include different types of materials......................	15.0	12.6	9.3
4. Furnishes opportunity for the student-teachers to secure more adequate preparation for teaching a variety of subjects:			
a. Familiarizes them with different types of subject-matter, teaching techniques, and educational procedures...................	8.6	10.2	3.7
b. Enables them to secure teaching experience in both drill and content subjects...........	6.0	7.3	5.6
c. Gives them better understanding of different techniques and skills necessary for teaching different subjects......................	3.5	4.4	5.6
d. Helps them to build up skills in different types of subjects........................	3.5	2.9	3.7
5. Provides greater opportunity for student-teachers to secure experience in all types of work of elementary teachers......................	6.0	2.4	7.4
6. Gives student-teachers better understanding of child development through different types of subject-matter............................	4.5	2.4	....
7. Meets the demand for grade specialization rather than subject-matter specialization.......	1.0	1.5	11.1
8. Helps them to make adjustments more easlly...	2.0	1.5	1.9
9. Promotes more extensive study of the curriculum for the elementary grades...............	.5	1.0	1.9

courses. The following reasons, which are listed according to frequency of mention, were proffered by student-teachers in support of their conviction that ample opportunity for teaching a variety of subjects should be provided:

1. Provides more nearly adequate preparation for teaching the different subjects of the elementary grades.
    a. Prepares more definitely for teaching several subjects.
    b. Helps prospective teachers to acquire better working knowledge of procedures for teaching different subjects.
    c. Aids in interpreting difficulties and problems encountered in teaching different subjects.
2. Helps prospective teachers to obtain better conception of the work of the teacher.
    a. Provides wider range of experiences, better foundation, and richer background in teaching.
    b. Aids in acquiring better vision and better insight into real teaching situations.
    c. Furnishes more definite ideas of the scope of the work of elementary teachers.
3. Helps prospective teachers to become better qualified to meet real situations in the public schools of the state.
4. Affords opportunities for better integration of subjects.
    a. Gives clearer conception of ways in which to integrate subject-matter and materials.
    b. Provides more opportunities to experience teaching as a whole and to see the interrelation of different subjects.
5. Aids in acquiring better understanding of children.
    a. Provides more opportunities to study children's abilities and reactions in different subjects.
    b. Aids in discovering special aptitudes of individual children.
6. Promotes wider study of the curriculum.
    a. Affords more opportunity for students to become familiar with various phases of the curriculum.
    b. Inspires the teacher with greater self-confidence as a result of broader knowledge of the curriculum.
7. Furnishes more extensive preparation under expert guidance.
8. Helps in the placement of teachers.

Reports further indicated that (1) student-teachers should have practice in both "drill" and "content" subjects in order to develop skills and to master techniques necessary for the successful teaching of these; (2) they should experience planning and carrying out large developmental units of instruction in connection with literature and

Table LII in Volume II, which is on file in manuscript form in the Library of Teachers College, Columbia University, presents in detail the following data: the college year in which the student-teaching was done; the type of organization under which it was conducted; the number of primary and intermediate student-teachers, both inexperienced and experienced, who reported each of the reasons for which student-teachers should obtain practice in teaching a variety of subjects.

social science, as well as drill work in connection with arithmetic, reading, and spelling; (3) those who obtained practice in the drill phases of subjects without a comparable amount of experience in developmental work and creative activities were likely to leave the teachers colleges with very narrow views of elementary teachers' responsibilities; and (4) it was imperative for student-teachers to obtain practice in teaching several subjects because they needed rounded experiences for their future work in the field.

Justifications Offered for Devoting Entire Student-Teaching Time to the Teaching of Only One Subject

Less than 2% of the student-teachers and laboratory-school faculty members recommended that student-teachers should devote their entire student-teaching time to the teaching of only one subject in preference to a larger number. Most of these individuals worked under the one-hour-a-day student-teaching plan, in the intermediate or upper elementary grades, and taught departmentalized subject-matter. The justifications offered for limiting practice to only one subject are:

1. Avoids waste of time produced by changing from one subject to another.
2. Leads to specialization in one subject.
3. Conserves the student-teacher's time and energy.

E. Helping Children to Build Up and Develop Desirable Personal and Social Habits, Interests, Appreciations, Ideals, and Attitudes

Educators have long realized the growing importance of helping children to cultivate and develop those interests, appreciations, ideals, and attitudes of mind that will help each one to build up a well-integrated personality and become a useful member of society. The diminishing influence of the church and the home has placed upon the school a large share of the responsibility for training children in habits of right living. Conflicting trends of thought as to the most effective means of moulding character and developing personalities of children prevail in the different state teachers colleges. The greatest number of faculty members favored the indirect method of approach; a few advocated the direct method of attacking these problems; and some maintained that a combination of these two methods would best serve to inculcate in the children those habits, attitudes, interests, and ideals which are most desirable.

TABLE

Average Per Cent of Student-Teachers Who Obtained Actual Experience
Routine According to Reports from

Activities in Connection with School and Classroom Routine

1. Arranging work on blackboards and bulletin boards.........................
2. Regulating physical factors of the room
   a. Regulating heat, ventilation, and lighting................................
   b. Adjusting seats and desks to meet individual needs of children...............
3. Tending to schoolroom housekeeping
   a. Keeping floor, desks, tables, bookcases, blackboards, and other classroom equipment neat and clean..
   b. Arranging pictures and other decorations................................
   c. Arranging furniture, books, magazines, etc.................................
   d. Arranging and decorating classroom to suit special occasions, days, weeks, holidays, months, seasons, etc..
   e. Tending to flowers, plants, pets, etc..
4. Selecting and displaying children's work
   a. Selecting and displaying samples of the children's work.....................
   b. Planning and arranging exhibitions of the children's work...................
5. Keeping records and making reports
   a. Making charts showing the progress made by the children.................
   b. Keeping attendance records..
   c. Keeping card indexes for individual children, e.g., of books read, work completed, progress made, etc..
   d. Making out report cards or promotion cards...........................
   e. Making monthly or annual reports to be sent to the principal's office or to the superintendent of schools..
6. Selecting and ordering materials and equipment
   a. Selecting supplies, materials, and equipment for art, costumes, pageants, plays, projects, programs, games, etc..
   b. Seeing if supplies meet all the needs of a well-equipped school..............
   c. Taking inventories of supplies and materials...........................
   d. Sending for materials and samples..
   e. Collecting money from pupils for materials, fees, excursions, social functions, etc.
   f. Making requisitions for necessary materials................................
   g. Selecting texts and reference books..
7. Making programs and schedules
   a. Making daily programs..
   b. Making schedules for class and extra-class activities........................

The student-teachers were brought into contact with many perplexing problems while attempting to provide and to utilize opportunities that presented themselves for developing in the children well-rounded personalities and high ideals of character. They were faced

XXXI

in Each of the Activities in Connection with School and Classroom
Laboratory-School Faculty Members

Approximate Per Cent of Student-Teachers							
1–2 Hours		½ Day		All Day		Total Average	
P	I	P	I	P	I	P	I
98	100	99	100	100	100	99	100
98	92	98	100	100	100	98	96
87	83	85	83	95	100	87	85
96	92	100	100	100	100	98	96
88	81	98	99	100	100	93	89
88	81	98	100	100	100	93	89
88	81	95	86	91	90	91	84
72	64	90	81	100	100	81	74
92	92	98	92	100	100	95	93
85	82	98	89	100	100	91	87
84	88	85	94	85	97	85	91
73	71	91	93	90	90	81	80
53	66	75	81	71	80	62	73
52	64	73	77	67	80	61	70
15	16	40	38	50	50	27	27
36	25	45	48	60	56	41	36
25	25	48	47	45	50	35	35
16	25	43	47	50	50	28	35
26	24	43	34	50	56	34	30
18	21	31	30	41	52	24	26
10	11	16	20	26	25	14	15
2	3	8	7	9	10	5	5
25	30	36	38	50	54	31	35
20	20	33	35	50	45	27	27

with many delicate situations in helping children to develop initiative, self-expression, self-reliance, and the finest characteristics of
ethical conduct. The abilities of the student-teachers were especially
challenged in their efforts to guide the children in the intricacies of

co-operative living, social and civic responsibilities, and constructive leadership. Reports indicated that it was highly essential for student-teachers to secure definite training and efficient guidance in these activities.

Table XXIII enumerates some of the dominant personality traits and evaluates some of the activities that might be used in developing these traits.

F. *Taking Charge of Activities in Connection with School and Classroom Routine*

All the student-teachers obtained some experience in performing routine duties. Practically all had considerable practice in each of the following activities:

1. Arranging work on blackboards and bulletin boards.
2. Regulating physical factors of the classroom.
3. Attending to schoolroom housekeeping.
4. Selecting and displaying children's work.
5. Keeping records and making reports.

Approximately 99% of those majoring in the primary grades and 100% of those in the intermediate grades arranged work on blackboards and bulletin boards. About 98% of those in the primary grades and 96% of those in the intermediate grades obtained practice in regulating light and ventilation, and in keeping floors, desks, bookcases, blackboards, and other schoolroom equipment neat and clean. Reports indicated that many student-teachers devoted so much time and energy to mechanical routine and janitorial duties that they lost sight of the more valuable educational activities in the elementary school.

Less than one-third of the student-teachers obtained actual practice in the following administrative activities:

1. Making monthly or annual attendance reports.
2. Making daily programs and class schedules.
3. Taking inventories of supplies and materials.
4. Making requisitions for materials.
5. Sending for supplies and materials.

Less than 5% of the student-teachers obtained actual practice in selecting texts and reference books to be purchased by the school.

Table XXXI lists some of the specific activities in connection with *school and classroom routine;* and shows the average per cent of student-teachers, under the different forms of student-teaching organization, who obtained actual practice in each of these activities according to reports from laboratory-school faculty members.

Contacts with Children's Extra-Class Activities

The supervised civic, social, and spiritual activities outside of the regular school subjects are referred to as extra-class activities in some institutions. In some of the most progressive schools these extra-class activities are fast becoming part of the regular class activities. Some of the laboratory-school faculty members specified that a properly supervised activity program was one of the best means of (1) setting standards and fostering ideals; (2) discovering and developing talents and interests of the children; (3) awakening the sense of social and civic responsibility; (4) teaching worthy use of leisure time; and (5) developing strong moral character and well-rounded personality. Many implied that the school could be made a happier place in which to live, work, and grow, if more effective use were made of assembly programs, pageants and festivals, school parties and picnics, clubs and organizations of different kinds, field trips and excursions, and various phases of physical education.

Table XXIII shows that, although faculty members recognized the value of these extra-class activities, most of the student-teachers obtained very little actual practice in them. The median student-teacher under the half-day and whole-day student-teaching plans obtained considerably more experience in connection with these activities than did those under the one-hour-a-day plan.

1. *Planning and directing programs and festivals*

    a. *Planning, directing, and staging assembly presentations and programs in the elementary grades*

Although the median student-teacher obtained few contacts and very little actual experience in planning and directing children's assembly programs or presentations, many of the critic teachers offered ample justification for providing practical preparation in this phase of the teacher's work. They specified that prospective teachers should obtain sufficient contacts and experiences in connection with these activities to gain understanding of how constructive assembly programs could be made valuable for the following purposes: establishing more friendly relations and more willing co-operation between teacher and pupils; furnishing good incentives for activity work both in and out of the classroom; planning, selecting, organizing, integrating, and developing suitable subject-matter; co-ordinating all other school work; forming conclusions for activity units in which music, art, handwork, physical education, literature, reading, history, and other school subjects are all integrated for the solution and enrichment of vital educational and social problems; measuring the results of their teaching; ascertaining the means by which closer co-operation could be brought about between the different grades and departments; and promoting contacts with the community.

In some of the more progressive laboratory schools, where the assembly was the center of the school community and provided opportunity for a great many activities of general school interest, student-teachers secured considerable practice in this type of work. In these schools the assemblies were not merely entertaining, but were also of educational, social, and inspirational value.

Many believed that assembly programs were most valuable when they grew out of the regular school work or fulfilled a definite child need. The assembly programs that grew out of real situations or real needs in the daily work usually presented the greatest difficulties to the student-teachers because these required more creativeness, initiative, resourcefulness, and sense of responsibility than did the more formal types.

b and c. Planning and coaching pageants and festivals

Reasons were given both for and against the necessity of student-teachers' obtaining experience in directing children's pageants and festivals. Some faculty members contended that if these activities were well planned and were the outgrowth of the children's actual school work, they could be of definite value in the preparation of teachers for the elementary grades. The arguments in favor of providing practical experience in connection with festivals and pageants were fundamentally the same as those enumerated under "Planning, directing, and staging assembly presentations and programs." (See pages 105–106.) Some, on the other hand, stated that these activities take too much time in proportion to the educational values derived, often interfere too much with the regular schoolroom activities, interrupt the scheduled class routine, excite the children, and upset the discipline of the room. It was generally conceded, however, that the real educational value to be derived from these activities depended on the nature and worth of the undertakings.

2. *Participating in children's school parties, picnics, and similar activities*

Participation in these activities helped the students to secure a more sympathetic understanding of the social life of the children.

3. *Planning and conducting excursions and field trips*

Student-teachers were confronted with many trying problems in conducting groups of children on field trips and excursions. Difficulties encountered were usually caused by their lack of definite preparation for this type of work and by their limited knowledge of how to guide children in informal situations outside of the classroom.

Many faculty members suggested that it was essential for student-teachers to secure experience in conducting field trips and excursions because these activities require very careful preparation and constructive follow-up work, and are among the best activities for stimulating interest in classwork. Some specified that every student-teacher should be led to realize that the highest development of the pupils is not achieved in the classroom alone, nor produced by the presentation of materials of instruction, but is the result of working together, living together, and playing together.

Even though critic teachers recognized the importance of these extra-class activities, most of the student-teachers obtained very little practice in taking children on field trips and excursions. The median student-teacher, in fact, never conducted a group of children on a field trip.

4. *Directing and participating in children's organizations*

It was conceded by critic teachers in the intermediate and upper grades that organizations and clubs furnish excellent outlets for children's pent-up energies, and are of inestimable value in the formation of right civic habits, ethical standards, and social qualities. The amount and type of preparation required to enable student-teachers to direct effectively the various activities in connection with children's organizations and clubs, however, gave rise to divergent points of view. While it was contended by some that the training of student-teachers in these activities should proceed along conventional lines, experiences with informal teaching situations had convinced others that formal training could be obviated by an enrichment of teaching situations to the point at which these activities became an integral part of the regular daily work.

5. *Supervising children in various phases of physical education*

A comparison of the amounts of experience obtained by primary and intermediate student-teachers in these activities revealed a significant variation, the mean being considerably higher for the former. It appeared that the difference in the levels at which learning takes place in the primary and intermediate grades was responsible for this divergence. The median student-teacher in the primary grades obtained some experience in such physical recreational activities as supervising playground work and group games, posture work, and relaxation exercises. Inasmuch as teachers in the public elementary schools are usually required to assume responsibility for directing play periods, faculty members recommended that prospective elementary teachers should obtain adequate practice in directing children in various types of physical education activities.

6. *Assisting with children's school publications*

Student-teachers on the whole obtained practically no experience in connection with children's school publications. The median critic teacher considered it advisable for student-teachers to secure some experience in this activity, however, because if rightly conducted, such work can be used as an agency of integration for enriching the various school subjects.

ACTIVITIES PERTAINING TO THE DEVELOPMENT OF DESIRABLE TEACHING PERSONALITY

Personality is usually thought of as the sum total of one's qualities of body, mind, and character. As an aggregate of qualities it quite invariably represents more or less of need for the further cultivation of or perhaps for the elimination of certain traits and attitudes. For this reason, and also because teaching is an art rather than a combination of skills, a large place should be provided in teacher-education for the development of desirable teaching personality.

There were diversified ideas as to the best methods of developing the personalities of prospective teachers. Many faculty members believed that the direct method of approach should be used in personality guidance, contending that it was better to concentrate on only a few characteristics or traits at a time, and step by step to build up a well-rounded personality; or that a combination of synthetic and analytic procedures should be used—first considering a student-teacher's personality in its entirety, then analyzing the constituent parts, and finally reconstructing the whole. Some, on the other hand, advocated the indirect method of dealing with personality development.

In addition to the student-teaching activities and procedures given in the *Master Activity Check List,* Table XXIII, a number of others were utilized for the specific purpose of developing personality. Different types of contacts, experiences, and activities were stressed by the various teachers colleges. A summary of the reports from the different schools provides the following composite list of additional activities and procedures that were experienced by different student-teachers in the development of personality.

Activities in Connection with the Direct Approach to Personality Development

The development of desirable personality through conscious effort has long been recognized as a definite function of teacher-preparing institutions. Methods have evolved in this as in other fields, with several rather well-established procedures being in general use. The laboratory-school faculty members, who deemed it wisest to give special attention to individual traits rather than to promote personality development almost entirely through the more general processes of cultivation, used the direct method of approach to personality study.

1. *Attending and participating in conferences*
    a. Participating in group conferences between faculty members and student-teachers.
        (1) Helping to carry on general discussions dealing with the following topics and problems relative to personality:
            (a) Different types of personalities.
            (b) Personality traits—social, mental, physical, emotional—of prominent characters and outstanding leaders.
            (c) Qualities that make for good teaching personalities.
            (d) How student-teachers can analyze themselves.
            (e) How to develop important personality traits.
        (2) Working with groups to formulate self-rating sheets.
        (3) Setting up standards by which to evaluate personality traits.
    b. Interviewing and conferring with faculty members relative to personality development.
        (1) Discussing personal problems with critic teachers and other faculty members.

    (2) Discussing with critic teachers and supervisors the following problems relative to personality development:

      (a) Why student-teachers encountered certain difficulties and how these could best be overcome.

      (b) How to build up and improve on strong points.

      (c) How to recognize, analyze, and overcome the individual's deficiencies or weak points.

      (d) How to acquire a more refined, pleasing, and attractive personal appearance.

      (e) How to improve the voice, posture, and general health.

      (f) How to make better social adjustments.

      (g) How to develop certain important personality traits, such as adaptability, alertness, breadth of interest, co-operativeness, dependability, discernment, forcefulness, good taste, initiative, leadership, open-mindedness, progressiveness, poise, refinement, resourcefulness, self-confidence, self-control, self-direction, sense of responsibility, sociability, tactfulness, and thoroughness.

      (h) What type of activities would be most valuable in the development of the student-teacher's total personality.

      (i) How to develop a well-integrated personality.

      (j) How to use self-rating schemes effectively.

    (3) Accepting criticisms from critic teachers and other faculty members. (Being receptive to constructive criticism.)

Most of the student-teachers welcomed constructive, analytical, and inspiring criticisms that helped them to build up more positive attitudes. The student-teachers usually responded in direct ratio to the attitudes and interest shown by faculty members. For example, they gained a greater degree of self-assurance when the critic teacher's attitude toward them was one of confidence rather than one of doubt. Critic teachers implied that the most effective results in personality development could be obtained when student-teachers were encouraged to build up on their strong traits, rather than to concentrate on their weaknesses.

    c. Participating in conferences held among the student-teachers.

In some schools the student-teachers were encouraged to hold conferences among themselves for the purpose of discussing their problems in connection with personality development and other phases of teaching.

  2. *Making personality studies*

    a. Approaching personality study through analysis of the traits of others.

      (1) Observing master teachers—elementary grades, high school, or college—and analyzing wherein their success lies.

(2) Studying personality traits of teachers and educators who have been outstanding throughout the ages, and endeavoring to determine why these people were so successful.

(3) Observing public speakers and other prominent personages.

(4) Observing other student-teachers, finding strong and weak points, and offering remedial suggestions.

Some faculty members suggested that student-teachers could be made conscious of their strong and weak points by studying the personality traits of others, and that the weaker student-teachers could learn much by carefully directed observation of the stronger ones.

b. Studying, analyzing, and diagnosing their own personalities in light of the objectives and principles of modern education.

c. Evaluating their own personality traits by use of rating devices.

(1) Discovering strong and weak points in own personality by means of definite check lists.

(2) Evaluating and rating own personality traits with the aid of objective measurements, such as rating sheets.

(3) Using suggestions set forth in student-teaching manuals.

(4) Keeping records of personal progress on regular rating charts.

(5) Formulating check lists for personal use.

(6) Using rating cards designed to aid in maintaining certain standards.

(7) Studying personality traits listed in the *Commonwealth Teacher-Training Study* by Charters and Waples.

The forms and uses of rating schemes varied in the different schools. Some used published rating devices while others formulated their own. In a number of the laboratory schools definite rating sheets were given to the student-teachers so that they might analyze and rate their own personalities, while in a few schools the student-teachers were required to devise such forms for themselves. In formulating and in using these rating schemes, the student-teachers usually started with very simple activities and gradually undertook more difficult ones. A common procedure was to work on one point at a time and gradually build up a list of personality traits.

In some schools the critic teachers periodically filled out for each student-teacher rating sheets which were subsequently discussed in conferences between the departmental supervisors and the individual student-teacher. Both strong and weak points were considered, together with suggestions for improvement. Student-teachers were then sent back to the critic teachers for definite remedial work. At the close of a stated period of time the rating sheets were again checked to indicate the progress that had been made. This process continued throughout the student-teaching period.

Some teachers colleges had not developed any systematic self-rating schemes for student-teachers. Many faculty members believed that the development of personality traits should be approached more informally than could be done through definitely set up rating schemes. Some implied that these devices were not necessary when student-teachers worked closely with the critic teachers, and that self-rating and analysis of personality traits could be overdone unless carefully supervised. They did not deem it wise for student-teachers to use definite rating sheets because (1) the student-teachers were often inaccurate in their ratings; (2) it was difficult to obtain an honest expression from many of them; and (3) it tended to make them too introspective, bewildered, and self-conscious. Some student-teachers rated themselves too low, and others too high, through the influence of one or more of the following factors: (1) lack of standards by which to evaluate; (2) inadequate background for accurate judgment and comparison with others; (3) the fear that their ratings might influence their grades; and (4) the nature of their own personal experiences and cultural backgrounds.

The types of student-teachers who had a tendency to overrate themselves were (1) the over self-confident or those who had a great deal of social poise; (2) those who were unwilling to put forth the necessary effort and who resorted to bluffing as a means of obtaining good grades; (3) the weak students; and (4) those whose social standards were very low and who lacked desirable standards by which to evaluate themselves.

The types of student-teachers who usually underrated themselves were (1) the overconscientious who knew a great deal and held very high standards; (2) the timid and self-conscious ones; and (3) those with inferiority complexes.

Reports indicated that in order to obtain the most effective results from the use of rating devices, the active participation and close co-operation of student-teachers with faculty members were highly essential.

3. *Obtaining and applying suggestions and special instruction for the improvement of personality*

    a. Reading books and reference materials.
        (1) Making annotated bibliographies on needed personality development.

    (2) Reading professional literature.

    (3) Reading books and materials of cultural value—social, intellectual, and aesthetic.

  b. Obtaining assistance in overcoming defects.

    (1) Taking special work in voice and diction.

    (2) Improving motor co-ordination, carriage, and posture through special instruction.

  c. Keeping records in connection with personality development.

    (1) Listing suggestions given by faculty members and others interested in the professional progress of the student-teachers.

    (2) Recording reactions of the children to certain personality traits in the student-teachers.

    (3) Noting improvements that they themselves made in holding the attention and interest of the pupils.

    (4) Keeping records of personal progress.

  d. Focusing attention and effort on the improvement of a different personality trait each week.

  e. Building up on suggestions given to them relative to their personality development.

Activities in Connection with the Indirect Approach to Personality Development

In the accumulation of data, it became apparent that most of the teachers colleges utilized a combination of direct and indirect methods for guiding student-teachers in the development of desirable teaching personalities. In defense of the indirect approach some faculty members maintained that it is the synthesis, under competent guidance, of a wide variety of activities, contacts, and experiences in life situations that constitutes the most successful procedure in personality development. They pointed out that teachers' extra-school life—in that it largely regulates their health, happiness, and emotional stability—directly affects their reactions to individuals and to groups of children as a whole, and thereby in great measure determines their ultimate success. It was implied that only through well-balanced living in a representative environment does any teacher develop a well-integrated personality with proper emphasis upon the physical, mental, social, and spiritual aspects thereof.

Faculty members employing the indirect approach to personality problems frequently found it possible to help their students to develop desirable personality traits by raising general requirements or by improving the teaching and learning environments: for example, some faculty members helped their students to develop habits of intellectual curiosity, industry, thoroughness, and accuracy by stressing high standards of scholarship and by requiring genuine excellency of workmanship; some were successful in securing attitudes of open-mindedness, understanding, and tolerance on the part of student-teachers by presenting the opinions of great leaders and a great variety of ideas from miscellaneous sources; while others stimulated in their student-teachers a recognition of and an appreciation for things of aesthetic and intellectual values largely by providing the right settings.

Although well-balanced living was considered the ideal formula for securing maximum and permanent results in the personality development of prospective teachers, it was also recognized that certain activities in which they participated contributed materially in this connection. Those most frequently suggested for this purpose are given below.

1. *Living a rich, cultural life*
    a. Living in a wholesome, pleasant, and cultural environment.
    b. Living with other people in an atmosphere of refinement.
    c. Associating with people of cultivation and wide social experience.
    d. Attending and otherwise participating in the functions of church and community organizations; taking part in certain types of religious and social work in the community.
    e. Doing wide reading of a cultural nature.
    f. Attending plays, high grade moving pictures, and other entertainments.
    g. Attending operas, concerts, and other musical programs.
    h. Attending teas, luncheons, and dinners.
    i. Visiting fairs, exhibits, and expositions of local, national, and international scope.
    j. Traveling and visiting places of interest.
2. *Studying economically and effectively in order to hold up high scholastic standards and yet have sufficient time for social and recreational activities*
    a. Acquiring habits of concentration that permit the accomplishment of required work in a minimum of time.
    b. Conserving time and energy for the most valuable things in life.
3. *Originating ideas and initiating activities*
4. *Accepting responsibility in a variety of situations*
    a. Assuming responsibility for the success of various types of activities.
    b. Taking full responsibility for groups of children during designated periods of time.
5. *Attending and participating in extra-class activities, both in and out of school*
    a. Participating in extra-class activities within the school, such as clubs,

social and civic organizations, publications, assembly programs, entertainments, school plays, festivals and pageants, orchestra and choir, school parties and dances, picnics, and various types of physical education work.

b. Taking excursions and field trips.

c. Acting as hostesses at parties and teas for the mothers of pupils in the laboratory school, thus meeting and conversing with them.

d. Attending lectures and chautauquas.

e. Attending such sporting events as races, football and baseball games, tennis tournaments, track meets, and other athletic contests.

Although many of the student-teachers had very limited experience in connection with extra-curricular activities outside the school during their attendance at the teachers college, most of them attended or participated in some extra-class activities within the school.

Some faculty members implied that too many student-teachers had not yet learned the art of living, and suggested that such students be drawn away from humdrum routine and be provided opportunities to emerge and to establish themselves as individuals. Some indicated that student-teachers did not know how to take advantage of their surroundings and needed constructive guidance in developing a deeper appreciation and better realization of the advantages of their environment, human and physical. Some implied that students needed to make finer social adjustments and to develop keener understanding of those with whom they came in contact.

Some of the more progressive faculty members, therefore, made special efforts to provide opportunities for the student-teachers to attend different types of functions where they could obtain such experiences as coming in contact with many people, carrying on conversations, seeing a tasteful choice of the right types of clothes to wear for different occasions, meeting people of prominence, and displaying special aptitudes or talents.

CONTACTS WITH THE STAFF-PERSONNEL AND WITH THE ADMINISTRATIVE PHASES OF ELEMENTARY SCHOOLS

Reports indicated that prospective teachers for the elementary grades should make more adequate contacts with the staff-personnel and with the administrative phases of school systems. Many desirable activities for establishing closer relations with the staff-personnel and for obtaining broader perspective of the school as a whole were suggested. The median student-teacher, however, obtained very limited contacts with these phases of the teacher's work. Some of the important activities in which it was recommended that student-teachers obtain definite experience are: (1) becoming acquainted with an entire school system, including the school plant, equipment, and staff-personnel, as well as the instructional phases; (2) obtaining an understanding of the organization and management under regular school conditions; (3) studying the available educational facilities; (4) co-operating with the school authorities; and (5) co-operating with both the regular school staff and the student-teachers, for example, attending and participating in faculty meetings and conferences, working with various types of committees, participating in educational research, participating in revising courses of study, and assisting in caring for school property.

The number and types of conferences with which student-teachers have contacts during student-teaching courses are summarized in Tables VI and VII, and a brief discussion of these statistics is given on pages 21–23. The ratings given in Table XXIII indicate that it is highly essential for student-teachers to attend and participate in conferences of a constructive nature.

On the pages immediately following, the typical activities of student-teachers in collaborating on committees and in various branches of educational research are given a more extended treatment.

Working on Committees or in Group Activities with Other Student-Teachers

Approximately 70% of the critic teachers and supervisors of student-teaching who participated in this particular phase of the report stated that most of their student-teachers obtained some practice in working on one or more committees or group activities with other student-teachers. The types of committees or group projects in which different student-teachers participated are listed below. The major headings are ranked according to frequency of mention.

1. Instruction.
    a. Units of instruction.
    b. Activity units or projects.
    c. Subject-matter and reference materials.
    d. Lesson planning.
    e. Child study, for example, case studies of children.
    f. Evaluation and grading of pupils' work.
    g. Testing programs of various types.
2. Classroom management and housekeeping routine duties.

3. Extra-class activities.
  a. Assembly programs (program committees, costume committees, stage committees).
  b. Entertainments and parties (social committees, refreshment committees, reception committees).
  c. Playground and physical education work.
  d. Excursions and field trips.
  e. Cafeteria and lunchroom committees.
  f. Club work and room organizations.
  g. Publicity committees.
  h. Special fund committees.
4. Personality development.
5. Professional contacts.
  a. Professional reading committees.
  b. Educational research and investigations.

The remaining 30% of those who gave information on this topic stated that their student-teachers had practically no experience in working on committees or in group activities with other student-teachers.

Working on Committees with Laboratory-School Faculty Members

Approximately 32.0% of the critic teachers and supervisors of student-teaching, who contributed to this phase of the study, indicated that their student-teachers had some practice in working on one or more committees with faculty members in the laboratory schools. The types of committees or the group activities in which they engaged are listed according to frequency of mention.

1. Instructional activities.
  a. Units of work or activity units.
  b. Child study.
  c. Testing programs of various types.
2. Extra-class activities.
  a. Entertainment committees.
  b. Program committees.
  c. Social committees.
  d. Refreshment committees.
  e. Reception committees.
  f. Publicity committees.
  g. Welfare committees.
  h. Special fund committees.
  i. Auditing committees.
3. Professional contacts and activities.
  a. Educational research work.
  b. Revision of curriculum.

Approximately 68.0% stated that their student-teachers had practically no experience in working on committees with faculty members. The faculty members, however, acted in supervisory capacities on most of the student-teachers' committees. Under present conditions in many places, the critic teachers and supervisors of student-teaching necessarily become directors of student-teachers rather than co-workers with them. This state of affairs is generally the result of overcrowded conditions in the laboratory schools; namely, inadequate laboratory facilities, too large a number of student-teachers for each critic teacher, and excessive teaching and supervisory loads on the part of the supervisory staff members.

Participating in Educational Research

According to the reports from laboratory-school faculty members, less than 10% of the student-teachers participated in educational research. Most of those who obtained practice in this activity were seniors in four-year elementary curricula. The research problems in which these student-teachers participated are listed according to frequency of mention.

1. Studying, investigating, and experimenting with different types of units of work or units of instruction.
2. Studying syllabi and courses of study, and accumulating materials for use in building up and revising the curriculum.
3. Investigating and studying different types of activity programs.
4. Helping to investigate, promote, and carry into effect extensive testing programs for the purpose of classifying children according to their abilities, special aptitudes, and achievements along various lines.
5. Investigating and analyzing the factors that condition the learning activities and the conduct of children; then finding the proper types of remedial measures in cases of problem or unadjusted children.
6. Investigating, finding, and listing the best reading materials to be used in teaching different subjects in the elementary grades.
7. Studying vocabularies used by children at various age levels.

More than 90% of the student-teachers never participated in research work that could be properly designated as such. Their activities were usually limited to the study of assigned lessons or units of work, subject-matter—materials of instruction of all types, methods of instruction, child study, school management, and other problems that were of immediate value to them in teaching.

Most of the student-teachers lacked knowledge of essential research techniques, and were not prepared to carry on educational research work.

Contacts of Student-Teachers with Community Activities

The critic teachers, for the most part, were not in a position to state exactly the number of contacts and the amounts of experience that the student-teachers obtained in connection with community activities, because (1) attendance at community functions was generally a matter of personal choice; and (2) participation in community activities was usually determined by individual initiative, independent of the teachers college requirements.

With the exception of attendance and participation in local religious services, the median student-teacher's contacts with community activities were very limited. Only a small per cent made a representative variety of contacts, and some made no contacts whatsoever; less than 5% of the student-teachers reported participation in the established social, civic, and welfare organizations. Only seventeen out of fifty-seven state teachers colleges reported that the student-teachers attended and participated in parent-teacher meetings; almost none of the student-teachers reported attendance at mothers' meetings in the capacity of hostesses; and few visited the homes of the children in the campus schools, either by assignment or by personal inclination.

Recognizing that these contacts form an essential part of teacher-education and that the present situation is far from satisfactory, leaders in elementary teacher-education recommended increased contacts with community life. Some suggested a careful guidance program designed to acquaint students with community resources available for educational purposes and to introduce them to various phases of community life; experiences with Red Cross and public welfare agencies, local clubs, church and Sunday School work, community drives and surveys were specified as cases in point. "Parents' visiting days in the schools" were mentioned as valuable in helping student-teachers to make first-hand contacts with the parents of the pupils.

Professional Contacts Outside the Teachers Colleges

The fifty-seven state teachers colleges participating in this study reported that (1) only a small per cent of the student-teachers attended professional meetings other than those connected with the teachers colleges; (2) practically none of the student-teachers, except those with previous teaching experience in the field, were members of national or state educational organizations; (3) very few contributed to the professional programs of these educational organizations; and (4) a still smaller number prepared educational articles for publication outside the school papers. These educational articles usually dealt with the use of supplementary materials, child study, and the teaching of different subjects.

Reports indicated that the following per cents of student-teachers obtained experience in each of the specified activities pertaining to professional contacts outside the teachers colleges: attending sectional, district, or city educational organizations during attendance at the teachers colleges, about 5%; joining professional organizations, less than 5%; attending state or national educational meetings, about 1%; contributing to these educational meetings, about .5%; writing educational articles that were published in other than school papers, less than .5%.

Faculty members recommended that greater effort should be put forth to provide opportunity for students to (1) attend and participate in professional educational meetings; (2) prepare articles for publication; and (3) obtain contacts with experts in various fields.

Summary of Ratings of the Principal Activities That Help to Make Up Content of Student-Teaching Courses in State Teachers Colleges

The activities in the *Master Activity Check List* were, for the most part, selected with reference to their difficulty and importance in the content of student-teaching. Most of the activities listed were selected because they had been considered important by the critic teachers and other educators who helped to make up the original check list. There was frequently wide variation, ranging from high positive to high negative correlation, between the ratings given to the value of an activity in the preparation of teachers for the elementary grades and to the amount of experience which the student-teachers actually obtained in that activity during student-teaching. The correlation between the ratings given to the difficulty encountered by student-teachers in skillfully carrying out an activity and to the amount of experience secured by the student-teachers in that activity also ranged from high positive to high negative. Many of the critic teachers who filled out the final activity check list indicated that their student-teachers obtained very little experience in some activities that were rated the highest (1) in degree of difficulty encountered by student-teachers in carrying out the activities;

and (2) in value of such activities for the preparation of elementary teachers. Some, on the other hand, reported that their student-teachers obtained much experience in the activities that were rated average or below in difficulty and in value.

Types of activities rated consistently high in the degree of difficulty encountered by student-teachers in skillfully carrying out an activity, in the value of that activity in the preparation of teachers for the elementary grades, and in the amount of experience which student-teachers obtained during student-teaching courses are:

1. Planning the selection and organization of materials of instruction.
2. Selecting and adapting materials of instruction in daily work.
3. Selecting, planning, and adapting methods of instruction.

Types of activities which were rated high in the degree of difficulty encountered by student-teachers and high in value for the preparation of elementary teachers, but in which the amount and type of experience obtained by student-teachers in different schools varied greatly, are:

1. Securing perspective and understanding of elementary school curricula.
   a. Planning and developing units of instruction of relatively comprehensive scope.
   b. Thinking out each day's work in terms of large units of instruction.
   c. Building up the curriculum from day to day through the combined initiative and co-operation of pupils and teacher.
2. Studying and analyzing personality traits of children; and dealing effectively with their individual differences.
3. Utilizing activities and procedures involved in the more progressive methods of instruction, such as:
   a. Stimulating appreciation, admiration, and enjoyment of things of intellectual, social, and aesthetic values.
   b. Guiding children in creative construction, dramatic expression, developmental problem-solving, and socialized activities.
   c. Individualizing learning activities to meet the capacities, interests, and needs of the children.
   d. Initiating and carrying to completion, with the co-operation of the pupils, large units of instruction which include the integration and drawing together of various phases of subject-matter, different types of activities, and many human experiences within the comprehension of the children.
      (1) Guiding children in initiating and carrying into effect such purposeful learning activities as large centers of interest, developmental units of instruction, and constructive activity units of a broad scope.
      (2) Recognizing and making effective use of children's leads, questions, and contributions.

(3) Leading children to suggest, to choose, and to plan methods for developing or solving problems, and for working out large units of instruction.

(4) Guiding children in the execution and progress of learning activities that a high purpose may be maintained consistently under changing conditions.

(5) Utilizing assignments as effective guides for study.

e. Setting up situations which provide opportunities and utilizing those which present themselves for helping children to develop the highest types of (a) co-operative living, (b) social responsibility, (c) self-confidence and self-reliance, (d) self-expression, and (e) ethical conduct.

Types of activities which were rated high in the degree of difficulty encountered by student-teachers and high in value for the preparation of elementary teachers, but in which the median student-teacher obtained an average or above average amount of experience, are:

1. Dealing with problems of child behavior; and handling discipline of children.

2. Guiding children in making effective use of different types of books and recorded matter; leading them to form the habit of searching in various sources for related materials.

3. Studying, analyzing, and diagnosing the student-teacher's own personality in light of objectives and principles of modern education.

Types of activities which were rated about average in degree of difficulty encountered by student-teachers and in value for the preparation of elementary teachers, but in which the median student-teacher obtained an average or above average amount of practice, are:

1. Applying such teaching techniques as exposition, inductive-deductive types of procedure, memorization of materials, review, textbook work, and supervised or directed study.

2. Keeping illustrative materials and supplies in order and available for use when needed.

3. Directing children in attending to routine school activities.

Types of activities which were rated high in degree of difficulty encountered by student-teachers and high or above average in value for the preparation of elementary teachers, but in which the majority of student-teachers obtained few contacts and very little actual experience, are:

1. Obtaining understanding of individual differences of children in a group by (1) studying and analyzing each child's social and experiential

backgrounds; and (2) investigating and studying their home, neighborhood, and community environments.

2. Planning and directing children's assembly presentations and programs; staging or taking charge of special day, week, or holiday programs.
3. Planning and conducting children's school journeys, excursions, and field trips.

Types of activities which were rated low in difficulty, but in which the majority of the student-teachers obtained much practice, are:

1. Regulating physical factors of the classroom, and attending to schoolroom housekeeping.
2. Selecting and displaying children's work.
3. Keeping records and making reports of a routine nature.

The amount of emphasis placed on each of the different types of activities was not consistent for all the elementary grades. Some activities were more characteristic of the primary grades, while others were more so of the intermediate grades.

Types of activities in which student-teachers in the primary departments obtained more contacts and experiences than did those in the intermediate departments are:

1. Studying and analyzing personality traits of individual children; and adjusting to such individual differences.
2. Applying methods of instruction suitable to children in the primary grades.
   a. Utilizing such educational procedures as activity units, constructive creative work, dramatic play, drill exercises in the language arts—including both oral and silent reading—and number work, exposition and story telling, and socialized activities.
   b. Teaching the following subjects: reading, social studies (designated as such), art, music and rhythms, and writing.
3. Supervising the children in various types of recreational activities, such as playground work, group games, dancing and rhythm, posture work, relaxation exercises, rest periods, and lunch periods.

Student-teachers in the intermediate departments obtained more contacts and experiences in the following types of activities than did those in the primary departments:

1. Acquiring adequate command of subject-matter in order to direct effectively the learning activities of children.
2. Applying certain methods of instruction in directing the learning activities of children.
   a. Utilizing such educational procedures as inductive-deductive techniques, organized question and answer recitations, problem-solving,

reviews or reorganization of subject-matter, study-test plans, supervised or directed study, textbook work, and testing.
  b. Teaching children to study.
    (1) Utilizing assignments as effective guides for study.
    (2) Helping children to develop proper techniques for reference work.
    (3) Helping children to develop skill in specific study habits.
  c. Teaching the following subjects: arithmetic, geography, history, language, and spelling.
3. Dealing with problems of child behavior; and handling discipline of children.

Types of activities in which more than 95% of all the student-teachers obtained practice are:

1. Preparing materials of instruction for daily work.
  a. Selecting and adapting materials of instruction in daily work.
  b. Preparing and writing lesson plans.
2. Utilizing different methods of instruction.
  a. Selecting and adapting methods of instruction.
  b. Applying a variety of educational procedures in directing the learning activities of children.
  c. Directing the learning activities of a group of children; motivating individual and group instruction.
3. Taking charge of school and classroom routine.
  a. Arranging work on blackboards and bulletin boards.
  b. Regulating physical factors of the classroom.
  c. Attending to schoolroom housekeeping.
  d. Performing mechanical classroom routine.
  e. Caring for supplies and materials.

Types of activities in which the student-teachers obtained very few contacts and practically no actual experience during student-teaching courses are:

1. Obtaining understanding of individual differences of children by means of:
  a. Giving behavioristic, affectivity, and motor co-ordination tests.
  b. Studying the home and community environments of children.
  c. Giving intelligence tests and utilizing the results of such tests.
  d. Examining certain conditions of health and physical equipment of individual children.
  e. Investigating reasons for deficiencies in school education.
2. Directing or participating in such children's extra-class activities as pageants and festivals.
3. Co-operating with the personnel of the school in extra-class professional activities, such as:
  a. Attending and participating in faculty meetings.
  b. Helping to build up or revise the curriculum.
  c. Participating in educational research.
4. Making contacts with the community.

    a. Participating in the established social, civic, and welfare organizations of the community.
    b. Attending and participating in parent-teacher meetings.
    c. Visiting the homes for the purpose of interviewing the parents of the pupils in the campus laboratory schools.
5. Making professional contacts outside the teachers colleges.
    a. Attending sectional, state, and national educational meetings.
    b. Joining professional organizations.
    c. Contributing to professional meetings or to educational programs.
    d. Preparing educational articles for publication.

Less than 5.0% of the student-teachers obtained actual practice in connection with the following types of activities during attendance at the teachers colleges:

1. Making professional contacts outside the teachers colleges through such activities as:
    a. Attending meetings of sectional and state educational organizations.
    b. Joining professional organizations.
2. Participating in the established social, civic, and welfare organizations of the community.
3. Selecting texts and reference books to be purchased by the school.

Less than .5% of the student-teachers reported practice in the following types of activities:

1. Contributing to professional meetings or to educational programs outside the teachers colleges.
2. Preparing or writing educational articles that were published in other than school papers.

The scope and richness of the content of student-teaching was directly dependent upon the adequacy of the provision therefor. The content was usually enriched in direct ratio to the comprehensiveness of the background preparation of the student-teachers and to the adequacy of the laboratory facilities. The student-teachers in the four-year curricula obtained broader experiences with progressive educational procedures, secured more numerous and varied contacts in connection with all types of educational activities, and developed clearer understanding of the elementary teacher's work as a whole than did those in the two-year programs. Student-teachers scheduled for whole-day student-teaching, likewise, obtained more extensive contacts and richer experiences in connection with the work and responsibilities of teachers in the elementary schools than did those scheduled for one-hour-a-day student-teaching.

CHAPTER FOUR

AN ANALYTICAL CONSIDERATION OF THE FUNCTIONING OF
THE LESSON PLAN IN STUDENT-TEACHING

THE use of lesson plans in connection with student-teaching was almost unanimously endorsed by the 2,383 student-teachers (1,190 from the primary and 1,193 from the intermediate or upper elementary grades) and 459 laboratory-school faculty members who participated in this phase of the survey. They recognized that effective planning was a prerequisite to successful teaching and gave evidence that the preparation of lesson plans was an integral part of student-teaching activities. More than 95% of these student-teachers reported that they prepared lesson plans during student-teaching courses. There remained, however, much to be determined as to the details of the practices of the various teachers colleges in regard to lesson planning: the types or forms used, the length of time during which plans were required, the use made of plans, the flexibility of requirements—extent to which allowance was made for the development of teaching skill, and the reactions of student-teachers and faculty members to the lesson-planning programs of their respective institutions.

ADMINISTRATIVE ASPECTS OF LESSON PLANNING

Different Types and Forms of Lesson Plans Prepared Prior to the Presentation of Materials of Instruction

More than 95% of the student-teachers stated that they had obtained practice in writing lesson plans prior to the presentation of materials of instruction; and many had prepared several types or forms of lesson plans during their student-teaching courses. The median student-teacher obtained some experience in preparing detailed daily lesson plans, partly detailed plans, daily outlines, brief memoranda or high points to be taught, and units of instruction. The per cents of student-teachers who obtained actual experience in preparing each of the different types of lesson plans specified in the inquiry sheets are summarized in Table XXXII.

TABLE XXXII

Per Cent of Primary and Intermediate Student-Teachers Who Answered "Yes" or "No," or Who Failed to Answer at All, When Asked if They Obtained Experience in Preparing Each of the Designated Types of Lesson Plans during Student-Teaching Courses

Types of Plans Prepared by Student-Teachers during Student-Teaching Courses	Per Cent of Student-Teachers						
	YES		No		SUM TOTAL		
	P	I	P	I	Yes	No	Blank
1. Partly detailed plans.......	85.6	87.3	8.7	8.6	86.5	8.7	4.8
2. Brief memoranda..........	82.3	87.8	12.9	7.6	85.1	10.2	4.7
3. Detailed daily plans........	73.8	78.7	18.8	14.9	76.3	16.8	6.9
4. Daily outlines.............	70.0	74.0	21.4	18.9	72.0	20.1	7.9
5. Units of instruction........	67.9	64.4	26.0	27.4	66.1	26.7	7.2
6. Weekly outlines...........	33.8	30.0	53.4	58.1	31.9	55.8	12.3
7. Term or semester outlines...	26.0	21.6	61.0	64.8	23.8	62.9	13.3

The following per cents of student-teachers reported that they had obtained practice in preparing each of the specified types of lesson plans during student-teaching courses: partly detailed plans, 86.5%; memoranda of high points in procedure and materials of instruction, 85.1%; detailed daily plans, 76.3%; daily outlines, 72.0%; units of instruction which included work in one or more subjects for periods of time ranging in length from several days to several weeks, 66.1%; weekly outlines, 31.9%; and a whole term's work in one or more subjects, 23.8%. Many substituted brief memoranda for more formal lesson plans during the latter part of their student-teaching work; approximately 54% of the student-teachers scheduled for one-hour- and two-hours-a-day, more than 66% of those scheduled for half-day, and about 68% of those scheduled for whole-day student-teaching prepared only memoranda or very brief plans for daily work during the latter part of their final student-teaching courses. Table XXIV, item A, shows the per cent of student-teachers under different types of administrative organization who answered "yes" or "no," or who failed to answer at all, when asked if they obtained practice in writing each of the specified types of lesson plans during student-teaching.

Approximately 82% of the student-teachers followed definite forms in writing lesson plans. The form of these plans usually varied with different teachers colleges or with the critic teachers and student-teachers in each school. Printed forms for lesson plans were used by the student-teachers in a few teachers colleges. In some schools the plans varied with different critic teachers or with individual student-teachers. In most of the laboratory schools, however, they were determined by the critic teachers in charge of each grade. Table XXIV, item A, 3, shows the per cent of student-teachers under different types of student-teaching organization who obtained practice in writing lesson plans according to definite forms.

In the lesson plan forms * used by the majority of the beginning student-teachers, provision was usually made for the inclusion of the following topics:

1. Aims, purposes, or objectives.
2. Subject-matter or content.
3. Materials and references.
4. Methods of procedure.
    a. Approach or introduction.
    b. Presentation of subject-matter.
        (1) Significant or pivotal questions.
        (2) Special devices or techniques.
    c. Pupil-teacher activities.
    d. Summaries or conclusions.
    e. Assignments.
5. Results or outcomes.

Induction into the Preparation of Lesson Plans

A large proportion of the student-teachers proceeded gradually from the stage of the detailed daily lesson plans to the brief outlines or memoranda, but some wrote outlines during the early part and then gradually worked up to the more detailed daily plans. Some prepared units of work from the beginning and continued to do so throughout their student-teaching courses, while others did not obtain practice in connection with units of work. Some outlined large units of instruction from the beginning and then subdivided these into smaller units, while others dealt with small units at first and gradually undertook more comprehensive ones. Some prepared whole units of instruction at first and then wrote daily lesson plans based upon the subject-matter and activities outlined in these, while others wrote only formal plans during the early part of student-

* Samples of various forms of lesson plans which were used in the different state teachers colleges are presented in Appendix B in Volume II of this study, which is on file in manuscript form in Teachers College Library.

teaching and outlined units of instruction during the latter part.

According to reports from both student-teachers and critic teachers, the median student-teacher obtained practice in outlining units of instruction and then writing daily plans based upon the subject-matter and activities in these units. The planning and writing of these units began during the first four weeks of the regular student-teaching courses.

Time Element in the Preparation of Lesson Plans

The median student-teacher wrote the daily plan about two days before applying it in teaching activities. Table XXXIII summarizes the reports from 2,152 student-teachers who answered the question, "How many days in advance did you generally write your daily plans before you applied them in teaching."

TABLE XXXIII

Per Cent of Student-Teachers under Different Administrative Organizations Who Wrote Their Daily Plans for Each of the Specified Number of Days or Weeks Before Applying Them in Teaching

Number of Days or Weeks	Per Cent of Student-Teachers								Sum Total
	1–2 HOURS		½ DAY		ALL DAY		TOTAL		
	P	I	P	I	P	I	P	I	
Days									
1	31.8	27.5	36.9	32.1	44.4	39.2	34.2	29.6	31.9
2	26.7	25.0	27.9	28.9	25.4	24.6	27.0	26.2	26.6
3	19.5	20.4	19.6	22.0	12.7	18.8	19.1	20.8	20.0
4	1.5	1.7	1.9	1.5	3.2	2.9	1.7	1.7	1.7
5	3.2	3.3	2.2	2.6	....	....	2.7	2.9	2.8
Weeks									
1	17.3	22.1	11.5	12.8	14.3	14.5	15.3	18.8	17.1

The student-teachers were also asked to answer the question, "For how long did you write detailed or partly detailed lesson plans?" Table XXXIV presents the distribution of replies from 2,120 student-teachers.

The median of these student-teachers wrote detailed or partly detailed daily plans for approximately ten weeks. Some, however, wrote detailed or formal daily lesson plans throughout their entire student-teaching work. The median student-teacher who taught in schools requiring whole-day student-teaching prepared plans that were somewhat detailed in nature for approximately eight weeks.

TABLE XXXIV

Per Cent of Student-Teachers under Different Administrative Organizations Who Wrote Detailed or Partly Detailed Lesson Plans for Each of the Specified Number of Weeks

Number of Weeks	Per Cent of Student-Teachers								
	1–2 Hours		½ Day		All Day		Total		Sum Total
	P	I	P	I	P	I	P	I	
31 and up......	2.1	3.2	....	....	....	....	1.4	2.0	1.7
28–30..........	1.2	1.6	....	....	....	....	.8	1.0	.9
25–27..........	1.2	2.0	....	....	....	....	.8	1.3	1.0
22–24..........	6.8	6.7	.3	.3	....	....	4.4	4.4	4.4
19–21..........	2.7	4.3	.6	1.9	....	....	1.9	3.3	2.6
16–18..........	9.3	13.9	7.6	8.6	1.6	2.9	8.3	11.6	10.0
13–15..........	6.1	4.1	8.2	9.9	1.6	2.9	6.2	5.7	5.9
10–12..........	30.2	28.4	35.9	35.5	25.4	39.7	32.4	31.2	31.8
7– 9..........	14.3	10.4	21.0	17.6	30.2	23.5	17.2	13.4	15.3
4– 6..........	13.3	11.7	15.3	12.6	25.4	17.7	14.4	12.4	13.4
1– 3..........	12.7	13.8	11.1	13.6	15.9	13.2	12.2	13.7	13.0

The lengths of time for which student-teachers were required to write the various types and forms of lesson plans and the amounts of time devoted to the writing of these varied greatly in the different teachers colleges, as a result of numerous important factors. Chief among these factors were the following: (1) administrative phases of teacher-education, for example, student-teachers who were scheduled in student-teaching courses for one hour a day for thirty-six weeks generally wrote formal daily lesson plans over a much longer period of time than did those who were scheduled for whole-day student-teaching for twelve weeks; (2) requirements and standards set up by supervisors and critic teachers in different grades or schools; (3) the nature and scope of the materials of instruction; and (4) the teaching skill, together with the subject-matter and technical background preparation, acquired by the student-teachers.

Use Made of Lesson Plans during Teaching Periods

There were 2,142 student-teachers who answered the question, "How closely did you follow your prepared daily lesson plans during class periods?" The distribution of replies is summarized in Table XXXV. Approximately 10.9% of the student-teachers usually followed their previously prepared plans exactly as they had planned them; about 57.4% carried them out for the most part; about 30.0%

followed them in general; and 1.7% practically ignored them. The median student-teacher followed prepared lesson plans *for the most part* during class periods. Some student-teachers carried their plans into effect much more successfully than others, due partly to the fact that some prepared plans which were flexible and adaptable in nature while others adhered rigidly to lesson-plan forms regardless of subject-matter and teaching situations.

A slightly larger per cent of the student-teachers in the inter-mediate grades than of those in the primary grades adhered rigidly to prepared lesson plans while teaching groups of children. Student-teachers scheduled for one-hour-a-day student-teaching had a tend-ency to follow their lesson plans more closely than did those scheduled for half-day and whole-day student-teaching.

TABLE XXXV

Per Cent of Student-Teachers under Different Administrative Organizations Who Indicated to What Extent Previously Prepared Lesson Plans Were Usually Followed in Actual Teaching

Extent to Which Previously Prepared Plans Were Followed during Teaching	Per Cent of Student-Teachers								Sum Total
	1–2 Hours		½ Day		All Day		Total		
	P	I	P	I	P	I	P	I	
Exactly as planned......	10.6	13.5	8.8	10.5	5.8	6.9	9.7	12.1	10.9
For the most part.......	57.1	56.7	57.5	58.1	60.3	59.7	57.4	57.3	57.4
In general..............	31.0	27.6	32.4	29.6	32.4	31.9	31.5	28.5	30.0
Slightly................	1.3	2.2	1.3	1.8	1.5	1.4	1.4	2.0	1.7

Different Types of Records, Reports, and Plans Written Subsequent to the Teaching Activities

Some of the student-teachers prepared several forms of records, reports, outlines, and plans subsequent to their teaching activities. The median student-teacher listed outcomes or results after the completion of certain daily lessons, and also wrote summaries of work after the completion of certain units of instruction. Only 8.8% of the student-teachers reported that they wrote outcomes, sum-maries, outlines, or plans for most of the lessons subsequent to the teaching of them. Table XXXVI presents the distribution of answers given by student-teachers to the section of questions contained in the inquiry sheets relative to the types of records and plans that were prepared subsequent to teaching activities.

TABLE XXXVI

Per Cent of Primary and Intermediate Student-Teachers Who Answered "Yes" or "No," or Who Failed to Answer at All, When Asked if They Obtained Practice in Writing Each of the Specified Types of Records Subsequent to Teaching Activities during Student-Teaching

Types of Records Written Subsequent to Teaching Activities	Per Cent of Student-Teachers						
	YES		No		TOTAL		
	P	I	P	I	Yes	No	Blank
1. Outcomes or results of:							
a. Daily lessons...........	62.3	57.5	28.5	31.3	59.8	30.0	10.2
b. Whole units............	44.4	41.3	44.4	46.7	42.8	45.5	11.7
c. Activity units.........	42.3	35.3	43.2	51.0	38.8	47.1	14.1
d. Sub-units..............	38.3	33.9	47.9	50.5	36.1	49.2	14.7
e. Term's work...........	24.8	27.1	57.9	52.8	26.0	55.3	18.7
2. Summaries of:							
a. Units of work.........	50.5	49.6	40.4	44.3	50.1	42.4	7.5
b. Term's work...........	27.3	29.1	57.4	56.4	28.2	57.1	14.7
3. Outlines and records of units of work as carried out in class.	39.9	35.5	48.9	52.6	37.7	50.8	11.5
4. Records of daily class work actually completed and of activities carried out by pupils.	39.3	36.4	53.4	57.3	37.8	55.4	6.8
5. Records of daily work completed, written in the form of definite plans..............	33.5	31.5	58.6	60.2	32.5	59.4	8.1

A larger per cent of the student-teachers majoring in the primary grades than of those in the intermediate or upper elementary grades obtained practice in keeping records or reports subsequent to the teaching activities. A much larger per cent of the student-teachers scheduled for half-day and whole-day student-teaching than of those scheduled for only one-hour-a-day teaching wrote different types of records and reports subsequent to the presentation of subject-matter and materials. (See Table XXIV, item B.)

THE VALUE OF LESSON PLANS AS APPRAISED BY STUDENT-TEACHERS AND LABORATORY-SCHOOL FACULTY MEMBERS

Student-teachers and laboratory-school faculty members were requested to state arguments for and against the use of lesson plans. There was almost unanimous agreement that lesson plans of the right types were helpful to student-teachers during the early part of student-teaching. Written plans were, however, considered less essential as the work in teaching progressed.

The specific reasons given both for and against the use of lesson plans were grouped under appropriate major headings with subtopics under each. The bases on which the use of lesson plans during the early part of student-teaching was justified are listed below, ranging from high to low, according to the average per cent of answers from both student-teachers and laboratory-school faculty members.

Justifications for the Use of the Lesson Plan during Early Part of Student-Teaching According to Reports from Student-Teachers and Laboratory-School Faculty Members

A. *Assures more effective planning and more thorough preparation for teaching; helps student-teachers to organize subject-matter and activities in their total possibilities; gives more comprehensive understanding of total situations.*

1. Guarantees planning in advance and gives a working basis to the immature teacher.
   a. Aids student-teachers in planning and thinking through the subject-matter, the classroom activities, and the teaching procedures in advance.
   b. Helps student-teachers to know definitely what they are going to teach; how they are going to present materials; and when they are going to teach various phases of the work.
   c. Serves as a medium for developing skill in planning.
   d. Helps prospective teachers to form habits of systematic planning that will carry over to future teaching in the elementary schools.

2. Promotes careful and systematic organization.
   a. Insures more careful and systematic organization of subject-matter, instructional materials, activities, ideas, and teaching techniques.
   b. Helps to establish good working organization.
   c. Provides opportunities to organize whole units of work before presenting them to the children.
   d. Gives student-teachers practice in organizing and in determining which type of organization is best suited to a given unit of subject-matter and to the children to be taught.

3. Clarifies educational principles and increases grasp of teaching techniques.
   a. Helps student-teachers to determine and to fix in mind suitable teaching techniques and activities.
   b. Insures that provision has been made for significant questions, suitable assignments, summaries, and conclusions.
   c. Makes student-teachers conscious of teaching techniques that can be used in different types of teaching situations.
   d. Insures better understanding of educational principles.
   e. Requires the giving of attention to proper learning processes.

4. Assures better working knowledge of subject-matter and other educative materials to be used in teaching.
    a. Helps to arouse interest and shows the need for ready command of subject-matter.
    b. Promotes clearer understanding and more thorough mastery of materials of instruction.
    c. Aids in discriminating between major and minor points, and in remembering essentials of subject-matter to be presented.
5. Makes student-teachers conscious of objectives and results that should be accomplished.
    a. Aids in determining, in setting up, and in realizing desired objectives and expected outcomes.
    b. Helps in knowing exactly what should be covered or completed during each class period, in light of definite objectives.
6. Promotes unity and integration of subject-matter.
    a. Helps to develop each part of a unit in relation to every other part; aids in relating parts of subject-matter units to the whole, and in seeing the relation of the "daily plan" to the "unit plan."
    b. Gives experience in unifying and integrating subject-matter in developing large units of work.

B. *Serves as valuable aid and definite guide in teaching, thus inspiring feeling of security and self-confidence that comes with thorough preparation.*
    1. Gives student-teachers something constructive to follow.
    2. Helps the beginning teacher to keep to the point in teaching and to keep the work moving smoothly towards a definite goal.
    3. Gives the teacher tangible means of comparison and evaluation.
    4. Serves as a memorandum directly helpful in teaching.

C. *Serves as medium for stimulating thinking; helps student-teachers to develop forethought and to make necessary adjustments.*
    1. Aids student-teachers in thinking more clearly and systematically in connection with teaching situations.
    2. Helps to clarify, organize, systematize, and crystallize their own thinking.
    3. Promotes logical, independent, and reflective thinking.
    4. Aids student-teachers in analyzing situations, in foreseeing difficulties that might arise and in making provision for these, in anticipating problems and in determining possible solutions; thus increasing ability of student-teachers to make necessary adjustments.
    5. Helps to develop better mental habits.

D. *Aids critic teachers in inducting student-teachers into the art of lesson planning.*
    1. Serves as a check on the planning and preparation of student-teachers.
    2. Provides opportunity for checking student-teachers' preparation so that necessary corrections and revisions can be made, thus preventing undue errors and faulty procedures in teaching.

3. Gives critic teachers and supervisors an opportunity to check on the progress and development of each student-teacher so that proper individual guidance may be given.

4. Forms a medium of communication and understanding between critic teachers and student-teachers.

E. *Safeguards and protects the welfare and interests of the children.*

1. Insures more careful consideration of the abilities, interests, problems, difficulties, and needs of the children.

2. Aids in making necessary provisions and adaptations for individual differences of the children.

3. Leaves the teacher free to deal with the needs and interests of the pupils during class periods.

4. Helps in utilizing children's leads, questions, contributions, and experiences.

5. Prevents exploitation of children.

F. *Conserves time and energy during class periods as a result of thorough preparation.*

1. Insures that materials and plans are ready when needed.

2. Prevents wandering and side-tracking during class periods, thus saving time.

3. Aids in budgeting time so as to accomplish the maximum amount of work.

4. Frees the teacher from much detailed work while teaching a class.

5. Helps student-teachers to encounter classroom problems with minimum loss of time during teaching periods.

G. *Serves as a written cumulative record of work accomplished; forms basis upon which to build.*

1. Helps to keep cumulative records of objectives accomplished and of work covered.

2. Opens up many possibilities and leads to future work.

H. *Insures greater progress, and helps to keep the work well-balanced.*

1. Brings forth effort that would not otherwise be secured.

2. Keeps student-teachers more alert and prevents slackness.

I. *Orients student-teachers into teaching.*

Table XXXVII presents the per cent of student-teachers and laboratory-school faculty members whose statements were placed under each major heading giving justifications for the use of the lesson plan during early part of student-teaching.

The bases on which the use of lesson plans during the advanced or latter part of student-teaching was justified are listed on pages 137 and 138.

TABLE XXXVII

Per Cent of Student-Teachers and Laboratory-School Faculty Members Whose
Statements Were Placed under Each Major Heading Presenting
Justifications for the Use of the Lesson Plan during
Early Part of Student-Teaching

Justifications for the Use of the Lesson Plan during Early Part of Student-Teaching	Per Cent of Student-Teachers and Faculty Members						
	STUDENT-TEACHERS		SUPERVISORS AND CRITICS		DIRECTORS OF TRAINING	TOTAL	
						Student Teachers	Faculty Members
	P	I	P	I			
A. Assures more effective planning and more thorough preparation for teaching; helps student-teachers to organize subject-matter and activities in their total possibilities; gives more comprehensive understanding of total situations..............	59.0	64.1	51.0	54.3	37.7	61.6	51.0
B. Serves as valuable aid and definite guide in teaching, thus inspiring feeling of security and self-confidence that comes with thorough preparation..........	19.0	16.8	18.0	19.5	18.8	17.9	18.8
C. Serves as medium for stimulating thinking; helps student-teachers to develop forethought and to make necessary adjustments....	12.3	11.3	7.2	7.7	11.3	11.8	7.9
D. Aids critic teachers in inducting student-teachers into the art of lesson planning...............	5.9	4.4	8.2	5.8	13.2	5.1	7.7
E. Safeguards and protects the welfare and interests of the children.	....	....	8.8	6.8	5.6	....	7.5
F. Conserves time and energy during class periods as a result of thorough preparation..........	3.0	2.6	1.5	2.0	3.8	2.8	2.0
G. Serves as a written cumulative record of work accomplished; forms basis upon which to build..	.9	.9	3.0	3.0	5.7	.8	3.4
H. Insures greater progress, and helps to keep the work well-balanced.......................	....	....	2.0	1.0	1.9	....	1.5
I. Orients students into teaching...	....	....	....	....	1.9	....	.2

Table LIII in Volume II of this study, which is on file in manuscript form in Teachers College Library, presents in detail the following data: the college year in which the student-teaching was done; the form of organization under which it was conducted; the number of primary and intermediate student-teachers, both inexperienced and experienced, who reported each of the reasons for the use of lesson plans during early part of student-teaching.

Table LIV in Volume II shows the number of laboratory-school faculty members, under different forms of student-teaching organization, who reported each of the reasons for the use of lesson plans during early part of student-teaching.

Justifications for the Use of the Lesson Plan during the Advanced or Latter Part of Student-Teaching Courses According to Reports from Student-Teachers and Laboratory-School Faculty Members

A. *Assures more effective planning and more thorough preparation for teaching; helps student-teachers to organize subject-matter and activities in their total possibilities; gives more comprehensive understanding of total situations.*

  1. Develops greater skill in planning, in organizing, and in adapting subject-matter, activities, and procedures.
  a. Provides opportunity for long-view planning.
  b. Establishes systematic planning and good working organization.
  c. Guarantees that some activities have been planned in advance.
  d. Necessitates daily preparation based on the preceding activities.
  e. Promotes more effective organization and adaptation of both subject-matter and methods of instruction.

  2. Insures more thorough command of both subject-matter and methods of instruction.
  a. Encourages wider use of libraries and other sources of supply in finding suitable references and supplementary materials; promotes more intensive and extensive reading.
  b. Helps to determine and to fix in mind essentials of subject-matter.
  c. Gives more assurance that suitable procedures and activities will be used in different types of teaching situations.

    (1) Gives student-teachers a clear conception of what to do and how to proceed during class periods.
    (2) Helps student-teachers to determine and to fix in mind suitable techniques and activities.
    (3) Helps student-teachers to formulate vital and thought-provoking questions, to make purposeful and suitable assignments, to provide for summaries, and to form conclusions.

  3. Promotes unity and integration of materials of instruction.
  a. Provides better opportunity for developing whole units of work or large centers of interest; helps in seeing a unit as a whole.
  b. Aids in seeing the relation of the "daily plan" to the "unit plan."
  c. Affords opportunity for unifying and integrating subject-matter and instructional materials in developing large units of instruction.

  4. Helps to determine and to formulate basic principles, definite objectives, and desired outcomes.

B. *Serves as a means for stimulating thinking; and for helping student-teachers to develop forethought and to make necessary adjustments.*

  1. Serves as an incentive for student-teachers to do systematic, independent, and reflective thinking.
  2. Helps to clarify, organize, and crystallize ideas.
  3. Aids in anticipating problems, in analyzing situations, in seeing relation-

ships, in determining possible solutions, and thus increasing ability of student-teachers to make necessary adjustments to situations.

4. Promotes thoughtful consideration of all the possibilities inherent in any particular group situation.

C. *Safeguards and protects the welfare and interests of the children.*

1. Insures more careful consideration of the interests, experiences, problems, capacities, and needs of the children; aids in making necessary provisions and adaptations for individual differences of children.

2. Aids in utilizing children's leads, questions, contributions, and experiences.

3. Frees the student-teacher for better classroom teaching, thus preventing exploitation of the children.

D. *Serves as a valuable aid and definite guide; inspires self-confidence.*

1. Forms a guide to use when necessary, thus inspiring self-confidence.

2. Serves as an aid in teaching, thus giving a feeling of security.

3. Helps to keep to a definite point and to accomplish desired objectives.

4. Furnishes a good organization to fall back on when a lesson takes an unforeseen or confusing direction.

5. Gives a tangible means of comparison and evaluation.

6. Furnishes a memorandum of high points in subject-matter.

E. *Aids faculty members in inducting student-teachers into the art of teaching.*

1. Serves as a check on the planning and preparation of student-teachers; helps to reduce errors in teaching in consequence of necessary corrections and revisions made possible by thorough checking of plans.

2. Gives faculty members an opportunity to check the work and progress of student-teachers, thus making possible constructive guidance.

F. *Serves as a written cumulative record; forms a basis upon which to build.*

1. Aids in keeping cumulative records of objectives accomplished, subject-matter covered, activities carried out, and references used.

2. Opens up possibilities and leads to further activities.

G. *Insures greater progress in consequence of adequate preparation, and helps to keep the work well-balanced.*

H. *Conserves time and energy during class periods.*

Table LV in Volume II of this study, which is on file in manuscript form in Teachers College Library, presents in detail the following data: the college year in which the student-teaching was done; the form of organization under which it was conducted; the number of primary and intermediate student-teachers, both inexperienced and experienced, who reported each of the reasons for the use of lesson plans during the latter part of student-teaching.

Out of the 2,181 student-teachers who gave reasons for or against lesson planning during the latter part of student-teaching, 88.1% gave arguments in favor of lesson planning while only 11.9% stated objections. From the criticisms offered by this latter group of students it was evident that they did not object to lesson planning as such, but rather to the types and forms of written lesson plans that they were required to prepare and to use during student-teaching. The major headings, under which the individual objections were summarized, are arranged according to the number of times that each was mentioned by these student-teachers at the close of their student-teaching courses.

Objections Raised by 11.9% of the Student-Teachers to the Use of Lesson Plans during the Advanced or Latter Part of Student-Teaching

A. *Student-teachers spent much time in writing plans that were encumbered with structural complications and deficiencies.*

   1. Excessive amounts of time and energy were devoted to writing plans that were not adapted to immediate needs, problems, and situations.
   2. Considerable time and energy were wasted in writing daily plans that were described as being:
      a. Similar in form and content; a repetition of old plans from day to day.
      b. Detailed in nature; lacking in discrimination between essential and nonessential points, and between major and minor questions.
      c. Formal and mechanical in organization.
      d. Complicated and elaborate.
      e. Narrow in scope.
      f. Poorly organized.
   3. Extremely detailed, formal, and elaborate plans defeated their own purposes because they were:
      a. Time- and energy-consuming in proportion to value derived.
      b. Cumbersome to use while teaching.
      c. Difficult to scan and review.
      d. Burdensome and unprogressive, consequently losing their value.

B. *Plans were written in too small units; frequently for daily work only.*

C. *Advanced student-teachers had already acquired ability to teach without written plans.*

Table LVI in Volume II, which is on file in manuscript form in Teachers College, Columbia University, shows in detail the following data: the college year in which the student-teaching was done; the type of organization under which it was conducted; the number of primary and intermediate student-teachers, both experienced and inexperienced, who suggested each of the reasons why lesson plans were not helpful to student-teachers during the latter or advanced part of student-teaching.

     1. Student-teachers had acquired confidence and efficiency in presenting materials and had gained ability to proceed without written plans.

     2. Student-teachers were accustomed to the routine and could keep materials in mind without written plans.

D. *The time schedule for writing plans was not adjusted to the needs of student-teachers.*

     1. Plans were not written far enough in advance to make possible the necessary criticisms and revisions.

     2. Plans were written too far in advance to be of value in teaching.

E. *Previously prepared plans could not be followed during class periods because pupils' responses, arguments, and leads upset definitely formulated questions and answers.*

     1. Lessons seldom turned out as student-teachers had previously planned.

     2. Plans did not provide for the emergencies that always came up during the class period.

F. *Written lesson plans handicapped initiative and spontaneity in class.*

     1. Children's interests and needs were sacrificed when student-teachers attempted to follow written plans in all details.

     2. Formalism in planning produced formalism in instruction; the following results attended the use of very formal plans:

        a. The children's spontaneous reactions and contributions were ignored.

        b. Self-expression and initiative were inhibited.

        c. The teacher was bound to a definite procedure, thus making the lessons stilted and formal.

     3. Plans encouraged teacher initiative rather than pupil initiative.

     4. Student-teachers were required to adhere too strictly to written plans.

     5. Plans were written on the teacher's level rather than on the pupil's level.

G. *Plans were frequently not corrected, criticized, nor returned.*

     1. Critic teachers were too busy to correct or to constructively criticize lesson plans, thus little progress was made.

     2. Plans were seldom returned and, therefore, could not be used during teaching periods.

WAYS IN WHICH LESSON PLANS COULD BE MADE MORE HELPFUL TO STUDENT-TEACHERS ACCORDING TO REPORTS FROM STUDENT-TEACHERS AND LABORATORY-SCHOOL FACULTY MEMBERS

Although most of the student-teachers and faculty members recognized that the resultant benefits justified the use of the lesson plan as a teaching aid, they were also conscious that limitations were being imposed upon these benefits through the existing deficiencies in the lesson-planning programs as administered in their respective teacher-preparing institutions. Questions pertaining to the most effective ways in which lesson plans could be made more helpful to student-teachers elicited answers from 2,103 student-teachers and 459 laboratory-school faculty members. In order to facilitate tabulation and study, these replies were grouped under appropriate major headings. Table XXXVIII presents the per cent of student-teachers and laboratory-school faculty members, under different administrative organizations, whose answers were grouped under each main heading showing ways in which lesson plans could be made more helpful to student-teachers. These major headings were first listed according to frequency of mention; then the detailed suggestions of both student-teachers and laboratory-school faculty members were inserted below the proper heading, to be organized finally into the outline given below—forming ultimately a composite statement that includes many of the most essential phases of an effective lesson-planning program.

A. *Lesson-planning should be in accord with the best educational principles. The form, content, and application of written plans should be suitably adapted and intelligently applied to particular needs, problems, and situations.*

    1. Lesson plans should be purposeful, practical, workable, flexible, and intelligent.

       a. Written plans should be adapted and suited to various factors, such as:

          (1) The needs, abilities, experiences, and skill of the student-teachers.

          (2) The interests, needs, and abilities of the children.

          (3) The subject-matter and instructional materials to be used.

          (4) The activities to be carried out.

          (5) The teaching techniques and the educational procedures to be applied.

          (6) The teaching situation and the learning environment.

       b. The application and use of plans should be flexible and elastic enough to:

          (1) Meet the interests, needs, and abilities of the children in class and extra-class activities.

          (2) Provide for active participation of children in class work.

          (3) Promote freedom and adaptability on the part of the teacher.

          (4) Develop initiative, self-expression, and resourcefulness on the part of student-teachers and children.

TABLE

Per Cent of Student-Teachers and Laboratory-School Faculty Members
in Which Lesson Plans Could Be Made

Ways in Which Lesson Plans Could Be Made More Helpful to Student-Teachers	1-2 Hours				Per ½	
	Student-Teachers		Supervisors and Critics		Student-Teachers	
	P	I	P	I	P	I
A. Lesson-planning should be in accord with the best educational principles. The form, content, and application of written plans should be suitably adapted and intelligently applied to particular needs, problems, and situations	22.6	19.2	32.5	26.0	29.5	21.9
B. Adequate guidance should be given to student-teachers in the preparation and revision of large units and daily plans	36.8	27.4	5.1	5.5	27.5	21.6
C. Adequate opportunity should be provided for the preparation of long-view plans—the planning of large units of work, selection and organization of broad units of subject-matter, integration of materials of instruction, and development of comprehensive units of instruction	7.4	10.5	19.7	23.6	9.6	11.1
D. Thorough preparation in connection with lesson plans should be required of student-teachers	5.8	13.9	8.5	17.3	6.3	10.2
E. Systematic and effective induction into the preparation of lesson plans should be provided during student-teaching	11.1	8.3	12.8	9.4	12.2	10.5
F. Lesson plans should be more inclusive	11.9	16.7	10.2	11.0	10.3	20.3
G. Definite follow-up work should be done in connection with lesson-planning; careful records should be kept of daily activities and of significant events in the development of units of work	4.4	4.0	2.6	2.4	4.6	4.3
H. Lesson plans should be of such a nature as to serve as valuable aids and helpful guides to student-teachers in actual teaching	....	....	3.4	2.4	....	....
I. Plans should be so organized and applied as to insure continuous growth in both student-teachers and pupils; they should form a work basis and guide for future work	....	....	2.6	.8	....	....
J. Samples of lesson plans may be helpful under proper conditions	....	....	2.6	1.6	....	....

XXXVIII

Whose Answers Were Placed under Each Major Heading Showing Ways More Helpful to Student-Teachers

Cent of Student-Teachers and Laboratory-School Faculty Members

DAY		ALL DAY				TOTAL				Directors of Training	SUM TOTAL	
Supervisors and Critics		Student-Teachers		Supervisors and Critics		Student-Teachers		Supervisors and Critics			Student-Teachers	Faculty Members
P	I	P	I	P	I	P	I	P	I			
32.3	28.3	38.1	23.6	33.3	25.0	25.8	20.3	32.5	26.6	31.0	22.9	29.6
3.2	3.3	22.2	19.4	11.1	5.0	33.1	25.1	5.1	4.8	7.3	29.1	5.2
19.4	23.3	11.1	15.3	27.8	30.0	8.2	11.0	20.3	24.2	29.1	9.6	23.1
8.1	15.0	9.5	16.7	....	15.0	6.2	12.9	7.6	16.4	14.5	9.6	12.4
16.1	13.3	6.3	13.9	16.7	15.0	11.2	9.3	14.2	11.1	7.3	10.2	12.0
4.8	6.7	11.1	7.0	....	5.0	11.4	17.2	7.6	9.2	....	14.4	7.4
1.6	3.3	1.6	4.1	....	....	4.3	4.2	2.0	2.4	1.8	4.2	2.2
6.5	5.0	....	....	5.6	....	....	....	4.6	2.9	5.5	....	3.9
8.1	1.7	....	....	5.6	5.0	....	....	4.6	1.4	3.6	....	3.1
....	....	....	....	....	....	....	....	1.5	1.0	....	....	1.1

(5) Stimulate constructive imagination, originality, and creativeness.

(6) Provide for emergencies, unusual problems, unexpected situations, and unforeseen difficulties that might arise.

(7) Take into account possible new developments and activities.

(8) Adjust to various directions that a lesson might take.

(9) Arouse enthusiasm over modern progressive methods in education.

   c. The forms of plans should be modified from time to time to keep pace with:

(1) Changing trends in the objectives of education.

(2) Revisions in the curriculum.

(3) The new administrative policies of the school.

Extremely formal, elaborate, and stereotyped plans should be avoided; rigid systems of planning should be eliminated.

2. Written daily plans should be clear-cut and brief, yet adequate.

   a. Daily plans should be simple, concise, and to the point.

   b. Brief plans that can be easily scanned and followed in teaching should be stressed; major and essential points should be emphasized, but minor details should be omitted from written plans.

   c. The amount of detail in written lesson plans should be determined by the various factors comprising the total teaching situation.

3. Students and faculty members should study the best practices in lesson planning, and then build on these.

B. *Adequate guidance and intelligent help should be given to the student-teachers in the preparation and revision of large units and daily plans.*

1. Well-prepared conferences in connection with lesson-planning should be held frequently with student-teachers.

   a. Stimulating guidance, valuable suggestions, practical ideas, and sympathetic advice should be given to the students for the preparation of:

(1) Large activity units.

(2) Large units of instruction or comprehensive units of work.

(3) Daily plans.

   b. Constructive criticisms of lesson plans should be given to student-teachers:

(1) From the beginning of the student-teaching work.

(2) Both prior and subsequent to teaching.

   c. Instructional materials and educational procedures observed by students during demonstration periods should be evaluated and discussed in light of modern educational principles.

2. Lesson plans should serve as a check on the preparation of the student-teachers.

   a. Written plans and outlines should be submitted to critic teachers for approval before lessons are taught.

    b. Corrections, suggestions, and criticisms of plans should be given to student-teachers in ample time to make necessary revisions.

    c. Plans should always be returned to student-teachers prior to the teaching periods in which they are to be used.

3. Efficient guidance should be given in connection with materials of instruction.

    a. Laboratory-school staff members and other college instructors should be ready to furnish available materials in their respective fields and to offer suggestions in the selection, organization, adaptation, and presentation of subject-matter.

    b. Instructors need adequate working knowledge of content subject-matter, educative materials, and references in order to guide the student-teachers effectively and without loss of time.

C. *Adequate opportunity should be provided for the preparation of long-view plans—the planning of large units of work, selection and organization of broad units of subject-matter, integration of materials of instruction, and development of comprehensive units of instruction.*

1. Opportunity should be provided for preparation of long-range plans in which student-teachers secure broad views of whole units of work. Students need longer periods of growth.

2. Adequate practice should be given in connection with planning, outlining, and organizing whole units of instruction or large activity units; then dividing these into smaller units to be used in daily work.

3. Close co-operation and integration between the college departments and the laboratory schools are highly essential in organizing and adapting units of subject-matter to different age levels of children.

    a. Organization of broad units of subject-matter should begin in connection with subject-matter courses in the teachers colleges.

    b. A series of large units of subject-matter should extend throughout the sophomore and junior years in connection with subject-matter and professional courses.

    c. Students should be provided opportunities to observe various units of subject-matter as they are carried out in the different grades in the laboratory schools.

    d. After students have participated in organizing large units of subject-matter in the college classes, they should be given opportunities to select and to organize those phases of subject-matter that could be used in the different elementary grades.

    e. During junior participation or preliminary teaching, the junior participants should assist the critic teachers in making units of work and daily plans to be used in the laboratory schools.

4. Integration of various types of subject-matter in the elementary grades should be emphasized in working out units of instruction.

D. *Thorough preparation in connection with lesson plans should be required of student-teachers.*

    1. Adequate time and effort should be spent in connection with such activities as thinking through plans, searching for materials, reading extensively, preparing materials, organizing high points in units of work or in daily lessons, mastering subject-matter, and obtaining broad background. Students should become acquainted with the best educative materials, such as textbooks, drill books, supplementary readers, reference and illustrative materials.

    2. Adequate working knowledge of child development, materials of instruction, educational principles, and teaching techniques are prerequisites to the preparation of effective lesson plans.

    3. Plans should be so well worked out that student-teachers will be free to concentrate upon the needs and interests of the children rather than upon the knowledge of the subject-matter and the teaching techniques during the class periods.

    4. The greatest proportion of the time allotted to preparation of lesson plans should be devoted to mastery of subject-matter and to acquisition of ready command of instructional materials; only a small proportion of the time should be devoted to the actual writing of the plans.

    5. Thorough preparation is highly essential to successful teaching; student-teachers must not be permitted to trust to inspiration of the moment nor to hurried and careless daily reading of the materials.

E. *Systematic and effective induction into the preparation of lesson plans should be provided during student-teaching.*

    1. The rate of induction into lesson planning should depend on the ability and skill that the student-teacher demonstrates in writing plans.

    2. Lesson planning should lead progressively toward a minimum of detailed and formal work.

        a. Students should never cease to plan, but they should be trained to write gradually less detailed plans as they show ability to organize and present materials with a reasonable degree of skill; thus detail should be reduced as skill is gained.

        b. Students should proceed gradually from the stage of the somewhat detailed lesson plan to that of the brief outline or memorandum.

    3. The following graded steps of induction into the preparation of lesson plans during student-teaching were suggested:

First step: Student-teachers should acquaint themselves with the teaching situation, observe the critic teacher, write observation reports on lessons observed, and discuss problems with the critic.

Second step: Student-teachers and critic teacher should confer and plan jointly a whole unit of work, with daily lessons based on that unit; the critic teacher should teach each lesson planned in relation to the whole unit.

Third step: Student-teachers should plan lessons and critic teacher should carry them out in teaching. After introductory survey of the entire unit, student-teachers should plan daily work with sufficient detail to show the critic teacher what the general procedures for the day should be.

Fourth step: Several students should co-operatively plan a unit; each one should participate in directing a part of the unit or in teaching a lesson in relation to the whole.

Fifth step: Each student-teacher should plan individually, and finally take over full responsibility for carrying on complete planning and teaching activities.

4. During the period of responsible teaching, student-teachers should be permitted to use their own originality and initiative in writing plans; they should be held responsible for final forms of plans.

5. Memoranda and checks should be used in preference to more detailed plans during the latter part of student-teaching.

F. *Lesson plans should be more inclusive.*

1. Lesson plans should include such items as:
   a. Objectives.
   b. Subject-matter outlines.
   c. Illustrative, supplementary, and reference materials for both student-teachers and children; sources of supply.
   d. Activities to be carried out.
   e. Procedures to be used, such as:

   (1) Leading problems to be solved.
   (2) Key type, pivotal, thought-provoking, and significant questions.
   (3) Possible solutions of vital problems.
   (4) Explicit directions, in case of unusually complex problems.
   (5) Detailed information essential to the clarification of an important point.
   (6) Stimulating, purposeful, and suitable assignments.
   (7) Concise summaries and important conclusions.

2. Beginning students should be required to state the following:

   a. How things are to be done as well as what is to be done.
   b. How materials are to be introduced, presented, and used.
   c. The most important answers and reactions that they expect the children to give. (This is a direct check upon student-teachers' knowledge of the psychology of the learner. The immature teachers usually know the subject-matter in terms of their own experiences and must be led to think of objectives and subject-matter in terms of the children to be taught.) The beginning student-teacher should be required to attempt to predict actual questions and answers.

G. *Definite follow-up work should be done in connection with lesson-planning; careful records should be kept of daily activities and of significant events in the development of units of work.*

1. Analysis and evaluation of each plan taught should be the preliminary step to the planning of the following ones.

2. Careful records should be kept of all activities in order to enable student-teachers to:

   a. Form a basis for each day's work.
   b. Make each day's lesson an outgrowth of the previous one.
   c. See growth in both the student-teachers' and the children's work.
   d. Keep the work well-balanced.

3. Daily checks should be made of:

   a. New leads opened up.
   b. Questions and problems raised.
   c. Activities proposed.
   d. High points in subject-matter covered.
   e. Problems solved.
   f. Conclusions reached.

4. Cumulative records should be kept of:

   a. Objectives and outcomes accomplished.
   b. Subject-matter covered.
   c. References and supplementary materials used.
   d. Techniques and procedures applied.
   e. Reactions to plans.
   f. Suggestions for improvement.
   g. Evaluation of progress made.

H. *Lesson plans should be of such a nature as to serve as valuable aids and helpful guides to student-teachers in actual teaching.*

1. Students need carefully organized plans to fall back on in case they become confused when teaching. It is better to follow a well-organized plan rather closely than to permit the class to become disorderly, confused, and uninterested. Disorder and confusion due to lack of definite planning permits the formation of undesirable habits, attitudes, and learnings.

Table LVII in Volume II shows in detail the following data concerning the student-teachers who suggested each of the ways in which lesson plans could be improved: the college year in which student-teaching was done; the type of organization under which it was conducted; the number of primary and intermediate student-teachers, both experienced and inexperienced.

Table LVIII in Volume II presents in detail the number of laboratory-school faculty members, under the different forms of administrative organization, who suggested each of the ways in which lesson plans could be improved.

Volume II of this study is on file in manuscript form in the Library of Teachers College, Columbia University.

2. Plans should be used as instruments to free the teacher and to give self-confidence based on thorough preparation.

3. Plans should help students to continue orderly sequence after a digression is terminated.

I. *Plans should be so organized and applied as to insure continuous growth in both student-teachers and pupils; they should form a work basis and guide for future work.*

J. *Samples of lesson plans may be helpful under proper conditions.*

1. Critic teachers should first arouse curiosity, stimulate thinking, and challenge students to write the best plans within their abilities; they should then give them samples of good plans for comparison.

2. Student-teachers should see many samples of lesson plans for each subject that they are to teach.

SUMMARY

In recognition of the importance attached to the lesson plan in the preparation of teachers, a consideration of certain significant details in the conduct of lesson-planning programs in different teacher-preparing institutions was undertaken. While the use of the lesson plan was unequivocally endorsed, there were permeative deficiencies to be overcome. A final overview of the situation pointed to clearly defined trends of thought along several lines.

1. Lesson-planning programs varied widely in response to the differences in purpose, detail, and scope of the types or forms of plans used, but the following general conditions prevailed:

a. More than 96% of the student-teachers prepared some type or form of lesson plan at some time during their student-teaching courses. More than 95% obtained practice in writing plans previous to the presentation of work to the pupils, while less than 9% regularly prepared plans as a follow-up procedure.

b. Although almost two-thirds of the student-teachers obtained some practice in the preparation of units of instruction, the contacts of the median student-teacher with long-range planning were relatively limited. The major part of lesson-planning experiences was obtained in connection with daily plans. The daily plan used by the median student-teacher was usually (1) prepared in some detail two days before using it in teaching; (2) written according to some definite form, guide, or outline; and (3) followed "for the most part" by the student-teacher during the class period.

c. The total period of time during which daily plans were required by the different teacher-preparing institutions varied according to the form of administrative organization under which student-teaching was done, ranging from one to more than thirty-one weeks—the median requirement being ten weeks.

2. The reactions of student-teachers and faculty members clearly vindicated the use of lesson plans as an integral part of the preparation of teachers for the elementary grades.

a. The justifications for the use of the lesson plan during the early part of student-teaching were concerned principally with the basic phases of teaching—the benefits accruing from a preview of the contemplated teaching situation: predetermination of purposes or goals to be attained; clarification of educational principles and command of teaching techniques; preparation and organization of materials of instruction to be presented; interrelation of the daily lesson to the whole unit of instruction; the safeguarding of the children's welfare; the incipience of the development of teacher-poise; and economy of time and effort in the classroom.

b. The justifications offered in support of the use of lesson plans during the more advanced or latter part of student-teaching were in general classified under headings similar to those used in the treatment of arguments favoring the use of lesson plans during the early part of student-teaching, but some of the specific suggestions included under these headings have more far-reaching implications.

c. The objections lodged against the use of plans during the latter or advanced part of student-teaching were concerned principally with deficiencies in the administration of the lesson-planning programs of the different teachers colleges, rather than with the use of lesson plans as a teaching aid. Those who offered objections implied that differentiation between the function of the lesson plan in the earlier and in the later stages of student-teaching was lacking, inasmuch as proper allowance was not made for the development of teaching skill on the part of the student-teacher nor for variations in the factors that comprise teaching situations.

3. The recommendations proposed by student-teachers and laboratory-school faculty members centered attention upon the need for

greater flexibility and intelligence in the preparation, adaptation, and use of lesson plans; and upon the effectiveness of a plan that was sufficiently individualized in both form and function to meet simultaneously the needs of teachers, pupils, and particular teaching situations.

In enumerating the factors which are essential to the construction of a satisfactory planning program, both student-teachers and laboratory-school faculty members emphasized that greater stress should be placed upon the following: the development of comprehensive understanding of total situations; long-view planning; the enrichment of the subject-matter content; integration and organization of subject-matter into large units of instruction; the relating of the daily plan to the large unit of instruction; individualization; and the initiation of that final orientation of students into the teaching process which enables them to deviate from the details of the prepared plan and yet maintain uninterrupted progress in the predetermined general direction. It was further advised that the lesson-planning program should provide proper induction into planning techniques; promote assurance of continuous growth on the part of both pupils and student-teachers through the co-ordination of all the contributing factors; and utilize follow-up procedures in capitalizing on progress made and in eliminating errors and deficiencies revealed in this process.

In these recommendations it was made clear that the attainment of these highly desirable ends in lesson-planning could be achieved only as student-teachers obtained the expert guidance and skillful assistance of experienced faculty members in the preparation and revision of large units of instruction and daily lesson plans.

CHAPTER FIVE

STUDENT-TEACHING ACTIVITIES, DIFFICULTIES, AND PROBLEMS
REPORTED AS OUTSTANDING BY STUDENT-TEACHERS AND
LABORATORY-SCHOOL FACULTY MEMBERS

BOTH student-teachers and laboratory-school faculty members who participated in this study filled out inquiry sheets in which they specified the most helpful activities and phases of student-teaching, as well as the least helpful ones; the most difficult problems encountered by student-teachers, together with the chief underlying causes of these difficulties; and the most important problems that student-teachers should investigate and study.

Specific questions that were answered by the laboratory-school faculty members are:

1. What activity or phase of student-teaching is most helpful in the preparation of elementary teachers?
2. What activity or phase of student-teaching is least helpful in drawing out and developing the average student-teacher's ability to teach?
3. What is the most difficult problem that your student-teachers encounter in student-teaching?
4. What is the chief underlying cause of the most difficult problem encountered by your student-teachers?
5. What is the most important problem that student-teachers should investigate and study in student-teaching?

The nature and content of the questions presented to the student-teachers were comparable to those for the faculty members, except that the former called for personal information from each student-teacher.

These questions were given a place in the inquiry sheets in order to secure specific data that would serve as a more accurate basis for analyzing the needs and difficulties of student-teachers; interpreting the ratings of the activities set forth in the *Master Activity Check List* and filling in omissions; and determining the activities and problems that should receive the greatest amounts of time and emphasis in student-teaching.

This part of the study presents the activities and phases of student-teaching which were designated as being either most helpful or least helpful in the preparation of elementary teachers.

Most Helpful Activities and Phases of Student-Teaching

The distribution of replies from 2,439 student-teachers and 455 laboratory-school faculty members to the question, "What activity or phase of student-teaching is most helpful in the preparation of elementary teachers?" is summarized in Table XXXIX.* To facilitate tabulation and interpretation of data, the first answer from each person was placed under an appropriate major heading.

Actual teaching of children under expert supervision and competent guidance was considered the most helpful phase of student-teaching for the preparation of elementary teachers. The answers of 64.8% of the student-teachers and 84.2% of the laboratory-school faculty members were classified under this major heading. To aid in the interpretation of data, the following sub-headings were used:

1. Actual teaching of children under expert supervision; practical experiences with children in teaching and learning situations.
   a. Teaching children under the direction of critic teachers or supervisors.
   b. Working with children in teaching and learning situations.
   c. Participating in various types of class and extra-class activities in the elementary grades.
2. Actual teaching of children under competent guidance; assumption of considerable responsibility in teaching.
   a. Assuming gradually increased responsibilities in teaching until the student-teacher is capable of taking complete charge of a group or a whole class of children.
   b. Teaching children and assuming responsibility for the development, growth, and progress of each individual in the group; assuming responsibility for a group of children over a period of time.
   c. Assuming full responsibility in teaching situations; assuming the responsibilities of a teacher in the elementary grades.

* Table LX in Volume II shows in detail the following data: the college year in which the student-teaching was done; the type of organization under which it was conducted; the number of primary and intermediate student-teachers, both inexperienced and experienced, who specified each of the most helpful activities and phases of student-teaching.

Table LXI in Volume II presents in detail the number of laboratory-school faculty members, under the different forms of administrative organization, who specified each of the most helpful activities and phases of student-teaching.

A number of specific activities were reported as most helpful. The following activities, dealing with actual teaching and learning situations, were classified under the above major heading.

1. Directing the different learning activities of the children.
    a. Applying effective and progressive methods of instruction in directing the learning activities of children.
        (1) Organizing school life around large centers of interest or important child activities.
            (a) Guiding children in working out developmental units of work or units of instruction of a broad scope.
            (b) Guiding children in carrying out large activity units.
        (2) Integrating subject-matter and methods of instruction.
            (a) Guiding children in applying and integrating materials of instruction—basic skills, content subject-matter, and fine and practical arts—in carrying out large child activities, in organizing their personal experiences, and in giving expression to their ideas.
            (b) Utilizing such educational procedures as creative construction, dramatic expression, developmental problem-solving, and socialized activities.

TABLE

Per Cent of Student-Teachers and Laboratory-School Faculty Members Whose Answers Were Placed under Each Major Heading Showing

| The Most Helpful Activities and Phases of Student-Teaching | 1–2 Hours | | | | ½ | |
| | Student-Teachers | | Supervisors and Critics | | Student-Teachers | |
	P	I	P	I	P	I
A. Actual teaching of children under expert supervision and competent guidance	65.8	61.7	86.4	80.3	67.0	66.3
B. Individual conferences with critic teachers and other faculty members	11.3	10.3	5.9	5.5	10.0	9.2
C. Planning, selection, organization, adaptation, and application of subject-matter	5.9	13.1	2.5	7.1	7.7	13.2
D. Well-directed observation of children and of expert teaching	12.9	9.2	4.2	3.1	10.0	7.5
E. Initiation of various types of class activities as an outgrowth of participation in extra-class activities	2.9	4.1	....	1.6	3.7	2.7
F. Activities relative to the development of desirable teaching personality	1.2	1.5	.8	1.6	1.7	1.1
G. Activities that force student-teachers to organize past experiences in terms of their present teaching jobs	....	....	....	.8	....	....

      (3) Individualizing the learning activities to meet the abilities, interests, and needs of the children.

   b. Applying the more fundamental methods of instruction.

      (1) Applying such educational procedures as asking effective questions, handling remedial work, conducting reviews and drill exercises, making suitable assignments, and supervising study.

      (2) Teaching the basic skill subjects, such as reading and arithmetic.

   c. Teaching geography, history, and science.

   d. Directing children in such recreational activities as playground work, group games, dancing and rhythms, and relaxation exercises.

  2. Dealing with child guidance.

   a. Managing and controlling children; dealing with problems of child behavior; and handling problems of discipline.

   b. Keeping all the children in a group interested and profitably engaged in suitable and purposeful learning activities.

   c. Establishing desirable teacher-pupil relations.

   d. Developing co-operative class spirit among the children.

   e. Maintaining wholesome, happy working atmosphere in the classroom.

  3. Studying and analyzing children as to personality traits, interests, special aptitudes, problems, difficulties, and needs.

XXXIX

in Primary and Intermediate Departments of State Teachers Colleges the Most Helpful Activities and Phases of Student-Teaching

Cent of Student-Teachers and Laboratory-School Faculty Members

DAY				ALL DAY		TOTAL				Directors of Training	SUM TOTAL	
Supervisors and Critics		Student-Teachers		Supervisors and Critics		Student-Teachers		Supervisors and Critics			Student-Teachers	Faculty Members
P	I	P	I	P	I	P	I	P	I			
88.3	81.3	66.2	66.3	94.4	90.0	66.2	63.4	87.8	81.6	81.1	64.8	84.2
3.3	5.1	9.1	8.9	....	....	10.7	9.8	4.6	4.8	5.7	10.3	4.8
3.3	6.8	10.4	15.7	....	5.0	6.7	13.5	2.5	6.8	3.8	10.2	4.5
3.3	3.4	9.1	7.9	5.0	5.0	11.8	8.6	4.1	2.9	3.8	10.2	3.5
....	3.4	3.9	1.1	....	....	3.2	3.4	....	2.4	1.9	3.3	1.3
....	....	1.3	....	....	....	1.3	1.3	.5	1.0	1.9	1.3	.9
1.7	....	....	....	....	....	....	....	.5	.5	1.9	....	.7

Individual conferences with critic teachers and other faculty members were reported as the most helpful phase of student-teaching by 10.3% of the student-teachers and 4.8% of the laboratory-school faculty members. Individual conferences in which the critic teachers and other faculty members offered constructive criticisms, helpful guidance, valuable suggestions, new ideas, definite aids, and real encouragement were specified as being of the greatest value to student-teachers.

The planning, selection, organization, integration, adaptation, and application of subject-matter were reported as the most helpful activities of student-teaching by 10.2% of the student-teachers and 4.5% of the faculty members. Many indicated that planning, organizing, developing, and executing comprehensive and developmental units of instruction were invaluable experiences to student-teachers.

Well-directed observation of children and of expert teaching was designated the most helpful phase of student-teaching by 10.2% of the student-teachers and 3.5% of the faculty members. Most of these student-teachers had taught in the elementary field prior to student-teaching. With this background of practical experience it was not surprising that they reported obtaining the greatest value from student-teaching by observing, under efficient direction and careful guidance, the work of master teachers and competent critics. Some of the student-teachers implied that observing and analyzing expert teachers to determine the qualities that make for success were the most valuable activities.

Initiation of various types of class activities as an outgrowth of participation in extra-class activities was reported as the most helpful phase of student-teaching by 3.3% of the student-teachers and 1.3% of the laboratory-school faculty members. Some stated that extra-class activities helped the student-teachers to create within their classrooms the friendly atmosphere that invites co-operation, spontaneity, and initiative.

Activities relative to the development of desirable teaching personality were given as the most helpful phase of student-teaching by 1.3% of the student-teachers and .9% of the laboratory-school faculty members. Activities suggested as especially helpful were: studying and diagnosing personality traits, setting up ideal personality standards, and then striving to achieve the desired goals. Many of the students have such meager social backgrounds that the teacher-preparing institutions should provide them with every possible opportunity for social cultivation and refinement.

Activities that force the student-teachers to organize past experiences in terms of their teaching jobs were reported by the remaining .7% of the laboratory-school faculty members as the most helpful phase of student-teaching.

The following types of activities and phases of student-teaching were reported as the most helpful by a much larger per cent (1) of the student-teachers in the two-year and three-year programs than of those in the four-year curricula; and (2) of student-teachers and laboratory-school faculty members under the one-hour-a-day student-teaching plan than of those under the whole-day plan:

1. Actual teaching of children under expert supervision; practical experiences with children in teaching and learning situations through such activities as:
   a. Dealing with certain phases of child guidance, such as:
      (1) Managing and controlling children; dealing with problems of child behavior; and handling discipline.
      (2) Keeping all the children in a group interested and profitably engaged in suitable and purposeful learning activities.
      (3) Establishing desirable teacher-pupil relations.
   b. Applying the more fundamental methods of instruction. (See page 155.)
   c. Teaching specific subjects, such as reading, arithmetic, geography, history, and language.
   d. Directing children in such recreational activities as playground work, group games, dancing and rhythms, posture work, and relaxation exercises.
   e. Studying and analyzing children; making individual case studies.
2. Individual conferences with critic teachers and other faculty members.
3. Preparation and adaptation of lesson plans.

Reflecting evidently the influence of richer background experiences, the student-teachers in the four-year teacher-education curricula attached more importance to the activities that required greater sense of responsibility and broader background experiences than did those in the two-year programs. Types of activities and phases of student-teaching reported by a large per cent of (1) the student-teachers in the four-year curricula; and (2) student-teachers and laboratory-school faculty members working under the whole-day student-teaching plan are:

1. Actual teaching of children under competent guidance; assumption of considerable responsibility in teaching.

    a. Teaching children and assuming responsibility for the development, growth, and progress of each individual in the group; assuming responsibility for a group of children over a period of time.

    b. Assuming full responsibility in teaching situations; assuming the responsibilities of a teacher in the elementary grades.

    c. Applying progressive methods of instruction in directing the learning activities of the children.

    (See activities listed under this heading on page 154.)

2. Preparation and adaptation of large units of instruction.

3. Initiation of various types of class activities as a result of participation in extra-class activities.

There was fairly close agreement between primary and intermediate departments as to the most helpful phases of student-teaching. A larger proportion of the student-teachers and critic teachers in the primary departments than of those in the intermediate departments, however, indicated the following types of activities and phases of student-teaching as the most helpful for the preparation of elementary teachers:

1. Actual teaching of children under expert supervision; assumption of considerable responsibility in teaching and learning situations through such activities as:

    a. Leading, guiding, and working with children in real teaching and learning situations.

    b. Organizing school life around large centers of interest or important child activities; guiding children in developing and in carrying out activity units of a broad scope.

    c. Keeping all the children interested, happy, and profitably engaged in purposeful and suitable activities.

    d. Utilizing such educational procedures as creative construction, dramatic expression, and socialized activities.

    e. Teaching such subjects as reading, social studies (designated as such), music, and art.

2. Well-directed observation of expert teaching.

A larger proportion of the student-teachers and critic teachers in the intermediate departments than of those in the primary departments designated the following types of activities and phases of student-teaching as the most helpful:

1. Actual teaching of children under competent guidance; asumption of considerable responsibility in teaching and learning situations through such activities as:

    a. Teaching and assuming responsibility for the progress of a group of children over a period of time.

    b. Managing and controlling children; dealing with problems of child behavior; and handling discipline.

    c. Directing children in working out large units of subject-matter.

    d. Utilizing such educational procedures as problem-solving, question and answer procedures, textbook work, reference techniques, and directed or supervised study.

    e. Teaching arithmetic, geography, and history.

2. Selection, organization, adaptation, and application of subject-matter.

Most of the inexperienced student-teachers as well as most of the laboratory-school faculty members specified activities and phases of student-teaching that could most appropriately be classified under the major heading *actual teaching of children under expert supervision and competent guidance.* Some of the experienced student-teachers—those who had taught in the public schools in the field prior to student-teaching—indicated that the following phases of student-teaching were the most helpful for their specific needs:

1. Individual conferences with critic teachers and other faculty members.
2. Well-directed and extensive observation of expert teaching.
3. Preparation and adaptation of large units of instruction.
4. Activities relative to the development of desirable teaching personality.

Least Helpful Activities and Phases of Student-Teaching

Each of the student-teachers and faculty members was requested to give the least helpful activity or phase of student-teaching. There were 2,298 student-teachers and 444 laboratory-school faculty members who answered the question, "What activity or phase of student-teaching is least helpful in drawing out and developing the average student's ability to teach?" * The reply from each person was placed under an appropriate major heading for the sake of convenience.

In some schools the activities reported as least helpful by the student-teachers were quite similar to those specified by the faculty

---

* Table LXII in Volume II presents in detail the following data: the college year in which the student-teaching was done; the type of organization under which it was conducted; the number of primary and intermediate student-teachers, both inexperienced and experienced, who reported each of the least helpful activities and phases of student-teaching.

Table LXIII in Volume II presents in detail the number of laboratory-school faculty members, under the different forms of administrative organization, who reported each of the least helpful activities and phases of student-teaching.

Volume II of this study is on file in manuscript form in the Library of Teachers College, Columbia University.

members. In some instances, however, there were conflicting opinions and noticeable variations in reactions; such divergence of judgment indicated the absence of a common basis for the evaluation of the different types of activities.

Of all the various activities suggested, those reported by 65.1% of the student-teachers and 82.9% of the laboratory-school faculty members were most appropriately classified under the five major headings listed below according to their frequency of mention:

A. Performing much mechanical routine work and tending to many house-keeping duties.
B. Observing without proper guidance and definite preparation, including too frequent observation of other student-teachers.
C. Attending conferences that lack definite purposes or for which no careful preparations have been made.
D. Preparing and memorizing detailed or elaborate forms of lesson plans over a prolonged period of time.
E. Correcting and grading numerous notebooks, papers, and tests.

Table XL shows the per cent of primary and intermediate student-teachers and laboratory-school faculty members who reported each of the activities and phases of student-teaching that were considered least helpful in the preparation of prospective elementary teachers.

Performing much mechanical routine work and tending to many housekeeping duties were activities that 17.3% of the student-teachers and 35.1% of the laboratory-school faculty members considered least helpful. These totals represented the summation of the following detailed percentages: 22.1% of the primary and 12.5% of the intermediate student-teachers, 40.0% of the primary and 31.2% of the intermediate critic teachers, and 32.7% of the directors of training. Some of the specific activities listed under this first major heading are:

1. Washing blackboards, cleaning erasers, sweeping floors, and doing other janitorial work.
2. Managing routine duties.
3. Taking care of supplies and equipment.

Many of the faculty members stated that the student-teachers wasted a great deal of time by (1) doing routine work or performing housekeeping and janitorial duties beyond the place where they could profit by these from an educational standpoint, that is, repeating the same type of work from day to day after skill has been acquired in these activities; (2) doing mechanical things that have no special

TABLE XL

Per Cent of Student-Teachers and Laboratory-School Faculty Members Who Reported Each of the Least Helpful Activities and Phases of Student-Teaching

Least Helpful Activities and Phases of Student-Teaching Courses	Student-Teachers		Supervisors and Critics		Directors of Training	Total	
	P	I	P	I		Student Teachers	Faculty Members
A. Performing much mechanical routine work and many housekeeping duties	22.1	12.5	40.0	31.2	32.7	17.3	35.1
B. Observing without proper guidance and definite preparation, including too frequent observation of other student-teachers	19.9	13.5	31.1	26.6	28.8	16.7	28.8
C. Attending conferences that lack definite purposes or for which no careful preparations have been made	8.8	12.6	8.8	17.1	7.7	10.7	12.4
D. Preparing and memorizing detailed or elaborate forms of lesson plans over a prolonged period	8.7	13.8	3.1	3.5	3.8	11.2	3.4
E. Correcting and grading numerous notebooks, papers, and tests	5.0	13.1	1.0	5.0	3.8	9.1	3.2
F. Using certain specific techniques of teaching	6.6	6.8	3.6	4.0	5.8	6.7	4.1
G. Filling out numerous child study charts, writing long or elaborate reports, and keeping many records that take much time from preparation for teaching	6.6	5.8	2.6	3.5	5.8	6.2	3.4
H. Assuming too little responsibility in teaching	4.1	6.5	1.6	2.5	1.9	5.3	2.0
I. Supervising or taking charge of yards, corridors, dressing rooms, and lunch rooms	8.9	4.9	....	....	....	6.9	....
J. Making and arranging charts, graphs, posters, bulletin board materials, etc	3.5	3.6	2.1	1.0	....	3.6	1.4
K. Reading and outlining a large number of professional articles and books without reference to immediate needs in teaching or to individual needs and interests of the student-teachers	3.3	4.8	....	1.0	....	4.0	.5
L. Teaching without proper supervision and constructive guidance	....	....	3.6	3.0	5.8	....	3.6
M. Handling only small groups of children throughout student-teaching	....	....	2.6	1.5	3.8	....	2.3
N. Receiving negative and discouraging criticisms	2.1	1.0	....	....	....	1.6	....
O. Helping backward children after school hours	.4	1.1	....	....	....	.7	....

educative value; and (3) performing routine work or attending to physical factors of the classroom beyond the place where these function as a part of the teaching and learning situations. There are certain activities of a routine nature, however, that are necessary to a well-organized schoolroom. These essential routine activities may vary in different teaching situations but should, in any case, be very carefully selected and reduced to habit in order to conserve the student-teachers' time and attention for the more valuable teaching activities.

Observing without proper guidance and definite preparation, including too frequent observation of other student-teachers, was specified as the least helpful activity by 16.7% of the student-teachers and 28.8% of the laboratory-school faculty members. Owing to the crowded conditions in some laboratory schools, these student-teachers devoted a large part of their student-teaching time to observing small groups of children, artificial teaching situations, and other student-teachers conducting classes—observations for which there were no definite purposes nor adequate preparation, and from which they did not, consequently, derive a great deal of benefit. The reports implied that if observation is to be of the greatest value to prospective teachers in the elementary field, it must be carefully directed, constructively guided, definitely prepared, and conducted in natural settings.

Attending conferences that lack definite purposes or for which no careful preparations have been made received its share of adverse criticism from 10.7% of the student-teachers and 12.4% of the laboratory-school faculty members. Specific mention was given the following types of conferences, the fundamental purposes of which were defeated by the predominance of avoidable defects: (1) those lacking in clearly defined purposes; (2) those conducted without adequate preparation; (3) those deficient in constructive value; (4) those wanting in progressive professional attitudes on the part of all present; and (5) those devoted to discussion of such problems as had no immediate value for the student-teachers. The main force of criticism was directed against the *large general or group conference,* which was characterized as the least helpful phase of student-teaching by approximately 10% of the student-teachers.

Preparing and memorizing detailed or elaborate forms of lesson plans over a prolonged period of time required too much effort for the educational value derived therefrom, according to 11.2% of the student-teachers and 3.4% of the laboratory-school faculty members. Some of the specific activities mentioned as being least helpful in connection with lesson planning are: (1) writing formal and complicated lesson plans; (2) working for correct grammar and sentence structure, rather than content; (3) memorizing detailed lesson plans; (4) adhering rigidly to prepared plans; and (5) making plans without objectives or ideas of what is to be done.

Correcting and grading numerous notebooks, papers, and tests were designated the least helpful activities by 9.1% of the student-teachers and 3.2% of the laboratory-school faculty members. Some of these student-teachers devoted a large part of their time and energy in student-teaching to correcting children's papers and notebooks, at the expense of richer educational activities in which they should have obtained considerable practice or have attained certain degrees of skill and mastery.

Using certain specific techniques of teaching was characterized the least helpful phase of student-teaching by 6.7% of the student-teachers and 4.1% of the laboratory-school faculty members. Some of the activities mentioned most frequently were: teaching routine subjects day after day with practically no variation in methods of procedure, using too many ready-made devices, conducting excessive numbers of similar drill exercises in spelling and writing, hearing children recite, directing free periods, taking charge of seat work, telling stories, lecturing to children, and adhering too closely to a specified textbook.

Filling out numerous child study charts, writing long or elaborate reports, and keeping many records that take much time from preparation for actual teaching were, in the judgment of 6.2% of the student-teachers and 3.4% of the laboratory-school faculty members, the least helpful activities in student-teaching. The above heading included such activities as doing an excessive amount of clerical work; writing long, tedious, and elaborate observation reports; and keeping diaries and records for each child in a class.

Assuming too little responsibility in teaching situations was recognized as one of the least helpful phases of student-teaching. It was, on the other hand, generally conceded that the assumption of greater and greater responsibilities in teaching and learning situations was one of the most valuable phases of student-teaching.

Supervising or taking charge of yards, corridors, dressing rooms, and lunch rooms were, in the opinion of 8.9% of the primary and

4.9% of the intermediate student-teachers, the least helpful activities. Most of these student-teachers devoted a large portion of their student-teaching time to similar activities and, consequently, obtained very limited practice in real teaching situations in the classroom. Some of these student-teachers implied that such activities were not of sufficient educative value to warrant the expenditure of a large share of the student-teaching time.

Making and arranging charts, graphs, posters, bulletin board materials, and so forth, beyond the stage where they are of educative value to the student-teachers, were specified as the least helpful activities by 3.6% of the student-teachers and 1.4% of the critic teachers. Some of these student-teachers were required to spend excessive amounts of time in working with materials, rather than with children. Some devoted much time and energy to mounting pictures, cutting stencils, typing materials, mending books, making tools and equipment, and other similar activities.

Reading and outlining a large number of professional articles and books without reference to the immediate needs in student-teaching or to the individual needs and interests of the student-teachers were reported as least helpful activities by 4.0% of the student-teachers, and .5% of the laboratory-school faculty members.

The remaining 2.3% of the student-teachers and 5.9% of the laboratory-school faculty members each gave activities that were classified under one of the following major headings:

Teaching without proper supervision or constructive guidance.

Handling only small groups of children throughout student-teaching.

Receiving negative and discouraging criticisms.

Helping backward children after school hours.

Most of these activities were classified as least helpful, not because they had no essential place in the teacher-education program, but because excessive application had robbed them of educative merit and had contributed to the neglect of other more valuable educational activities, such as, contacts with children in life situations.

Some activities were rated as the least helpful by a larger proportion of those in the primary departments than by those in the intermediate departments, and vice versa. In other instances there was a corresponding relation between the attitudes of student-teachers and critic teachers; and also between the attitudes of student-teachers and faculty members under various types of student-teaching organization. Attention must be called to the fact that those activities which were overdone at the expense of others were usually specified as the least helpful by the largest number.

Types of activities reported as least helpful in student-teaching by a larger per cent of student-teachers in the two-year and three-year programs than by those in the four-year curricula are:

1. Performing much mechanical routine work and tending to many house-keeping duties.
2. Preparing and memorizing detailed forms of lesson plans over a prolonged period of time.
3. Correcting and grading numerous notebooks, papers, and tests.
4. Using certain specific techniques, where the procedures were similar from day to day or from week to week.
5. Writing long observation reports and keeping many records that take much time from preparation for actual teaching.

Types of activities reported as least helpful in student-teaching by a larger per cent of student-teachers in the four-year curricula than by those in the two-year and three-year programs are:

1. Observing without proper guidance and without definite preparation, including too frequent observation of other student-teachers.
2. Attending conferences that lack definite purposes and for which no careful preparations have been made.
3. Assuming too little responsibility in teaching situations.
4. Reading and outlining a large number of professional books and articles without reference to their immediate value in student-teaching or to the individual needs and interests of the student-teachers.
5. Making charts, preparing illustrative materials, and other similar activities beyond the stage where they are of educative value to the student-teachers.

Types of activities reported as least helpful in student-teaching by a larger per cent of student-teachers assigned to student-teaching for one hour a day than by those assigned for units of whole days are:

1. Observing without proper guidance and without definite preparation, including too frequent observation of other student-teachers.
2. Attending general conferences of large groups of student-teachers.
3. Writing long and elaborate observation reports.
4. Assuming too little responsibility in teaching situations.
5. Handling only very small groups of children throughout student-teaching.

The following types of activities were reported as least helpful in student-teaching by a larger per cent of student-teachers and critic teachers in the primary departments than by those in the intermediate departments:

1. Performing much mechanical routine and many housekeeping duties.
2. Observing without proper guidance and without definite preparation for the work, including too frequent observation of other student-teachers.
3. Supervising yards, corridors, dressing rooms, and lunch rooms.
4. Filling out numerous child study charts; keeping diaries and records of each child in the class.
5. Handling only small groups of children throughout student-teaching.

The following types of activities were specified as least helpful in student-teaching by a larger per cent of student-teachers and critic teachers in the intermediate departments than by those in the primary departments:

1. Attending conferences that lack definite purposes or for which few preparations have been made; attending large group conferences.
2. Preparing and memorizing detailed and elaborate forms of lesson plans over a prolonged period of time.
3. Correcting and grading a large number of notebooks, papers, and tests.
4. Doing much undirected reading of professional materials of no immediate value to the student-teachers.
5. Helping backward children after school hours.

A larger proportion of the student-teachers than of the laboratory-school faculty members reported the following types of activities as least helpful in student-teaching:

1. Preparing and memorizing detailed or elaborate forms of lesson plans over a prolonged period of time; and adhering strictly to definite forms of lesson plans.
2. Correcting and grading a large number of notebooks, papers, and tests.
3. Filling out numerous child study charts, writing long reports, and keeping many records that take much time from preparation for actual teaching.
4. Supervising yards, corridors, dressing rooms, and lunch rooms.
5. Making and arranging charts, graphs, posters, and bulletin board materials; mounting pictures, typing materials, mending books, making tools and equipments, and other similar activities.

A larger proportion of the laboratory-school faculty members than of the student-teachers specified the following types of activities as least helpful in student-teaching:

1. Performing much mechanical routine work and many housekeeping duties at the expense of more valuable and more educative activities.

      a. Doing routine work beyond the stage of growth in the student-teach-
ers, or where it no longer functions as part of the teaching situation; attending to routine duties after these have become automatic processes for the student-teachers.

      b. Performing housekeeping and janitorial duties, where there is repe-
tition of the same types of work from day to day, after student-
teachers have acquired skill in doing them.

      c. Doing mechanical things that are of little educative value to the
student-teachers in the elementary departments.

2. Observing without proper guidance and careful preparation, including
too frequent observation of other student-teachers.

3. Attending individual and group conferences that lack definite purposes
or for which no careful preparations have been made.

4. Teaching without proper supervision and constructive guidance.

5. Handling only small groups of children throughout student-teaching
courses.

PART II

Most Difficult Problems Encountered by Student-Teachers During Student-Teaching

An analysis of the content of student-teaching would be incom-
plete without some consideration of the most difficult problems encountered by prospective teachers during student-teaching. Only
through careful study and intelligent understanding of these problems can effective suggestions for improvement be made.

In order to determine the most difficult problems, answers were
obtained from 2,518 student-teachers in reply to the question, "What
is the most difficult problem that you encountered in student-teaching?" and from 471 laboratory-school faculty members in reply to
the question, "What is the most difficult problem that your student-
teachers encounter in student-teaching?" These answers varied
greatly in content and scope, and necessitated classification under
appropriate major headings. In cases where more than one difficulty
was reported by the same person, only the first one was tabulated
and included in the per cents shown in this study. Table XLI * pre-

---

  * Table LXIV in Volume II of this study, which is on file in manuscript form
in Teachers College Library, presents in detail the following data: the college year
in which the student-teaching was done; the type of organization under which it
was conducted; the number of primary and intermediate student-teachers, both
inexperienced and experienced, who reported each of the most difficult problems
encountered in student-teaching.

  Table LXV in Volume II shows the number of laboratory-school faculty members, under different types of student-teaching organization, who reported each of
the most difficult problems encountered in student-teaching.

sents the per cent of student-teachers and laboratory-school faculty members, under the different forms of administrative organization, whose answers were grouped under each major heading showing the most difficult problems encountered by student-teachers. The distributions of answers of student-teachers in the two-year programs and in the three-year and four-year curricula are presented in Table XLII.

The most difficult problems have been listed in the form of activities, partly for purposes of convenient classification, but more largely because the student-teachers and faculty members reported them in that form.

TABLE

Per Cent of Student-Teachers and Laboratory-School Faculty Members Whose Difficult Problems Encountered by Student-

| Major Headings under Which the Most Difficult Problems Encountered by Student-Teachers during Student-Teaching Courses Were Grouped | 1–2 Hours | | | | ½ | Per |
| | Student-Teachers | | Supervisors and Critics | | Student-Teachers | |
	P	I	P	I	P	I
A. Directing the different learning activities of the children and leading them to develop desirable habits, traits, interests, attitudes, and ideals	35.6	31.0	42.6	32.6	41.4	39.7
B. Securing and maintaining high standards of conduct among the children, and establishing desirable teacher-pupil relations	27.8	37.3	17.2	24.3	17.7	24.6
C. Securing intelligent understanding of children and dealing efficiently with their individual differences	14.3	10.6	13.1	15.1	18.2	14.0
D. Planning, selecting, organizing, mastering, and adapting subject-matter	11.0	13.0	7.4	11.4	14.2	15.4
E. Assuming complete responsibility in teaching situations	1.6	1.0	3.3	3.8	2.5	2.3
F. Developing desirable teaching personality traits and wholesome professional attitudes	4.2	2.5	7.4	4.5	2.0	2.1
G. Securing a broad vision and an intelligent understanding of the teacher's work as a whole	1.1	1.0	7.4	6.0	....	....
H. Securing proper relations between critic teachers and student-teachers	2.5	1.3	....	....	2.4	1.2
I. Trying to do two jobs at one time, and finding time to prepare for daily work	1.0	1.5	.8	1.5	.8	.5
J. Making economical and effective use of time	.8	.8	.8	.8	.8	.2
K. Making effective use of special school equipment	....	....	....	....	....	....

The results shown in Tables XLI and XLII would no doubt have been different if a prepared list of problems had been submitted to the student-teachers and laboratory-school faculty members from which to select the most difficult problem. Since no such list was given in the inquiry sheets, the problems or activities reported in this study as being the most difficult for student-teachers are those specified by student-teachers and laboratory-school faculty members. The types of difficulties reported are, therefore, determined by the personal experiences and backgrounds of each individual participating in this study; and are especially significant in an analysis of the content of student-teaching.

XLI

Answers Were Classified under Each Major Heading Showing the Most Teachers during Student-Teaching Courses

Cent of Student-Teachers and Laboratory-School Faculty Members

DAY		ALL DAY				TOTAL				Directors of Training	SUM TOTAL	
Supervisors and Critics		Student-Teachers		Supervisors and Critics		Student-Teachers		Supervisors and Critics			Student-Teachers	Faculty Members
P	I	P	I	P	I	P	I	P	I			
50.8	37.7	41.1	32.6	66.6	50.0	37.8	33.6	47.3	35.7	43.6	35.7	41.6
11.1	18.1	12.9	22.8	11.1	15.0	23.8	32.4	14.8	21.6	18.2	28.1	18.3
17.4	16.4	15.3	13.0	5.6	5.0	15.5	11.8	13.8	14.5	12.7	13.7	14.0
6.3	13.1	14.1	17.4	5.6	20.0	12.2	13.9	6.9	12.7	5.5	13.1	9.3
4.8	6.5	14.2	13.0	11.1	10.0	2.7	2.3	4.4	5.2	9.1	2.5	5.3
4.8	3.3	1.2	....	....	....	3.2	2.3	5.9	3.7	1.8	2.7	4.5
3.2	3.3	....	....	....	....	.7	.6	5.4	4.7	7.3	.7	5.3
....	....	1.2	1.1	....	....	2.4	1.4	....	....	....	1.9	....
....	1.6	....	....	....	....	1.1	1.3	.5	1.4	1.8	1.2	1.1
....	....	....	....	....	....	.5	.4	.5	.5	....	.5	.5
1.6	....	....	....	....	....	....	....	.5	....	....	....	.2

TABLE XLII

Per Cent of Student-Teachers in Different Teacher-Education Curricula Whose Answers Were Classified under Each Major Heading Showing the Most Difficult Problems Encountered in Student-Teaching

Major Headings under Which the Most Difficult Problems Encountered in Student-Teaching Were Grouped	Per Cent of Student-Teachers											
	Two-Year Programs						Three-Year and Four-Year Elementary Curricula					
	1–2 Hours		½ Day		All Day		1–2 Hours		½ Day		All Day	
	P	I	P	I	P	I	P	I	P	I	P	I
A. Directing the different learning activities of children and leading them to develop desirable habits, traits, interests, attitudes, and ideals	31.0	27.2	41.5	37.1	38.7	29.4	43.2	37.3	41.2	43.1	44.4	36.7
B. Securing and maintaining high standards of conduct among the children, and establishing desirable teacher-pupil relations	36.8	45.5	20.3	28.0	14.3	25.5	13.3	24.2	12.7	17.4	11.1	19.5
C. Securing intelligent understanding of children and dealing efficiently with their individual differences	11.2	8.1	15.0	12.7	16.3	15.7	19.3	14.7	24.6	16.7	13.9	9.8
D. Planning, selecting, organizing, mastering, and adapting content subject-matter and other instructional materials	10.8	12.2	14.5	15.4	14.3	19.6	11.6	14.3	13.5	15.1	13.9	14.5
E. Developing desirable teaching personality traits and wholesome professional attitudes	4.3	2.4	2.4	2.8	2.0	....	3.9	2.6	.8	.9	....	....
F. Assuming complete responsibility in teaching situations	.6	.6	2.1	2.0	12.3	9.8	3.0	1.6	3.2	3.0	16.7	17.0
G. Securing proper relations between critic teachers and student-teachers	2.9	1.6	2.1	1.2	2.0	....	2.0	.7	3.2	3.0	....	2.5
H. Trying to do two jobs at one time, and finding adequate time to prepare for daily work; making economical and effective use of time	1.4	1.6	2.1	.8	....	....	2.3	3.6	.8	.9	....	....
I. Securing a broad vision and an intelligent understanding of the teacher's work as a whole	1.0	1.0	....	....	....	....	1.3	1.0	....	....	....	....

Directing the different learning activities of the children and leading them to develop desirable habits, traits, interests, attitudes, appreciations, and ideals presented some of the most difficult problems to a large proportion of student-teachers. The statements from approximately 35.7% of the student-teachers and 41.6% of the laboratory-school faculty members were classified under this major heading. A large number of these student-teachers encountered their greatest difficulties in connection with the following types of activities: presenting content subject-matter and other materials of instruction by the most interesting and effective methods within the comprehension of the children; motivating and vitalizing the work sufficiently to develop the interests of the children in a group; relating the work closely to the abilities, interests, and needs of the children in a grade; creating and holding the interest, attention, and enthusiasm of every child in a class so that high standards may be maintained; keeping all the members in a group profitably engaged in suitable and purposeful activities; and seeing subject-matter in terms of life activities.

A large per cent of the above student-teachers and faculty members implied that the most difficult problems encountered by student-teachers were in connection with educative activities involved in the more progressive methods of instruction, such as:

1. Initiating and carrying to completion, with the co-operation of the pupils, large developmental units of instruction which include the integration and drawing together of various phases of subject-matter, different types of activities, and many experiences within the comprehension of the children.
2. Handling activity programs; guiding children in carrying out large child activities.
   a. Stimulating pupil self-activity; guiding children in initiating purposeful learning activities, and then leading them to carry these into effect.
   b. Organizing children's experiences; recognizing and making effective use of children's leads, questions, and contributions.
   c. Guiding children in connection with such educational procedures as creative construction, dramatic expression, and socialized activities; and leading children to develop initiative, creativeness, imagination, originality, self-expression, leadership, and social responsibility through such activities.
   d. Leading children to assume responsibility for carrying activities to completion; and for maintaining high standards of workmanship.
3. Balancing pupil-teacher initiative and participation in class instruction.
4. Guiding children effectively in concomitant and associated learnings.
5. Understanding the philosophy underlying purposeful activity; seeing organization in relation to what it should do for the children being taught, and in terms of experiences which will be valuable for each individual in a group.

Some student-teachers specified that they encountered their greatest difficulties in connection with the more fundamental educational principles and teaching procedures, such as:

1. Setting up and accomplishing desired objectives and outcomes.
2. Formulating and asking effective, vital, stimulating, and thought-provoking questions.

3. Utilizing such teaching techniques as problem-solving, drill, and review; also handling remedial work.
4. Making skillful, suitable, and purposeful assignments.
5. Summarizing work and drawing conclusions.

Some reported that student-teachers encountered their greatest difficulties in connection with the teaching of the following subjects, which are listed according to frequency of mention:

1. Social sciences.
2. Reading in the primary grades.
3. Arithmetic in the intermediate and upper grades.
4. Literature.
5. The fine arts—music and art.

A much larger per cent of the student-teachers and laboratory-school faculty members under the half-day and whole-day student-teaching plans than of those under the one-hour-a-day plan indicated that educational activities involved in progressive methods of instruction presented the most difficult problems for student-teachers. According to the findings of this study, student-teachers scheduled for half-day and whole-day student-teaching in the four-year elementary curricula obtained much more experience in progressive types of educational activities than did those scheduled for one-hour-a-day teaching in the two-year programs. The inexperienced student-teachers who had only one-hour-a-day student-teaching in the two-year programs, in a large majority of the cases, had very meager backgrounds and were provided little opportunity for carrying out large units of instruction or large child activities and were not made conscious of these difficulties. The student-teachers who were scheduled for half-day or whole-day student-teaching in the four-year elementary curricula, on the other hand, usually had broader backgrounds, were provided greater opportunities for carrying out progressive educational procedures, and were thus made aware of these difficulties.

Although it is generally conceded that there is much overlapping between the art of instruction and the art of discipline, they really presented two distinct problems for many of the beginning student-teachers. *Presenting instructional materials to the children* demanded such large proportions of the attention and energy of some student-teachers that they were unable to make room for effective discipline and child management.

Securing and maintaining high standards of conduct among the children and establishing desirable teacher-pupil relations were, in the judgment of 28.1% of the student-teachers and 18.3% of the laboratory-school staff members, the most difficult problems for student-teachers. *Handling discipline* headed the list of specific difficulties. Approximately 23.8% of the primary and 32.4% of the intermediate student-teachers, 14.8% of the primary and 21.6% of the intermediate critic teachers, and 18.2% of the directors of training stated that handling discipline or managing and controlling children were the most difficult problems encountered by student-teachers. Some of the disciplinary difficulties enumerated by the student-teachers and faculty members were as follows: handling informal discipline; managing and controlling children; securing wholesome attitudes; obtaining willing and wholehearted co-operation; maintaining proper rapport between the student-teachers and the children; attempting to find happy mediums between the too formal and the too informal methods of discipline; learning to discriminate between true freedom and license; and maintaining a wholesome, happy working atmosphere in the classroom. Some of the more specific disciplinary troubles involved the elimination of such frequent causes of confusion as interference with class activities, the exercise of too many privileges, over-excitement, undue talking and laughing, incessant whispering, discourteous interruptions, impudence, rudeness, and general disorder on the part of the children.

Of the inexperienced student-teachers in the two-year programs, 33.1% of the primary and 40.9% of the intermediate student-teachers reported their greatest difficulties in connection with problems of discipline and management of pupils. These total percentages were organized in detail as follows: 40.4% of the primary and 48.0% of the intermediate student-teachers under the one-hour- and two-hours-a-day plans; 21.5% of the primary and 29.3% of the intermediate under the half-day plan; and 16.2% of the primary and 27.0% of the intermediate under the whole-day plan. Of the inexperienced student-teachers in the four-year curricula, a total of 14.8% of the primary and 25.8% of the intermediate student-teachers likewise reported problems in discipline and management of children as the most difficult. The distribution of these totals is as follows: 15.9% of the primary and 28.2% of the intermediate student-teachers under the one-hour- and two-hours-a-day plans; and 12.6% of the primary and 20.8% of the intermediate under the half-day and whole-day student-teaching plans. Reports from student-teachers who had taught in the field previous to student-teaching indicated that 17.6% of the primary and 29.1% of the intermediate in the two-year programs, and only 9.4% of the primary and 15.3% of the intermediate in the four-year elementary curricula encountered their most trying problems in maintaining high standards of conduct on the part of the children. Difficulties in connection with problems of discipline and management of children were consistently reported most frequently by inexperienced intermediate student-teachers who were scheduled for one-hour-a-day student-teaching in the two-year programs. These difficulties were reported least frequently by the experienced primary student-teachers who were scheduled for whole-day student-teaching in the four-year elementary curricula. These percentages would have been considerably higher if other related problems had been grouped under the heading *Handling problems of discipline and management of children,* instead of having been classified in other connections. The following related problems could have been included under this heading as appropriately as under the divisions in which they were actually placed: creating and holding the attention, interest, and enthusiasm of the children; keeping all the children profitably engaged in purposeful activities; and dealing efficiently with certain types of children.

Securing intelligent understanding of children and dealing efficiently with their individual differences were reported as the most difficult problems by 13.7% of the student-teachers and 14.0% of the laboratory-school faculty members. There was great variation in the scope of the content of these answers. Many of the student-teachers encountered considerable difficulty in securing necessary fundamental knowledge of the nature of individual ability, behavior, and learning. They frequently failed to assign due importance to the individuality of the children, and were not sufficiently conscious of their own responsibility in helping each child to become a well-rounded personality. Making effective use of individual differences gave rise to such difficult problems as recognizing and making adequate provision for the wide range of individual differences along lines of abilities, talents, interests, personality traits, problems, and needs; acquiring intelligent and human understanding of those individual differences attributable to the various stages of development and growth; obtaining a working analysis of individual difficulties as a basis for stimulating the development of each child to his fullest capacities; modifying classroom procedures and techniques to make definite place for individuals who are deficient mentally or who are socially unadjusted, as well as those who possess superior ability; and balancing instruction to meet the needs of both individuals and group.

Planning, selecting, organizing, mastering, and adapting content subject-matter and other instructional materials were indicated, by the reports of 13.1% of the student-teachers and 9.3% of the laboratory-school faculty members, as the most difficult problems encountered in student-teaching. The most trying of these problems were experienced in such activities as planning instruction wisely; visualizing, organizing, and working out large developmental units of instruction; integrating and unifying all the work, instead of teaching merely isolated facts; finding, selecting, evaluating, and adapting appropriate content subject-matter and other instructional materials to the needs and abilities of the children; and acquiring rich backgrounds in general education and sufficient mastery of subject-matter to stimulate, guide, and direct children effectively. All of the activities involved in vitalizing and humanizing subject-matter and seeing it in terms of life activities converged to create many challenging problems for the student-teachers.

Assuming complete responsibility in teaching situations was pronounced the most difficult problem encountered in student-teaching by 2.5% of the student-teachers and 5.3% of the laboratory-school faculty members. If this problem had been suggested in the inquiry sheets, a much larger per cent of those who participated in this study, no doubt, would have rated it as the most difficult. Student-teachers and faculty members are often too much concerned with specific problems to think in terms of the teaching situation as a whole.

Developing desirable teaching personality traits and wholesome professional attitudes was designated as the most difficult problem in student-teaching by 2.7% of the student-teachers and 4.5% of the laboratory-school faculty members. Phases of personal and professional orientation considered the most difficult were: developing such traits as adaptability, breadth of interest, forcefulness, foresight, good judgment, independence, initiative, leadership, openmindedness, originality, poise, progressiveness, resourcefulness, self-confidence, self-control, tact, and thoroughness; seeing possibilities and making effective use of opportunities when they come; interpreting and solving intricate problems with alacrity and efficiency; recognizing and assuming responsibility; developing pleasing and well-modulated voice, together with fluency of speech; cultivating personal charm, good taste, and refinement; establishing progressive professional attitudes toward the whole teaching process; and conserving personal strength, energy, and health.

Securing a broad vision and an intelligent understanding of the teacher's work as a whole was another problem set forth as the most difficult. Many of the student-teachers, especially those who worked under the one-hour-a-day student-teaching plan, obtained very limited experiences and, consequently, found difficulty in securing a wide perspective and an intelligent understanding of all that is involved in teaching. Their narrow and limited experiences tended to make them think of teaching in terms of small unrelated jobs, rather than as a unified whole.

Securing proper relations between critic teachers and student-teachers was the most trying problem encountered by 1.9% of the student-teachers. Meeting the requirements of the critic teachers and overcoming timidity when teaching in their presence were, for the inexperienced student-teachers in this group, outstandingly difficult. The most annoying problems, in the minds of a few of those who had teaching experience prior to student-teaching, were: getting opportunity to originate ideas, to initiate plans of work, and to carry these into effect in actual teaching situations; teaching under the supervision of critic teachers; accepting criticisms in the right spirit; and effecting harmony between student-teachers and critic teachers.

Trying to do two jobs at one time and finding adequate time to prepare for daily work were declared the most serious problems by 1.2% of the student-teachers and 1.1% of the laboratory-school faculty members. Another .5% of both the students and the critic teachers indicated that *making economical and effective use of time* was the most serious problem, and no doubt contributory to the first. Among the major difficulties enumerated under these headings were: meeting simultaneously the requirements of the college instructors and the critic teachers; budgeting time so as to accomplish a designated maximum of work in a minimum of time; and estimating the time necessary for children to complete assigned tasks.

Making effective use of special school equipment was also mentioned as a difficulty.

Student-teachers and laboratory-school faculty members working under different student-teaching organizations frequently reported diverse types of problems as being outstandingly difficult in student-teaching.

The following types of problems were reported as the most difficult by a much larger per cent (1) of student-teachers in the two-year and three-year programs than of those in the four-year curricula; and (2) of student-teachers and laboratory-school faculty members under the one-hour-a-day student-teaching plan than of those under the half-day and whole-day plans:

1. Securing and maintaining high standards of conduct among the children; and establishing desirable teacher-pupil relations.
   a. Handling discipline; and dealing with problems of child behavior.
   b. Managing and controlling children.
   c. Securing wholehearted co-operation of the pupils; gaining their respect and confidence; and establishing right attitudes between the student-teachers and the children.
   d. Creating in the children co-operative class spirit and right attitudes toward school work.
2. Directing the different learning activities of the children through such activities as:
   a. Motivating and vitalizing the work; creating and holding the interest, attention, and enthusiasm of all the children in class and extra-class activities; keeping all the children profitably engaged in purposeful and suitable learning activities.
   b. Applying the more fundamental educational procedures, such as setting up and accomplishing desired objectives, formulating and asking thought-provoking questions, making purposeful and suitable assignments, summarizing work, making effective use of tests, and supervising study periods.
   c. Utilizing techniques involved in teaching the basic skill subjects.
   d. Teaching specific subjects, such as reading, arithmetic, and social studies.
3. Acquiring adequate command and sufficient mastery of subject-matter to be taught; preparing well-organized, purposeful, and workable lesson plans.
4. Developing desirable teaching personality traits and wholesome professional attitudes, such as:
   a. Developing self-control, self-reliance, self-confidence, and poise in teaching situations.
   b. Making necessary adjustments to laboratory-school situations.
   c. Interpreting and meeting complex situations efficiently; seeing possibilities and grasping opportunities as they arise.
   d. Developing initiative, originality, and creativeness.
   e. Developing the right sense of responsibility; developing ability to do independent work in teaching situations.

   f. Obtaining the viewpoint of each child in the class; and making adjustments to these.
   g. Developing leadership necessary to control children.
   h. Being tactful in teaching situations.
   i. Conserving personal strength and health.
   j. Overcoming mannerisms in teaching.

Student-teachers in the four-year curricula usually reported difficult problems that showed broader understanding of a teacher's responsibilities than did the student-teachers with less academic and professional preparation. The following types of problems were reported as the most difficult by a much larger per cent (1) of the student-teachers in four-year curricula than of those in two-year and three-year programs, and (2) of the student-teachers and laboratory-school faculty members under half-day and whole-day student-teaching plans than of those under the one-hour-a-day plan.

   1. Directing the different learning activities of the children and leading them to develop desirable habits, traits, attitudes, appreciations, and ideals by means of:
      a. Applying progressive methods of instruction effectively. (See page 171 for list of specific activities that were represented and classified in connection with progressive education.)
      b. Balancing individual and group instruction; recognizing and providing for the wide range of individual differences of children relative to their abilities, interests, difficulties, problems, talents, and needs.
   2. Obtaining thorough command and adequate working organization of materials of instruction.
      a. Obtaining a rich background in subject-matter and a wide fund of general information.
      b. Planning, organizing, and developing large units of instruction.
      c. Preparing activity units of a broad scope.
   3. Assuming complete responsibility in teaching situations; assuming responsibility in all phases of a successful teacher's work.

Many problems and activities present greater difficulties to student-teachers in some grades than in others. The following types of activities were reported as the most difficult by a larger per cent of student-teachers and critic teachers in the primary departments than by those in the intermediate departments:

   1. Directing the different learning activities of the children and leading them to develop desirable habits, traits, interests, attitudes, and ideals through such activities as:
      a. Motivating and vitalizing the work; vitalizing and humanizing materials of instruction in order to bring these closer to the children.

    b. Keeping all the children happily and profitably engaged in purposeful and suitable activities.

    c. Guiding children in developing centers of interest of a broad scope; guiding them in carrying out large constructive activity units or developmental units of work.

    d. Directing children by means of such educational procedures as creative construction, dramatic expression, and socialized activities.

    e. Teaching the language arts—teaching children to read.

2. Gaining adequate understanding of the capacities, interests, and needs of little children.

3. Developing desirable teaching personality traits.

A larger per cent of student-teachers and critic teachers in the intermediate departments than of those in the primary departments specified that the following types of activities presented the greatest difficulties to student-teachers during student-teaching courses:

1. Securing and maintaining high standards of conduct among the children; and establishing desirable teacher-pupil relations.

    a. Handling discipline.

    b. Managing and controlling children.

    c. Establishing whole-hearted co-operation and wholesome attitudes between student-teachers and pupils; gaining the confidences, good-will, and respect of the children being taught.

2. Planning, selecting, organizing, mastering, and adapting subject-matter.

    a. Acquiring adequate command and sufficient mastery of subject-matter to stimulate, guide, and direct children effectively.

    b. Preparing well-organized and workable lesson plans.

3. Presenting content subject-matter in the most interesting and efficient ways within the comprehension of the children.

Some problems were considered much more difficult by inexperienced student-teachers than by those who had taught in the public schools prior to enrolling in student-teaching courses in the teachers colleges. Types of problems specified as most difficult by a larger per cent of inexperienced student-teachers than by those who had previously taught in the field are:

1. Handling discipline; dealing with problems of child behavior; and establishing desirable teacher-pupil relations.

2. Securing intelligent understanding of children and dealing effectively with their individual differences.

    a. Understanding interests, needs, and abilities of children at different stages of development.

    b. Diagnosing and analyzing individual differences and needs of children; leading each child to work and to progress to his fullest capacity.

    c. Dealing efficiently with certain types of children.

(1) Getting the slow and backward child up to standard.
(2) Helping the unadjusted child to find his place in the social group.
(3) Giving sufficient opportunity for the bright and superior children to work to their maximum capacities.

3. Developing desirable teaching personality traits, and establishing wholesome professional attitudes.
4. Assuming complete responsibility in teaching situations.
5. Securing broad vision and intelligent understanding of the teacher's work as a whole.

Problems in connection with progressive methods of instruction were specified as the most difficult by a large per cent of student-teachers who had taught in the public schools prior to taking student-teaching courses. Types of problems specified as most difficult by a larger per cent of experienced student-teachers than by the inexperienced ones are:

1. Applying progressive methods of instruction in directing the learning activities of children, such as:
   a. Carrying out activity programs or guiding children in developing activity units of a broad scope.
   b. Stimulating and promoting pupil self-activity.
   c. Balancing pupil-teacher initiative and participation in class instruction, and in extra-class activities.
2. Organizing and working out large developmental units of instruction.
3. Securing proper relations between the critic teacher and the student-teacher, such as adjusting to and meeting the requirements of the critic teachers; teaching under the supervision of critic-teachers; and accepting criticisms in the right spirit.

A larger proportion of the student-teachers than of the laboratory-school faculty members specified that the following types of activities presented the greatest difficulties in student-teaching:

1. Securing and maintaining high standards of conduct among the pupils.
   a. Handling discipline.
   b. Managing and controlling children.
   c. Dealing with problems of child behavior.
2. Applying the basic educational principles and the teaching techniques involved in the more fundamental methods of instruction, such as drill, memorization, review, and textbook work.
3. Planning, selecting, organizing, mastering, and adapting subject-matter.
4. Teaching specific subjects, such as reading in the primary grades and the social sciences in the intermediate grades.
5. Securing proper relations between critic teachers and student-teachers.

In view of the richer background and wider perspective of educational problems, the difficulties specified by many of the laboratory-school faculty members were more thought-provoking and of a broader scope than were those reported by the majority of the student-teachers. A much larger per cent of the laboratory-school faculty members than of the student-teachers indicated that the following types of problems presented the greatest difficulties to student-teachers:

1. Applying progressive methods of instruction effectively for directing the different learning activities of the children; and for leading them to develop desirable habits, traits, interests, appreciations, attitudes, and ideals. (See page 171 for list of procedures and activities specified in connection with progressive education.)
2. Providing for both the similarities and the wide range of individual differences of children in a group; balancing individual and group instruction; meeting successfully the needs of both the individual and the group.
3. Securing a broad vision and an intelligent understanding of the teacher's work as a whole.
   a. Securing wide perspective and broad view of the work as a whole.
   b. Understanding all that is involved in teaching instead of regarding it as so many unrelated jobs.
4. Assuming complete responsibility in teaching situations.
5. Developing well-integrated personalities; establishing high professional standards and wholesome professional attitudes; and building up sound philosophies of education.

Chief Underlying Causes of the Most Difficult Problems Encountered by Student-Teachers during Student-Teaching

Just as an analysis of the content of student-teaching required a study of the activities and problems producing the greatest difficulties for student-teachers, so the elimination of these difficulties is dependent upon a detailed consideration of the causal factors. Such an investigation reveals the influence of a body of conditioning forces, chief among which are: (1) the cultural, professional, and experiential backgrounds of the student-teachers; (2) the richness of the content of teacher-education curricula; and (3) the administrative organization of the teacher-preparing institutions. The extent to which other more detailed elements are determinants depends largely upon the particular situation, and upon the viewpoint of the source in question.

In order to discover what part each causal factor played in creating the most difficult problems of student-teaching, a reply was obtained from each of 2,508 student-teachers to the question, "What is the chief underlying cause of the most difficult problem that you encountered in student-teaching?" and from each of 468 laboratory-school faculty members to the question, "What is the chief underlying cause of the most difficult problem encountered by your student-teachers?" In cases where more than one cause was given by the same person, only the first one was tabulated and included in the per cents shown in the tables. The reports from about 83% of the student-teachers, 93% of the critic teachers and supervisors of student-teaching, and 98% of the directors of training were grouped under the following five major headings:

1. Limited cultural backgrounds and inadequate working knowledge of subject-matter on the part of student-teachers.
2. Inadequate working knowledge of modern educational principles and of progressive methods of instruction.
3. Inadequate working knowledge of children on part of student-teachers.
4. Insufficient time and opportunity to see and to experience a teaching situation as a whole, excessive numbers of student-teachers working with the same children, and inadequate supervision.
5. Immature and undeveloped teaching personalities—limitations in native ability, capacity for achievement, and character, as well as immaturity in years—on the part of student-teachers.

Table XLIII * presents the per cent of student-teachers and laboratory-school faculty members, in different types of student-teaching organization, whose answers were classified under each major heading showing the chief underlying causes of the most difficult problems encountered by student-teachers. Table XLIV enumerates twelve of the most difficult problems encountered by student-teachers and the seven major underlying causes of these difficulties, according to reports from laboratory-school faculty members.

The results shown in Table XLIII would no doubt have been different if the inquiry sheets had included a prepared list of causes underlying the major difficulties of student-teachers. Since no sug-

* Table LXVI in Volume II of this study, which is on file in manuscript form in Teachers College Library, presents in detail the following data: the college year in which the student-teaching was done; the type of organization under which it was conducted; the number of primary and intermediate student-teachers, both inexperienced and experienced, who reported each of the chief causes underlying the most difficult problems encountered in student-teaching.

Table LXVII in Volume II presents in detail the number of laboratory-school faculty members, under different forms of administrative organization, who reported each of the chief causes underlying the most difficult problems encountered by student-teachers during student-teaching courses.

gestions were made in the inquiry sheets as to student-teaching difficulties and the underlying causes of these, both student-teachers and faculty members answered the questions according to their own judgments. The discussions presented in this study, therefore, organize and summarize the opinions of student-teachers and faculty members as to the underlying causes of the most difficult problems encountered in student-teaching.

Although the inquiry sheets did not contain a list of "underlying causes of difficulties encountered in student-teaching," student-teachers and faculty members were requested not to use the terms "inexperience" or "lack of experience" in this connection. These terms are too general in scope, do not furnish a definite basis for the analysis of difficulties, and may be applied indiscriminately to the majority of student-teachers.

Limited cultural backgrounds and inadequate working knowledge of subject-matter on the part of student-teachers were, according to reports from a large number of student-teachers and faculty members, the chief underlying causes of many difficulties encountered by student-teachers during student-teaching. *Inadequate working knowledge of subject-matter* was specified, by 28.7% of the intermediate student-teachers, 30.2% of the intermediate critic teachers, and 29.6% of the directors of training, as the chief cause underlying the most difficult problems encountered by student-teachers. The reports indicated that a large number of student-teachers lacked rich cultural backgrounds, fund of general information, and broad command of content subject-matter and other materials of instruction essential to carry out effectively the functions of elementary teachers. Frequent reference was made to the following causes underlying difficulties encountered by student-teachers: meager acquaintance with suitable cultural materials for children of different age levels; inadequate working organization of instructional materials—the planning, selection, evaluation, organization, and adaptation of instructional materials to meet the children's abilities, interests, and needs; lack of background preparation for organizing subject-matter around comprehensive problems, for integrating information into larger units, and for developing large units of instruction; and inability to think through or to see relationships in several subjects at one time. The majority were also hampered, because of limitations in their cultural background experiences, in recognizing and using the fine and practical arts as inseparable parts of classwork in the elementary grades. The lack of understanding of a well-balanced curriculum was a major cause underlying difficulties encountered in student-teaching.

Inadequate working knowledge of modern educational principles and progressive methods of instruction was, in the judgment of

TABLE

Per Cent of Student-Teachers and Laboratory-School Faculty Members Whose
Underlying the Most Difficult Problems Encountered

Major Headings under Which the Chief Underlying Causes of the Most Difficult Problems Encountered by Student-Teachers Were Classified	1–2 Hours				Per ½	
	Student-Teachers		Supervisors and Critics		Student-Teachers	
	P	I	P	I	P	I
A. Inadequate working knowledge of subject-matter on part of student-teachers.........	16.9	26.9	18.2	31.5	21.8	30.8
B. Inadequate working knowledge of modern educational principles and of progressive methods of instruction...................	19.6	16.7	19.8	16.0	23.3	21.6
C. Inadequate working knowledge of children on the part of student-teachers..............	24.4	17.2	21.5	15.3	27.9	22.6
D. Insufficient time and opportunity to see and to experience a teaching situation as a whole, excessive numbers of student-teachers working with same children, and inadequate supervision...................................	13.8	9.3	20.7	21.3	3.4	2.5
E. Immature and undeveloped teaching personalities—limitations in native ability, capacity for achievement, and character, as well as immaturity in years—on the part of student-teachers...............................	10.2	6.0	13.2	10.7	10.6	6.3
F. Lack of respect for student-teachers on the part of the children.....................	6.6	13.3	1.6	3.1	4.3	8.1
G. Too heavy demands placed upon student-teachers and lack of time for adequate preparation...................................	4.3	6.6	1.6	.7	5.7	6.6
H. Lack of professional standards and ideals by which to judge and evaluate..............	1.7	1.7	1.6	.7	....	.5
I. Inadequate working knowledge of the use of materials and equipment in the laboratory schools................................	1.8	2.1	....	....	1.1	.5
J. Disillusionment about student-teaching before entering upon the work in student-teaching courses.............................	.7	.3	1.6	.7	.6	....
K. Too large classes for beginning student-teachers.................................	....	....	....	....	....	....
L. Over-supervision........................	....	....	....	....	1.1	.5

20.0% of the student-teachers and 22.6% of the laboratory-school faculty members, the chief underlying cause of the most difficult problems encountered by student-teachers. These student-teachers lacked the preparation necessary for progressive types of teaching and, prior to entering student-teaching courses, had no contacts nor

XLIII

Answers Were Classified under Each Major Heading Showing the Chief Causes by Student-Teachers during Student-Teaching Courses

Cent of Student-Teachers and Laboratory-School Faculty Members

DAY		ALL DAY				TOTAL				Directors of Training	SUM TOTAL	
Supervisors and Critics		Student-Teachers		Supervisors and Critics		Student-Teachers		Supervisors and Critics			Student-Teachers	Faculty Members
P	I	P	I	P	I	P	I	P	I			
15.9	26.2	28.2	36.0	16.7	35.0	19.1	28.7	17.3	30.2	29.6	24.0	24.6
31.7	26.2	30.8	24.4	27.8	25.0	21.4	18.7	24.2	19.8	27.7	20.0	22.6
23.8	18.0	26.9	19.8	22.2	15.0	25.6	19.0	22.3	16.0	16.7	22.3	18.8
9.5	8.2	....	....	....	....	9.9	6.6	15.4	15.5	13.0	8.2	15.2
12.7	11.5	8.9	8.1	27.8	20.0	10.2	6.3	14.3	11.8	11.1	8.2	12.8
1.6	1.6	3.8	5.8	....	....	5.8	11.2	1.5	2.4	....	8.5	1.7
1.6	3.3	....	3.5	....	....	4.5	6.4	1.5	1.4	1.8	5.4	1.5
1.6	1.6	....	....	....	....	1.1	1.2	1.5	.9	....	1.2	1.1
....	....	1.3	....	....	....	1.7	1.5	....	....	....	1.6	....
....	....	....	....	....	....	.6	.2	1.0	.5	....	.4	.6
1.6	1.6	....	....	5.5	5.0	....	....	1.0	.9	....	....	1.0
....	1.6	....	2.3	....	....	.3	.3	....	.5	....	.3	.2

TABLE XLIV

Twelve of the Most Difficult Problems Encountered by Student-Teachers and the Major Causes of Each of These Difficulties According to the Reports from Laboratory-School Faculty Members

The seven major causes underlying the most difficult problems encountered by student-teachers during student-teaching courses are arranged according to frequency of mention by laboratory-school staff members.

A* Limited cultural backgrounds and inadequate working knowledge of subject-matter.
B* Inadequate working knowledge of modern educational principles and progressive methods of instruction.
C* Inadequate working knowledge of children on the part of student-teachers.
D* Insufficient time and opportunity to see and to experience a teaching situation as a whole, excessive numbers of student-teachers working with same children, and inadequate supervision.
E* Immature and undeveloped teaching personalities—limitations in native ability, in capacity for achievement, and in character, as well as immaturity in years—on the part of student-teachers.
F* Lack of respect for student-teachers on the part of the children.
G* Too heavy demands placed upon student-teachers and lack of time for adequate preparation.

Twelve of the Most Difficult Problems Encountered by Student-Teachers Are Ranked according to Frequency of Mention by Laboratory-School Faculty Members	The Above Major Causes of Each of These Difficulties Are Ranked according to Frequency of Mention for Each Problem						
	1st	2nd	3rd	4th	5th	6th	7th
1. Managing, controlling, and directing children, including management of large classes	C*	E*	A*	B*	D*	F*	
2. Handling discipline	C*	E*	A*	D*	B*	F*	G*
3. Initiating and carrying to completion, with the coöperation of the pupils, large units of instruction which include the integration and drawing together of various phases of subject-matter, different types of activities, and many human experiences within the comprehension of the children	A*	B*	C*	E*	D*	G*	
4. Presenting subject-matter and instructional materials in interesting and efficient ways within the comprehension of the children	A*	B*	C*	E*	D*		
5. Providing efficiently for the wide range of individual differences of pupils in a class	C*	B*	A*	E*	D*	G*	
6. Guiding the pupils in initiating purposeful learning activities; and leading them to carry these into effect	B*	E*	C*	A*	D*		
7. Organizing children's experiences; recognizing and making effective use of children's leads, questions, and contributions	E*	B*	A*	C*	D*		
8. Balancing pupil-teacher initiation and participation in class instruction	B*	A*	C*	E*	D*		
9. Visualizing, planning, organizing, and working out whole units of instruction	A*	D*	B*	E*	C*	G*	
10. Creating and holding the interest, enthusiasm, and attention of all the pupils so that high standards of work may be consistently maintained	A*	B*	C*	E*	D*	F*	
11. Balancing individual and group instruction	B*	A*	C*	E*	D*		
12. Selecting, organizing, unifying, and adapting subject-matter to the children's interests, needs, and abilities as well as to the desired results	A*	C*	B*	D*	E*		

experiences in connection with creative and socialized activities or with informal work for groups of children. The reports indicated that some of these student-teachers encountered difficulties because they thought in terms of detailed subject-matter rather than in terms of the children's abilities, interests, and needs; were concerned with the mechanics of teaching to such an extent that their minds were not alert to the constructive leads of the children; wished to "pour in" subject-matter rather than to lead or guide their pupils; and failed to capitalize effectively the constructive leads and contributions of each individual in the group. Many failed to balance properly teacher-pupil activities and had a tendency to go to extremes, for example: presenting materials chiefly from the student-teacher's own standpoint or from the aspects of technical detail; telling or dictating rather than leading the children to discover for themselves; doing everything for the children rather than leading them to assume responsibility for learning activities; or permitting the children to do so much of the directing or to branch out into so many activities that confusion ensued and little was accomplished in any.

In some schools the failure to effect close integration between theory and practice was largely responsible for the following types of deficiencies on the part of many beginning student-teachers: inability to present subject-matter obtained in college classes; inability to apply to everyday situations the theories and methods of instruction that they had been taught in professional courses; absence of knowledge of aims or purposes, and limitations in their understanding of what was to be done; failure to recognize the time and place for applying different educational principles, theories, and techniques; inclination to use traditional methods and to teach as they themselves had formerly been taught while pupils in the elementary grades; and hesitancy to try out new ideas or to deviate from ready-made plans.

Inadequate working knowledge of children on the part of student-teachers was, according to the reports from 22.3% of the student-teachers and 18.8% of the laboratory-school faculty members, the chief cause of the major difficulties in student-teaching. A large number of student-teachers encountered their greatest difficulty in establishing desirable teacher-pupil relations because they lacked adequate understanding of children's capacities, characteristics, interests, difficulties, problems, and needs at different mental and chronological age levels; or because they lacked knowledge of the cultural, social, and experiential backgrounds of the children whom they were teaching. Difficult problems were also encountered, especially by beginning student-teachers, because they were unable to diagnose children's problems and difficulties and because they had insufficient knowledge of how to provide for the wide range of individual differences represented in a group. As a result of limited contacts and experiences with children, some failed to capitalize the children themselves or to think of boys and girls as real human beings.

Insufficient time and opportunity to see and to experience a teaching situation as a whole, excessive numbers of student-teachers working with the same children, and inadequate supervision were the chief causes underlying the most difficult problems encountered by student-teachers, in the opinion of 8.2% of the student-teachers and 15.2% of the laboratory-school faculty members. In many teachers colleges sufficient time and opportunity were not provided for students to see or to experience a teaching situation as a whole; nor was ample opportunity afforded for development of self-expression in co-ordinating theory and practice or for the exercise of their intelligence and energy to maximum capacity. In some of the schools that scheduled student-teaching on the one-hour-a-day basis, the contacts and experiences of the student-teachers with actual teaching situations were piecemeal in nature and limited in scope; the student-teaching work was not consecutive and continuous; assignments of work were too narrow and limited; the student-teachers were with the children for too short periods of time to become sufficiently acquainted with them, or to understand the conditions involved; too many student-teachers worked with the same children in the laboratory schools; too many student-teachers were assigned to each critic teacher or supervisor of student-teaching; and insufficient time was devoted to constructive observation of expert teachers as well as to responsible teaching. The critic teachers in these schools had supervisory loads too heavy to provide adequate time for guidance of individual student-teachers, and at the same time discharge their responsibilities to a grade of children.

Immature and undeveloped teaching personalities—limitations in native ability, capacity for achievement, and character, as well as immaturity in years—on the part of student-teachers were, according to reports from 8.2% of the student-teachers and 12.8% of the laboratory-school faculty members, the major underlying causes of

the difficulties encountered in student-teaching. In many instances
the teacher-preparing institutions did not provide sufficient opportunities for the development of well-integrated personalities in prospective teachers. One-fourth of these student-teachers indicated
that self-consciousness and timidity were their greatest handicaps;
and about one-fourth of the above laboratory-school faculty members stated that difficulties were due to the student-teachers' inexperience in taking initiative and in assuming responsibility. Other
limitations in personality that caused difficulties for some student-
teachers were: lack of self-confidence, self-assurance, and self-direction; insufficient power of self-expression; failure to see possibilities
and to grasp opportunities when they come; lack of foresight, insight, and vision in seeing through whole problems; inability to
anticipate unexpected problems and to adjust quickly to new
situations; lack of high standards of excellence in workmanship;
slack habits of thinking and reasoning; lack of originality, imagination, creativeness, aggressiveness, and resourcefulness; insufficient
energy, vitality, alertness, and enthusiasm; ineffective study habits;
inexperience with people; failure to make suspended judgments;
unattractive personal appearance; weak and uncontrolled voice,
poor health, and physical handicaps; inability to bring about a
happy, cheerful, and joyous atmosphere in the classroom; failure to
appeal successfully to children in the primary grades; sensitiveness
to criticism, carelessness, crudeness, dependence, impatience, inac-
curacy, inconsistency, indefiniteness, indifference, irresponsibility,
laxness, listlessness, nervousness, passiveness, tactlessness, unco-
operativeness, and vapidness.

Lack of respect for student-teachers on the part of the children
was the chief underlying cause of the major difficulties reported by
5.8% of the primary and 11.2% of the intermediate student-teachers.
The children evidenced their lack of respect through their attitudes
of indifference or by their efforts to "try out" and take advantage of
the student-teachers. The status of the student-teachers was only too
frequently a negative factor in discipline. Laboratory-school children
realized that the student-teachers lacked the authority that must go
with responsibility and took advantage of that fact; they knew that
the student-teachers held a position very different from that of the
critic or the regular teacher.

The extent to which student-teachers should assume responsibility
for the management, control, and discipline of pupils in the labora-

tory schools was argued by diametrically opposed factions. Some argued that training in the management of children should parallel that in methods of instruction, on the assumption that the proper type of classroom instruction will obviate disciplinary complications. Those of the opposite persuasion contended that to confront beginning student-teachers simultaneously with problems of discipline and instruction would be to invite failure, because: (1) *child management* and *subject-matter presentation* constituted two distinct problems for these student-teachers; (2) the tendency was to neglect instruction for the sake of discipline; and (3) inferior techniques of instruction and poor teaching habits were developed during the process of mastering the art of discipline. It was further maintained that economy of time would be effected by laying a solid foundation in instructional methods before attempting the intricacies of child management.

Most of the student-teachers who reported a *lack of respect on the part of the children* had been required to develop their own methods and devices for dealing with problems of discipline, without sufficient previous preparation and guidance in this important phase of teaching. Such a premature introduction to child management created an unnatural teaching situation, with major emphasis placed upon discipline rather than instruction proper.

Too heavy demands placed upon the student-teachers and lack of time for adequate preparation occasioned the greatest difficulties, according to the reports from 5.4% of the student-teachers and 1.5% of the laboratory-school faculty members. In some schools student-teachers were required to take a wide variety of college courses while they were scheduled for student-teaching. In some instances such heavy demands were placed upon them in college courses or in extra-class activities that they did not have sufficient time to make necessary preparation for and effective adjustment to the many new things with which they were confronted in teaching. In other instances, however, the student-teachers lacked proper training in skillfully budgeting time.

Lack of professional standards and ideals by which to judge and evaluate was denoted a cause for the difficulties encountered in student-teaching. Some student-teachers stated that they were handicapped in their planning because they were not ready to judge what was best for the children; they lacked standards by which to evaluate materials, subject-matter, and teaching techniques; and their contacts with current practices were utterly inadequate. Some manifested a tendency to undertake far more than could be accomplished and, consequently, failed to carry things to completion; while others thought of the work in terms of their own success to such an extent that they failed to delegate proper amounts of responsibility to the children. A lack of professional ethics, on the part of a few, was induced by a haphazard sort of preparation and poorly supervised student-teaching.

Inadequate working knowledge of the use of materials and equipment in the laboratory schools was reported as the most serious handicap by 1.6% of the student-teachers. These student-teachers did not have adequate knowledge of the use of the library, of available materials, or of various types of laboratory-school equipment.

Disillusionment about student-teaching before entering upon the work in student-teaching courses produced the most serious difficulties for a few student-teachers, according to the reports from .4% of the student-teachers and .7% of the critic teachers. These student-teachers had been placed at a serious disadvantage by reason of their confused states of mind and their distorted conceptions of the real purposes of student-teaching.

Too large classes for beginning teachers were, in the judgment of a few of the critic teachers, responsible for the major difficulties encountered in student-teaching. In cases where critic teachers in the campus laboratory schools had very large classes, usually in the city schools, the pupils were frequently organized into smaller groups for the purpose of providing teaching opportunities for more student-teachers.

Over-supervision produced the greatest difficulties for only a small number of the student-teachers. These individuals had been so circumscribed in their opportunities to exercise creative ability, initiative, resourcefulness, and sense of responsibility that they felt that their student-teaching experiences had been unnecessarily limited.

The following specific causes underlying the most difficult problems encountered in student-teaching were designated by a much larger per cent of the student-teachers in the two-year and three-year programs than by those in a four-year curricula:

1. Insufficient mastery of subject-matter on the part of student-teachers.
2. Limited contacts with and inadequate understanding of children.
3. Immature and undeveloped teaching personalities on the part of student-teachers.

    a. Self-consciousness and timidity.
    b. Lack of initiative, originality, and creativeness.
    c. Laxness and inconsistency.
    d. Lack of forcefulness.
    e. Weak and uncontrolled voice.
    f. Insufficient power of self-expression.
    g. Ineffective study habits.

4. Lack of respect for student-teachers on the part of the children.
    a. Children try out and take advantage of student-teachers.
    b. Lack of confidence in and respect for student-teachers.
    c. Indifferent attitudes toward student-teachers on the part of children.
    d. Disregard for authority on the part of children.

5. Lack of professional standards and ideals on the part of student-teachers.
    a. Indefinite requirements of student-teachers on the part of critic teachers and supervisors of student-teaching.
    b. Lack of definite standards for evaluating and judging work.
    c. Diverse standards set up by different critic teachers.
    d. Vague conceptions of purposes and aims.

6. Failure to make effective use of materials and equipment in the laboratory schools.
    a. Vague understanding of materials suitable to children of different age levels.
    b. Ineffective use made of libraries and of available materials.
    c. Lack of knowledge of available sources of supply and of suitable illustrative and reference materials.

The underlying causes of difficulties reported by student-teachers in the four-year curricula usually involved broader educational implications than did those reported by student-teachers in the two-year and three-year programs. The following specific causes were designated by a much larger per cent of the student-teachers in the four-year curricula than by those in the two-year or three-year programs:

1. Inadequate working organization of content subject-matter and other materials of instruction.
    a. Inexperience in long-range planning and in the organization of large units of work prior to student-teaching.
    b. Limited knowledge of how to unify and integrate content subject-matter and other materials of instruction.
    c. Lack of knowledge of how to organize materials of instruction around broad problems suitable to children in the elementary grades.

2. Inadequate working knowledge of underlying educational principles and progressive methods of instruction.
    a. Inability to apply successfully to everyday situations such progressive teaching techniques as creative construction, socialized activities, and informal work with large groups of children.

  b. Lack of proper balance between teacher and pupil activities—too much freedom allowed the children.
3. Inadequate working knowledge of children.
  a. Insufficient working knowledge of how to provide for the wide range of individual differences of children in a large group.
  b. Insufficient understanding of the capacities, interests, personality traits, difficulties, problems, and needs of children at various age levels.
  c. Limited knowledge of the experiential backgrounds, social activities, and home environment of the children in the laboratory-schools.
4. Too heavy demands placed upon student-teachers; too much work required of student-teachers by both the laboratory schools and the academic instructors during major student-teaching courses.

A much larger per cent of the student-teachers and laboratory-school faculty under the one-hour-a-day student-teaching plan than of those under the half-day and whole-day student-teaching plans specified the following as the chief underlying causes of the most difficult problems encountered in student-teaching:

1. Insufficient time and opportunity to see and to experience a teaching situation as a whole.
  a. Too short periods of time for student-teaching.
  b. Excessive numbers of student-teachers working with the same children during the same periods of the day.
  c. Piecemeal system of student-teaching; lack of continuity in teaching; and narrow student-teaching assignments.
  d. Limited observation work.
  e. Failure to see whole teaching situations.
2. Inadequate supervision; critic teachers have too heavy teaching and supervisory loads to give adequate constructive criticisms and definite help to individual student-teachers.
3. Lack of respect for student-teachers on the part of the children in the laboratory schools.
4. Lack of conception of standards and ideals by which to judge and evaluate.
5. Inadequate laboratory-school facilities and equipment.

A much larger per cent of the student-teachers and laboratory-school faculty members under the half-day and whole-day student-teaching plans than of those under the one-hour-a-day student-teaching plan specified the following causes as the chief ones underlying the most difficult problems encountered in student-teaching:

1. Inadequate working knowledge of materials of instruction.
  a. Lack of practice in long-range planning and in organizing large units of instruction prior to major student-teaching courses.

      b. Inadequate working knowledge of how to unify and integrate con-
tent, subject-matter and other materials of instruction.
2. Inadequate working knowledge of progressive methods of instruction.
      a. Lack of integration between theory and practice; work obtained in
theory courses does not function in actual practice.
      b. Inadequate preparation for progressive types of teaching.
3. Inadequate working knowledge of children in teaching and learning
situations.

Chief underlying causes reported by a larger per cent of student-teachers in the primary departments than by those in the intermediate departments are:

1. Inadequate working knowledge of progressive methods of instruction
on the part of student-teachers.
2. Inadequate understanding of little children on the part of student-teachers.
3. Excessive numbers of student-teachers working with the children.
4. Inadequate supervision in student-teaching.
5. Immature and undeveloped personalities on the part of the student-teachers.
6. Lack of knowledge of how to use materials and equipment in the
campus laboratory schools.

Chief underlying causes reported by a larger per cent of student-teachers in the intermediate departments than by those in the primary departments are:

1. Inadequate working knowledge of subject-matter on the part of student-teachers.
      a. Insufficient command and mastery of subject-matter to be taught.
      b. Limited knowledge of how to select, organize, integrate, and adapt
subject-matter.
2. Lack of respect for student-teachers on the part of children in the laboratory schools.
3. Too heavy demands placed upon the student-teachers; and lack of
time to make adequate preparation for teaching.

Chief underlying causes of difficulties reported by a larger per cent of inexperienced student-teachers than by those who had taught in the field prior to student-teaching are:

1. Inadequate working knowledge of materials of instruction.
2. Inadequate working knowledge of children.
3. Immature and undeveloped teaching personalities on the part of the
student-teachers.
4. Lack of respect for student-teachers on the part of the children.
5. Lack of professional standards and ideals by which to judge and evaluate.

Chief underlying causes of difficulties reported by a larger per cent of student-teachers who had taught in the field prior to student-teaching than by the inexperienced ones are:

1. Inadequate background for working out large units of instruction.
2. Insufficient understanding of progressive methods of instruction, including modern educational principles and theories; inadequate preparation for progressive types of teaching.
   a. Few contacts with creative construction, socialized activities, and informal work with large groups of children.
   b. Vague conceptions of how to carry out activity programs.
   c. Formal backgrounds of school experiences; tendency to teach as one was taught; inclination to use traditional methods.
   d. Failure to balance teacher and pupil initiative and participation effectively.
   e. Inability to adjust quickly to new ideas and progressive theories.
3. Insufficient understanding of the experiential backgrounds, social activities, and home environments of the children to be taught in the laboratory schools.

A larger per cent of the student-teachers than of the laboratory-school faculty members reported the following as the chief causes underlying the most difficult problems encountered in student-teaching.

1. Inadequate working knowledge of children on the part of the student-teachers.
2. Lack of respect for student-teachers on the part of the children in the laboratory schools.
3. Too heavy demands placed upon student-teachers; lack of time for adequate preparation.
4. Lack of knowledge of how to use materials and equipment in the campus laboratory schools.

A larger per cent of the laboratory-school faculty members than of the student-teachers reported the following as the chief causes underlying the most difficult problems encountered in student-teaching:

1. Limited cultural backgrounds on the part of the student-teachers.
2. Inadequate working knowledge of modern educational principles and progressive methods of instruction.
   a. Lack of integration between theory and practice; work obtained in educational courses does not function in actual teaching.
   b. Lack of right types of professional preparation for progressive education.
   c. Too few professionalized subject-matter courses.
3. Insufficient time and opportunity to see and to experience a teaching situation as a whole.

4. Immature and undeveloped personalities—limitations in native ability, capacities for achievement, and character, as well as immaturity in years—on the part of the student-teachers.
   a. Inexperience in taking the initiative and in assuming responsibility.
   b. Immaturity.
   c. Lack of creativeness, ideas, imagination, originality, resourcefulness, and tactfulness.
   d. Failure to see possibilities and to grasp opportunities when they come.
   e. Lack of vision and foresight in seeing through whole problems.
   f. Slack habits of thinking and reasoning; failure to make suspended judgments.
   g. Inexperience with people.
5. Too large classes for beginning student-teachers.

PART III

THE MOST IMPORTANT PROBLEMS THAT STUDENT-TEACHERS SHOULD INVESTIGATE AND STUDY

It was felt that the data would not be complete until an expression had been obtained from student-teachers and faculty members as to the most important problems that should engage the time and efforts of student-teachers during student-teaching courses. For this reason a question intended to evoke the desired reaction was incorporated into the inquiry sheets and directed to both student-teachers and laboratory-school faculty members.

The answers of 2,451 student-teachers and 470 laboratory-school faculty members to the question, "What is the most important problem that student-teachers should investigate and study in student-teaching?" were tabulated and classified in the usual fashion. The major headings under which the individual answers were grouped are listed according to frequency of mention. Table XLV * presents the per cent of student-teachers and faculty members whose statements were placed under each major heading showing the most important problems that student-teachers should investigate and study.

---

* Table LXVIII in Volume II, which is on file in manuscript form in Teachers College Library, presents in detail the following data: the college year in which the student-teaching was done; the type of organization under which it was conducted; the number of primary and intermediate student-teachers, both inexperienced and experienced, who reported each of the most important problems to be studied in student-teaching.

Table LXIX in Volume II shows in detail the number of laboratory-school faculty members, under different forms of administrative organization, who specified each of the most important problems which student-teachers should investigate and study.

TABLE XLV

Per Cent of Student-Teachers and Laboratory-School Faculty Members Whose Answers Were Classified under Each Major Heading Showing the Most Important Problems that Student-Teachers Should Investigate and Study

Major Headings under Which the Most Important Problems that Student-Teachers Should Investigate and Study Were Classified	Per Cent of Student-Teachers and Faculty Members						
	STUDENT-TEACHERS		SUPERVISORS AND CRITICS		DIREC-TORS OF TRAIN-ING	TOTAL	
						Stu-dent-Teach-ers	Faculty Mem-bers
	P	I	P	I			
A. How to direct the learning activities of the children; and to lead them to develop desirable interests, habits, traits, appreciations, attitudes, and ideals...........	41.8	38.1	45.5	38.7	41.1	40.0	41.9
B. How to obtain an intelligent understanding of child development; and to deal effectively with both individual differences and similarities of children.........	19.0	14.7	15.8	18.9	12.5	16.8	16.8
C. How to secure and maintain high standards of conduct among the children; and to establish proper teacher-pupil rapport..........	13.7	21.8	10.9	15.6	14.3	17.8	13.4
D. How to acquire rich cultural background; and to obtain broad working knowledge of materials of instruction to be taught in the elementary grades.............	8.2	11.8	5.9	11.8	8.9	10.0	8.9
E. How to assume full responsibility in teaching; and to meet successfully the problems, duties, and responsibilities of the elementary teacher......................	6.3	5.8	4.5	4.7	7.1	6.1	4.9
F. How to develop a desirable teaching personality..........	6.7	4.0	5.4	2.4	3.6	5.3	3.8
G. How to build up and establish wholesome professional attitudes, worthy professional ideals, desirable professional interests, and high professional standards.....	3.4	2.8	4.0	2.8	5.4	3.1	3.6
H. How to obtain a broad conception of the elementary school as a whole.........................	....	....	6.9	4.2	7.1	....	5.7
I. How to analyze and evaluate teaching and learning..........	.2	.6	1.0	.9	....	.4	.9
J. How best to economize on time and energy in teaching.........	.4	.2	....	....	....	.3	....
K. How to make the most effective use of courses of study........	.2	.3	....	....	....	.2	....

It was foreseen that the same factors that influenced other evaluations would also figure in this connection, and a careful comparative analysis of the student-teachers' replies substantiates such an assumption. It was just as difficult for student-teachers whose cultural, educational, and experiential backgrounds were deficient to secure and manifest a broad outlook regarding the most important problem in student-teaching as it was when the most difficult problem, or its cause, was concerned.

A. *How to direct the learning activities of the children; and to lead them to develop desirable interests, habits, traits, appreciations, attitudes, and ideals.*

1. How to apply the more progressive methods of instruction in directing the learning activities of children.

   a. How to utilize progressive education in directing and guiding children.

   b. How to initiate and develop large centers of interest and whole units of work from the progressive viewpoint.

   c. How to initiate and carry to completion, with the co-operation of the pupils, large units of instruction which include the integration and drawing together of various phases of subject-matter, different types of activities, and many experiences within the comprehension of the children.

   d. How to use materials of instruction in such ways as to provide the greatest possible development of child initiative, group co-operation, and social responsibility.

   e. How to place proper emphasis on socially significant materials.

   f. How to stimulate and promote pupil self-activity.

   g. How to recognize and make effective use of children's leads, questions, and contributions; how to organize children's experiences.

   h. How to direct and guide various types of purposeful educational activities, such as:

      (1) Creative and socialized activities.

      (2) Constructive activity units.

   i. How to lead children to assume responsibility in class activities and for the progress of the work.

   j. How to balance pupil-teacher initiative and participation in class and extra-class activities.

   k. How to teach children rather than subject-matter.

   l. How to guide children in actual living.

2. How to guide the concomitant and indirect learnings of the children; and to develop in the children desirable social, moral, physical, and intellectual interests, habits, traits, attitudes, and ideals.

   a. How to help children develop such traits and habits as:

      (1) Self-control, self-direction, and self-confidence.

      (2) Self-expression, creativeness, originality, and imagination.

      (3) Initiative and sense of responsibility.

      (4) Willing co-operation and participation.

      (5) Constructive leadership.

      (6) Good mental and physical health habits.

      (7) Adaptability and adjustment to different situations.

      (8) Independent, economical, and effective study habits.

      (9) Ability to think clearly and independently.

      (10) Thoroughness, accuracy, and perseverance.

   b. How to help children to live, to grow, and to develop in a wholesome and happy manner.

3. How to develop the interests of the children.

   a. How to keep all the children interested and profitably engaged in suitable and purposeful activities; how to create and hold the interest, attention, and enthusiasm of all the members in a group.

   b. How to motivate and vitalize the work, and to create true to life situations in teaching.

   c. How to make materials of instruction vital and living; how to vitalize and humanize subject-matter in order to bring it closer to the children.

   d. How to provide valuable and suitable experiences for child development.

   e. How to create in each child a desire to want to learn.

4. How to present content subject-matter and other materials of instruction by the most intelligent, interesting, and efficient methods to meet the abilities, interests, and needs of children.

5. How to apply educational procedures involved in the more fundamental methods of instruction, such as:

   a. Setting up and accomplishing desired objectives.

   b. Formulating and asking stimulating, thought-provoking, vital, and effective questions.

   c. Applying such teaching techniques as drill exercises, exposition methods, memorization of materials, question and answer procedures, review work, supervised or directed study, textbook work, and testing.

   d. Making purposeful, suitable, and skillful assignments.

   e. Helping children to set up high standards of work as a result of the teacher's own quality of work.

   f. Making learning function.

6. How to teach the basic skill subjects, such as:

   a. The language arts, including both oral and silent reading.

   b. Arithmetic, including number work in the primary grades.

7. How to develop good teaching techniques and to establish skill in teaching.

B. *How to obtain an intelligent understanding of child development; and to deal effectively with both individual differences and similarities of children.*

   1. How to secure intelligent and sympathetic understanding of children at different age levels.

2. How to diagnose each child's difficulties, problems, and needs; and then to use proper remedial measures based on these diagnoses.

3. How to provide effectively for the wide range of individual differences relative to abilities, interests, personality traits, talents, problems, difficulties, and needs.

    a. How to lead each child to make suitable progress commensurate with his mental, physical, and social needs and abilities; and to help each child develop to his fullest capacities.

    b. How to help the unadjusted child to find his place in the social group; and to appeal to and interest the problem child.

    c. How to adjust the work so as to help each child to succeed; how to prepare each one to become a good future citizen.

    d. How to make adjustments to children at different age levels and be able to see things from each child's point of view.

4. How to provide for both the individual differences and similarities of all the children in a group; how to balance properly individual and group instruction.

5. How to develop the child as a whole; and help each one to develop a well-integrated personality.

C. *How to secure and maintain high standards of conduct among the children; and to establish proper teacher-pupil rapport.*

  1. How to secure and maintain high standards of conduct among the children.

    a. How to handle problems of discipline.

    b. How to manage and control children.

    c. How to hold together and manage large groups of children.

    d. How to apply corrective treatment to problem cases.

    e. How to anticipate problems, thus avoiding disciplinary troubles.

    f. How to find a happy medium between the too formal and the too informal types of discipline.

    g. How to discriminate between true freedom and license in class management.

  2. How to secure and maintain a wholesome, happy working atmosphere in the classroom.

  3. How to create in the children co-operative class spirit and wholesome attitudes toward school work.

  4. How to establish wholesome attitudes and whole-hearted co-operation between student-teachers and children.

  5. How to command or gain the respect, good-will, and confidence of the pupils.

D. *How to acquire rich cultural background; and to obtain adequate working knowledge of materials of instruction to be taught in the elementary grades.*

  1. How to acquire the rich cultural background and the wide fund of general information essential to teaching in the public schools.

  2. How to acquire thorough mastery and ready command of subject-matter to be taught.

3. How to find, plan, select, evaluate, organize, integrate, and adapt materials of instruction to be used in the elementary grades.

4. How to initiate, organize, and work out large units of instruction; and then relate daily work to the whole unit.

5. How to prepare well-organized, effective, and workable teaching plans.

E. *How to assume full responsibility in teaching; and to meet successfully the problems, duties, and responsibilities of the elementary teacher.*

F. *How to develop a desirable teaching personality.*

1. How to develop desirable characteristics and traits, such as:
   a. Initiative, ingenuity, originality, and creativeness.
   b. Constructive leadership, self-confidence, self-assurance, self-reliance, self-control, and poise.
   c. Sense of responsibility.
   d. Tactfulness and good judgment.
   e. Adaptability and co-operativeness.
   f. Foresight, insight, and resourcefulness.
   g. Forcefulness, firmness, and decisiveness.
   h. Accuracy, thoroughness, and perseverance.
   i. Charm, animation, and alertness.
   j. Pleasing and well-modulated voice.
   k. Patience and calmness.

2. How to acquire attractive personal appearance.

3. How to analyze personality traits and to discriminate between desirable and undesirable qualities; how to build up strong points and overcome weak ones.

G. *How to build up and establish wholesome professional attitudes, worthy professional ideals, desirable professional interests, and high professional standards.*

1. How to build up a sound foundation for future growth and development in the teaching field.

2. How to establish wholesome attitudes and worthy ideals in the teaching profession.

3. How to carry on the work of the teacher in conformity with the highest standards of the profession.

4. How to build up a well-integrated and worthy teaching philosophy.

5. How to secure a scientific outlook in teaching.

H. *How to obtain a broad conception of the elementary school as a whole.*

1. How to secure a broad outlook of the teacher's work as a whole.

2. What constitutes the successful teacher's job.

I. *How to analyze and evaluate teaching and learning.*

1. How to build up principles and standards by which to evaluate work of both children and teachers.

2. How to evaluate teaching and learning, in light of large basic principles; how to analyze one's own work in order to promote continuous growth in teaching.

J. *How best to economize on time and energy in teaching.*
   1. How to get started quickly and efficiently, with the least amount of friction and waste of time.
   2. How to minimize routine factors in order to devote more time to actual teaching and educative activities.

K. *How to make the most effective use of courses of study.*
   1. How to enrich the curriculum which is made up of courses of study, so as to take into account the vital experiences of the children.
   2. How to determine materials of instruction that should be presented to children at various age levels.

It is interesting to note that the problems specified as the most important for student-teachers to study are similar in content to those designated as the most difficult.

The reports from both student-teachers and laboratory-school staff members implied that the greatest amounts of time and energy should be devoted to those educational problems and teaching activities in which student-teachers encountered their greatest difficulties. These relationships are of great significance to an analysis of the needs of student-teachers, to the formulation of the content of student-teaching, and to the organization of student-teaching courses in elementary teacher-education curricula.

SUMMARY

In this portion of the survey there has been a striking evidence of the manner in which the thinking and judgment of student-teachers have been colored by the quality and quantity of their whole previous educative structures. In the selection of the most important, the least helpful, and the most difficult activities, together with the chief cause of the difficulty specified in each instance, the reactions of student-teachers and laboratory-school staff members have been both characteristic and significant. The very nature of these responses constitutes a valuable guide in the formulation of the elementary teacher-preparatory programs in state teachers colleges. Keenness of insight into and breadth of understanding of educational problems and teaching activities depended largely upon the richness and scope of the cultural, professional, and experiential backgrounds of those by whom the evaluations were made.

   1. In determining which phases of student-teaching were most helpful, several consequential trends of thought appeared.

a. Primary and intermediate teachers tended to consider those activities of special significance which were particularly characteristic of their respective levels of work.

b. A larger per cent of the inexperienced student-teachers, than of those who had previously taught in the field, considered actual teaching and practical experience with children the most valuable phases of student-teaching; while a larger per cent of those who had previously taught in the field, than of those who were inexperienced, indicated that well-directed observations of expert teaching and personal conferences with critic teachers were the most valuable.

2. Numerous activities of a routine and mechanical nature were mentioned as being least helpful. These activities were so classified, not because they lacked potential worth but because excessive use diminished their educational value in the preparation of prospective teachers and at the same time displaced other more essential educational activities, such as guiding children in the execution and progress of learning activities. Valuable activities, such as observation and conferences, were sometimes listed as least helpful because they became ineffectual through lack of intelligent guidance and through inadequate previous preparation.

3. The problems specified by the student-teachers as the most difficult were generally indicative of the types of activities and contacts that they experienced in their student-teaching. The student-teachers who obtained broad experiences in the higher types of teaching activities were naturally more conscious of the difficulties encountered in these activities than were the students whose teaching contacts were limited and narrow. The student-teachers in the four-year curricula were more concerned with problems of broad educational value than were those in the two-year programs. The student-teachers under the half-day and whole-day student-teaching plans mentioned difficulties in connection with the more progressive educational activities more frequently than did those under the one-hour-a-day plan. Those who taught for only a portion of each day evidenced difficulty in their contacts with such specifically fundamental problems as discipline and management of children.

4. The difficulties encountered in student-teaching courses were usually the outgrowth of a body of causal factors, chief among which were: inadequacy of cultural and professional background prepara-

tion; insufficiency of laboratory-school facilities; and immaturity of personalities of student-teachers—limitations in native ability, capacity for achievement, and character, as well as immaturity in years.

5. The breadth and the scope of educational backgrounds and teaching experiences had a direct bearing upon the nature of the problems and activities suggested by student-teachers for special study: the more circumscribed the professional contacts and the range of teaching experiences, the more frequently was mention made of educational problems constricted in outlook, limited in real educational value, and rudimentary in purpose, difficulty, and effect. Problems necessitating rich cultural backgrounds and progressive educational concepts were suggested as the most important by a large per cent of the student-teachers in the four-year curricula, while problems dealing with the simpler and more elementary phases of teaching were mentioned by a large per cent of student-teachers in the two-year programs.

CHAPTER SIX

WAYS IN WHICH CONTENT OF STUDENT-TEACHING COURSES
COULD BE ENRICHED TO HELP STUDENT-TEACHERS MORE
EFFECTIVELY ACCORDING TO REPORTS FROM STUDENT-
TEACHERS AND LABORATORY-SCHOOL FACULTY

EDUCATORS have been brought into conflict on the subject of ways
and means by which faculty members could help student-teachers
to prepare more fully for effective teaching in the field. There is,
however, a consensus of opinion among instructors in state teachers
colleges that the education of teachers should be a co-operative
undertaking; and it is the almost unanimous contention of leaders
in elementary teacher-education that the members of the administrative, instructional, and supervisory staffs of any teachers college
should share the responsibility for the progress and growth of the
student-teachers in their respective schools.

Each student-teacher and laboratory-school faculty member participating in this study was requested to state the most important
way in which each of the following groups could enrich the content
of student-teaching in order to help student-teachers to a greater
extent: critic teachers, instructors in education, instructors in subject-
matter, directors of training, and student-teachers. Among the host
of answers and recommendations offered was a body of suggestions
sufficient to effect, in some schools, a considerable reorganization of
student-teaching courses on a much more practicable basis.

The recommendations of both student-teachers and laboratory-
school faculty members were first classified under appropriate major
headings in separate tables to show the trend of thought of each
group. These tables were then combined for the sake of brevity. In
the combined tables the major headings and recommendations were
arranged according to frequency of mention, determined by com-
puting the average per cent of the answers of all the student-teachers
and of all the laboratory-school faculty members.

PART I

WAYS IN WHICH CRITIC TEACHERS COULD MOST EFFECTIVELY ENRICH THE CONTENT OF STUDENT-TEACHING IN ORDER TO HELP STUDENT-TEACHERS TO A GREATER EXTENT

The term "critic teacher" in this study refers to all the teachers who have the double responsibility of teaching regular groups of children and directing student-teachers in observation, participation, and teaching. Their titles vary in different schools, for example, supervisors, supervising teachers, training teachers, and critic teachers.

It is generally agreed that student-teaching is one of the most important phases of the elementary teacher-education program and that the critic teachers' contributions to teacher-preparation are invaluable. Critic teachers usually assume the greatest responsibility for the following types of activities: guiding the development and progress of student-teachers in teaching situations; teaching and directing children in both class and extra-class activities; helping to keep the objectives of the elementary schools before the student-teachers; demonstrating teaching techniques and educational principles to college classes; trying out experiments relative to modern and progressive educational procedures; helping to determine the grade placement of materials and activities; trying out different types of visual aids, illustrative materials, and physical equipment to determine their value for desirable child development in the different grades; keeping records and reports of all kinds for both children and student-teachers; keeping the routine and management of their classrooms running smoothly; co-operating with parents of children, school nurses and doctors, social workers, principals and teachers in the elementary field, and so forth. Since the critic teachers' duties are so greatly diversified and their supervisory loads are so extremely heavy in some schools, many do not have adequate time and energy to give sufficient attention to the needs of their student-teachers. With this knowledge at hand, both student-teachers and faculty members were asked to answer questions relative to ways in which critic teachers could enrich the content of student-teaching in order to help the student-teachers to a greater extent.

There were 2,220 student-teachers and 459 laboratory-school faculty members who answered the question, "How could the critic teachers most effectively enrich the content of student-teaching in order to help student-teachers to a greater extent?" To facilitate tabulation and study these answers were classified under appropriate major headings. Table XLVI presents the per cent of student-teachers and laboratory-school faculty members whose answers were grouped under each major heading. In cases where several suggestions were offered by the same person, only the first one was tabulated and included in the percentages shown in Table XLVI.

Although the reports varied greatly in the different state teachers colleges, there was relatively high agreement between the content of the answers of student-teachers and critic teachers in the same curriculum within any one institution.

The answers from 66.7% of the student-teachers and 71.3% of the laboratory-school faculty members were grouped under the following five major headings:

1. Holding sufficient number of well-prepared, constructive, and helpful conferences with the student-teachers.
   a. Commenting more on worthy achievements; offering more constructive criticisms and helpful suggestions; giving more definite aids, specific illustrations, candid remarks, and valuable ideas; encouraging rather than discouraging; recognizing the student-teachers' good qualities and building on these.
   b. Holding more individual conferences with each student-teacher to discuss frankly and intimately both strong and weak points.
2. Giving student-teachers more opportunity to assume responsibility in various types of teaching situations.
3. Providing adequate opportunity for well-directed observation throughout student-teaching.
   a. Demonstrating to a greater extent the most efficient methods of teaching children; devoting more time to teaching.
   b. Guiding more carefully the student-teachers observing the work.
4. Dealing more efficiently with individual differences of student-teachers.
   a. Studying and securing better understanding of each student-teacher.
   b. Helping each student-teacher to develop to her fullest capacity by adjusting the work, guidance, and criticisms to each one's particular needs, problems, difficulties, interests, and abilities.
5. Supervising and observing more closely and efficiently the work of student-teachers.

Holding a sufficient number of well-prepared, constructive, and helpful conferences with student-teachers was recommended by 24.3% of the student-teachers and 27.7% of the laboratory-school faculty members as the most effective means by which critic teachers could help to enrich the content of student-teaching. The reports indicated that thoughtfully planned, inspirational, and constructive private conferences with critic teachers were invaluable to student-

TABLE XLVI

Per Cent of Student-Teachers and Laboratory-School Faculty Members Whose Answers Were Placed under Each Major Heading Showing Ways in Which Critic Teachers Could Most Effectively Help to Enrich the Content of Student-Teaching

Ways in Which Critic Teachers Could Most Effectively Enrich the Content of Student-Teaching	Per Cent of Student-Teachers and Faculty Members						
	STUDENT-TEACHERS		SUPERVISORS AND CRITICS		DIRECTORS OF TRAINING	TOTAL	
						Student-Teachers	Faculty Members
	P	I	P	I			
A. Holding sufficient number of well-prepared, constructive, and helpful conferences with student-teachers....................	25.3	23.2	30.1	25.7	26.0	24.3	27.7
B. Giving student-teachers more opportunity to assume responsibility in various types of teaching situations....................	13.4	14.2	12.1	15.0	11.1	13.8	13.3
C. Providing adequate opportunity for well-directed observation throughout student-teaching....	13.1	10.5	12.6	9.2	11.1	11.8	10.9
D. Dealing more efficiently with individual differences of student-teachers....................	9.4	8.1	11.5	8.7	9.2	8.8	10.0
E. Supervising and observing more closely and efficiently the work of student-teachers............	9.6	6.8	11.1	8.7	5.5	8.2	9.4
F. Helping student-teachers to obtain intelligent understanding of the children and to establish desirable teacher-pupil relations	5.3	9.4	3.0	7.8	1.9	7.2	5.0
G. Guiding student-teachers more effectively in the planning, selection, organization, and use of instructional materials.........	6.7	10.3	....	1.9	....	8.5	.9
H. Establishing relations based on perfect understanding between critics and student-teachers.....	1.3	1.3	7.0	7.8	9.3	1.3	7.6
I. Having student-teachers teach for a longer and more consecutive period of time....................	....	....	7.5	7.8	1.9	....	7.0
J. Providing gradual induction into all phases of the elementary teacher's work................	6.4	5.8	....	....	....	6.1	....

TABLE XLVI—(Continued)

Per Cent of Student-Teachers and Laboratory-School Faculty Members Whose Answers Were Placed under Each Major Heading Showing Ways in Which Critic Teachers Could Most Effectively Help to Enrich the Content of Student-Teaching

Ways in Which Critic Teachers Could Most Effectively Enrich the Content of Student-Teaching	Per Cent of Student-Teachers and Faculty Members						
	STUDENT-TEACHERS		SUPERVISORS AND CRITICS		DIRECTORS OF TRAINING	TOTAL	
						Student-Teachers	Faculty Members
	P	I	P	I	ING		
K. Requiring high standards of attainment and checking carefully the work of each student-teacher	3.4	3.9	1.0	3.4	3.7	3.6	2.4
L. Leading student-teachers to utilize the most effective educational procedures	3.7	4.1	....	....	....	3.9	....
M. Working for closer integration between college classes and laboratory schools	....	....	2.0	2.4	5.5	....	2.6
N. Preparing student-teachers to meet actual teaching situations in the field	....	....	1.5	1.0	3.7	....	1.5
O. Securing thorough preparation for critic work	....	....	.5	.5	7.4	....	1.3
P. Guiding student-teachers in extra-class activities	.8	1.2	....	....	....	.9	....
Q. Inspiring greater co-operation among student-teachers	1.0	.8	....	....	....	.9	....
R. Discussing rating sheets	.7	.4	....	....	....	.6	....
S. Assuming more responsibility for growth of each student-teacher	....	....	....	....	3.7	....	.4

teachers; that such conferences led to better understanding and closer co-operation between the critic teacher and the student-teacher; and that it was not the number and length of conferences that determined their adequacy, but thoughtful preparation and intelligent application of educational principles vital to the development of the individual student-teacher.

Many indicated that giving constructive, inspiring, and helpful criticism was one of the most important as well as one of the most difficult functions of the critic teacher. They stated that critic teachers should offer more frank and constructive criticisms, more helpful and clearly expressed suggestions, more definite aids, more specific illustrations, more candid remarks, more valuable ideas, more real encouragement at the right times, and more commendations of worthy achievements. Some added that better results would be obtained from the display on the part of the critic teacher of deeper sympathy, kindlier attitudes, and broader understanding of the individual student-teacher's difficulties. Some specified that good qualities and worthy efforts should be commended before deficiencies were pointed out; that adverse as well as favorable criticism may be necessary, but the critic teacher should first lead the student-teacher to see the cause for failure, and then suggest means for improvement; that criticism, whether oral or written, should be given in such a manner as to further the student-teacher's efficiency, skill, and independence in teaching and at the same time create a consciousness of the justice thereof and the need therefor; and that criticism should be given from a strictly impersonal standpoint and with a purely professional attitude on the part of the critic teacher.

The general opinion was that destructive criticism should never be given in the presence of the children; that although it might be necessary to point out weaknesses, constructive criticism should always be given in order to insure constant progress and maximum growth; and that the suggestions offered by the critic teacher should be directed toward making the student-teacher thoughtful about the work in light of the principles of the teaching and learning processes, rather than in terms of special methods or devices.

Giving student-teachers more opportunity to assume responsibility in various types of teaching situations was, in the judgment of 13.8% of the student-teachers and 13.3% of the faculty members, the most effective means by which critic teachers could help to enrich the content of student-teaching. It was advised that critics should lead their student-teachers to become a part of the school staff and to assume more responsibility in the types of activities that are required of successful teachers in the field. They should not, however, require student-teachers to undertake responsibilities that they themselves are unwilling to meet.

Providing adequate opportunity for well-directed observation throughout the student-teaching, and demonstrating the most efficient educational principles and teaching techniques were suggested by 11.8% of the student-teachers and 10.9% of the laboratory-school faculty members as the best means by which critic teachers could help to enrich the content of student-teaching. Inasmuch as demonstration is a fundamental method of instruction and as the ultimate skill of the student-teachers depends in such a large measure upon the quantity and quality of their observation, it was suggested that critic teachers demonstrate to a greater extent the best educational principles and the most effective methods of teaching children; that more opportunities for observation of expert teaching be provided by having demonstration teaching for longer periods of time at the beginning, and at more frequent intervals throughout student-teaching; that concrete examples be made of the things that student-teachers were expected to accomplish; and that more effectual observation be assured through more careful guidance and more intelligent discussion of the work. It is evident that the success of the critic teachers as supervisors of student-teaching depends in a large measure upon their ability to do expert classroom teaching.

Dealing more efficiently with individual differences of student-teachers was, in the judgment of 8.8% of the student-teachers and 10.0% of the laboratory-school faculty members, the most effective means by which critic teachers could help to enrich the content of student-teaching. The reports implied that the same principles that should guide the student-teachers in handling individual differences of children be applied by the supervisors in dealing with the student-teachers; that it was just as important for the critic teacher to know each student-teacher's social and experiential backgrounds, scholastic achievements, abilities, interests, talents, characteristics, habits, problems, and difficulties as it was for the student-teacher to know each child's; and that such information should be secured from a variety of sources. Critic teachers should thus continuously study and analyze the capacities, talents, needs, problems, and difficulties of each student-teacher in order to help each one develop to the utmost capacity. The consensus of opinion was that the more thorough the knowledge possessed by the critic teachers, the more capably could they guide their students to make proper adjustments and to develop well-rounded personalities; that the more complete the knowledge and understanding, the more objective could be their judgments and evaluations of each student; and that the work, criticisms, and guidance should in all cases be adjusted to the individual differences and needs of the student-teachers.

Supervising and observing more closely and efficiently the work of student-teachers were specified by 8.2% of the student-teachers and 9.4% of the laboratory-school faculty members as the most effective means by which critic teachers could enrich the content of student-teaching. Some students stated, "My critic teachers were willing and anxious to help, but they were usually too busy to supervise my work very closely." Both student-teachers and faculty members indicated that critic teachers needed more time to observe the work of each student-teacher carefully, consecutively, and frequently; that most student-teachers required close and skillful supervision during the early stages of student-teaching in order to develop the best teaching habits from the beginning; that close supervision should be gradually withdrawn as the student-teacher gained self-confidence and skill in teaching situations; and that increasingly enriched experiences should be provided as progress was manifested.

The reports indicated that, in some teachers colleges, so many duties and responsibilities were placed upon the critic teachers that they were compelled to neglect the supervision and guidance of the individual student-teacher. Such comments as the following were frequently made by the critic teachers in these institutions: "My teaching and supervisory loads together with other school responsibilities are entirely too heavy to give adequate time to individual guidance of student-teachers," and "If my teaching and supervisory loads were lighter, I would be less tired and more inspiring." It was recommended that the instructional load of the supervisory staff should be sufficiently light to permit adequate individual guidance throughout student-teaching.

Helping student-teachers to obtain intelligent understanding of the children and to establish desirable teacher-pupil relations was advanced by 7.2% of the student-teachers and 5.0% of the laboratory-school faculty members as the best means by which critic teachers could help to enrich the content of student-teaching. Some suggested that critic teachers should provide greater opportunities for student-teachers to obtain experience in such activities as studying the children's social, cultural, and experiential backgrounds; analyzing the children's intellectual, physical, social, and spiritual needs; securing insight into character development; recognizing and providing for individual needs and differences of children; and dealing with large groups of children in teaching and learning situations. In order that the education and general welfare of the children might be safeguarded, some recommended that critic teachers should carefully guide their student-teachers in problems of management, control, and discipline of their pupils.

Guiding and directing student-teachers more effectively in the planning, selection, organization, and use of instructional materials were, in the judgment of 8.5% of the student-teachers and .9% of the laboratory-school faculty members, the most effective means through which critic teachers could help to enrich the content of student-teaching. Students who entered student-teaching courses with limited working knowledge of subject-matter usually required a great deal of definite guidance in problems pertaining to the utilization and application of subject-matter. An important phase of the critic teacher's work, consequently, was to stimulate in the student-teachers an appreciation of and a desire for richer academic and cultural backgrounds. The relative inexperience of student-teachers in assembling, organizing, and applying subject-matter and educational materials rendered it necessary for critic teachers to provide constructive guidance in these activities. Some recommended that critic teachers should guide student-teachers more effectively in working out developmental units of instruction; offer more constructive help in lesson planning; assist in the selection and organization of content materials; acquaint student-teachers with the most appropriate and progressive materials to be used in a specific grade; suggest the most helpful references to be applied in teaching; and familiarize student-teachers with a variety of reliable sources of information and materials.

Establishing relations based on perfect understanding between critics and student-teachers was, according to reports from 1.3% of the student-teachers and 7.6% of the laboratory-school faculty members, the best means by which critic teachers could help student-teachers to become more efficient teachers. Some student-teachers gave such statements as: "My supervisor was always in a hurry and did not have time to talk about my difficulties"; "I did not know my supervisor very well and did not feel free to discuss my problems with her"; or "I did not feel at ease in the presence of my critic teacher." The causes for such comments by student-teachers should be remedied. It was suggested that thorough understanding and friendly co-operation should be the basis of student-critic relationships, so that the critic teachers might analyze more accurately each student-teacher's merits, difficulties, and weaknesses; and that the student-teachers might in turn discuss freely their own problems, difficulties, and ideas. Some indicated that the critic teacher and the student-teacher should work together in school situations as co-partners; and that mutual respect, courtesy, co-operation, obligations, helpfulness, and understanding should be promoted in order to inspire desirable attitudes and ethics for the teaching profession. Some specified that critics should use their opportunities for observation, and thus determine the types of social, cultural, and professional experiences that student-teachers need. These reports implied that critic teachers should know the personal and professional qualities that are fundamental to success, and should foster such attitudes of helpfulness, sympathy, tolerance, and interest as will inspire confidence and lead to real progress in the development of a desirable teaching personality; and that close and intimate contacts between critic teachers and student-teachers were highly essential if the student-teachers were to realize their maximum possibilities.

Having student-teachers teach for a longer and more consecutive period of time was, according to 7.0% of the laboratory-school faculty members, the best way in which greater assistance could be rendered to student-teachers. These faculty members specified that longer and more consecutive periods of student-teaching were essential for the proper induction of student-teachers into the major teaching activities of the modern elementary school; and for the development of high professional standards and ideals.

Providing more gradual induction into all phases of the elementary teacher's work was, in the opinion of 6.4% of the primary and 5.8% of the intermediate student-teachers, the best means by which critic teachers could help to enrich the content of student-teaching. The reports showed that there was considerable overlapping of the same types of work in the different student-teaching courses, and that many student-teachers experienced the same types of activities on the same levels of attainment in changing from one student-teaching assignment to another. In order to insure continuous growth on the part of student-teachers, critic teachers were advised to study records of the activities in connection with observation, participation, and teaching courses which their student-teachers had completed; to plan the sequence of the teaching activities so that each student-teacher might continuously grow in ability to initiate and to assume greater responsibilities; and to provide increasingly rich experiences in planning, initiating, and executing work in different situations.

Requiring high standards of attainment and checking more carefully the work of each student-teacher were, in the opinion of 3.6% of the student-teachers and 2.4% of the laboratory-school faculty members, the best ways in which critic teachers could help to enrich the content of student-teaching. It was suggested that critic teachers and supervisors of student-teaching could be of great assistance by acquainting student-teachers from the beginning with the definite requirements of student-teaching; by inspiring the student-teachers to attain the highest ideals of the profession; and by following up the work of each student-teacher to ascertain his success in maintaining the prescribed standards. Some stated that the efforts of the student-teachers should be checked at conferences held at frequent intervals, and that cumulative records should be kept of the progress of each individual.

Working for closer integration between college classes and laboratory schools was the most helpful way in which critic teachers could help to enrich the content of student-teaching, according to the reports from 2.2% of the critic teachers and 5.5% of the directors of training. They recommended that critic teachers should (1) obtain a broad understanding of what is taught in the subject-matter and professional courses in the college and then help student-teachers to make effective application of this background in student-teaching; (2) teach more professional courses in the college; and (3) demonstrate the best educational principles and progressive methods of instruction to college classes.

Preparing student-teachers to meet actual teaching situations in the field was recommended by 1.3% of the critic teachers and 3.7% of the directors of training as the critic teacher's greatest work. They implied that critic teachers could enrich the content to a greater extent by the following procedures: going out into the schools of the state and seeing what was actually going on in different types of situations; keeping informed about the latest educational research in the field; taking more active part in the life of the community; serving on regional and state educational committees; and giving student-teachers broader conceptions and clearer understanding of the work, duties, and responsibilities of teachers in the public schools of the state.

Securing thorough preparation for critic work was considered by .5% of the critic teachers and 7.4% of the directors of training as the most effective way in which critic teachers could help to enrich the content of student-teaching. These directors of training were in charge of schools in which most of the senior student-teaching was done in the city or in the affiliated schools of the state. Some stated that critic teachers should have more definite ideas of the objectives to be attained in student-teaching; of the types of activities through which these objectives could be accomplished; and of the standards by which to evaluate the work of student-teachers.

Assuming more responsibility for the growth of each student-teacher was, according to the reports from 3.7% of the directors of training, the best way for critic teachers to enrich the content of student-teaching.

The statement offered by each of the remaining 6.3% of the student-teachers was placed under one of the following headings:

Leading student-teachers to utilize the most effective educational procedures.

Guiding student-teachers in extra-class activities.

Inspiring greater co-operation among student-teachers.

Discussing personality rating sheets with student-teachers.

The following ways in which critic teachers could most effectively enrich the content of student-teaching, in order to help student-teachers to a greater extent, were suggested by a much larger per cent (1) of student-teachers in the two-year and three-year programs than of those in the four-year curricula; and (2) of student-teachers and laboratory-school faculty members under the one-hour-a-day student-teaching plan than of those under the half-day and whole-day plans:

1. Supervising more closely and efficiently; observing the work of each student-teacher more carefully, more consecutively, and more frequently; giving more individual attention and devoting more time to each student-teacher, thereby necessitating lighter teaching and supervisory loads on the part of the critic teachers.
2. Helping student-teachers to establish desirable teacher-pupil relations; aiding them more effectively in the management, control, and discipline of the children; recognizing the fact that children react differently to student-teachers than they do to regular teachers.
3. Guiding student-teachers more effectively in the planning, selection, organization, and use of instructional materials.
4. Checking carefully the work of each student-teacher and requiring higher standards of attainment.
5. Inspiring greater co-operation among the student-teachers.

There was fairly close agreement between the types of suggestions offered by student-teachers and laboratory-school faculty members within each teachers college. A slightly larger proportion of those in the primary departments than of those in the intermediate departments, however, suggested the following ways in which critic teachers could most effectively enrich the content of student-teaching in order to help student-teachers to a greater extent:

1. Commenting more on worthy achievements; giving more constructive criticisms and helpful guidance; offering more valuable suggestions and ideas; giving more definite aid and specific illustrations; encouraging rather than discouraging; and recognizing good qualities and building on these.
2. Providing adequate opportunity for well-directed observation throughout student-teaching.
   a. Demonstrating to a greater extent the most efficacious methods of teaching children.
   b. Devoting more time to teaching children.
   c. Guiding student-teachers more carefully in connection with observation work.
3. Dealing more efficiently with individual differences of student-teachers.
4. Supervising and observing more closely and efficiently the work of each student-teacher.
5. Providing gradual induction into all phases of the elementary teacher's work.

A slightly larger proportion of those in the intermediate departments than of those in the primary departments suggested that critic teachers could help student-teachers to a greater extent by enriching the content of student-teaching in the following ways:

1. Giving student-teachers more opportunity to assume responsibility in various types of teaching situations.
2. Aiding the student-teachers more effectively in the management, control, and discipline of the children; helping student-teachers to establish desirable teacher-pupil relations.
3. Guiding student-teachers more effectively in the planning, selection, organization, adaptation, and presentation of subject-matter.
4. Setting up higher standards and making more definite requirements.
5. Guiding student-teachers in extra-class activities; providing opportunities for student-teachers to participate in and to direct children in various types of extra-class activities, such as, assembly programs, field trips, club work, and suitable recreational activities.

A larger proportion of student-teachers than of laboratory-school faculty members suggested the following ways in which critic teachers could most effectively enrich the content of student-teaching in order to help student-teachers to a greater extent:

1. Providing more opportunity for well-directed observation throughout student-teaching.
2. Leading student-teachers to obtain more intelligent understanding of the children to be taught; aiding them in managing and controlling the children; helping them in dealing with problems of child behavior; and in handling discipline.
3. Guiding student-teachers more effectively in the planning, selection, organization, and use of instructional materials.
4. Leading student-teachers to utilize the best educational procedures.
5. Providing gradual induction into all phases of a teacher's work.
6. Holding up higher standards of attainment in student-teaching.
7. Providing more opportunities for student-teachers to obtain actual experience in connection with children's extra-class activities.

A larger proportion of faculty members than of student-teachers suggested the following ways in which critic teachers could most effectively enrich the content of student-teaching:

1. Holding sufficient number of well-prepared, constructive, and helpful conferences with student-teachers; making conferences more vital.
2. Dealing more efficiently with individual differences of student-teachers.
3. Supervising more closely and efficiently; observing the work of each student-teacher more carefully, more consecutively, and more frequently; giving more individual attention and devoting more time to each student-teacher, thereby necessitating lighter teaching and supervisory loads on the part of the critic teachers.
4. Establishing relations based on perfect understanding between critic teachers and student-teachers.
   a. Being more sympathetic, friendly, human, tolerant, and understanding, thus inspiring confidence in the student-teachers; encouraging student-teachers to regard the critic teachers as helpful counselors and real friends.
   b. Working with each student-teacher as a co-partner; working side by side in all phases of the teacher's work.
   c. Promoting the idea that the student-teacher is one of the teaching staff and a part of the community.

Table LXX in Volume II presents in detail the following data: the college year in which the student-teaching was done; the type of organization under which it was conducted; the number of primary and intermediate student-teachers, both inexperienced and experienced, who reported each of the ways in which critic teachers could most effectively enrich the content of student-teaching in order to help the student-teachers to a greater extent.

Table LXXI in Volume II presents in detail the number of laboratory-school faculty members, under the different forms of administrative organization, who reported each of the ways in which critic teachers could most effectively enrich the content of student-teaching.

Ways in Which Instructors in Educational and Professional Courses Could Help Most Effectively to Enrich the Content of Student-Teaching

A large proportion of student-teachers encounter difficulties in teaching because of inadequate working knowledge of modern educational principles and progressive methods of instruction. The work offered in educational and professional courses frequently fails to function in actual teaching because of lack of integration between theory and practice. It also fails to function because of lack of unity between different college courses. Professional courses are too frequently taught as isolated phases of work without reference to the whole field of education, with the result that students are not led to acquire a feeling for the whole, nor to experience continuity in learning.

In the light of these facts, student-teachers and laboratory-school faculty members were requested to answer questions relative to ways in which instructors in educational and professional courses could most effectively help to enrich the content of student-teaching. There were 2,322 student-teachers and 457 laboratory-school faculty members who replied to the question, "How could the instructors in educational and professional courses most effectively enrich the content of student-teaching in order to help student-teachers to a greater extent?" To facilitate tabulation and study, the first reply given by each individual was placed under an appropriate major heading. Table XLVII * presents the per cent of student-teachers and laboratory-school faculty members whose answers were grouped under each major heading showing ways in which instructors in educational and professional courses could help most effectively to enrich the content of student-teaching.

* Table LXXII in Volume II shows in detail the following data: the college year in which student-teaching was done; the type of organization under which it was conducted; the number of primary and intermediate student-teachers, both inexperienced and experienced, who reported each of the ways in which instructors in educational and professional courses could most effectively help to enrich the content of student-teaching.

Table LXXIII in Volume II presents in detail the number of laboratory-school faculty members, under different forms of administrative organization, who reported each of the ways in which instructors in educational and professional courses could most effectively help to enrich the content of student-teaching.

Volume II is on file in manuscript form in Library of Teachers College, Columbia University.

TABLE XLVII

Per Cent of Student-Teachers and Laboratory-School Faculty Members in the Primary and Intermediate Curricula Whose Answers Were Placed under Each Major Heading Showing Ways in Which Instructors in Professional Courses Could Most Effectively Help to Enrich the Content of Student-Teaching

Ways in Which Instructors in Professional Courses Could Help Most Effectively to Enrich the Content of Student-Teaching	Per Cent of Student-Teachers and Faculty Members						
	STUDENT-TEACHERS		SUPERVISORS AND CRITICS		DIRECTORS OF TRAINING	TOTAL	
	P	I	P	I		Student-Teachers	Faculty Members
A. Presenting and clarifying practical educational procedures, effective teaching techniques, and workable educational principles.	26.1	26.8	19.4	21.8	21.8	26.4	21.0
B. Integrating and co-ordinating their work with that of the laboratory schools.............	7.8	4.3	30.6	25.2	41.8	6.0	29.5
C. Providing more carefully planned and well-directed observation of children and of expert teaching.	18.5	14.8	8.7	6.3	5.5	16.6	7.0
D. Leading students to acquire more intelligent understanding of children in teaching and learning situations....................	18.9	16.8	7.7	4.7	1.8	17.8	5.5
E. Preparing students to do more effective planning, more critical evaluation, and more skillful organization and integration of subject-matter and materials...	8.9	15.5	8.7	14.6	1.8	12.2	10.5
F. Becoming better acquainted with real teaching situations; then helping students obtain broad understanding of the responsibilities of teachers...............	....	....	16.3	10.7	20.0	....	14.2
G. Familiarizing the students with the most helpful instructional materials in the field; then training them to make efficient use of different sources of supply	8.2	11.1	2.0	6.8	....	9.7	3.9
H. Leading students to build up and attain higher scholastic and professional standards............	3.8	3.2	1.5	3.4	3.6	3.5	2.6
I. Encouraging active class participation among students........	1.9	1.6	2.0	1.9	....	1.8	1.8

TABLE XLVII—(Continued)

Per Cent of Student-Teachers and Laboratory-School Faculty Members in the Primary and Intermediate Curricula Whose Answers Were Placed under Each Major Heading Showing Ways in Which Instructors in Professional Courses Could Most Effectively Help to Enrich the Content of Student-Teaching

Ways in Which Instructors in Professional Courses Could Help Most Effectively to Enrich the Content of Student-Teaching	Per Cent of Student-Teachers and Faculty Members						
	STUDENT-TEACHERS		SUPERVISORS AND CRITICS		DIRECTORS OF TRAINING	TOTAL	
						Student-Teachers	Faculty Members
	P	I	P	I			
J. Leading students to develop wholesome professional attitudes, worthy professional ideals, and desirable professional interests			3.1	3.4	3.6		3.3
K. Holding more individual conferences with students	3.0	1.6				2.3	
L. Devoting more time to work on the curriculum	1.1	1.6		1.4		1.4	.7
M. Training students in the application and uses of different types of testing materials and scientific data	1.0	2.4				1.7	
N. Inspiring co-operation among student-teachers	.8	.3				.5	

Presenting and clarifying practical educational procedures, efficacious teaching techniques, and workable educational principles were suggested as the most effective ways in which instructors in professional courses could help to enrich the content of student-teaching. The answers from 26.4% of the student-teachers and 21.0% of the laboratory-school faculty members were classified under this major heading. There was a consensus of opinion that courses in education should be made more valuable and comprehensive, and that they should give students those professional skills and concepts essential to teaching proficiency. The reports suggested that instructors in educational courses could help students to become more efficient teachers by the following means: making the work in their courses more concrete, practical, realistic, and applicable by being less theoretical, general, and abstract; leading students to acquire strong foundation in theory and intelligent understanding of guiding educational principles, then seeing that their instruction functions in actual teaching; introducing and clarifying more efficient ways of presenting subject-matter and other instructional materials to children at different age levels; giving specific examples and concrete illustrations of classroom problems, and then indicating workable means of coping with these; making use of actual classroom situations in illustrating problems; presenting activity units and activity programs as carried out in the best schools; preparing students to guide children in carrying out large developmental units of instruction; being master teachers themselves in order to demonstrate the most effective methods of teaching children; and then applying the most efficient and progressive methods of instruction in teaching their own classes. Both student-teachers and laboratory-school faculty members stated that instructors in professional courses should teach groups of children at frequent intervals in order to understand fully the application of large basic principles underlying progressive education.

Some of the directors of training urged that the students should be trained to think in terms of principles involved in both the teaching and the learning processes, rather than in terms of specific devices and methods. They implied that observation of some of the best demonstration teaching failed to carry over into student-teaching because emphasis was placed upon specific methods and devices, rather than upon underlying educational principles of teaching and learning.

Many contended that theory and practice were absolutely interdependent; that methods and techniques of teaching were valuable only to the degree that they were associated with definite objectives, appropriate content subject-matter and other instructional materials, and knowledge of pupil-growth; and that educational methods, however essential when developed in connection with definite objectives and suitable content materials, became useless when ineffectively related to these.

Integrating and co-ordinating their work with that of the laboratory schools were, according to reports from 6.0% of the student-teachers and 29.5% of the laboratory-school faculty members, the most effective ways in which instructors in professional courses could help to enrich the content of student-teaching. These faculty members indicated that instructors in educational courses could help to bring about closer co-ordination, co-operation, and integration between the laboratory schools and the professional courses in the college by the following means: securing better understanding of what the laboratory schools are doing, having more contacts with them, spending more time visiting the classrooms, holding more conferences with laboratory-school faculty members, planning and discussing demonstration lessons with critic teachers; relating the work in educational courses to the best practices in the laboratory schools; observing student-teachers at work in the classrooms and studying their problems; and making the laboratory schools the pivot on which professional courses are centered. Some contended that the content of educational courses should originate in the laboratory schools, either on or off the campus, first through well-directed observation and later through increased forms of participation. These faculty members suggested that the typical laboratory or public school furnishes adequate problems and questions to be dealt with in any course in education. Some suggested that instructors in professional courses should assume considerable responsibility for the progress of student-teachers and that they should help to eliminate students who did not show promise in the teaching field.

Such statements as the following show definitely that critic teachers were desirous of help from these college instructors: "Instructors in professional courses could help the critic teachers by furnishing authentic information and reliable references"; "They should help the laboratory school to keep informed about the latest investigations and developments in the field"; and "The busy critic teacher should be able to draw upon the skill of a specialist in each field."

Providing more carefully planned and well-directed observation of children and of expert teaching was given as the most effective means by which instructors in educational courses could help to enrich the content of student-teaching, according to the reports from 16.6% of the student-teachers and 7.0% of the laboratory-school faculty members. Reports indicated that these instructors should make provision for more well-directed observation, which would serve the following purposes: exemplifying and testing educational principles and teaching techniques; presenting different types of work in a variety of teaching situations; leading students to obtain a broad perspective of teaching; and securing background by which to build up standards for determining the effectiveness of the teaching and learning processes. It was advised that thoughtful preparation and careful follow-up work be done in connection with all observation.

Leading students to acquire more intelligent understanding of children in teaching and learning situations was indicated by 17.8% of the student-teachers and 5.5% of the laboratory-school faculty members as the best way in which instructors in professional courses could help to enrich the content of student-teaching. They suggested that instructors in education should devote more time and effort to the following activities: obtaining intimate contacts with children's interests, problems, difficulties, and needs in order to help their students develop intelligent understanding of child life; leading students to obtain keener understanding of the abilities, interests, reactions, tendencies, and problems of children at different mental and chronological age levels; directing students in attaining clearer working knowledge of both individual differences and similarities of children; guiding students in developing sympathetic understanding of child development; dealing with problems pertaining to management and discipline of children; and providing opportunities for students to make individual and group case studies. Progressive critic teachers urged that instructors in education should build their courses on the principle of "growth of the child."

Preparing students to do more effective planning, more critical evaluation, and more skillful organization and integration of subject-matter and materials was reported by 12.2% of the student-teachers and 10.5% of the laboratory-school faculty members as the most helpful means by which instructors in professional courses could help to enrich the content of student-teaching. There was special demand for definite education in connection with the following: the collection, selection, evaluation, organization, and integration of subject-matter, including all types of materials of instruction to be used in the elementary grades; the systematic cataloging and filing of materials; the preparation of activity units; and the planning and organization of comprehensive units of instruction. Most of these faculty members implied that content and theory are inseparable, and that methods of teaching subject-matter could be learned through professionalized subject-matter courses.

Becoming better acquainted with real teaching situations, and then helping the students to obtain broad understanding of the responsibilities of teachers were, in the estimation of 16.3% of the primary and 10.7% of the intermediate critic teachers and 20.0% of the directors of training, the most important means by which instructors in professional courses could help to enrich the content of student-teaching. These faculty members implied that professional courses were frequently too far removed from actual classroom situations to be effective. It was recommended that instructors in educational courses should visit elementary schools in the field and thereby secure better understanding of the problems and needs of elementary teachers; that they should relate their work more directly to the real problems, duties, and responsibilities of teachers in the elementary grades; and that they should lead their students to get in touch with the practical side of teaching, to think in terms of real experiences, to see underlying principles of education beyond the specific needs, and to participate in the actual work of elementary teachers.

Familiarizing their students with the most helpful instructional materials in the field and training them to make efficient use of sources of supply were, according to 9.7% of the student-teachers and 3.9% of the laboratory-school faculty members, the most helpful ways in which instructors in education could enrich the content of student-teaching. Many prospective teachers devoted much time and energy to finding and assembling various types of illustrative materials that were practically useless to them because they had no conception of objectives to be attained through their use. Some also wasted much time and energy through careless and inefficient study habits, faulty reference techniques, and inadequate working knowledge of sources of supply. It was suggested that instructors in professional courses could be of great assistance to prospective teachers in the following ways: familiarizing them with the best instructional materials in the field, together with a clear understanding of significant objectives to be attained through these materials; acquainting them with the best sources of supply, for example, libraries, museums, current literature, documents, and reports; training them in the efficient use of references; and helping them to develop economical and effective study and reading habits.

Leading the students to develop wholesome professional attitudes, worthy professional ideals, and desirable professional interests was, in the judgment of 3.3% of the laboratory-school faculty members, the best way in which instructors in professional courses could help to enrich the content of student-teaching. It was asserted that these instructors could help the students to a greater extent by the following means: leading them to develop desirable professional points of view and sound philosophies of education; helping them to build up and to keep clearly in mind professional goals; guiding them in placing major emphasis upon underlying principles of teaching and learning rather than upon devices by which to do specific things; and leading them to see that professional growth should be continuous.

Each of the remaining 11.2% of the student-teachers and 5.1% of the laboratory-school faculty members suggested one of the following ways in which instructors in professional courses could help prospective teachers to a greater extent, thus enriching the content of student-teaching:

Leading students to build up and attain higher scholastic and professional standards.

Encouraging active class participation among students.

Holding more individual conferences with students; dealing with the individual student as well as with the group.

Devoting more time to work on the curriculum.

Training students in the application and use of different types of testing materials and scientific data.

Inspiring co-operation among student-teachers.

The following ways, in which instructors in educational or professional courses could most effectively help to enrich the content of student-teaching, were suggested by a much larger per cent (1) of the student-teachers in the two-year and three-year programs than of those in the four-year elementary curricula; and (2) of the student-teachers and laboratory-school faculty members working under the one-hour-a-day student-teaching plan than of those under the whole-day plan:

1. Presenting and clarifying practical educational procedures and effective teaching techniques that could be applied in teaching children.
   a. Teaching their students effective methods of presenting subject-matter to children in the elementary grades.
   b. Giving specific examples and concrete illustrations of classroom problems, and suggesting workable means for handling such problems.
   c. Discussing common difficulties encountered in teaching, and specifying ways of overcoming such difficulties.
2. Providing more carefully planned and well-directed observation; requiring more definite preparation and more careful follow-up work for observation periods.
3. Helping their students to obtain better understanding of children; placing greater emphasis on child behavior, and on the management and discipline of children.
4. Familiarizing their students with helpful instructional materials in the field; and training them to make use of different sources of supply.

    a. Acquainting students with useful instructional materials suitable to children in the different elementary grades.

    b. Assigning more valuable reading materials and more specific references which would be helpful in teaching children.

    c. Telling students about available sources of supply.

    d. Helping students to make efficient use of libraries and other sources of supply.

    e. Teaching students to use reference techniques.

5. Holding more individual conferences with students, both before and during student-teaching; and showing greater interest in the work and progress of student-teachers.

The suggestions offered by student-teachers in the four-year curricula usually involved broader educational problems than did those offered by student-teachers in the two-year programs. The following ways, in which instructors in educational or professional courses could most effectively help to enrich the content of student-teaching, were reported by a much larger per cent (1) of the student-teachers in four-year curricula than of those in two-year and three-year programs; and (2) of the student-teachers and laboratory-school faculty members working under half-day and whole-day student-teaching plans than of those under the one-hour-a-day plan.

1. Presenting underlying educational principles and progressive methods of instruction that could be applied successfully in directing the learning activities of children.

    a. Helping students to gain intelligent understanding and sound working knowledge of underlying principles of modern education.

    b. Preparing their students to guide children in carrying out large developmental units of instruction.

    c. Preparing their students to organize school life around large child activities.

    d. Illustrating successful activity programs and activity units that are carried out in the best schools; and explaining reasons for the success of such undertakings in these schools.

    e. Leading their students to gain intelligent understanding of the philosophy underlying progressive education.

2. Preparing students to do more effective planning, more critical evaluation, and more skillful organization and integration of content subject-matter and other materials of instruction.

    a. Placing more emphasis on long range planning and on the preparation of large units of work.

    b. Teaching students to evaluate materials of instruction in light of underlying educational principles.

    c. Helping students to gain clear conceptions of ways in which to integrate materials of instruction.

3. Leading students to acquire broad working knowledge of children in teaching and learning situations.
   a. Placing more emphasis on child development and child guidance.
   b. Helping students to obtain working knowledge of ways in which to diagnose children's difficulties and needs, and ways in which to provide effectively for the wide range of individual differences of children in a group.
4. Training students in the application and uses of different types of testing materials and scientific data.
5. Devoting more time to work on the curriculum; helping their students develop intelligent understanding of activities and problems involved in curriculum revision and construction.

A larger per cent of student-teachers and critic teachers in the primary departments than of those in the intermediate departments reported that instructors in educational courses could best help to enrich the content of student-teaching by the following means:

1. Integrating and co-ordinating their work with that of the laboratory schools.
2. Providing more well-directed observation of children and of expert teaching.
3. Leading their students to acquire better working knowledge of child life and development.
   a. Coming in closer contact with children in order to help students acquire intelligent understanding of child life and development.
   b. Helping their students acquire sympathetic understanding of the capacities, interests, traits, characteristics, problems, difficulties, and needs of children at different mental and chronological age levels.
   c. Providing more opportunity for individual case studies.
4. Becoming better acquainted with real teaching situations; and then helping their students obtain broad understanding of the responsibilities of teachers in the primary grades.
5. Holding more individual conferences with student-teachers.

A larger per cent of student-teachers and critic teachers in the intermediate departments than of those in the primary departments indicated that instructors of educational or professional courses could best help to enrich the content of student-teaching by the following means:

1. Presenting and clarifying practical methods of instruction.
2. Preparing students to do more effective planning, more critical evaluation, and more skillful organization and integration of subject-matter.
   a. Helping their students to become more proficient in finding, selecting, evaluating, organizing, and applying materials of instruction.

     b. Giving students practice in planning, organizing, and developing whole units of work.

     c. Presenting ways in which to integrate subject-matter.

     d. Placing greater emphasis on long-range planning.

     e. Teaching students ways in which to prepare effective lesson plans.

3. Familiarizing the students with the most helpful instructional materials in the field, and training them to make efficient use of different sources of supply.

4. Placing more emphasis on child behavior, and on problems dealing with management and discipline of children.

5. Training students in the application and uses of different types of testing materials and scientific data.

The content and scope of the answers of the faculty members were, on the whole, of a richer and broader nature than were those of the student-teachers. This can be attributed partly to inexperience and lack of vision of the whole teaching field on the part of the student-teachers. The following statements, relative to ways in which instructors in educational or professional courses could most effectively help to enrich the content of student-teaching, were made by laboratory-school faculty members:

1. Integrating and co-ordinating their work with that of the laboratory schools.

     a. Working for closer co-ordination, co-operation, and integration between the laboratory schools and the professional courses.

     b. Securing better understanding of what the laboratory schools are doing, having more contacts with them, spending more time visiting the classrooms; and then connecting their work more closely with the best practices in these schools.

     c. Making the laboratory schools the pivot on which the professional courses should be centered.

2. Becoming acquainted with real teaching situations; then helping students to obtain broad understanding of the responsibilities of teachers.

     a. Being in touch with what is going on in actual classrooms in the field —state and nation.

     b. Visiting public schools in order to secure better understanding of the needs and problems of teachers in the elementary field; and then preparing their students to meet these problems more effectively.

     c. Relating their work and discussions more directly to real problems, duties, and responsibilities of teachers; and leading their students to understand underlying educational principles beyond the specific needs.

     d. Providing opportunities for their students to come in touch with the practical side of teaching; guiding them to think in terms of real experiences.

    e. Providing opportunities for their students to participate in some of the major teaching activities.

3. Utilizing underlying educational principles and applying progressive methods of instruction in teaching their own college classes; being master teachers themselves in order to demonstrate the most efficient methods of teaching children.

4. Leading students to develop wholesome professional attitudes, worthy professional ideals, and desirable professional interests.

5. Avoiding repetition and overlapping of materials offered in different college courses.

WAYS IN WHICH INSTRUCTORS IN SUBJECT-MATTER COURSES COULD MOST EFFECTIVELY HELP TO ENRICH THE CONTENT OF STUDENT-TEACHING

A large proportion of the student-teachers were handicapped in their student-teaching work by inadequate working knowledge of content subject-matter and other instructional materials. Both student-teachers and laboratory-school faculty members contended that instructors in subject-matter courses could do much to help college students become more efficient teachers. Suggestions and recommendations were therefore proposed, delineating ways in which these instructors could help student-teachers to a greater extent before and during student-teaching. It was advised that instructors in subject-matter who are helping to prepare teachers for the elementary field give due consideration to some of the recommendations offered in this study.

There were 2,158 student-teachers and 455 laboratory-school faculty members who answered the question, "How could instructors in subject-matter courses most effectively enrich the content of student-teaching in order to help student-teachers to a greater extent?" * To facilitate tabulation and study, these answers were grouped under appropriate major headings. In cases where more

* Table LXXIV in Volume II, which is on file in manuscript form in Teachers College Library, shows in detail the following data: the college year in which the student-teaching was done; the type of organization under which it was conducted; the number of primary and intermediate student-teachers, both inexperienced and experienced, who specified each of the ways in which instructors in subject-matter courses could most effectively help to enrich the content of student-teaching.

Table LXXV in Volume II presents in detail the number of laboratory-school faculty members, under the different forms of administrative organization, who specified each of the ways in which instructors in subject-matter courses could most effectively help to enrich the content of student-teaching.

than one answer was given by the same person, only the first one was tabulated and included in the per cents shown in this study. Table XLVIII presents the per cent of student-teachers and laboratory-school faculty members whose answers were placed under each major heading showing ways in which subject-matter instructors could help most effectively to enrich the content of student-teaching.

Providing opportunities for students to obtain broad vision and rich backgrounds, requiring thorough command of subject-matter, and stimulating high standards of accomplishments were recommended as the most effective means by which instructors in subject-matter could help to enrich the content of student-teaching. The answers of approximately 21.7% of the student-teachers and 24.0% of the laboratory-school faculty members were grouped under this major heading. The consensus of opinion indicated that a comprehensive view of an entire field of subject-matter was highly essential, and that intelligent grasp and thorough knowledge of subject-matter to be taught in the elementary grades were primarily needed.

Such comments as the following were frequently made by laboratory-school faculty members: "Students should acquire richer cultural backgrounds"; "Students need broader views of subject-matter"; "Student-teachers are unprepared in subject-matter; they may know unrelated facts but cannot apply them to life situations"; "Students in college classes are not led to see the need for subject-matter in light of future teaching"; "Many student-teachers encounter great difficulties in carrying out large units of instruction because of inadequate knowledge of subject-matter"; "College instructors place emphasis on the accumulation of facts rather than upon the understanding of relationships in subject-matter, and it is the tying-up process that they fail to get across to their students"; "There should be greater unity between courses in subject-matter so that students could see relationships, for example, relationships between one era in history and the next"; "Subject-matter instructors should work for the accomplishment of important objectives, and should bring unity out of the college work rather than so many courses in the curriculum"; "There is too much overlapping and repetition in college classes"; "Higher standards of attainment should be stressed in college classes."

Such remarks as the following were made by a number of the student-teachers: "My subject-matter background was inadequate for effective teaching"; "My work in student-teaching has made me

TABLE XLVIII

Per Cent of Student-Teachers and Laboratory-School Faculty Members in the Primary and Intermediate Curricula Whose Answers Were Classified Under Each Major Heading Showing Ways in Which Subject-Matter Instructors Could Most Effectively Enrich the Content of Student-Teaching

Major Headings under Which the Answers, Showing Ways in Which Subject-Matter Instructors Could Most Effectively Enrich the Content of Student-Teaching, Were Classified	Per Cent of Student-Teachers and Faculty Members						
	STUDENT-TEACHERS		SUPERVISORS AND CRITICS		DIRECTORS OF TRAINING	TOTAL	
						Student-Teachers	Faculty Members
	P	I	P	I			
A. Providing opportunities for students to obtain broad vision and rich backgrounds, requiring thorough command of subject-matter, and stimulating high standards of accomplishments..	17.2	26.1	18.6	30.1	20.0	21.7	24.0
B. Teaching students to find, select, evaluate, organize, integrate, and adapt subject-matter..........	19.8	23.1	12.4	18.0	7.3	21.5	14.3
C. Acquainting students with the most valuable references, the most suitable educative materials, and the best sources of supply; and training them to use these effectively..............	17.8	14.7	6.2	9.2	1.8	16.2	7.0
D. Acquainting students with the most efficient methods of presenting subject-matter.........	12.0	9.5	10.8	9.2	7.3	10.7	9.7
E. Providing greater amount of carefully directed observation......	17.8	11.2	4.6	2.9	1.8	14.5	3.5
F. Working for greater integration between college classes and laboratory schools..............	2.0	2.4	16.0	7.8	21.8	2.2	13.0
G. Professionalizing subject-matter	....	....	11.3	7.8	18.2	....	10.5
H. Training students to take more initiative and to assume more responsibility.................	3.7	2.6	4.6	2.4	1.8	3.1	3.3
I. Obtaining better understanding of the problems and needs of elementary teachers by visiting elementary schools in the field..	.6	.6	6.2	2.4	7.3	.6	4.6
J. Making subject-matter more vital, helpful, purposeful, practical, and applicable...................	....	....	3.6	4.5	9.1	....	4.6
K. Acting as advisers on problems of subject-matter; providing more							

TABLE XLVIII—(Continued)

Per Cent of Student-Teachers and Laboratory-School Faculty Members in the Primary and Intermediate Curricula Whose Answers Were Classified Under Each Major Heading Showing Ways in Which Subject-Matter Instructors Could Most Effectively Enrich the Content of Student-Teaching

Major Headings under Which the Answers, Showing Ways in Which Subject Matter Instructors Could Most Effectively Enrich the Content of Student-Teaching, Were Classified	Per Cent of Student-Teachers and Faculty Members						
	STUDENT-TEACHERS		SUPERVISORS AND CRITICS		DIRECTORS OF TRAINING	TOTAL	
						Student-Teachers	Faculty Members
	P	I	P	I			
opportunities for individual conferences with student-teachers..	2.4	4.0	....	1.5	1.8	3.2	.9
L. Having contacts with children in order to understand their interests and needs................	....	....	5.1	1.8	....	....	3.1
M. Offering more help relative to the problems and organization of the curriculum..................	1.1	1.8	.5	1.5	1.8	1.5	1.1
N. Showing more sympathetic attitudes toward student-teachers and feeling more vital interest in their problems..............	2.8	1.9	....	....	....	2.2	....
O. Helping students develop economical and effective study habits......................	1.1	1.5	....	1.0	....	1.3	.4
P. Teaching subject-matter within comprehension of students....	1.7	.8	....	....	....	1.3	....

realize the great need for a rich fund of general information"; "I completed some college courses just for credit, not realizing the need for thorough command of subject-matter until I was assigned to teach a class of children"; "I crammed to pass subject-matter tests, but the facts were so unrelated that I could not apply them in teaching children"; "College instructors assigned so many pages to be read each day that we had no time to assimilate or to think about the materials which we read"; "We need more thoroughness in college classes."

While the quantity of subject-matter background is being adjusted, care should also be exercised that the quality is desirable. Many recommended that courses in subject-matter should be expanded and enriched in order to provide a wide fund of information and a broad outlook on the field as a whole; that student-teachers should be impressed with the absolute need for sound mastery and ready command of subject-matter to be taught in the field; that fulfillment of subject-matter requirements should be insisted upon; that mastery of subject-matter should include more than the accumulation of facts; that higher scholastic standards should be built up and maintained; that in acquiring facts, students should be led to see the relation of those facts to life and to actual situations, and to think in terms of large objectives rather than in terms of pages in books; and that instructors in subject-matter should assume the responsibility for seeing that the work is satisfactorily accomplished.

Some specified that students should be encouraged to investigate the various types of subject-matter, to read widely, and to develop a real intellectual curiosity; and that an interest in travel and an eagerness to realize more of the opportunities which are contained in their environments should be valuable aids in increasing the fund of general background information. Thus, although the students must work in conjunction with the subject-matter instructors, they have several avenues through which they may attain the establishment of more desirable subject-matter standards.

Some of the directors of training urged that overlapping and repetition in the different college courses should be eliminated in order to enrich the curriculum to the fullest extent.

Teaching students to find, select, evaluate, organize, integrate, and adapt subject-matter was proffered by 21.5% of the student-teachers and 14.3% of the laboratory-school faculty members as the most effective way in which subject-matter instructors could help students to become more efficient teachers. Many stated, "Students are not given adequate training in finding and selecting materials"; "Student-teachers lack ability to discriminate between essentials and non-essentials in subject-matter"; and "Students have not been trained to organize or adapt subject-matter." In order to acquire adequate working knowledge of content subject-matter and other materials of instruction essential for teaching in the public elementary schools, many recommended that prospective teachers should be provided ample opportunities to participate in the following activities in connection with subject-matter courses: collecting and finding materials; learning the fundamentals of subject-matter evaluation, selection, organization, integration, and unification; evaluating data and information, discriminating between essentials and nonessentials, and discerning the relationships of parts to the whole; planning and organizing large units of work and important problems in subject-matter;

unifying and integrating subject-matter obtained from different sources—textbooks and reference materials; verifying the reliability of conclusions drawn for vital problems; carrying out essential activities in preparing activity units or units of instruction as an integral part of their college work; and obtaining the assistance and guidance necessary to develop adequate skill in dealing with units of subject-matter. Inasmuch as an important part of the elementary teacher's work is in connection with the adaptation and application of subject-matter, the instructors in subject-matter were considered to be in a position to render the most effectual service in this phase of the teacher-educational program.

Acquainting students with the most valuable references, the most suitable educative materials, and the best sources of supply; and training them to use these effectively were, in the judgment of 16.2% of the student-teachers and 7.0% of the laboratory-school faculty members, the best ways in which subject-matter instructors could help to enrich the content of student-teaching. Subject-matter instructors, more than other faculty members, should be in a position to give students the tools with which to work; to direct student-teachers and critic teachers to the most recent, useful, and valuable references and sources of supply in their own respective fields; to furnish bibliographies of collateral reading and educative materials that would be helpful to teachers; to furnish authentic information about the latest research, discoveries, findings, inventions, and literature in the field; and to familiarize students with the best current literature in their chosen fields. Assistance was specifically requested in connection with such activities as finding, selecting, and evaluating reference and supplementary materials; determining which textbooks and references are most reliable and useful; forming intelligent acquaintance with new texts and supplementary materials; and determining what texts, references, and materials are most suitable and practical in the different elementary grades. It was suggested that college instructors should keep informed about the latest and the best books in the elementary grades in order to be of the utmost service to both critic teachers and students; that they should have at hand the best and the latest materials in their respective fields; and that they should be able to refer others to source materials.

Reports indicated that it was not sufficient for the students to acquire and to possess a fixed reserve of information, but it was necessary for them constantly to expand that fund of knowledge by reading and studying the works of a large range of acknowledged authorities. *Offering a wider selection of materials* in each course was recommended as one means towards this end. Subject-matter instructors were requested to teach students to apply the various source materials; to familiarize students with the literature in their respective fields of subject-matter; to train them to take advantage of library facilities—library card catalogs, *The Reader's Guide,* card indexes, and so forth; and to place on the students more responsibility for doing real reference and research work. The theory and practice of effective continuous study should thus be made an essential part of the equipment of every teacher.

Acquainting students with the most effective methods of presenting subject-matter was suggested by 10.7% of the student-teachers and 9.7% of the laboratory-school faculty members as the most effective means by which instructors of subject-matter courses could help to enrich the content of student-teaching. Some critic teachers stated, "The instructors in subject-matter are not as up-to-date as they might be"; "Subject-matter instructors still use the old traditional methods of teaching"; "The subject-matter teachers are entirely too far behind in their methods of presenting materials"; "They lecture too much or the lecture periods are too prolonged"; and "They do not have the point of view of children in the grades." Some specified that subject-matter instructors could help student-teachers to a greater extent by familiarizing them with effective methods of adapting and presenting appropriate subject-matter to the abilities, interests, and needs of children at various age levels; by giving students some working knowledge of ways in which to apply subject-matter to different grade levels, especially to the primary grades; and by utilizing more progressive methods of instruction in connection with their own college classes—for example, organizing their courses around comprehensive units of instruction. Some stated that subject-matter courses should be taught from the standpoint of progressive needs of teachers, rather than as a process of pouring in facts.

Providing more carefully directed observation prior to student-teaching was, in the opinion of 14.5% of the student-teachers and 3.5% of the laboratory-school faculty members, the best means by which instructors in subject-matter could help to enrich the content of student-teaching. It was suggested that these instructors should provide opportunity for their students to observe various units of subject-matter, in a diversity of teaching and learning situations and on different grade levels; that they should always inform the critic teachers as to the purposes of each observation period, and then invite them to participate in the class discussions following the observations; and that they should demonstrate a variety of methods of teaching subject-matter to children.

Working for greater integration between college classes and laboratory schools was recommended by 2.2% of the student-teachers and 13.0% of the laboratory-school faculty members as the most effective way in which subject-matter instructors could help to enrich the content of student-teaching. Some specified that these instructors could help both student-teachers and critic teachers to a greater extent by the following means: keeping in closer touch with the laboratory-school situation and having better understanding of its aims, purposes, and work; observing student-teachers and critic teachers; discussing plans and units of work with student-teachers and critic teachers; following up their own instruction to see if it functions in teaching; and using the laboratory schools more effectively. Student-teachers and critic teachers should thus be able to draw upon the skill of a specialist in each of the subject-matter departments.

Professionalizing subject-matter was a term used by approximately 10.0% of the critic teachers and 18.2% of the directors of training. (It should be borne in mind, however, that professionalization of subject matter is not a distinct activity, but that it is included in most of the specific recommendations that are presented in this discussion of ways in which subject-matter instructors could help to enrich the content of student teaching. In the interest of preserving statistical accuracy, it was deemed wisest to allow this suggestion to stand as worded in its original form, rather than to attempt to allocate the percentages under a variety of other headings.) These faculty members implied that there should be very close connection between the content and the methods of presenting subject-matter, that subject-matter could not be taught in one compartment and methods in another; that there should be a definite connection between the content and its use in the classroom; and that elementary teachers need a distinctive type of professional preparation in subject-matter, especially during the latter part of undergraduate work.

Training students to take more initiative and to assume more re-

sponsibility was, according to 3.1% of the student-teachers and 3.3% of the laboratory-school faculty members, the best way in which subject-matter instructors could help to enrich the content of student-teaching. These student-teachers and faculty members specified that in order to prepare prospective teachers for progressive types of education, subject-matter instructors should provide more opportunities in their college classes for student initiative, participation, self-expression, creativeness, committee and group work, and assumption of responsibility.

Obtaining better understanding of the problems and needs of elementary teachers by visiting elementary schools was, according to reports from .6% of the student-teachers and 4.6% of the laboratory-school faculty members, the best way in which subject-matter instructors could help to enrich the content of student-teaching. It was recommended that these instructors visit public schools and study their needs and problems; that they be in touch with actual teaching in the field and come in contact with the practical side of teaching; that they develop more sympathetic understanding of the elementary teacher's responsibilities and take more interest in the problems of the elementary school; and that they learn more accurately the problems which the prospective teachers will meet in actual teaching and prepare them to meet these more effectively.

The remaining 9.5% of the student-teachers and 10.1% of the laboratory-school faculty members gave answers that were placed under the following headings:

Making subject-matter courses more vital, helpful, purposeful, practical, and applicable; being more open-minded in their views.

Acting as advisers on problems of subject-matter; providing more opportunities for individual conferences to clear up difficulties that constantly arise in teaching.

Having closer contacts with children in order to understand their interests and needs at different age levels.

Offering more help relative to the problems and organization of the curriculum.

Showing more sympathetic attitudes toward student-teachers and feeling more vital interest in their problems.

Helping students to develop economical and effective study habits.

Teaching subject-matter within the comprehension of the students.

Ways in Which Directors of Training Could Most Effectively Help to Enrich the Content of Student-Teaching According to Reports from Student-Teachers

Many valuable suggestions were given as to ways in which the directors of training could help to enrich the content of student-teaching. The statements, which indicated how the directors could help the student-teachers to a greater extent, were classified under major headings for the sake of convenience in tabulating the data. These major headings, together with the chief subdivisions placed under each, are here arranged according to frequency of mention by 2,096 student-teachers.

A. Providing opportunities, under expert guidance, for the development of teaching skill adequate for the beginning teacher in the field.
   1. Providing opportunity for student-teachers to do more actual teaching of children.
   2. Affording more opportunities for the student-teachers to assume responsibility in different types of teaching situations.
   3. Placing the final student-teaching course on the half-day or whole-day basis to enable student-teachers to obtain experience in whole teaching and learning situations.

B. Making adequate provision for well-directed observation.
   1. Providing opportunity for prospective teachers to obtain carefully directed observation prior to, during, and subsequent to major student-teaching courses.
   2. Furnishing adequate opportunity for the student-teachers to see teaching and learning situations as a whole.
   3. Providing variety in observation.

C. Observing the student-teachers frequently and offering helpful suggestions, stimulating comments, constructive criticisms, definite aids, and specific instructions for improvement.

D. Having more personal contacts with the student-teachers and providing adequate opportunity for private conferences.
   1. Holding more personal conferences with the student-teachers both prior to and during student-teaching.
   2. Becoming acquainted with the background, personality, interests, abilities, talents, problems, and difficulties of each student-teacher; and then helping each one according to individual needs.

E. Helping student-teachers to understand the laboratory-school standards and requirements.
   1. Giving student-teachers a clear understanding of:
     a. The laboratory-school situation.
     b. What is expected of the student-teachers.

2. Explaining and clarifying standards and requirements.
3. Analyzing and discussing different types of difficulties and problems which student-teachers encounter in student-teaching.

F. Planning for more gradual and continuous induction of student-teachers into teaching.

G. Fostering in the children of laboratory schools a more genuine feeling of respect for student-teachers.

H. Obtaining more nearly adequate laboratory-school facilities; striving for less crowded conditions in the campus laboratory schools; assigning fewer student-teachers to the same group of children and to the same critic teacher.

I. Promoting unity of purpose and co-operative relations among the teachers college departments.
   1. Promoting greater interrelation between the laboratory-school and the college staff members.
   2. Working for closer integration between the work of the college classes and that of the laboratory schools.
   3. Encouraging willing co-operation and sympathetic understanding between student-teachers and faculty members.

J. Guiding student-teachers more carefully in the selection of valuable courses that will more fully prepare them for student-teaching.

K. Supplying adequate equipment and more useful materials for the laboratory schools.

The nature of the recommendations was greatly influenced by the type of student-teaching organization. A larger number of negative criticisms and a greater variety of suggestions for improvement were offered by student-teachers assigned for one-hour-a-day student-teaching than by those assigned for half-day or whole-day student-teaching. Such recommendations as the following were usually proffered by those under the one-hour-a-day student-teaching plan:

1. Providing opportunity for student-teachers to devote a longer portion of each day to teaching during the final student-teaching course.
2. Fostering in the children a more genuine feeling of respect for student-teachers.
3. Striving for less crowded conditions in the campus laboratory schools.

Table LXXVI in Volume II, which is on file in manuscript form in Teachers College Library, shows in detail the following data: the college year in which the student-teaching was done; the type of organization under which it was conducted; the number of primary and intermediate student-teachers, both experienced and inexperienced, who suggested each of the ways in which directors of training could help to enrich the content of student-teaching.

WAYS IN WHICH STUDENT-TEACHERS COULD MOST EFFECTIVELY HELP TO ENRICH THE CONTENT OF STUDENT-TEACHING

The necessity of proper example if maximum development is to be achieved is conceded to be a fundamental principle of education, and the really great teacher is the one who can exemplify the highest moral, ethical, and social qualities of character and life. The eminently and truly successful teachers are those whose lives have been full, rich, and meaningful; those whose lives have been enhanced by wide reading, intensive observation, profitable contacts with worthy people and interesting places, participation in all types of activities, and numberless contacts with life as it is. The lack of the requisite cultural, experiential, and professional backgrounds almost inevitably limits teaching success, but the situation is readily subject to improvement in the case of most individuals.

It was with these facts in view that student-teachers and faculty members were asked, "How could the student-teachers most effectively help to enrich the content of student-teaching?" The first answer reported by each of 2,408 student-teachers and 457 laboratory-school faculty members was classified under an appropriate major heading. A study of these replies revealed that there was at least a fair agreement between the suggestions offered by the two groups. The answers of the faculty members, however, gave evidence of broader experiences and more mature judgment.

Table XLIX * summarizes the per cent of answers, of student-teachers and laboratory-school faculty members, that were placed under each major heading showing ways in which student-teachers could most effectively help to enrich the content of student-teaching.

Knowing the field, and preparing more judiciously and thoroughly for teaching were, in the judgment of 35.5% of the student-teachers and 28.2% of the laboratory-school faculty members, the means by which student-teachers could most effectively help to enrich the con-

---

* Table LXXVII in Volume II, which is on file in manuscript form in Teachers College Library, shows in detail the following data: the college year in which the student-teaching was done; the type of organization under which it was conducted; the number of primary and intermediate student-teachers, both inexperienced and experienced, who specified each of the ways in which student-teachers could most effectively help to enrich the content of student-teaching.

Table LXXVIII in Volume II presents in detail the number of laboratory-school faculty members, under the different forms of administrative organization, who reported each of the ways in which the student-teachers could most effectively help to enrich the content of student-teaching.

TABLE XLIX

Per Cent of Student-Teachers and Laboratory-School Faculty Members in the Primary and Intermediate Curricula Whose Answers Were Classified Under Each Major Heading Showing Ways in Which Student-Teachers Could Most Effectively Help to Enrich the Content of Student-Teaching

Major Headings under Which the Answers, Showing Ways in Which Student-Teachers Could Most Effectively Help to Enrich the Content of Student-Teaching, Were Classified	Per Cent of Student-Teachers and Faculty Members						
	STUDENT-TEACHERS		SUPERVISORS AND CRITICS		DIRECTORS OF TRAINING	TOTAL	
						Student-Teachers	Faculty Members
	P	I	P	I			
A. Knowing the field, and preparing more judiciously and thoroughly for teaching	30.6	40.2	25.0	34.0	18.2	35.5	28.2
B. Working more conscientiously to develop desirable teaching personality traits	26.6	22.1	26.0	21.8	14.5	24.3	22.8
C. Taking more initiative and assuming more responsibility in various types of teaching situations	13.8	13.1	18.3	16.0	20.0	13.4	17.4
D. Observing more carefully, intently, and extensively	14.5	10.7	6.6	4.4	5.5	12.6	5.5
E. Developing wholesome professional attitudes, desirable professional interests, and worthy professional ideals	....	....	11.7	7.8	20.0	....	10.9
F. Interviewing and consulting with faculty members more frequently relative to problems in teaching	7.9	6.6	2.0	2.9	5.5	7.2	2.8
G. Scheduling lighter college programs while doing student-teaching	5.4	5.9	1.0	1.5	1.8	5.6	1.3
H. Conserving time carefully so as to accomplish a maximum of work in a minimum of time	.7	.7	2.6	3.9	1.8	.7	3.2
I. Setting up and striving for high standards of scholarship, of work, and of living	....	....	2.6	3.9	9.1	....	3.9
J. Doing careful follow-up work in teaching, for example, analyzing, criticizing, evaluating, and comparing daily work or units of instruction	....	....	2.6	2.4	3.6	....	2.6
K. Making wider use of environment—availing themselves of opportunities to see and to hear good things, and participating more extensively in extra-class activities	.6	.7	1.5	1.5	....	.7	1.3

tent of student-teaching. Just as inadequate working knowledge of the fundamental elements in teaching was recognized as the outstanding cause for student-teaching difficulties, so more judicious and thorough preparation was recommended as the avenue to greatest improvement. While a great variety of activities would enter into the ideal preparation, the following were specified as needful of additional emphasis: (1) obtaining broader viewpoints and richer backgrounds by putting forth greater effort and devoting more time to investigation, reading, and study; (2) acquiring more thorough grasp and sounder mastery of subject-matter before entering upon student-teaching; (3) securing broader acquaintance with and more intelligent understanding of children; (4) obtaining more comprehensive and practicable knowledge of educational principles and teaching techniques; (5) determining more accurately the extent of need for adaptation of procedures to provide for children's individual differences; (6) preparing more completely the integration of all materials of instruction for a grade, and organizing such materials into units of instruction and plans for daily work; and (7) obtaining, prior to student-teaching, more intelligent acquaintance with the laboratory-school situation. Some indicated that a clear working knowledge of children—their community and home environments, experiential backgrounds, social activities, personality traits, abilities, attitudes, interests, tendencies, difficulties, and needs—might be secured from actual contacts, from analytical observation, from reading of children's literature, from study of child psychology, and from investigation and analysis of child development. Many stated that students should make more efficient use of cultural and professional materials; of subject-matter in texts, reference books, supplementary materials, and current literature; and of professional books, magazines, articles, and bulletins.

Working more conscientiously to develop desirable teaching personality traits was, in the opinion of 24.3% of the student-teachers and 22.8% of the laboratory-school faculty members, the most effective means by which student-teachers could help themselves to become more efficient teachers. Student-teachers were advised to analyze more carefully and conscientiously their personality traits and to make definite efforts at self-improvement. Student-teachers and faculty members alike suggested the cultivation of such traits as adaptability, alertness, considerateness, creativeness, enthusiasm, forcefulness, open-mindedness, originality, receptiveness to suggestions, refinement, resourcefulness, self-confidence, self-criticism, and tactfulness. Student-teachers more frequently than faculty members specified such traits as calmness, common sense, courtesy, good judgment, optimism, and patience; while faculty members more frequently specified such traits as accuracy, ambition, energy, foresightedness, pliability, serious mindedness, and thoroughness. Other channels of self-improvement named were: studying and applying qualities that make for good teaching, building system and concentration into habits of study and thought, directing energies with more efficiency, developing and exhibiting leadership in teaching situations, and being more sensitive to the fine things in life.

Taking more initiative and assuming more responsibility in various types of teaching situations were advanced by 13.4% of the student-teachers and 17.4% of the laboratory-school faculty members as the means by which student-teachers could most effectively help to enrich the content of student-teaching. Statements from their reports indicated that there are numerous ways in which student-teachers might more fully take advantage of the responsibilities already entrusted to them. The following were particularly suggested: by entering into teaching with greater initiative and more whole-hearted enthusiasm; by utilizing sound educational principles; by more effectively applying materials and methods of instruction; and by displaying more vital interest in the growth and development of each child in the class.

Observing more carefully, intently, and extensively was the most fruitful means that student-teachers could employ in helping themselves to become more efficient teachers, according to the reports from 12.6% of the student-teachers and 5.5% of the laboratory-school faculty members. It was particularly advised that expert teachers be observed in as great a variety of teaching situations and in as many different rooms, grades, and schools as possible. Throughout the entire teacher-education curriculum—before, during, and after responsible student-teaching courses—observation of master teaching was recommended as very helpful. Care in observation work was considered fundamental and, for maximum benefit, it was recommended that a technique for observing be developed.

Developing wholesome professional attitudes, desirable professional interests, and worthy professional ideals was, in the judgment of 10.9% of the laboratory-school faculty members, the most effective means by which student-teachers could help themselves to become more efficient teachers. Fundamental to the continued success of every teacher is the cultivation of desirable and progressive professional attitudes toward teaching. Presumably with this in mind, the majority of the above faculty members recommended a more sympathetic attitude and a more personal interest in each pupil; a willingness to devote to the work the requisite time and energy; and open-mindedness toward the profession as a whole. In this connection faculty members mentioned the development of worthy professional ideals and of a wholesome philosophy of education; the adoption of a scientific outlook on teaching; an appreciation of the problems and responsibilities of the teacher; and the conception of student-teaching as an opportunity to learn to teach, and a real job, not merely another course to be completed. That student-teachers failed to consider these and other less obvious factors in self-improvement is in all probability caused by their limited concept of the field of teacher-education as a whole.

Interviewing and consulting with faculty members more frequently relative to problems in teaching was indicated by 7.2% of the student-teachers and 2.8% of the faculty members as the most effective means by which student-teachers could help to enrich the content of student-teaching. The reports implied that student-teachers could help themselves to a greater extent by interviewing critic teachers more frequently regarding personality traits, progress in teaching, and possible means of improvement; and by consulting instructors in subject-matter and professional courses for special advice on specific problems within their respective fields.

Scheduling lighter college programs while doing student-teaching was suggested by 5.6% of the student-teachers and 1.3% of the laboratory-school faculty members as the most productive means that student-teachers might employ in helping to enrich the content of student-teaching.

Conserving time carefully so as to accomplish a maximum of work in a minimum of time was, in the opinion of .7% of the student-teachers and 3.2% of the laboratory-school faculty members, the most effective means of self-help for student-teachers. To this end, faculty members suggested that a practicable budget of time be prepared and followed, and that further economy of time be insured by the use of only the most efficient methods of work.

Each of the remaining .7% of the student-teachers and 7.8% of the laboratory-school faculty members suggested one of the following ways in which student-teachers could most effectively help to enrich the content of student-teaching:

Setting up and striving for high standards of scholarship, of work, and of living.

Doing careful follow-up work in teaching, for example, analyzing, criticizing, evaluating, and comparing daily work or units of instruction.

Making wider use of environment—availing themselves of opportunities to see and to hear good things, and participating more extensively in extra-class activities.

PART II

The first part of this chapter has been devoted to suggestions relative to ways in which different faculty members and student-teachers could enrich the content of student-teaching to help student-teachers to a greater extent. The latter part deals with recommendations of a more general nature in connection with the improvement of student-teaching courses. In order to show more clearly the trends of thought of both student-teachers and faculty members, their recommendations for changes and improvements in student-teaching have been classified under separate headings.

Changes and Improvements That Were Recommended by Student-Teachers for the Enrichment of the Content of Student-Teaching Courses in Elementary Teacher-Education Curricula

There were 2,345 student-teachers who answered the concluding question for student-teachers, "What change or improvement, if any, do you consider most essential for the enrichment of the content of student-teaching courses in your state teachers college?" * To facilitate tabulation and study, these answers were classified under appropriate major headings. The per cents of student-teachers, under

* Table LXXIX in Volume II of this study, which is on file in manuscript form in Teachers College Library, Columbia University, presents in detail the following data: the college year in which the student-teaching was done; the type of organization under which it was conducted; the number of primary and intermediate student-teachers, both inexperienced and experienced, who specified each of the recommendations for the enrichment of the content of student-teaching.

different types of administrative organizations whose answers were classified under each major heading, are presented in Table L. In cases where several answers were given by the same individual, only

TABLE L

Per Cent of Student-Teachers in Different Administrative Organizations Whose Answers Were Classified under Each Major Heading Showing Changes and Improvements Recommended for the Enrichment of the Content of Student-Teaching Courses

Major Headings under Which Answers, Showing Changes and Improvements Recommended for Enrichment of Content of Student-Teaching Courses, Were Classified	Per Cent of Student-Teachers								
	1–2 Hours		½ Day		All Day		Total		Sum Total
	P	I	P	I	P	I	P	I	
A. More extensive contacts in various types of teaching situations should be provided.	20.5	28.6	19.4	27.4	19.5	24.7	20.1	28.0	24.1
B. More nearly adequate laboratory-school facilities and more effective supervision should be assured to every student-teacher throughout student-teaching courses.	21.5	13.3	14.1	9.5	13.0	9.4	18.8	11.9	15.4
C. Greater amounts of time in teachers-college curricula should be devoted to student-teaching courses.	14.5	10.7	17.9	15.0	11.7	11.8	15.3	12.0	13.6
D. More well-directed and carefully guided observation of expert teaching should be provided.	14.8	9.9	16.4	10.4	27.3	22.4	16.1	10.9	13.5
E. Individual and group conferences should be adequate in number and in length; and should be well-prepared, purposeful, and constructive.	14.3	16.0	11.7	11.8	3.9	3.5	12.8	13.9	13.3
F. The scheduling and content of college courses should be readjusted to serve more effectively in the preparation of teachers for the elementary grades.	5.2	11.2	8.6	14.7	7.8	12.9	6.4	12.4	9.4
G. More gradual and more careful induction into student-teaching should be stressed.	4.0	2.9	5.1	3.4	7.7	4.7	4.6	3.2	3.9
H. Closer integration and co-ordination between the college classes and the laboratory-schools should be promoted.	1.9	2.4	3.0	2.9	1.3	7.1	2.2	2.9	2.5
I. More credit should be offered for student-teaching courses.	1.1	1.5	1.5	1.7	5.2	2.4	1.5	1.6	1.5
J. More uniformity should be required in the grading of student-teachers.	1.3	1.5	.9	.3	....	....	1.0	1.0	1.1
K. Greater emphases should be placed on co-operative group activities and on committee work among student-teachers.	.7	.9	1.2	1.2	2.6	1.2	1.0	1.0	1.0
L. Greater opportunities for specialization in one field should be offered.	.1	1.1	.3	1.7	....	....	.2	1.2	.7

the first one was included in the distribution of per cents shown in Table L.

The results shown in this table would, no doubt, have been different if the student-teachers had been presented with a prepared list of recommendations from which to select the one most applicable to a specific situation. Since the inquiry sheets did not include any suggestions as to changes or improvements that might be offered, the recommendations reported by the student-teachers were evidently those foremost in their minds.

A. *More extensive contacts in various types of teaching situations should be provided.*

    1. Student-teaching courses should make place for more opportunity to initiate activities and to assume responsibility in different types of teaching situations.

    2. Student-teaching should be enriched by the inclusion of experiential contacts in which student-teachers assume responsibility for a variety of activities in different types of situations.

        a. Teaching children in representative groupings, such as:

           (1) A whole classroom of children.

           (2) A whole group of children representing a typical situation in the public elementary schools of the state.

           (3) Two or more groups of children in a classroom.

        b. Organizing and carrying out large activity units or units of instruction of a broad scope.

        c. Teaching several or all the subjects in a grade.

        d. Directing or taking charge of children's extra-class activities.

        e. Teaching in two or more different grades.

        f. Teaching in two or more different schools.

    3. A schoolroom atmosphere more nearly paralleling real life should be created by releasing student-teachers from much of the routine work and by permitting them greater latitude in such activities as (*a*) directing the learning activities of the children; and (*b*) managing and controlling children, and handling discipline.

B. *More nearly adequate laboratory-school facilities and more effective supervision should be assured to every student-teacher throughout student-teaching.*

    1. The numbers of student-teachers assigned to each grade and to each critic teacher should be reduced so that more effectively individualized guidance may be given each student, and so that conditions under which student-teaching is done may be made more natural and true to life.

    2. Those supervising student-teaching should strive to make their suggestions more concrete and constructive, especially with regard to child guidance and to the carrying out of units of instruction.

3. Critic teachers and other supervisors of student-teaching should issue to students definite information concerning the work expected of them: observers and participants should be furnished guides and standards in connection with their work, while those engaged in responsible teaching should be given syllabi or outlines of the subject-matter to be covered by the children during any given time.

C. *Greater amounts of time in teachers-college curricula should be devoted to student-teaching courses.*

1. The following amounts of time were variously suggested as a minimum of student-teaching work essential to enable student-teachers to develop clear conceptions of teaching as a whole, to acquire necessary teaching skills, and to establish wholesome professional attitudes:
   a. Whole day for a semester.
   b. Half day for a semester.
   c. Two or more hours a day for a year.
   d. More than one hour a day for a year.
   e. Whole day during the latter part of senior student-teaching.
2. Student-teachers should be allowed to remain longer with each group of children, in order that better relations may be established between the student-teachers and the children.
3. The amount of time devoted by teacher-education curricula to theory and methods courses should be reduced, and the time allotment for actual teaching correspondingly increased.

D. *More well-directed and carefully guided observation of expert teaching should be provided.*

1. There should be ample opportunity to observe, under competent guidance, a representative cross-section of teaching situations. Such a program would include observation of:
   a. Critic teachers at work with children during regular student-teaching courses.
   b. Expert teaching in all the grades and in different teaching situations.
   c. Units of work in various grades.
   d. Various types of work in different public schools.
2. Carefully directed observation in connection with subject-matter and professional courses should precede and serve as foundational preparation for responsible teaching.
3. A skillfully supervised course in observation should be afforded all students, upon the completion of responsible teaching in the senior year.

E. *Individual and group conferences should be adequate in number and in length; and should be well-prepared, purposeful, and constructive.*

1. More opportunity should be provided for individual conferences with faculty members; greater time and effort should be spent in preparing for these individual conferences, thus making it possible for the student-teachers to receive the personal commendations, constructive

criticisms, helpful suggestions, and definite aids which are so necessary if progress is to continue without interruption.

2. The number of general conferences for all the student-teachers should be reduced to a minimum; and the helpfulness of those that are retained should be enhanced by devoting them to more purposeful work of immediate value to student-teachers.

3. Individual conferences should be assigned a definite time and place, and be made an integral part of student-teaching.

F. *The scheduling and content of college courses should be readjusted to serve more effectively in the preparation of teachers for the elementary grades.*

1. More thorough command and sounder mastery of subject-matter is essential; entrance upon senior student-teaching courses should be postponed until the student-teachers have obtained that command of subject-matter which will free them from the difficulties arising out of inadequate subject-matter preparation.

2. Professional courses that precede student-teaching in point of time should be made more concrete and helpful.

3. Technique courses, if required, should be offered simultaneously with student-teaching.

G. *More gradual and more careful induction into student-teaching should be stressed.*

1. The sequence of induction into the student-teaching activities should be more carefully planned in order that student-teachers may continuously develop clearer conceptions of teaching problems.

2. Gradually increased responsibilities should be provided throughout student-teaching in order that there may be continuous growth in the ability to assume the work of a teacher.

H. *Closer integration and co-ordination between the college classes and the laboratory schools should be promoted.*

1. Greater inter-relation between the college courses and the laboratory-school work would help to bring about more rapid progress in the growth of the student-teachers.

2. The college instructors should take more interest in the work of the student-teachers in the laboratory schools.

I. *More credit should be offered for student-teaching courses.*

1. A greater number of term-hours or semester-hours of credit should be allowed for student-teaching courses in elementary teacher-education curricula.

2. In proportion to the vast amount of work required in student-teaching courses, more college credit should be afforded.

J. *More uniformity should be required in the grading of student-teachers.*

1. Certain standards and criteria should be set up by which to grade student-teachers at the close of each student-teaching course.

2. The requirements set up for the attainment of high marks in student-teaching should be more nearly uniform throughout the laboratory schools—campus and co-operative schools.

K. *Greater emphasis should be placed on co-operative group activities and on committee work among student-teachers.*

1. Provisions should be made for all the student-teachers to work co-operatively in various types of group undertakings, such as organizing the school life around large centers of interest.
2. More experience should be obtained in connection with various types of committee work, such as entertainment, assembly, publicity, and curriculum committees.

L. *Greater opportunities for specialization in one field should be offered.*

1. Provisions should be made for specialization in such subjects as music, physical education, and art for the elementary grades.
2. More specialized work in connection with child guidance should be offered.

CHANGES AND IMPROVEMENTS THAT WERE RECOMMENDED BY LABORA-
TORY-SCHOOL FACULTY MEMBERS FOR THE ENRICHMENT OF THE
CONTENT OF STUDENT-TEACHING IN ELEMENTARY TEACHER-
EDUCATION CURRICULA

The following question was submitted to and answered by 450 laboratory-school faculty members, "What changes and improvements, if any, do you consider most essential for the enrichment of the content of student-teaching in the elementary teacher-education curricula in your teachers college?" In an effort to reduce to some semblance of working order the host of individual recommendations offered by these faculty members for changes and improvements in student-teaching courses, procedures similar to those used elsewhere in this study were utilized. Recognizable trends of thought were organized into main headings under which were placed in some detail the explanatory and clarifying suggestions. Hence, the outline given below presents in much reduced form but with no loss of value the recommendations and suggestions which were offered for increasing the utility of elementary teacher-education. Both main headings and sub-units have been arranged according to the frequency with which they appeared among the suggestions made by critic teachers, supervisors of student-teachers, directors of training, and teachers college administrators.

A. *The elementary teacher-education curricula should be lengthened, expanded, and enriched to prepare prospective teachers more adequately for teaching.*

1. Cultural, scholastic, and professional backgrounds should be adequate in quantity and quality before students enter upon major student-teaching courses.

        a. Richer cultural and sounder scholastic backgrounds should be built up.

        b. Wider outlook and broader general education should be stressed.

        c. More thorough command of content subject-matter and other materials of instruction to be used in the elementary schools should be required; subject-matter instructors should assume more responsibility for the student-teacher's working knowledge of subject-matter.

        d. More nearly adequate professionalization in subject-matter is desirable; special emphasis should be placed upon professionalization of subject-matter during the latter half of the elementary teacher-education curricula.

        e. Professional courses should be more practical and should strive for higher levels of attainment.

    2. The elementary teacher-education curricula should be extended beyond the two-year and three-year programs; four years should constitute a minimum preparation for elementary teachers.

    3. Some system of evaluating the adequacy of prospective teachers' background preparation should be devised so as to minimize later failures.

B. *Greater amounts of time should be provided in elementary teacher-education curricula for the various phases of student-teaching.*

    1. Sufficient length of time should be provided to insure initial competency in actual teaching situations and for the acquisition of skill needed by beginning teachers in the field.

    2. Major student-teaching courses should be scheduled for longer periods daily and for a greater total number of weeks. The following set-ups were suggested:

        a. Whole day for one semester.

        b. Half day for one year.

        c. Half day for twenty-four weeks or two terms.

        d. Half day for one semester.

        e. Whole day for twelve weeks.

        f. One hour a day during the first semester; two hours a day during the second semester.

        g. One hour a day for a year. (Schools from which this suggestion emanated offered less than 120 hours of work in student-teaching.)

    3. More time should be apportioned to well-directed observation and to competently supervised participation in teaching and learning situations.

        a. More time—prior to, during, and subsequent to major student-teaching—should be provided for observation of expert demonstration teaching in the campus schools and of master teachers in the field.

        b. Participation in teaching activities should parallel observation in point of time and difficulty.

C. *More nearly adequate laboratory-school facilities, and sufficient numbers of competent critic teachers and supervisors of student-teaching, should be provided.*

1. The laboratory-school facilities in each teachers college should be expanded sufficiently to allow all prospective teachers adequate opportunities for observation, participation, and teaching.
   a. The campus laboratory schools should be used chiefly for demonstration, observation, participation, and experimental purposes.
   b. Responsible student-teaching should be done in schools separate from those used for observation and participation so that sufficient practice facilities may be assured.
2. Fewer student-teachers should be assigned to each critic teacher and to each room in the campus laboratory schools, in order to make possible more natural teaching situations and more effective guidance.
3. More competent supervision of student-teachers is essential; critic teachers, in both the campus laboratory schools and the co-operative urban and rural schools, should be more adequately prepared for their guidance work and supervisory responsibilities in connection with student-teaching.
   a. Critic teachers should be thoroughly conversant with the principles and purposes of the student-teaching programs.
   b. Critic teachers should consistently demonstrate and emphasize the most effective modern methods of instruction.
   c. Principles underlying progressive education should be applied in all of the critic teacher's guidance and supervisory activities.

D. *Broader views of teaching, more varied contacts with educational problems, and richer experiences in teaching and learning situations should be afforded.*

1. Student-teachers should be helped to see teaching as a whole and to obtain wider views of whole situations—instructional, administrative, routine, and extra-class.
2. Provision should be made for broad contacts—through observation, participation, and teaching—in a variety of situations, such as:
   a. Contacts with all the elementary grades.
   b. Experiences in a variety of subjects, in several grades, in a diversity of teaching situations, and under the direction of more than one critic teacher.
   c. Opportunity to see growth and progress in children at various age levels
   d. Contacts with a variety of educational problems.
3. Greater opportunities should be afforded the student-teachers for the development of initiative and for the assumption of responsibility in teaching situations.
   a. Student-teachers should be required to assume more responsibilities in all phases of the elementary teacher's work.
   b. Student-teachers should assume responsibility for handling such pupil groupings as:

(1) A whole classroom.

(2) Large groups of pupils that would represent the typical situation in the field.

(3) Two or more groups of pupils in a classroom.

(4) Two sections at one time.

E. *A more helpful and constructive conference program should be adopted.*

1. Greater provision should be made for individual and group conferences; more time should be spent in planning and preparing for these conferences, as unprepared conferences require an amount of the student-teacher's time that is entirely disproportional to the value derived.

2. More time should be devoted to purposeful and constructive individual conferences between student-teachers and critic teachers or supervisors of student-teaching.

F. *Closer integration and co-ordination between college classes and laboratory schools should be promoted.*

1. Greater unity of purpose and more mutual co-operation among all the faculty members in the elementary teacher-education curricula should be encouraged.

2. The instructors in subject-matter and professional courses should be enabled to share and to appreciate to a greater degree the viewpoint of the laboratory schools.

3. Both college and laboratory-school staff members should collaborate in the organization of professionalized subject-matter and educational courses, in order that a program of maximum helpfulness may be evolved.

G. *More gradual, more continuous, and more careful induction into all phases of the elementary teacher's work should be provided.*

1. Responsibility in teaching should be gradually and continuously increased; the second term of student-teaching should be done on a more advanced level than that of the first term.

2. More continuity and integration, together with more consecutive experiences in teaching, should be emphasized.

3. More economical induction into actual teaching could be secured by eliminating routine activities which are of little educational value to the student-teachers.

H. *Individual differences of student-teachers should be dealt with more effectively.*

1. More effective guidance programs should be provided.

   a. Individualized guidance should be stressed to a greater extent; more time should be devoted to discovering and meeting each student-teacher's interests, problems, difficulties, and needs.

   b. More effective techniques for handling individual differences of student-teachers should be evolved.

c. Wisdom and tact should be exercised in guiding students in curriculum selection, so that they may be placed in the work for which they are best adapted by natural endowment and preparation and in those courses that will allow them to develop to the fullest extent.

2. The number of weeks of responsible teaching required should be adjusted to the rate and the level of each student-teacher's progress; and prospective teachers should be required to continue to teach under guidance until they have developed acceptable teaching skill, regardless of the time consumed and with no additional credit.

I. *Higher standards of achievement should be required of student-teachers.*

J. *Greater emphasis should be placed upon development of desirable teaching personality and upon the establishment of wholesome professional attitudes; student-teachers should be led to build up sound and workable philosophies of education.*

K. *More careful and more judicious selection of students for the elementary teaching field should be made.*

SUMMARY AND CONCLUSIONS

This chapter has presented the principal recommendations offered by student-teachers and laboratory-school staff members as to how the content of student-teaching could be enriched to a greater extent through the efforts of members of the various departments in the teacher-preparing institutions.

1. The principal ideas which seem to dominate throughout the major part of the recommendations for enriching the content of student-teaching courses are: (1) more nearly adequate pre-teaching preparation, to be obtained through such means as college courses of a broad cultural nature, appropriate and thorough subject-matter courses, valuable and applicable professional courses, and a great variety of cultural contacts and professional experiences; (2) more nearly adequate professional contacts and teaching experiences in preparation for actual service in the elementary field, to be obtained through well-organized and competently supervised student-teaching courses—skillfully directed observation and teaching courses which provide a representative cross section of all phases of the elementary teacher's work and responsibilities; and (3) closer co-ordination and integration between the laboratory-school and the college departments in teacher-preparing institutions.

a. The reports from both student-teachers and laboratory-school faculty members implied that the entrance upon major student-teaching courses should be postponed until adequate foundations had been laid in cultural and subject-matter backgrounds and in professional equipment. It was maintained that more nearly adequate opportunities should be provided to make possible the acquisition of broad cultural backgrounds, thorough working knowledge of materials of instruction, intelligent understanding of child development, and appropriate professional and technical equipments; and that more emphasis should be placed upon the development of well-integrated personalities.

b. In the provision for more nearly adequate professional contacts and pre-service teaching experiences, the recommendations for improvement dealt largely with the administration and supervision of student-teaching courses. The following were specified most frequently:

(1) Greater amounts of time in the elementary teacher-education curricula should be allotted to well-organized and efficiently supervised student-teaching courses. More time should especially be apportioned to (1) actual teaching of children and assumption of responsibility in various types of teaching situations; and (2) well-directed observation of children and of expert teaching.

(2) More extensive contacts with various types of educational problems and richer experiences in connection with the major teaching activities should be required.

(3) Adequate laboratory-school facilities should be provided to prepare prospective teachers effectively for their work in the public elementary schools of the state.

(4) Higher order of supervision and more competent guidance of student-teachers should be afforded.

(5) More constructive conference programs—more purposeful individual conferences and more economical arrangement of work for group conferences—should be adopted.

(6) Individual differences and needs of the student-teachers should be dealt with more effectively.

(7) More gradual, more continuous, and more careful induction of student-teachers into all phases of the elementary teacher's work, duties, and responsibilities should be provided and realized.

c. It was recommended that the work in the laboratory school should be an integral part of the elementary teacher-education curricula; that there should be closer integration and more mutual co-operation among the various departments in the teacher-preparing institutions; and that all the faculty members connected with the preparation of elementary teachers should have some share and responsibility in carrying forward the work of student-teaching.

2. Some of the significant suggestions that were made for the enrichment of the content of student-teaching might serve as useful guides to the various members of the supervisory, instructional, and administrative staffs in their efforts to function more efficiently and to render to prospective teachers more effective service.

3. Many of the student-teachers proposed changes that would greatly improve the elementary teacher-preparing programs within their respective institutions. An analysis of the recommendations offered by the student-teachers revealed a direct relationship between the number of suggestions for improving conditions in student-teaching and the types of organization under which the student-teaching was conducted. Student-teachers whose major work in responsible teaching was obtained in units of whole days in the four-year curricula recommended the fewest revisions, while those who taught for only one hour a day in the two-year programs suggested the most numerous and varied changes. The findings of this study must lead to the assumption that major student-teaching courses conducted on the whole-day plan are more completely adapted to the needs of the student-teachers than is any one of the types of organization which provide only a portion of a day for responsible student-teaching; and that the four-year curricula more nearly meet the needs of student-teachers than do any programs offering a shorter period of preparation.

CHAPTER SEVEN

SUGGESTIONS AND RECOMMENDATIONS PROPOSED FOR ENRICH-
ING THE CONTENT OF STUDENT-TEACHING COURSES
IN STATE TEACHERS COLLEGES

THE principal functions of this study have been to analyze experiences and contacts of student-teachers; to determine some of the representative activities and essential problems which should be included in the content of student-teaching; and to make recommendations for enriching the content of student-teaching in elementary teacher-education. The dependence of the quality and quantity of the content upon a large number of influencing factors, however, made imperative an investigation of some of these factors.

The findings of this survey have been thoroughly studied and critically assimilated over an extended period of time so that the suggestions offered are the product of much careful deliberation and thought. The recommendations set forth in this concluding chapter have been formulated on the following assumptions: (1) that competently supervised student-teaching is essential in the preparation of teachers for the elementary grades; (2) that certain objectives, principles, and practices are fundamental in the conduct of sound student-teaching; and (3) that the application of the objectives and the principles set forth will largely determine the content of student-teaching. The general substance of these recommendations has been derived through the following media: personal visits to fifty-seven state teachers colleges located in twenty-seven states; interviews with leading educators throughout the United States; inquiry sheets filled out by student-teachers and faculty members in state teachers colleges; evaluation of student-teaching activities by laboratory-school staff members; professional literature; first-hand observations; and actual experience in the elementary teacher-education field. An attempt has subsequently been made to set up worthy objectives and purposes, to propound sound principles underlying student-teaching, and to suggest theories for applying principles.

Objectives and Purposes of Student-Teaching

Objectives and purposes of student-teaching recommended as being fundamentally important in the preparation of teachers for the elementary grades are:

I. OBJECTIVES OF STUDENT-TEACHING RELATIVE TO THE ORGANIZATION AND ADMINISTRATION OF TEACHER-EDUCATION IN STATE TEACHERS COLLEGES

    A. To serve as the testing point for all other work in the teacher-education curricula, and to determine the students' preparation and readiness to do successful teaching in the field.

    B. To serve as the laboratory for determining experimentally the types of subject-matter preparation that are most conducive to effective and successful teaching in the modern elementary school.

    C. To provide opportunities for prospective teachers to synthesize, rationalize, and utilize the other aspects of their professional preparation in actual teaching situations; and to furnish students with concrete illustrations of the principles of teaching, learning, and administration which are essential requisites to teaching.

II. OBJECTIVES RELATIVE TO THE LABORATORY-SCHOOL FACILITIES AND TO THE ADMINISTRATION, ORGANIZATION, AND SUPERVISION OF STUDENT-TEACHING COURSES

    A. To give prospective teachers a broad vision of teaching as a whole, and an intelligent understanding of the responsibilities of teachers in the elementary grades.

    B. To bring student-teachers into contact with (1) children at various stages of development and under different types of circumstances; (2) effective progressive educational ideas and theories; (3) the best types of school buildings and equipment; and (4) types of actual school situations which they are likely to meet in the field.

    C. To provide opportunities for students to observe, participate in, and do responsible teaching under expert supervision and constructive guidance.

    D. To make provision for individual differences in the abilities, problems, needs, talents, and special interests of prospective teachers.

    E. To provide opportunities for effective integration of observation, participation, and teaching.

    F. To furnish adequate teaching experience, under expert supervision, to insure initial competency on the part of prospective teachers.

III. OBJECTIVES RELATIVE TO THE ACTIVITIES THAT HELP TO MAKE UP THE CONTENT OF STUDENT-TEACHING

    A. To induct student-teachers by gradual, continuous, and economical processes into the art of teaching.

    B. To give prospective teachers increasingly wider and richer contacts with all the important educative activities of elementary teachers; to create constantly keener interest in the work, problems, and responsibilities of teachers in the modern elementary schools.

1. To guide student-teachers in acquiring intelligent understanding of major objectives and basic principles underlying the modern elementary school.

2. To give student-teachers continuously broader perspective of the elementary school curriculum.

3. To help student-teachers acquire adequate working knowledge of materials of instruction.

   a. To help student-teachers develop increasingly greater skill in planning, selecting, evaluating, organizing, adapting, and applying appropriate materials of instruction.

   b. To show student-teachers ways in which to integrate the elementary school subjects into a comprehensive and well-rounded school program.

4. To lead student-teachers to obtain increasingly broader understanding of the factors which produce individual differences; to train them to cope successfully with both the similarities and the wide range of individual differences of children in a group.

5. To increase progressively the student-teachers' understanding of and skill in applying the best modern methods of instruction.

   a. To lead student-teachers to acquire adequate working knowledge of effective progressive methods for directing the learning activities of children.

   b. To give student-teachers opportunity to study and to experiment with different types of teaching techniques and educational procedures.

   c. To help student-teachers to develop continuously greater skill in applying effective methods of teaching children.

   d. To lead student-teachers to assume increasingly greater responsibilities for the development and progress of both individuals and groups of children.

   e. To train student-teachers to evaluate and judge teaching and learning activities in light of modern educational principles.

6. To develop in student-teachers increasingly greater ability to guide children in establishing desirable habits, traits, interests, attitudes, appreciations, and ideals.

7. To aid student-teachers in establishing proper rapport in child guidance; to give them constantly wider experiences in managing and controlling children in various types of teaching and learning situations.

   a. To guide student-teachers in establishing co-operative relations with the children; to direct them in securing and maintaining desirable teacher-pupil rapport.

   b. To help student-teachers to build up and maintain high standards of conduct among the children in a group.

   c. To teach student-teachers to deal effectively with discipline and behavior problems of children.

8. To familiarize student-teachers with the routine and mechanics

of the classroom; to aid them in acquiring clear understanding of valid principles underlying classroom management.

9. To provide increasingly richer opportunities for student-teachers to observe, participate in, and direct children's extra-class activities.

10. To give student-teachers experience in establishing desirable relations with the staff-personnel of an elementary school.

   a. To show student-teachers ways in which they might relate themselves to the school as a whole.

   b. To develop in prospective teachers a willingness to co-operate in all the activities of the school.

11. To provide opportunities for student-teachers to have contacts with the administration and routine of the whole school.

12. To give student-teachers experience in participating in the community life of which the school is a part.

C. To lead prospective teachers to acquire wider understanding, richer knowledge, and deeper appreciation of the essential factors of the elementary teacher's personal and professional equipment.

1. To help student-teachers to develop well-integrated personalities; to encourage them to be human, understanding, and skillful leaders of children.

2. To lead student-teachers to build up habits and skills with enough perfection so that they can further develop them in the field.

3. To equip student-teachers with the professional knowledge and understanding necessary for successful teaching in the elementary grades; to help student-teachers in each of the following:

   a. To develop a desire for continuous professional growth and personal development.

   b. To develop constructive professional interests.

   c. To develop a spirit of inquiry and investigation toward problems in teaching.

   d. To build up a high order of professional ethics.

   e. To establish worthy ideals and high standards in teaching.

   f. To establish wholesome professional attitudes.

   g. To formulate and to build up a sound philosophy of education.

If student-teaching is to function effectively in the preparation of elementary teachers, conditions must be made such that desired objectives can be realized. How best can these objectives and purposes be carried into effect and accomplished? The solution of this question requires intelligent understanding of teacher-education problems in general, thorough knowledge of existing conditions within any particular teacher-preparing institution, resourceful planning of programs to meet the individual needs of both the prospective teachers and the institution, and judicious execution of these plans. It calls for sound principles underlying student-teaching, and needs practical methods for working out the application of these principles.

PRINCIPLES UNDERLYING SOUND STUDENT-TEACHING IN ELEMENTARY TEACHER-EDUCATION CURRICULA

Numerous principles have recently been advocated as fundamental in the conduct of student-teaching. Some have been found practical, many are still in the experimental stages, and others have never been practically applied. The following underlying principles of sound student-teaching, which have been promulgated by leading educators in the field of teacher-education, form the basis for the recommendations and suggestions offered in this study:

I. PRINCIPLES RELATIVE TO THE ORGANIZATION AND ADMINISTRATION OF TEACHER-EDUCATION IN STATE TEACHERS COLLEGES

    A. The elementary teacher-education curricula should be sufficiently lengthened, expanded, and enriched to equip teachers to cope successfully with the problems incident to the modern elementary school.

    B. A distinctive type of preparation in subject-matter is essential to prospective teachers for the elementary grades.

    C. The work of the laboratory schools and the college departments should be carefully integrated and economically co-ordinated in order to secure the richest and broadest content of student-teaching.

II. PRINCIPLES RELATIVE TO THE LABORATORY-SCHOOL FACILITIES AND TO THE ADMINISTRATION, ORGANIZATION, AND SUPERVISION OF STUDENT-TEACHING

    A. Laboratory-school facilities must be provided adequate to prepare prospective teachers effectively for work in the public schools.

    B. The contacts of students with educational problems should be long and continuous, with sufficient amounts of time apportioned to the various phases of student-teaching.

    C. All phases of student-teaching—observation, participation, conferences, and teaching—should be carefully integrated.

    D. Individual interests, traits, aptitudes, capacities, and needs of the student-teachers should serve as criteria for the differentiation in student-teaching.

    E. Adequate guidance and competent supervision are essential to sound student-teaching.

III. PRINCIPLES RELATIVE TO THE ACTIVITIES THAT HELP TO MAKE UP THE CONTENT OF STUDENT-TEACHING

    A. Student-teachers should be inducted by gradual, continuous, and economical processes into the art of teaching.

    B. Student-teaching courses should give student-teachers contacts with all the important educational activities of elementary teachers.

Application of Principles Underlying the Content of Student-Teaching

The recommendations suggested in this study are based on the assumption that all of these principles must operate co-operatively and simultaneously in a successful student-teaching program. The quality, type, and scope of the content of student-teaching are determined by the application of all these principles.

I. Principles Relative to the Organization and Administration of Teacher-Education in State Teachers Colleges

A. *The elementary teacher-education curricula should be sufficiently lengthened, expanded, and enriched to equip teachers to cope successfully with the problems incident to the modern elementary school.*

Recent studies show that the constantly increasing responsibilities placed upon the modern elementary schools have produced a correspondingly growing demand for broadly cultured, well-informed, and professionally educated teachers. The elementary schools of today need teachers who have cultural background preparation and professional equipment far beyond the amount and level required for the actual teaching in the grades, and who are prepared to take their places as useful citizens in society.

The tendency today is to lengthen elementary teacher-education curricula. Many teachers colleges are increasing the number of courses of broad cultural and social values. The leading teacher-preparing institutions are attempting to make more nearly adequate provision for cultural background, well-rounded general education, the essential tools of learning, professionalization, techincal skills, and a variety of social and physical activities.

Although the emphasis is toward broader and more extensive courses in the major fields of knowledge, the reports from student-teachers and laboratory-school faculty members indicated that *limited cultural backgrounds and inadequate working knowledge of subject-matter and of modern methods of instruction* were the chief underlying causes of many of the student-teachers' difficulties. In many schools the student-teachers had devoted a large proportion of the student-teaching time to the acquisition of instructional materials—including the fine and practical arts as well as the regular academic subjects—that should have been mastered in subject-matter and professional courses. In some teachers colleges many of the student-teachers had taken courses that were very restricted in outlook and narrow in scope; that were in no way related to the problems of modern life or to the current social trends; that failed to develop proper perspective and broad understanding of materials; and that were lacking in the principles of synthesis and integration. In teachers colleges where elementary teachers were trained in two-year and three-year curricula, the opportunities for obtaining the rich cultural backgrounds that progressive teachers need were limited; for the vast amount of subject-matter and the great quantity of professional materials now available for use in the elementary grades are too great to be comprehended or mastered in two or three years.

The following recommendations, which give a synopsis of those proffered by leaders in the elementary teacher-education field, are based on the assumptions that the real value to be derived from student-teaching is in direct ratio to the quantity and quality of the content of student-teaching; and that the depth and the richness of the content are restricted in direct ratio to the quantity and quality of the cultural background preparation, the professional equipment, and the personal development of both student-teachers and faculty members:

1. Prospective elementary teachers should be afforded opportunities to cultivate breadth of interests in many types of human activities, to obtain broad general background in the major fields of organized knowledge, and to secure rich social experiences. The elementary teacher-education curricula should provide opportunities for:

a. Liberal cultural and well-rounded general education that will help prospective teachers to:

(1) Acquire broad historical background and gain intelligent understanding of developments in culture, religion, politics, industry, science, education, and the other fields of activity which comprise our present social structure.

(2) Interpret the social heritage; understand the evolution of society and the life implications of race experiences.

(3) Understand logical causal relationships; see relationships between forces.

(4) Obtain broad vision and open-minded understanding of contemporary problems; gain intelligent and cosmopolitan concepts of affairs.

(5) Become constructively critical of the current status of society, of contemporary modes of living, and of present-day problems and issues.

(6) Develop insight into both individual and social behavior.

(7) Recognize both background and instructional functions of knowledge.

(8) Become active participants in the major fields of human activities.

(9) Obtain adequate working knowledge of social, civic, and professional activities of the types in which they will be expected to participate in a community.

(10) Cultivate discrimination, suspended judgment, and tolerance.

(11) Develop sensitiveness, appreciation, and enjoyment of things of intellectual, social, and aesthetic values.

(12) Develop broadened interests, intelligent attitudes, intellectual curiosity, and ability to think clearly on vital problems.

b. Thorough command of the essential subject-matter and adequate working knowledge of instructional materials to be taught in the elementary grades.

2. In addition to rich cultural background and well-rounded general education, elementary teacher-education curricula should provide adequate professional preparation.

a. A general overview of elementary-school education and broad technical information, with emphasis upon the basic principles and major objectives in modern education, should first be obtained. Such a professional program should be set up as will afford opportunity for prospective elementary teachers to:

(1) Acquire wide scope of professional information.

(2) Secure intelligent understanding of the educative process; obtain broad conception of educational theories; and acquire adequate technical equipment.

(3) Obtain comprehensive knowledge of child development and growth at various age levels.

(4) Develop sympathetic understanding of individual differences and similarities of children.

(5) Gain experiences in making adjustments to abilities, interests, and needs of children at various age levels in the elementary grades.

(6) Develop ability to analyze and to criticize constructively present practices and new proposals in school organization, child guidance, and curriculum construction.

(7) Gain understanding of desirable standards of accomplishment.

(8) Obtain training in scientific inquiry.

(9) Cultivate genuine interest in and appreciation of fundamental problems of teaching.

(10) Study ways in which to integrate education with changing social life.

(11) Study ways in which to make education serve as a potent instrument in effecting the elevation of individual and social living to a higher plane.

(12) Build up a sound working philosophy of education.

b. A more specialized working knowledge of education suitable to a definite elementary school level should then be acquired.

c. Sufficient technical skill in teaching to insure initial competency in the field should finally be attained.

The professional preparation should be of such a nature as to equip prospective teachers with the needed professional knowledge, insights, techniques, aptitudes, and skills; and to help them to build up wholesome attitudes and a sound working philosophy of education. In order that the professional preparation may take place on a high level of achievement, the general educational and cultural backgrounds of prospective teachers should be expanded and enriched far beyond that possible in two-year and three-year curricula. The period of preparation should, therefore, be lengthened and intensified so that the teachers will be more fully prepared to meet successfully the problems confronting the elementary school.

3. Provision should also be made for the development of prospective teachers as individuals. Greater attention should be given to the development of latent talents, potential aptitudes, and con-

comitant learnings of students in teachers colleges in order to help each one become a well-integrated personality. Prospective teachers should obtain rich experiences of social and aesthetic values, as well as those of intellectual and professional character. Through careful integration of all their activities and contacts, students should be led to develop desirable interests, attitudes, appreciations, and ideals, as well as knowledge and skills.

B. *A distinctive type of preparation in subject-matter is essential to prospective teachers for the elementary grades.*

It has been evident throughout this study that a large proportion of student-teachers lacked sound working knowledge of a wide scope of instructional and cultural materials essential to successful teaching in the modern elementary school. Teaching in the elementary field usually requires a less highly specialized knowledge in any one particular academic subject and a more general background preparation in a variety of subjects than does teaching in the secondary schools.

On the assumption that elementary teachers require a broad general education, and that adequate mastery of the right type of subject-matter and intelligent understanding of its use are essential to successful teaching, the following recommendations—embracing those advocated by leaders in teacher-education—are made:

1. In the elementary field the amount and nature of specialization should be determined by numerous factors, such as individual differences of the students, the purpose of the teacher-preparing institution, the particular teacher-education curriculum, and the objectives and requirements of the schools in which the students will later be placed as teachers.

2. Prospective teachers should be adequately prepared to teach on the elementary school level a wide range of subjects, such as the language arts—reading, language or English, spelling, and writing; the social studies or the social sciences—geography, history, and citizenship; arithmetic and number work; elementary science; fine and practical arts—music, art, and industrial arts; health and physical education.

3. Through a well-integrated and highly co-ordinated curriculum which provides for broad general education as well as the essential subject-matter, prospective teachers should obtain wealth of back-

ground information for the enrichment of instruction in the various elementary school subjects.

a. A few well-organized and efficiently taught survey courses, given in sequential order, would help prospective teachers to obtain a comprehensive overview and a representative cross-section of the most essential and usuable fields of human knowledge.

b. In addition to scholarly command of the essential subject-matter to be taught in the elementary grades, each elementary teacher-education curriculum should equip its prospective teachers with a comprehensive scope of subject-matter of a cultural nature, broad fund of general information, wealth of reference and supplementary materials, and wide informational resources.

c. Modern education further requires versatility and adaptability in the use of information and materials.

4. Professionalization of subject-matter should constitute an integral part of the latter half of four-year and five-year elementary teacher-education curricula.

a. Elementary teachers should acquire adequate working knowledge of subject-matter in their own fields and should be sufficiently acquainted with related instructional materials to enable them to plan and carry out comprehensive units of instruction; to guide effectively the learning activities of children; and to participate intelligently in all the other educational work of teachers.

b. Certain phases of subject-matter should be offered from the standpoint of both content and methods of instruction.

c. Adequate professionalization should especially be afforded in the language arts, the natural and the social sciences, the fine arts, and physical education.

The richness of the content of student-teaching is in a large measure influenced by the scope of the general education and the thoroughness of the subject-matter and professional backgrounds that the students have obtained. Professionalized courses should be made vital, helpful, purposeful, practical, and applicable to teachers in the elementary grades; and should be of such a nature that they will continuously open up fields of knowledge essential to background preparation for advanced professional training.

C. *The work of the laboratory schools and the college departments should be carefully integrated and economically co-ordinated in order to secure the richest and broadest content of student-teaching.*

The great aim of elementary teacher-education curricula in state teachers colleges should be to turn out efficient teachers, who can successfully cope with the problems of the modern elementary school. The achievement of this highly important goal should be a co-operative undertaking of all concerned.

This study revealed a great lack of integration in the functions of the subject-matter, professional, and laboratory-school departments. In some teachers colleges there was a lack of integration between different departments—subject-matter and theory, subject-matter and student-teaching, and theory and student-teaching—and a further lack of co-ordination among the different courses within each department. The reports indicated that student-teachers frequently entered student-teaching courses inadequately prepared for teaching because they had not been trained to integrate the knowledge acquired in different subject-matter courses, nor to relate their technical equipment to appropriate subject-matter. The lack of close integration among the various college departments also explains the difficulties that many beginning student-teachers encountered in unifying and interrelating subject-matter; in simultaneously applying theory and materials of instruction; and in applying theory to actual practice. In many schools the student-teaching was done almost entirely under the direction of the laboratory-school staff members, whereas instructors in subject-matter and professional courses assumed practically no responsibility for this important phase of the elementary teacher's preparation.

In view of the apparent need for better functioning between the laboratory schools and the other college departments, the following recommendations—digested from those proffered by faculty members of teachers colleges and other leaders in elementary teacher-education—are made for the promotion of closer integration, co-ordination, and unity:

1. There should be unity of purpose and continuous whole-hearted co-operation among all the faculty members in elementary teacher-education curricula.

    a. Each department in the teacher-preparing institution should be closely articulated and economically co-ordinated with all other departments, and should be effectively related to the whole.

b. A central administrative control of all the college courses and of the work in the laboratory schools is essential. One person —the president of the teachers college, the director of instruction, the director of the laboratory schools, or some other highly trained specialist in co-ordination—should act as a co-ordinating director of the whole teacher-preparing institution.

c. Definite provision should be made for the promotion of mutual understanding of what is being done in all the various departments of the teachers college. There should be free and constant interchange of ideas and activities. Continuous co-ordination and closer harmony between the laboratory schools and the college departments could be promoted by means of constructive observations, frequent intervisitations, and conferences in which all work jointly for a common end. Conferences between supervisory and instructional staff members should be a part of the regular program.

2. The work in the laboratory schools should be an integral part of elementary teacher-education curricula, and should promote the professional development of both students and faculty members. The content of student-teaching courses should be so enriched, through the collaboration of all the faculty members, as to furnish a sound basis for the integration of all the other courses.

a. The laboratory-school curriculum should be a joint product of the laboratory-school and college departments.

b. In elementary teacher-education curricula, the instructors in subject-matter courses should so organize and direct their work as to help prospective teachers gain broad cultural knowledge and secure information that will significantly contribute to the enrichment of teaching in the elementary grades. A clear conception and an appreciation of the great need for wide variety of cultural activities and broad scope of instructional materials, essential to effective teaching in the modern elementary school, should be stimulated by subject-matter courses and evolved through adequate use of the laboratory schools for observation.

c. Instructors in professionalized subject-matter courses should awaken in their students an awareness of the principal teaching problems that are common to a group of subjects, as well as of those that are characteristic of a specific subject. They should help prospective teachers gain knowledge of how to integrate and utilize numerous instructional materials, and how to adapt and interrelate different kinds of subject-matter and educative activities. These instructors should frequently participate in demonstration teaching and should occasionally teach children in the laboratory schools for the purposes of illustrating current practices and of definitely exemplifying before their college groups certain educational principles or phases of work.

d. Instructors in professional and educational courses should, at every opportunity, make it a point to observe and to teach groups of children. They should make frequent visits to the laboratory schools and to public schools in the field for the purpose of making those close contacts with children in teaching and learning situations that will promote the effectiveness of their own instruction in preparing prospective teachers to cope with the problems of the modern elementary school, and that will be of material assistance in the continuous reconstruction of the elementary curriculum.

e. All courses in education should have laboratory phases, including various forms of participation. Laboratory courses on the undergraduate level in teachers colleges should be taught by instructors who are specially prepared for the work, and who are in close and intimate contact with children in teaching and learning situations. This applies particularly to such courses as child guidance, child and curriculum, principles and techniques of teaching, primary methods courses, and directed observation and participation. Orientation courses in education should be taught by directors of training or by other persons who have a thorough understanding of the laboratory-school situation as a whole and who can give the students an intelligent perspective of the teaching profession in its various aspects.

f. The work of critic teachers and supervisors of student-teaching should be so organized as to constitute an active force in bringing about harmony among the various departments.

(1) Demonstration teaching for college classes is an essential part of the critic teachers' work. Demonstration lessons should be planned co-operatively by the critic teachers and the observing instructors, so that they might agree upon points of technique and methods of organizing materials. Critic teachers should be informed in advance as to what points the observation group wishes to study, and should be given opportunity to participate in the discussions which follow the observations. These follow-up class discussions should, when necessary, be preceded by private conferences between the critic teachers and the college instructors for the purpose of clearing up difficulties and conflicting points of view.

(2) The most capable and best qualified critic teachers and supervisors of student-teaching in the campus laboratory schools should, when possible, be relieved of part of the laboratory-school load and assigned to teach professional courses. It was recommended that critic teachers scheduled to conduct college classes should take charge of their regular grades for not more than three hours a day; and that during this time they should demonstrate the best educational procedures in teaching children, carry out experiments in elementary education, induct observers and participants into teaching situations, et cetera. They should devote about one hour daily to conferences with observers, participants, and student-teachers; and another hour to teaching a professional course. A regular grade teacher of superior quality should be employed for every two grades for the purpose of assisting and alternating with the aforesaid critic teachers. Such an organization would promote closer integration and unification of theory and practice; provide opportunity for instructors of theory to use their own pupils for demonstration purposes; and to make possible the origination of a larger part of the content of educational courses from actual classroom situations in the laboratory schools. The conduct of observation and participation under such conditions would stimulate and bring out many questions and numerous problems, and would gradually lead to larger centers of

interest and to more comprehensive units of work. The solution of these problems would require increasingly wider reading, keener interest in various types of materials, more intensive study of real situations, and more first-hand experience.

(3) Critic teachers, in both campus and co-operative laboratory schools, should thoroughly acquaint themselves with the types of instruction that are being offered in professionalized subject-matter and educational courses.

g. Various types of experimental work should be carried out in the laboratory schools through the co-operative efforts of college and laboratory-school staff members.

h. Students should be encouraged to take active part in interchanging ideas and activities between college classes and laboratory schools.

3. Every faculty member in elementary teacher-education curricula should take active interest in and assume some responsibility for integrating and carrying forward the work of student-teaching. The National Survey of the Education of Teachers recommends that, "Proficiency in teaching should be the final test of a prospective teacher's right to graduate and the work of the laboratory school should also be the final test of the institution's ability to educate teachers. For this reason every staff member whose courses are required of prospective teachers should have an interest in or some responsibility for the work of the training schools." [1]

a. Instructors of subject-matter and professional courses should assume partial responsibility for the supervision and progress of student-teachers. These instructors should observe student-teachers in campus and co-operative laboratory schools in order to determine to what extent their instruction functions in actual situations. They should lead their students to see the need for subject-matter and professional materials in light of future teaching; and should stimulate and promote high standards of scholarship and professional ethics. They should be prepared and willing to give active and continuous aid along their respective lines of work; and should act within

[1] *National Survey of the Education of Teachers,* Vol. II, p. 213, Bulletin 1933, No. 10. Office of Education, U. S. Department of the Interior, Washington, D. C., 1933.

their own fields of specialization as advisors for student-teachers on difficult problems as need may arise.

b. Critic teachers, who teach children in campus and co-operative laboratory schools, and supervisors or directors of student-teaching should assume the major supervisory responsibilities for student-teachers in the primary and intermediate departments.

4. In order to effect the necessary preparation of elementary teachers, all faculty members in teachers colleges should be in close touch with the schools in the field. Understanding of elementary school situations might be obtained through various media, such as personal visitations to public and private schools, conferences and interviews with teachers in the field, professional meetings, committee work—regional, state, and national—current professional literature, and educational research in the elementary field.

II. PRINCIPLES RELATIVE TO THE LABORATORY-SCHOOL FACILITIES AND TO THE ADMINISTRATION, ORGANIZATION, AND SUPERVISION OF STUDENT-TEACHING

A. *Laboratory-school facilities should be provided adequate to prepare prospective teachers effectively for their work in the public schools.*

Adequate laboratory-school facilities constitute one of the most essential factors in the professionalization of the teachers college. Through efficient use of well-organized laboratory schools, the professional development of both students and faculty members can be promoted; the fitness of students to undertake teaching responsibilities can be determined; the initial competency of prospective elementary teachers can more nearly be insured; and the professional effectiveness of the whole teacher-preparing institution can be intensified and advanced.

During the past two decades many state teachers colleges have greatly expanded their practice facilities in order to make more nearly adequate provision for the preparation of elementary teachers. Some of the state teachers colleges have increased their facilities to the extent that most of the student-teachers are assigned to off-campus and co-operative laboratory schools in the local and neighboring communities for their practice in responsible student-teaching, thus leaving the campus schools almost exclusively for such purposes as observation, demonstration teaching, experimental work, participation, and preliminary teaching. Although there has recently been a decided expansion in laboratory-school facilities, most of the state teachers colleges had inadequate facilities for observation and student-teaching at the time when data for this study were obtained. In some teachers colleges inadequate laboratory-school facilities permitted only short periods of student-teaching, with the result that the variety and scope of the content of student-teaching were correspondingly restricted. In other institutions where student-teaching courses spread over a long period of time, many student-teachers obtained little actual practice in the major activities of teachers in the elementary schools. These conditions were usually caused by one or more of the following factors: excessive numbers of student-teachers working with the same children; the scheduling of too large a number of student-teachers to a room during the same period of the day; the assignment of too many student-teachers to a critic teacher; the devotion of too large a proportion of the student-teaching time to undirected observation of other student-teachers handling the classroom; and the piecemeal nature of the student-teaching work. In some state teachers colleges there were more students who should be enrolled in student-teaching courses than there were pupils in the laboratory schools.

In light of the fact that the content of student-teaching is definitely affected by the amount and type of laboratory-school facilities, and in conformity to the suggestions of a large body of teachers college administrators and other leaders in the teacher-education field, the following recommendations are made:

1. Laboratory-school facilities should be provided adequate to prepare effectively all teachers needed for the elementary schools.

    a. Laboratory-school facilities should be increased until there is a minimum ratio of four pupils to each student doing 180 hours of student-teaching. Until adequate facilities have been provided, the enrollment of students in any teacher-preparing institution should be restricted.

    b. There should be adequate facilities to provide ample opportunities for instructors of subject-matter and professional courses to participate in such professional activities of the laboratory schools as observation, demonstration teaching, group experiments, and co-operative supervision of student-teaching.

c. Leaders in teacher-education contended that practice facilities might be expanded in one or more of the following ways: affiliating with the schools in the local and neighboring communities; utilizing the schools of the state; enlarging the campus laboratory schools; enlarging or building off-campus laboratory schools under the direct control of the teachers college; subsidizing private schools; and using potentialities of the community, such as religious, social, civic, and welfare organizations.

d. The ideal situation would be one in which the director of training would be the administrative head of a public school area large enough to provide sufficient laboratory facilities for student-teaching. It is decidedly advantageous to have student-teaching concentrated in school buildings located close to the teachers college, rather than scattered over a wide territory; for it is difficult for the teacher-preparing institution to maintain close and expert supervision of student-teachers when the laboratory schools are widely separated.

e. When affiliated public or private schools are used for student-teaching purposes, the teachers college should have sufficient control in each situation to select or approve the teachers with whom the student-teachers are placed; to modify the curriculum and the methods of instruction to meet the student-teaching needs; to supervise the student-teaching activities; to guide the development of each student-teacher; to evaluate the achievements and to determine the final fitness of the prospective teachers.

2. Laboratory facilities should be sufficiently varied to provide prospective teachers contacts with all types of work that they will later perform as responsible teachers in the field.

a. Demonstration teaching for college classes and preliminary participation should, whenever possible, be conducted in schools or rooms separate from those in which major student-teaching courses are carried on.

(1) The demonstration school should be located as conveniently as feasible to all the other buildings on the campus, and should be used chiefly for observation, demonstration, participation, and experimentation.

(2) Laboratory schools for responsible teaching by student-teachers might be located on or off the campus. Sufficient

facilities should be provided so that not more than one student-teacher, who is scheduled to do responsible teaching, would be assigned to the same room during the same period of the day. Not more than five student-teachers, each of whom does 180 hours of responsible student-teaching, should be assigned to a room teacher during a year.

b. Provision should be made for adequate and competently supervised student-teaching situations (1) characteristic of the best practices in the elementary field, and (2) in schools typical of the regions and of the socio-economic conditions among which the prospective teachers will subsequently be placed.

c. Prospective elementary teachers should have contacts with all the elementary grades; and should obtain directed teaching experience in connection with several subjects and a variety of instructional materials, in a diversity of teaching situations, in two or more grades, and in two or more different schools.

d. Adequate laboratory facilities should be provided so that every prospective teacher has opportunity to assume responsibility for the progress of one or more groups of children over a sufficient length of time to assure understanding of a teaching situation as a whole.

3. The laboratory schools should demonstrate the best in education and should be the leaders in the teaching field, thus setting high standards for the elementary schools of the state.

a. It should be the function of laboratory schools in connection with teacher-preparing institutions to typify and exemplify the best modern educational principles and practices.

b. The faculty members in charge of student-teaching should be superior teachers of children and competent supervisors of student-teachers.

c. The campus laboratory-school buildings and equipment should conform to the highest standards attained by public schools; and additional rooms, offices, and equipment needed for student-teaching purposes should be supplied.

d. Pupils enrolled in these schools should be typical of those in the public schools; serious problem cases, however, should not be admitted to the rooms regularly used for student-teaching purposes.

e. In all schools used for student-teaching purposes, courses of study and methods of instruction should be under the control of the teachers college in order that they may be kept in accord with the latest and the best in education.

B. *The contacts of students with educational problems should be long and continuous, with sufficient amounts of time apportioned to the various phases of student-teaching.*

In some teachers colleges a large per cent of the students were scheduled in student-teaching courses for only one term or one semester. This was decidedly too short a time for most of the students to acquire intelligent understanding of all phases of the major problems of elementary teachers and for the establishment of wholesome professional attitudes. In a number of institutions where regularly scheduled student-teaching courses spread over a long period of time, the contacts with teaching situations were too limited and too superficial to prepare prospective teachers to do the most effective work in the field. Long-view planning, for example, was considered very essential in the preparation of teachers, yet the limitations in professional contacts prohibited its application in some teachers colleges. The periods of student-teaching, including observation, participation, and teaching—and all other contacts with children in the teacher-education curriculum—were inadequate and entirely too short in numerous cases for the attainment of the objectives set up for sound student-teaching. The following recommendations, which recapitulate those advocated by many progressive educators in the teacher-education field, are based on the assumption that adequate pre-service preparation requires a long period of careful study of child development and of varied contacts with educational problems:

1. The approach of students to educational problems should be gradual and continuous.

2. There should first be a careful study of individuals and groups of children in a variety of activities both in and out of school.

a. Inadequate working knowledge of children is one of the major causes for student-teachers' difficulties in establishing desirable relations with their pupils and in handling individual differences. Prospective teachers should be led to realize that children are not all alike, but are very different; and that the chief purposes and objectives of education are to discover, to bring out, and to develop effectually the innate powers and native abilities of each individual. They should be given as comprehensive a view as possible of children's intellectual, physical, social, and spiritual needs; and should be helped to obtain sympathetic understanding of the interests and preferences, personal habits and traits, possibilities and limitations, and the social and recreational activities of groups of children and of individuals in a group. They should be led to see that individual differences are produced by environment and heredity; and to trace the consequent influences of these factors upon the acquisition of knowledge, skills, traits, attitudes, and appreciations. Intelligent understanding and real appreciation of individual differences and similarities among children as to abilities, characteristics, interests, difficulties, problems, needs, and potential aptitudes, at different mental and chronological age levels, require many types of contacts over a long period of child study.

b. Observation of and contacts with individuals and groups of children should be made in connection with courses in child study, biology, health, psychology, and sociology.

c. Contacts should be made with boys and girls in out-of-school as well as in-school situations, because children are often under too much restraint in the classroom to be natural and frequently surround themselves with defensive barriers that are difficult for the beginning student-teacher to penetrate; and because it is essential for every teacher to know how to handle children outside of the regular schoolroom situations. Students should begin to study individuals and groups of children during the freshman year and should obtain increasingly broader experiences in these connections throughout their teacher-preparatory work. Child study and close contact with child life should continuously permeate their professional education, because knowledge of and experience with children vitalizes all the other work. Students can secure outside contacts with children through such activities as the following: teaching Sunday School classes, directing young people's religious organizations, participating in children's library story hours, entertaining children in hospitals and sanitariums, caring for children, tutoring children outside of school, attending children's picnics and parties, supervising city or community playgrounds, assisting at children's camps, participating in community gatherings, helping with Junior Red Cross, directing Girl Scout and Boy Scout organizations, and assisting with child clinic and social welfare work.

3. Competently supervised observation and efficiently guided participation in the essential teaching activities should constitute an important part of the elementary teacher-education curricula, in order that prospective teachers may secure experiential background for the proper understanding of educational problems confronting the elementary school.

a. Carefully planned and skillfully guided observation in all the grades and simple forms of participation in teaching situations should begin early in the elementary teacher-education curricula. Professionalization, however, should be very slight during the first college year. A guidance program should be provided to direct the students into the right types of work; but they should have at least one year, and if possible two or more years, for orientation before deciding upon a definite line of preparation.

(1) Prospective teachers should be afforded opportunities to obtain an overview of the whole elementary school, in order that the selection of a particular teaching field will emanate from a clear understanding of the requirements of that field and of the adequacy of their own personal equipments in relation thereto.

(2) Constructively guided contacts with children in various types of learning situations in all the elementary grades constitute the most direct means by which the students acquire a first-hand knowledge of the plan and the scope of the elementary school. A practicable understanding of child nature at various levels of growth requires acquaintance with the development of pupils, both above and below the age levels at which the teaching is to be done.

b. Throughout the latter half of the elementary teacher-education curricula—primary and intermediate—provision should be made for increasingly difficult problems in observation and for gradually expanding responsibilities in participation in all phases of the elementary teachers' work—instructional, children's extra-class, administrative, staff-personnel, extra-class professional, and community activities.

4. Ample time and opportunities should be afforded prospective teachers for becoming proficient in the planning of their work. There should be provision for adequate practice in long-view planning, with special emphasis upon such phases as selection and organization of broad units of subject-matter and integration of materials of instruction. Thoughtful and purposeful planning is essential to successful teaching, and should serve as an instrument to free the teacher and to inspire self-confidence based on thorough preparation. The ability to prepare intelligent plans requires a long period of practice.

   a. Effective induction into long-view and daily planning should be provided.

   (1) Induction into lesson planning should begin in connection with subject-matter courses. The students should have broad experiences in organizing subject-matter around vital problems that will help them to obtain comprehensive views of whole situations. They should also secure extensive practice in developing large units of work that will help them to build up sense of values and proper balance in the use of subject-matter and materials. A series of large units of subject-matter, carefully directed observations of various types of activities, and well-planned conferences should be offered in connection with both subject-matter and professional courses. Such a program would necessitate very close articulation between the laboratory school and the different college classes.

   (2) During student-teaching the general organization of the long-range or the large unit plans should be worked out carefully in order to give an overview of the whole, but the details of unit and daily plans should be reduced according to the stage of progress reached by the student-teachers in directing the learning activities, of the children.

   (3) The subject-matter and technical backgrounds for major unit plans should largely be secured prior to entering

upon responsible teaching courses. During the period of responsible teaching in the senior year, the student-teachers should be encouraged to use their own originality and initiative in writing the plans needed.

(4) The rate of induction into lesson planning should depend upon the ability and skill that the student-teachers demonstrate in writing and applying lesson plans.

b. Adequate guidance and intelligent help should be given to student-teachers in the preparation and revision of large units and daily plans.

c. Thorough preparation in connection with lesson planning should be required of student-teachers.

(1) Command of instructional materials, knowledge of educational procedures, and understanding of children are prerequisites to effective planning.

(2) The time and effort spent in preparing plans should be adequate to insure effective teaching.

d. Lesson planning should be in accord with the best educational principles. Lesson plans should be purposeful, practical, workable, and intelligent. The form, content, and application of written plans should be effectively adapted and intelligently applied to particular needs, problems, and situations.

(1) The form of lesson plans should be modified from time to time to keep pace with (a) the changing trends in the objectives of education, (b) the revisions in the curriculum, and (c) the new administrative policies in the schools. Extremely formal, elaborate, and stereotyped forms of plans should be avoided; rigid systems of plans should be eliminated.

(2) Lesson plans should be organized and developed in such a manner that desirable objectives and aims are provided for and determined in light of criteria set up; that environment, subject-matter, and materials are effectively used; that those educational procedures and teaching techniques which will promote the best growth of the pupils are applied; that valuable leads and contributions of the pupils are recognized and utilized; and that individual children, as well as the group, are taken into consideration.

(3) The content of written plans should be adaptable to various factors, such as needs, abilities, experiences, and skills of the student-teachers; abilities, experiences, and needs of the children; content subject-matter and other instructional materials to be used; activities to be carried out; teaching techniques and educational procedures to be applied; and teaching situation and learning environment.

(4) The application of lesson plans should be sufficiently flexible to meet the interests, abilities, experiences, and needs of the children; promote freedom, adaptability, and versatility on the part of the student-teachers; develop initiative, originality, sense of responsibility, and resourcefulness; make room for emergencies, unusual problems, unexpected situations, and unforeseen difficulties that might arise; adjust to different directions that a lesson might take; utilize effectively the contributions and reactions of the pupils in a class; and provide for the active participation of children in class work.

e. Definite follow-up work should be done in connection with lesson planning.

(1) Careful records should be kept of all activities for the purposes of assisting student-teachers in forming a basis for each day's work; making each day's lesson an outgrowth of the previous one; seeing growth in both student-teachers' and children's work; keeping the work well-balanced; and promoting self-evaluation and criticism.

(2) Cumulative records of subject-matter covered and of significant events in the development of units of work should be diligently kept and systematically filed.

5. Prospective teachers should be provided sufficient time and opportunities for actual teaching under competent supervision.

a. Practice in connection with the teaching of children should, for the median prospective teacher, be extended over a period of several terms.

b. Student-teachers should spend an adequate length of time in each grade or room to which they are assigned for directed teaching in order to orient themselves effectively into each situation, to secure a feeling of self-confidence, to know the children and their needs, and to handle teaching situations with some degree of skill.

c. The advanced work in directed teaching, or the final term of responsible teaching, should take place during the last year of professional preparation but, if possible, early enough to permit the taking of some integrating or summarizing courses subsequent to the teaching period.

d. The final term of responsible teaching should be scheduled on the whole-day basis in view of the resultant benefits which accrue to the student-teachers. In contrast to student-teaching conducted on the one-hour-a-day plan, student-teaching organized on the whole-day basis would provide student-teachers more time and opportunities for the following types of activities: seeing continuity in teaching; experiencing a teaching situation as a whole; obtaining consecutive experiences in all types of school situations; studying and knowing children in many types of activities both in and out of the schoolroom, thereby placing themselves in a position to develop in their pupils higher interests in scholarship, health, character building, citizenship, and extra-class activities; obtaining a more complete view of the entire teaching process; securing more intelligent understanding of the responsibilities and duties of teachers in the elementary grades; participating in many activities that are of vital importance in the life of the successful teacher; and becoming an integral part of school and community life.

e. During the final period of responsible teaching each student-teacher should be afforded time and opportunity to work out some comprehensive problem or constructive experiment in connection with the teaching of children. This work should give the prospective teachers acquaintance with scientific methods of attacking educational problems.

C. *All phases of student-teaching—observation, participation, conferences, and teaching—should be carefully integrated.*

Student-teaching courses, which embrace directed observation and participation together with constructive conferences and responsible teaching, rightly constitute one of the most important phases of teacher preparation. These courses should permeate and color the entire elementary curricula, but their effectiveness as individual activities and as a composite whole is largely determined by the extent to which they are integrated with each other and interrelated to the other teacher-educative courses and activities.

In some laboratory schools, the beginning student-teachers devoted considerable time to observation of other student-teachers and to observation in which they had no active participation in teaching situations; the more advanced student-teachers likewise spent a great deal of time in observing other student-teachers and obtained few opportunities to observe expert teaching done by critic teachers or by supervisors of student-teaching. Failure to participate actively in teaching situations during observation periods, lack of opportunity to observe expert teaching throughout student-teaching courses, and time-consuming conferences of no real educative value resulted in low standards of teaching on the part of some student-teachers.

In light of the findings of this study, and on the assumption that more careful integration of observation, participation, conferences, and teaching would greatly intensify and enhance the content of student-teaching, the following recommendations are made:

1. Student-teachers can best be guided in observation work through some form of participation in which they are intimately connected with immediate teaching situations.

2. Student-teachers should be exposed repeatedly throughout all the student-teaching courses to expert demonstration work, because carefully integrated and competently supervised observation work aids the student-teachers in securing working knowledge of children; in becoming mentally active in teaching situations; and in obtaining an intelligent understanding of the teacher's work.

3. Demonstration teaching should be as nearly perfect as possible and should manifest the very highest types of classroom instruction, because the skill of the student teachers will depend in a large measure upon the kind of teaching that they have observed.

4. The following are procedures suggested by Thomas Alexander for co-ordinating and integrating observation, participation, and teaching:

The best observation is possible while one is participating in teaching. Real observation possibly can only be carried on as a form of participation. We best see what is going on when we are intimately connected with the situation at hand. It seems to me a weakness in American practice-teaching that we have divided student-teaching into three steps of observation, participation, and practice, with the implication that observation comes first, participation second, and student-teaching third. To me they should run side by side throughout the entire period of training. A student never should cease to observe. His participation should be continuous throughout his training and I can imagine very worthwhile observation being carried on after full classroom teaching has been experienced. In fact, I think that the best time to do observation work as an independent exercise is after full teaching experience.[2]

D. *Individual interests, traits, aptitudes, capacities, and needs of the student-teachers should serve as criteria for the differentiation of student-teaching.*

When this study was made, student-teaching courses in the elementary teacher-education curricula were commonly organized into blocks consisting of a definite number of weeks of observation, participation, and teaching. In most of the teacher-preparing institutions differentiation was based principally upon grade level (primary and intermediate), subjects taught by the student-teachers, and type of school (rural or urban), while differences in student-teachers as individuals were frequently ignored. Student-teachers pursuing the same curriculum within each teachers college were usually required to take an equal number and the same kind of student-teaching courses regardless of differences in their native abilities, cultural backgrounds, scholastic achievements, and special aptitudes. As a result of such practices, the more capable students frequently wasted time through needless repetitions and were neither encouraged nor provided opportunity to develop their maximum powers; while the less promising students were overtaxed and so limited in time that they failed to secure the well-rounded preparation essential to successful teaching in the field.

The following recommendations are based on the assumption that student-teaching should be differentiated according to the individual interests, traits, aptitudes, capacities, needs, intellectual industry, and integrity of the student-teachers:

1. Careful provision should be made for differentiation in units of observation, participation, and teaching to meet the individualities of student-teachers.

2. Individual differences of student-teachers should determine the time when student-teaching is done, the number of hours assigned to

[2] Thomas Alexander, "Application of Some of the Principles Which Underlie Practice Teaching." Address delivered before the New York Association of Teachers Colleges and Normal School Faculties at Syracuse, October 13, 1930.

student-teaching, the activities in which each obtains experience while teaching, the levels in skill at which each one secures practice, and the type of teaching position for which preparation is being made.

a. Variations might be made in student-teaching time requirements, ranging from a longer period for the less capable students to a shorter period for the more capable ones. In any case, the time allotted student-teaching courses should be sufficient to give each prospective teacher a reasonable mastery of control and skills needed.

b. The rate of induction into the more complex teaching activities and into the more advanced educational work should be commensurate with the abilities and capacities of the student-teachers. Differentiation in activities might be made on a basis of comprehensiveness and difficulty, the work being so graded as to evoke the best efforts of all groups—the superior, the average, and the below-average.

3. Continuous growth and progress on the part of beginning teachers in the field is in large measure dependent upon their powers of self-analysis and self-direction. These in turn are considerably limited by the foundation in habits and skills which has been acquired throughout the teacher-preparing work. Student-teaching courses should therefore be sufficiently long and intensive, varying with the individual, to build up skills and habits to that degree of perfection where prospective teachers can further and continuously develop them in the field.

Through recognition of and provision for individual differences of student-teachers, the most economical induction into the art of teaching can be brought about. It should be borne in mind that not all students enrolled in the same curriculum need the same amounts of observation, participation, and teaching; that not all are ready to begin to teach at the same time; and that not all need an equal amount nor the same kinds of experiences in the same types of activities. Consideration must be given to the fact that some student-teachers gain proficiency with less effort than do others; and that some develop teaching skills much more rapidly than do others. The more capable student-teachers should, therefore, be provided opportunities to deal with broader problems relating to teaching and to participate in wider fields of investigation.

E. *Adequate guidance and competent supervision are essential to sound student-teaching.*

The value of student-teaching is in large measure dependent upon the skill and wisdom with which student-teachers are guided and supervised throughout their laboratory-school experiences. Assuming that the student-teachers' academic backgrounds together with their professional and personal equipments are all that need be desired, the most satisfactory results in student-teaching are obtainable under the direction of and through intimate contacts with critics and supervisors whose personal qualifications, specialized preparation, professional attitudes, and ethical standards are of a high order of excellence.

The reports from student-teachers and faculty members showed that in some laboratory schools the mass production of student-teachers practically eliminated the intimate contacts that are so essential between student-teachers and critic teachers. The excessive teaching and supervisory loads in these schools definitely limited the opportunities of critic teachers and other faculty members to help student-teachers develop to their fullest capacities. The following are some of the contributing factors that made the critic teachers' loads immoderately heavy: (1) the assignment to each critic teacher of a greater number of student-teachers—observers, participants, and teachers—than could be effectively supervised; (2) the responsibility for teaching such large groups of children as to exhaust time and energy that should have been given to the constructive supervision of student-teachers; (3) the demand for constant adjustment and readjustment to keep pace with progressive educational ideas and for leadership in the elementary teaching field; (4) the expenditure of too much time and energy on clerical work, lunchroom supervision, classroom management, and other routine duties; (5) the large number of extra-class activities, such as curriculum work, faculty and professional meetings, community problems, and responsibilities to the school as a whole. In some cases the critic teachers were also handicapped because they lacked the professional preparation necessary for the most effective supervision of student-teachers.

On the assumptions that sufficient guidance and competent supervision are highly essential factors in the preparation of teachers, and that the quality and effectiveness of the content of student-teaching are greatly influenced by the adequacy of the supervision; and in light of the findings of this study, the following recommendations are offered as a condensation of those made by laboratory-school faculty members and student-teachers participating in this survey:

1. A sufficient number of highly qualified and thoroughly competent critic teachers and supervisors of student-teaching should be employed to provide adequate supervision for every student-teacher. The teaching and supervisory staff of the laboratory schools should be composed of persons who are specifically prepared for their work, enthusiastic and skillful in their guidance, and discriminating in their recognition of and in their provision for individual differences of student-teachers.

2. The selection of the laboratory-school faculty members, in all the schools used for student-teaching purposes, should be vested in the state teachers college in order that the needs of the teacher-preparatory work may be more fully met.

3. Principles underlying sound supervision of student-teaching should be applied.

Teaching student-teachers to teach children by the most effective methods of instruction is essentially the fundamental principle underlying the supervision of student-teaching in the elementary grades. In order to make student-teaching of maximum value to prospective teachers, the work in supervision should be maintained at a very high level of achievement. Critic teachers and other supervisors of student-teaching should, therefore, faithfully carry out the following duties, responsibilities, and activities:

a. Establish the relationships between the faculty members and the student-teachers on a basis of perfect understanding.

b. Deal intelligently and efficiently with individual differences of student-teachers.

c. Hold sufficient number of vital, well-prepared, constructive, and helpful conferences to guide effectively the student-teachers.

d. Practice the best educational principles, demonstrate progressive and effective methods of instruction, and provide opportunities for well-directed observation of expert teaching throughout student-teaching courses.

e. Provide for gradual, continuous, and economical induction into the art of teaching.

f. Help student-teachers to acquire intelligent understanding of and to establish desirable relations with their pupils.

g. Guide constructively the student-teachers in adapting, integrating, and applying suitable materials of instruction and effective modern educational procedures.

h. Plan and teach co-operatively with the student-teachers until they are able to work independently.

i. Observe closely, supervise competently, and assume responsibility for the work and the progress of student-teachers.

j. Provide sufficient opportunities for student-teachers to initiate activities, to assume responsibility in various types of teaching situations, and to obtain rounded-out experiences.

k. Lead student-teachers to obtain broad perspective of the whole teaching situation; guide them in obtaining clear conception of the problems and situations that they will meet in the field, and prepare them to meet these effectively.

l. Lead the student-teachers to develop a high order of professional ethics; and to build up wholesome professional attitudes, worthy professional interests and ideals, and a sound working philosophy of education.

III. PRINCIPLES RELATIVE TO THE ACTIVITIES THAT HELP TO MAKE UP THE CONTENT OF STUDENT-TEACHING

A. *Prospective teachers should be inducted by gradual, continuous, and economical processes into the art of teaching.*

Some teachers colleges required their student-teachers to assume teaching responsibilities with no preliminary participation, while others provided for gradual induction into teaching situations. The term "gradual induction" has been interpreted in numerous ways and its interpretation has largely determined the approach to the content of student-teaching in state teachers colleges. In some laboratory schools, the student-teachers were inducted into teaching by gradual steps which first introduced them to a long series of classroom-routine and school-management units. Many student-teachers devoted much time and energy, which should have been applied to participation in the more difficult phases of teaching or to practice in the more complex teaching situations, to such activities as classroom routine and housekeeping duties, undirected and promiscuous observation of other student-teachers handling classes, and repetition of the same types of activities on the same levels of attainment in changing from one student-teaching course to another. Many of the activities in which the student-teachers obtained experience were of a routine nature and added very little to their experiences when repeated in two subjects or in two grades.

In light of these findings, and on the assumption that close articulation and careful gradation of the work in all student-teaching courses are highly essential in promoting constant professional growth and development in each student-teacher, the following recommendations are offered:

1. The sequence of induction into the teacher's activities should be so carefully planned and systematically organized that each student-teacher may continuously develop better understanding of the elementary teacher's work and responsibilities. Each new student-teaching assignment should secure the careful attention of critic teachers and supervisors of student-teaching, especially during the orientation period.

2. Students should be introduced into teaching by means of observation and participation in which they are guided to see all the factors that help to make up the classroom environment, in relation to the actual teaching and learning situations.

3. Induction into participation and teaching should begin with a gradation of thought phases of teaching and learning rather than a gradation of management units. There should first be an introductory acquaintance with the activities that involve the thought phases and the most vital problems of teaching, because acquisition of skill in these requires the greatest amount of time, energy, and thought. The major emphasis should thus be given to such phases of teaching as child guidance, thorough working knowledge of materials of instruction and of modern educational procedures, efficient teaching skills, personality development, professional growth, and community relations.

4. Experience should be obtained in those teaching techniques and educative activities that are unique in different subjects and in different grades. These techniques and activities should be carefully selected and arranged according to difficulties encountered by student-teachers in each grade. Except for a few typical activities required of all teachers, care should be exercised to avoid repetition of experiences beyond the point of educative value to the student-teachers.

5. Before attempting to assume complete responsibility for teach-

ing a whole group of children, student-teachers should acquire adequate command of the subject-matter and the methods of instruction to be applied and should obtain intelligent understanding of the children to be taught. Well-organized induction of student-teachers into the intricacies of teaching protects the pupils in the laboratory schools and promotes systematic mastery of teaching techniques on the part of the student-teachers.

6. Student-teachers should obtain increasingly broader experiences in the actual work of the teacher, and each experience should be put on a higher level than the preceding one. They should thus be led by gradual induction to the assumption of greater and greater responsibility for all the major activities of elementary teachers.

B. *Student-teaching courses should give student-teachers contacts with all the important educational activities of elementary teachers.*

According to the findings of this study, the types of activities in which student-teachers obtained practice during student-teaching and the emphasis placed upon many of them were determined by such factors as the following: the length of the elementary teacher-education curriculum and the background preparation of the student-teachers; the amount of time devoted to student-teaching courses; the administration of student-teaching; the adequacy of the laboratory-school facilities; the integration and co-ordination between college departments and the laboratory schools; the competency of the supervision of student-teaching; and the effectiveness of the organization of the content of student-teaching courses with reference to the types of activities stressed. Student-teaching in many teachers colleges concerned itself almost entirely with activities that might be classified as instructional. In some institutions even the instructional activities in which the student-teachers obtained practice were limited as to content, variety, and scope.

In light of the findings of this study; in conformity to the evaluation of the content of the *Master Activity Check List*; in harmony with the suggestions made by both student-teachers and laboratory-school staff members included in this survey; in keeping with the author's own teaching and supervisory experience; and on the assumption that prospective teachers need a broad vision of the whole teaching situation and that well-organized student-teaching courses are highly essential in the preparation of elementary teachers, the following recommendations are made:

1. Intensive, extensive, and comprehensive preparation for elementary teachers should be provided in our state teachers colleges throughout the country. Students preparing to teach in the elementary grades should have contacts with all the important educational activities of elementary teachers.

2. Student-teaching should introduce the student-teachers to all phases of the elementary teacher's work and should include all those contacts which the successful teacher must make both inside and outside the school. It should be so planned and organized as to provide for instructional, extra-class, personality, personnel, administrative, community, and extra-class professional contacts.

(I) *Activities Concerned with Instructional Phases of Teaching*

Student-teachers should obtain experience in dealing with all phases of instruction in connection with the elementary school. The following is a suggested list of student-teaching activities of an instructional nature. The extent to which these activities are carried out should depend upon the individual abilities, interests, and needs of the student-teachers.

A. Developing clear perspective and broad understanding of the elementary school curriculum.
   1. Studying and utilizing the guiding educational principles.
   2. Studying, formulating, and endeavoring to achieve desired objectives in teaching and learning.
      a. Selecting and setting up
         (1) General objectives to be accomplished.
         (2) Specific objectives in harmony with general objectives.
      b. Evaluating the educational principles and objectives in light of definite criteria.
      c. Working toward the achievement of desired objectives.
   3. Making analytical study and constructive use of curriculum materials.
      a. Investigating and examining curriculum materials.
      b. Becoming familiar with courses of study, syllabi, textbooks, references, and other instructional materials of recognized excellence for use in modern elementary schools.
      c. Selecting and arranging the sequence of units to be taught in the elementary grades.
      d. Applying the content of courses of study in actual teaching.
   4. Preparing, writing, revising, and recording units of instruction and daily teaching plans.
      a. Outlining, preparing, and writing long-range plans, such as:
         (1) Large developmental units of instruction or broad units of work.

(2) Activity units of comprehensive scope.
b. Thinking out each day's work in terms of large units.
c. Preparing and writing short units or daily teaching plans.
d. Making necessary revisions and corrections in lesson plans.
e. Recording plans subsequent to teaching.
  (1) Keeping daily records of such factors as new leads opened up, questions and problems raised, activities proposed, problems solved, and conclusions reached.
  (2) Keeping cumulative records of achievements, such as objectives and outcomes accomplished, subject-matter covered, references and materials used, activities carried to completion, and procedures and teaching techniques applied.
  (More detailed treatment of lesson planning is given on pages 281–283)

5. Helping to build up the curriculum from day to day through the combined initiative and co-operative efforts of pupils and teacher.

B. Acquiring adequate command and establishing working organization of content subject-matter and other materials of instruction in order to carry out effectively the instructional functions of elementary teachers.

1. Securing mastery of materials of instruction.
  a. Obtaining broad fund of general information that might be applied in teaching.
  b. Becoming familiar with important contributions in each field of subject-matter to be taught in a grade.
  c. Acquiring thorough command of subject-matter to be taught.
  d. Gaining broad working knowledge of supplementary materials that might be applied in teaching.
  e. Developing skill in using appropriate supplementary materials.

2. Finding and accumulating suitable materials and pertinent information for specific lessons, problems, activities, and units of instruction.
  a. Utilizing different types of techniques in collecting information, such as observation, reading, interviewing, and traveling.
    (1) Reading as a means of securing information.
    (2) Interviewing people for the purpose of securing information that would apply definitely to problems in connection with student-teaching.
    (3) Visiting places of interest for the purpose of securing information relative to the work in student-teaching. (Visiting places of industrial, commercial, scientific, geographical, historical, civic, social, recreational, and scenic interest.)
  b. Making practical use of environmental materials.
  c. Becoming acquainted with and utilizing various types of school equipment, materials, and supplies; determining circumstances under which each is necessary for efficient teaching.
  d. Making effective use of such reference guides as card catalogs, The Readers' Guide, study guides, reading lists, bibliographies,

dictionaries, encyclopedias, periodicals, bulletins, atlases, annals, chronicles, and archives.

e. Using different sources of supply, such as libraries, publishing houses, business and industrial concerns, transportation companies, geographical and historical societies, social and civic organizations, museums and art galleries, aquariums and zoos, gardens and parks, and outdoor nature and scenery.

3. Arranging, recording, and filing materials of instruction.

a. Adding to the files already in the laboratory schools.

b. Building up filing systems for the prospective teacher's own future use; adding to the student-teacher's own files.

c. Keeping illustrative materials and supplies in order and available for use when needed.

d. Arranging reference materials for specific problems so that they may be found with minimum time and effort when needed in teaching.

e. Recording important elements of data or information for future use.

f. Filing important materials topically, with minor classifications under each major topic.

4. Planning the selection, the organization, and the integration of materials of instruction; weighing and planning subject-matter so that it may become a tool for the ultimate development of the children.

5. Selecting, evaluating, interpreting, and adapting content subject-matter and other instructional materials with reference to:

a. The basic educational principles.

b. The desired objectives and outcomes sought.

c. The abilities, background experiences, immaturities, interests, difficulties, problems, and needs of the children to be taught.

d. The environment in which teaching and learning activities take place.

e. Present-day life and problems.

6. Organizing content subject-matter and other materials of instruction.

a. Organizing materials of instruction into coherent units that could be applied in teaching particular groups of children.

b. Relating the daily work to the large unit.

c. Reorganizing subject-matter to meet particular situations that arise during progress of work, in order to make these experiences more meaningful to the children.

7. Integrating the elementary school subjects into a comprehensive and well-rounded school program.

C. Obtaining comprehensive knowledge and sympathetic understanding of individual differences and similarities of children by studying and analyzing factors that condition their learning.

1. Acquiring knowledge of scientific techniques for studying both individual differences and similarities of children.

2. Making psychological and personality studies of children.
   a. Recognizing children as individuals with different aptitudes, capacities, traits, and interests.
   b. Studying, observing, analyzing, and recording personality traits of individuals and groups of children.
      (1) Making case studies of individual children; studying each individual scientifically in order to discover his potentialities.
      (2) Making scientific studies of groups of children.
      (3) Recording accurately observations made of children; filing these records for future use.

Intelligent understanding of the children to be taught is a prerequisite to guiding and teaching them. The student-teachers should become conscious of each child's abilities and talents, habits and traits, possibilities and limitations, conflicts and difficulties, problems and needs, interests and ambitions, and attitudes and ideals. It is, therefore, highly essential for student-teachers to obtain adequate experience in studying and diagnosing personality traits and characteristics of individuals and groups of children.

3. Developing sympathetic understanding and acquiring working knowledge of children by studying their interests, experiences, social and cultural backgrounds, environments, and heredity.
   a. Interviewing critic teachers and other faculty members in order to acquire desired information concerning children.
   b. Making personal contacts with children in and out of school.
   c. Obtaining frequent opportunities to observe individuals of the age to be taught, and in situations similar to those which the prospective teachers will encounter.
   d. Acquiring knowledge and understanding of the next-younger and the next-older age groups of the children to be taught, through observation, reading, and interviews.
   e. Holding individual conferences with the children to be taught.

Well-planned and purposeful conferences are valuable means through which friendly relations and willing co-operation can be established between the student-teachers and their pupils. Careful records should be kept of all that goes on in each of these conferences in order that student-teachers may secure better understanding of each child; gain more complete knowledge of each child's work habits; analyze and diagnose difficulties more intelligently; locate causes of difficulties and weaknesses; determine corrective measures; develop preventive methods of teaching to avoid the formation of undesirable habits in the children; and determine the progress made from time to time.

   f. Interviewing the parents relative to the children.

Interviews with parents relative to their children should be handled most diplomatically, and a very careful background should be built up for this phase of the teacher's work. Visiting days in which parents are encouraged to visit laboratory schools furnish student-teachers valuable means for making contacts and holding interviews with the parents.

g. Securing necessary information through records and reports.

   (1) Formulating check lists that call for the desired information concerning the children to be taught.

   (2) Directing children in recording information relative to their activities, habits, interests, and personality traits.

   (3) Developing and keeping individual and group records of the children.

   (4) Studying and interpreting records on file which give pertinent information about each child.

Through proper filing systems, student-teachers should have access to necessary information relative to individual children.

h. Determining special interests and aptitudes of children at different age and grade levels through such means as:

   (1) Discussing with children a variety of illustrative materials, books, and current literature; various types of literature, music, art, recreational and social activities, the manual arts and crafts; personal affairs and matters of interest to individual children.

   (2) Discovering children's tastes in reading.

   (3) Studying children's general outside social interests.

   (4) Observing and studying types of activities that appeal to groups of children and to individuals in a group.

   (5) Taking part in the children's recreational activities; playing different types of games with them.

i. Learning about the home conditions of the children whom they teach, and studying their home problems.

j. Visiting, under competent guidance of critic teachers or other faculty members, the homes of children in the laboratory schools.

k. Interviewing specialists in the various fields of child study relative to individual case studies.

4. Measuring the mental development of children.

a. Participating in various types of standard intelligence testing programs.

b. Classifying and grouping children for instructional purposes in accordance with the results of standard intelligence tests.

Student-teachers should be technically trained before attempting to give intelligence tests or to apply the results of such tests for diagnostic purposes. They should know the values and limitations of various types of intelligence tests, and should develop the right mental attitudes toward them.

5. Studying and observing conditions of mental and physical health; examining the physical, mental, and emotional equipment of individual children from the standpoint of health.

    a. Assisting with health inspections.

    b. Weighing and measuring children at stated intervals; recording weights and measurements; and making effective use of these findings in promoting the health of the children.

    c. Noting defects in vision, hearing, speech, posture, and motor co-ordination.

    d. Watching for, recognizing symptoms of, and making allowances for health deficiencies.

    e. Keeping records of absences caused by illness.

    f. Studying the emotional and mental balance of individual children.

    g. Maintaining and promoting desirable health standards among the children in a group.

The teacher-education program should equip student-teachers to provide and maintain desirable health standards in their classrooms, and to discover and make allowance for common defects in the physical and mental equipment of children.

6. Developing a reasonable degree of skill in applying the basic principles of biology, physiology, psychology, and sociology in order to obtain sympathetic and intelligent understanding of children.

7. Maintaining an intelligent interest in problems arising from individual differences of children; studying authoritative references and reading current literature pertaining to these topics.

D. Acquiring adequate working knowledge of modern methods of instruction and developing skill in the application of a variety of teaching techniques.

  1. Studying the best current educational procedures and the most modern teaching techniques.

  2. Planning methods of instruction.

    a. Planning methods of developing interests.

    b. Planning types of procedures and activities by which desired objectives can most effectively be attained.

    c. Planning methods of providing sufficient opportunities for the children's activities.

    d. Planning types of questions, reviews, summaries, assignments, and tests.

    e. Planning work for both individual differences and similarities of children in a group.

    f. Planning methods of evaluating the children's interests, achievements, progress, and needs.

  3. Selecting, evaluating, organizing, and adapting methods of instruction.

    a. Selecting, evaluating, and adapting methods of instruction, including all educative activities, with reference to:

      (1) The basic educational principles.

      (2) The desired objectives and outcomes.

      (3) The children's abilities, background experiences, interests, attitudes, problems, and needs.

(4) The content subject-matter and other materials of instruction to be used.

(5) The learning activities to be undertaken.

(6) The environment in which the teaching and learning activities take place.

(7) The needs, abilities, experiences, and skill of the student-teachers.

b. Organizing and developing appropriate activities to be used in connection with daily work, activity units, and units of instruction.

c. Setting up criteria and making effective use of them for determining value of materials and methods of instruction to be applied in teaching a particular group of children.

4. Integrating and applying effective methods of instruction.

a. Applying basic principles underlying modern educational procedures; and directing instruction toward the attainment of desired goals.

b. Helping children to develop interests; and leading them to progress according to their maximal capacities.

(1) Helping children to develop appropriate mental-set for purposeful learning activities to be undertaken.

(2) Recognizing the abilities, aptitudes, interests, desires, goals, problems, and needs of the children to be taught; and relating the teaching process closely to these factors.

(3) Creating and maintaining pleasant and effective learning situations; providing true to life learning activities.

(4) Motivating and vitalizing the work—providing effective stimulation for each child in a group and furnishing adequate incentives for sustained effort on the part of each one; arousing and holding the children's interest, enthusiasm, and attention in order that high standards of work may be maintained; challenging children to want to take active part in purposeful activities; vitalizing and humanizing subject-matter, and bringing it close to those being taught.

(5) Providing maximal activities for all the members in a group; keeping all the children continuously interested and profitably engaged in suitable and purposeful learning activities.

c. Utilizing the more creative types of instruction that demand high degree of skill and understanding—the mastery of which requires considerable time, effort, and concentration—such as:

(1) Activity units

(a) Gaining understanding of activity units for different elementary grades.

(b) Directing children in connection with activity units.

(c) Guiding children in initiating, organizing, and carrying out large activity units which complement the integration of a variety of subjects in forming large units of instruction.

(d) Stimulating and promoting pupil self-activity.

(e) Organizing school life around constructive activity units.

The emphasis upon a school set-up that parallels life situations has made it necessary for teachers, planning to teach in progressive schools, to obtain practical preparation in the organization and integration of content subject-matter and other materials of instruction into large activity units of a constructive nature. Activity units may be divided into the "content activity" unit which deals with the organization of subject-matter, and the "project activity" unit which deals with activities and problems leading from the subject-matter and from the children's experiences. Care should be exercised, however, lest the activity unit become an end in itself rather than a means to an end.

(2) Appreciation

    (a) Stimulating in children an appreciation, admiration, and enjoyment of things of aesthetic, intellectual, and social values.

    (b) Incorporating into daily work references to materials of aesthetic and intellectual values, in such a manner as to help children become appreciation-conscious.

The acquisition of rich cultural and broad experiential backgrounds, together with the development of attitudes of sympathetic understanding, are prime requisites on the part of the teacher who would stimulate and develop in others appreciation, admiration, and enjoyment of things of æsthetic, intellectual, and social values.

(3) Creative and expressive activities

    (a) Stimulating and helping children to develop imagination, originality, creativeness, and self-expression through a variety of experiences.

    (b) Guiding children in activities of a creative nature.

    (c) Utilizing the creative aptitudes and abilities of the children to further group activities as well as individual achievement.

A careful background and a definite philosophy must be built up for carrying out creative activities. The intrinsic values in the right types of creativity as a means of developing self-expression, as well as the inherent difficulties which creative and expressive activities represent for inexperienced teachers, combine to make constructive guidance in these activities a necessity. Appreciation and creativity should especially be emphasized in connection with literature and the arts.

(4) Dramatic play and dramatic expression

    (a) Guiding children in dramatic play.

    (b) Re-creating in play form stories and incidents of interest to children.

    (c) Directing children in the preparation and the presentation of simple dramatizations and plays.

    (d) Directing children in planning and in carrying out debates and other types of forensics.

Preparation of teachers in the construction and direction of the right kind of dramatic play is made urgent by the universal appeal of this activity to the child-mind, and by the skill which is required on the part of teachers to realize its maximum possibilities.

(5) Individualized instruction
   (a) Diagnosing individual as well as class needs to determine the basis for each teaching plan.
   (b) Individualizing learning activities to provide for the wide range of differences relative to abilities, interests, talents, personality traits, difficulties, problems, and needs of children in a group; for example, making necessary adaptations to those of high mentality as well as to those of low mental capacity.
   (c) Presenting instructional materials on such graded levels of difficulty as to elicit the best efforts of all the children in a group.
   (d) Leading each child in a group to make suitable progress commensurate with his mental, physical, and social abilities.
   (e) Balancing individual and group instruction; meeting successfully the needs of both the individual and the group.

Modern educational trends necessitate more effective individualization of learning activities to meet the capacities, interests, and needs of children. Provision for individualities must be so skillfully made, with minimum of differentiation that could be recognized as such by any member of the group, that maximum effort is evoked from each child. Successful individualization of instruction to meet the potentialities of each child in the class requires that the teacher be able to think in terms of both individuals and the group, an ability which is developed only through prolonged practice of a constructive nature.

(6) Problem-solving and developmental phases of work
   (a) Leading children to recognize and to formulate vital, thought-provoking, and challenging problems.
   (b) Guiding children in studying and developing problems.
   (c) Directing children in the solution of problems.

As an essential factor in carrying out units of instruction, problem-solving represents a definite need for practice under competent guidance.

(7) Socialized procedures
   (a) Creating social situations in non-individual instruction.
   (b) Encouraging children to take initiative in class discussion.
   (c) Providing opportunity for each child in a group to work co-operatively with the other children.
   (d) Working with children in preparing group activities, such as sand table scenes, puppet shows, murals, co-operative

folios, friezes, models, museum collections, and units or projects of many types.

Real social situations might be created through such means as language communication, conversational groups and socialized discussions, co-operative planning, group and committee activities, projects, and other activities in which the children become real participants in the total learning situation. Inasmuch as many materials are more effectively presented by using other techniques, only socially valuable content and activities should be selected for these types of teaching. Socialized procedures of educative value demand a high level of constructive leadership and co-operative guidance, and therefore necessitate the right type of preparation on the part of the teacher.

(8) Visual instruction
- (*a*) Using visual appeals intelligently to stimulate interest and self-expression on the part of the children.
- (*b*) Preparing visual materials, such as hand slides, charts, graphs, maps, pictures, posters, objects, and specimens.
- (*c*) Operating lantern slides, motion picture projectors, duplicating machines, printing outfits, and other visual materials.
- (*d*) Displaying suitable materials that will further stimulate interest among the children.
- (*e*) Utilizing visual experiences to bring within the comprehension of the children concepts, contacts, and information that are not available to the group in any other form.
- (*f*) Enriching the curriculum through the use of a wide variety of visual materials and pictorial experiences.

The use of a wide variety of visual aids would help to bring about a broader and more flexible curriculum, so essential in our complex social structure. Prospective teachers should gain specific knowledge of illustrative techniques and should have experience in the correct use and care of various types of visual aids, such as silent and talking motion pictures, flat pictures, stereographs, cartoons, objects, globes, maps, charts, graphic materials, posters, newspapers, periodicals, and exhibits. They should know the sources of supply for various types of visual aids—illustrative materials and projection apparatus.

d. Utilizing the more fundamental types of instruction that require considerable skill on the part of the teacher.

(1) Assimilation of the ideas of an author
- (*a*) Developing purposeful and effective study techniques for assimilating the ideas of an author.
- (*b*) Helping children to assimilate the ideas of an author.

(2) Drill lessons and exercises
- (*a*) Making drill work functional and meaningful to children.

      (*b*) Applying economical and effective drill techniques suitable to the children to be taught.

Most educators agree that some drill work is essential to produce perfection in the necessary skills; and that wholesome attitudes toward drill work should be developed. Certain habits and skills, which may be most economically automatized through drill, require that student-teachers obtain at least elementary proficiency in the application of various types of drill techniques.

(3) Exposition methods, including story telling

      (*a*) Imparting information to children by means of exposition.

      (*b*) Describing, explaining, illustrating, and interpreting different types of materials on the children's level of understanding.

      (*c*) Telling, reading, and interpreting stories and poems to children; presenting fairy tales, fiction, folklore, mythology, biography, hero tales, and narratives in connection with literature and the social studies—geography, history, and citizenship.

(4) Inductive-deductive types of procedures

      (*a*) Determining types of materials that could be effectively developed by inductive-deductive procedures.

      (*b*) Applying inductive-deductive procedures in developing certain concepts and rules in connection with such subjects as arithmetic, geography, language, and spelling.

(5) Memorization of materials

      (*a*) Applying effective modern techniques pertaining to the memorization of materials in the elementary grades.

      (*b*) Guiding children in memorizing interesting and suitable selections in literature and music.

      (*c*) Helping children to memorize important phases of subject-matter as a means to an end, rather than as an end in itself.

(6) Question and answer procedures

      (*a*) Formulating and asking stimulating, significant, thought-provoking, intelligent, and suitable questions.

      (*b*) Answering questions on the language level of the children being taught.

      (*c*) Recognizing and using the children's answers and responses as a basis for further work.

(7) Review work and reorganization of old knowledge

      (*a*) Making review work purposeful and interesting to the children being taught.

      (*b*) Teaching various types of review lessons, each of which requires different techniques and activities.

(*c*) Guiding children in reorganizing materials of instruction for review purposes.

(8) Supervised or directed study

(*a*) Utilizing assignments as effective guides for study.

1. Adapting assignments to abilities, interests, and needs of individual children and the group.
2. Assisting children in developing proper conceptions of and desirable attitudes toward assignments.
3. Determining, with the co-operation of the children in a group, methods for attacking assignments.
4. Guiding children in initiating their own assignments.

(*b*) Providing for purposeful pupil activity during independent study periods as well as for class work.

(*c*) Helping children to develop proper techniques for reference work.

1. Directing children in making surveys of suitable materials and available equipment to be used in carrying out activities.
2. Guiding children in finding, collecting, assembling, and selecting materials.
3. Directing children in learning the use of the library.
   a. Explaining how to use card indexes, card slips, *The Reader's Guide,* and encyclopedias.
   b. Showing children how to find reference books, current magazines, and bound volumes of periodicals.
4. Directing children in learning economical and effective ways in which to use books.
   a. Teaching children how to take care of books.
   b. Guiding children in finding and using the essential parts of a book, i.e., title, author, illustrator, publisher, date of publication, pages, table of contents, chapter headings, index, glossary, footnotes, and marginal notes.
   c. Guiding children in making effective use of different types of books and recorded matter.
   d. Leading children to form the habit of searching in various references for related materials.
   e. Guiding children in judging the validity and reliability of materials and information.

(*d*) Helping children, especially those in the intermediate grades, to develop some skill in the following specific study habits: deciding what is to be done; studying with some definite aim in view; concentrating on the work at hand; organizing subject-matter; discriminating between essentials and nonessentials in subject-matter; connecting ideas in their proper relationships; searching for information through thoughtful and reflective reading; outlining and recording useful materials and information;

assimilating the ideas of an author; memorizing important phases of subject-matter; formulating summaries and conclusions; verifying conclusions drawn; maintaining critical attitudes toward materials studied; and correcting errors made in their own work.

(e) Leading children to make economical and effective use of time during class and study periods.

(9) Textbook work

(a) Using textbooks as guides, but avoiding formal adherence to them in teaching.

(b) Teaching children to make effective use of textbook materials.

(10) Testing

(a) Constructing, administering, and scoring various types of tests suitable to children in the elementary grades.

(b) Interpreting the results of tests.

(c) Utilizing the results of tests for the following purposes: selection, adaptation, revision, or reorganization of materials to meet the needs of the children; selection, adaptation, and evaluation of methods of instruction; evaluation of the children's progress and growth for a specified period of time; and grade placement of children.

5. Teaching a variety of subjects.

a. Teaching the basic skill subjects.

(1) Guiding children in developing situations and conditions from which will emerge the need for habits, skills, and more formal learning.

(2) Helping children to gain mastery of those essential fundamental skills that are within the scope of their comprehension, in the use of which they could manifest spontaneous interest.

(3) Helping children to increase comprehension, accuracy, and speed in such subjects as the language arts—oral and silent reading, language, spelling, and writing; also in arithmetic and number work.

(4) Handling remedial and diagnostic work.

(a) Discovering and diagnosing individual difficulties, problems, and needs in the mastery of skills and habits.

(b) Determining and applying appropriate remedial instruction.

b. Teaching content subjects required in the elementary grades; imparting and presenting content subject-matter in the most interesting, efficient, and intelligent ways within the comprehension of the children.

(1) Presenting and developing units of instruction in the social studies or social sciences—geography, history, and citizenship.

(a) Leading children to obtain broad outlook; presenting each topic in relation to the larger whole of which it is a part.

(b) Directing children in acquiring knowledge about real people living on a real earth; guiding them in obtaining vivid mental pictures of the world in which they live; and helping them to build up certain geographical concepts.

(c) Helping children, especially those in the intermediate grades, to build up concepts of places and of times different from their own; helping them to re-create scenes and people of other places and of other times.

(d) Helping children to develop clearer understanding of the close relation between the past and the present, and between people and their environment; and leading them gradually to gain better conceptions of their own status and place in a constantly changing world.

(e) Leading children to comprehend the interdependence of countries in different parts of the world.

(2) Teaching suitable units in elementary science and health.

(3) Presenting selections and masterpieces in children's literature.

c. Guiding children in the fine and practical arts—music, art, and industrial arts.

(1) Leading children to develop appreciation, imagination, and creative ability through the fine arts.

(2) Leading children to see that art is another language of expression.

(3) Directing children in art; directing them in the use and care of various types of materials, such as cardboard, paper, clay, wood, chalk, crayons, paints and brushes, utensils, and various other types of objects.

(4) Teaching certain fundamentals of music; taking charge of rhythm work; directing children in learning rote songs.

(5) Integrating the fine and practical arts with other elementary school subjects and extra-class activities in carrying out large child activities.

(a) Vitalizing other school subjects through art and music.

(b) Guiding children in manipulation of raw materials and construction of various types of objects.

(c) Applying art and music in the preparation of school assemblies, special programs, plays, and various types of entertainment.

6. Guiding children in applying and integrating materials of instruction—basic skills, content subject-matter, and fine and practical arts—in carrying out large child activities, in organizing their personal experiences, and in giving expression to their ideas.

a. Helping children to understand objectives and purposes of work to be accomplished; leading them to see implication in work to be completed; and inducing them to formulate and set up standards to be attained.

b. Initiating and carrying to completion, with the co-operation of the pupils, large units of instruction which include the integration and drawing together of various phases of subject-matter, different types of activities, and many human experiences within the comprehension of the children; and which provide for active participation on the part of each child in the group.

(1) Guiding children in initiating and carrying into effect such purposeful learning activities as:
  (a) Centers of interest, vital problems, and units of work which will draw upon many phases of human experiences within the grasp of the children.
  (b) Appropriate and constructive activity units which will give color, life, reality, and vitality to the different subjects in a grade.
(2) Directing children in making surveys of what they should do or accomplish during stated periods of time.
(3) Recognizing and making effective use of children's leads, questions, and contributions; taking into account vital experiences of the children and helping them to organize these effectively.
(4) Leading the children to suggest, to choose, and to plan effective methods for working out units or projects.
(5) Leading children to develop sequence of ideas, associations, and experiences.
(6) Encouraging departure from textbooks, thus helping the children to cultivate constructive and critical thinking.
(7) Challenging the children with questions, problems, and difficulties that will stimulate and enable them to evaluate their choices, and to test their convictions.
(8) Leading children to integrate their experiences and information through such activities as acting, applying, appraising, appreciating, associating, balancing, classifying, collecting, constructing, contrasting, correlating, creating, dancing, dramatizing, drawing, evaluating, exemplifying, experimenting, figuring, generalizing, grouping, illustrating, interpreting, judging, listening, memorizing, modeling, outlining, painting, planning, playing, questioning, reading, reasoning, singing, studying, talking, thinking, and writing.
(9) Guiding children in the execution and progress of learning activities that a high purpose may be maintained consistently under changing conditions.
(10) Leading children to assume responsibility in class activities and for progress of work.

c. Balancing teacher-pupil initiative and participation; leading children to be independently active under adequate teacher guidance.

E. Guiding the concomitant, associate, and indirect learnings of the children; guiding children in developing and establishing desirable habits, traits, interests, attitudes, appreciations, and ideals.

1. Leading children to build up desirable personality qualities—physical, mental, social, and moral.

    a. Discovering and encouraging the more desirable spontaneous interests and appreciations of the children.

    b. Inculcating sound mental and physical health habits; helping children to develop habits and attitudes that are involved in healthful living.

    c. Helping children to develop such traits as the following: self-control, self-confidence, and self-direction; adaptability and adjustment to different situations; willing co-operation and participation; constructive leadership; initiative and sense of responsibility; ability to think clearly and independently; thoroughness, accuracy, and perseverance.

    d. Leading children to develop positive attitudes, concepts, habits, and traits through a great variety of experiences suited to their respective interests and capacities.

    e. Helping children to correct undesirable or annoying habits, and to eliminate negative mannerisms.

       (1) Creating opportunities for children to appraise their own traits and tendencies objectively, in order that they may more intelligently cultivate positive elements and subordinate or sublimate the others.

       (2) Utilizing opportunities that arise for helping children to develop desirable habits and traits.

       (3) Interpreting for and discussing with children underlying principles of good social and ethical standards.

       (4) Giving kindly advice to children on personal problems.

       (5) Showing children results of practices that they should not be performing by referring them, insofar as advisable, to concrete examples.

2. Helping children to unify in themselves physical, mental, social, emotional, and aesthetic elements; realizing that any learning must be fully integrated with all other learnings.

F. Establishing proper rapport in child guidance; and building up and maintaining high standards of conduct among the children in a group.

1. Creating and maintaining wholesome teacher-pupil relationships.

    a. Securing the respect, good will, whole-hearted co-operation, and confidence of the children to be taught.

    b. Creating and maintaining a happy, healthful, working atmosphere in the classroom; helping the children to establish wholesome class spirit and the right attitudes toward the school work.

2. Establishing desirable relations among the children in a group; developing a spirit of co-operation, harmony, happiness, and security among the children.

3. Managing and controlling children; and handling discipline.

   a. Managing and controlling children in various types of situations.

   b. Directing children in such groupings as:

      (1) Individualized instruction.

      (2) Small groups.

      (3) Large groups.

      (4) Two or more groups in a classroom at one time.

      (5) Heterogeneous groups.

   c. Dealing with problems of child behavior; and handling remedial discipline of children.

      (1) Eliminating as far as possible any conscious consideration of discipline by directing effort and attention towards the ends to be achieved.

      (2) Finding a happy medium between the too formal and too informal types of discipline; drawing the line between true freedom and license.

      (3) Appealing to the best in each child.

      (4) Handling remedial discipline.

         (*a*) Seeking the cause of maladjustment in a child in light of the whole individual and the whole situation.

         (*b*) Developing an appreciation of the forces at work that frequently cause a child to seek satisfaction in socially unaccepted ways.

         (*c*) Seeking a child's viewpoint in seeing through problems.

         (*d*) Adjusting treatment to each child, but without any appearance of partiality and without violating previously established policies.

         (*e*) Managing situations so that approved reactions of conduct yield satisfying results and that undesirable ones are made annoying to the child; removing from the necessary disciplinary measures that which provides any satisfaction to the individual or group concerned.

         (*f*) Providing a variety of socially approved activities for the disciplinary-problem child; helping the unadjusted individual to find his place in the social group.

      (5) Maintaining high standards of conduct through the willing co-operation of the children in a group.

         (*a*) Establishing, in co-operation with the children, certain desirable rules of conduct.

         (*h*) Settling disciplinary situations by obtaining the co-operation of the children.

G. Dealing with the principal problems of schoolroom management and routine.

   1. Helping to create in the children an awareness of the school environment; securing their co-operation in caring for physical and mechanical factors of the classroom that contribute to the teaching and learning processes.

    a. Safeguarding the physical welfare of the children, and familiarizing them with established standards in the care of the physical factors of the classroom.

      (1) Maintaining proper ventilation, heating, and lighting.

      (2) Arranging the most advantageous seating of the children in a classroom; adjusting seats and desks to meet individual needs of children.

      (3) Administering first aid when necessary.

    b. Keeping the classroom attractive, clean, and interesting.

      (1) Attending to and performing schoolroom housekeeping.

      (2) Guiding children in making and keeping the schoolroom attractive and clean; directing them in arranging artistically such things as furniture, fixtures, books, materials, flowers, exhibits, and decorations.

      (3) Guiding children in decorating the classroom or assembly hall for holidays or special occasions.

    c. Directing children in cleaning, storing, and otherwise caring for various types of materials, supplies, and apparatus.

    d. Preparing and arranging bulletin board materials; directing children in performing these activities.

    e. Taking charge of the selection and display of children's work, and the exhibition of project work and collections.

2. Preparing blackboard work; writing on blackboards.

3. Taking charge of such routine factors as:

    a. Distributing and collecting materials in the classroom.

    b. Dismissing children at intermissions.

(II) *Contacts with Children's Extra-Class Activities*

It is highly essential that prospective teachers for the elementary grades obtain rich experiences in connection with activities that are commonly termed "extra-class," since these play such an important part in the life and interests of children in the modern elementary school. Student-teachers should make active efforts to secure contacts with as many such activities as possible and to equip themselves for this work; for the mastery of the necessary techniques involved in originating, planning, guiding, and directing extra-class functions requires a thorough background of experience and child study—more than can be obtained through perfunctory attendance at these affairs or through casual contacts. This need for preparation is further emphasized by the tendency on the part of our more progressive schools to incorporate these "extra-class" activities into the regular school program.

It is recommended that student-teachers obtain experience in as many as possible of the following activities, most of which should grow out of and should help to enrich the regular school work and fulfill definite child needs.

A. Making effective use of school journeys, excursions, and field trips.
1. Guiding the children in planning, organizing, and participating in excursions and field trips.
2. Utilizing school journeys and field trips for the purposes of:
    a. Interrelating the life in and out of school.
    b. Helping the children to know the world in which they live.
       (1) Guiding them in securing direct contacts with industries, occupations, practices, and customs.
       (2) Helping them to understand better the interdependence of peoples, places, and countries.
    c. Vitalizing, enriching, and improving the quality of instruction.
       (1) Initiating, stimulating, and promoting interest in connection with school activities.
       (2) Integrating the various school subjects.
       (3) Making visual-sensory materials easily available.

B. Obtaining adequate experience in the various activities involved in children's assemblies, programs, pageants, festivals, and other similar forms of extra-class activities.
1. Guiding children in originating, planning, and staging assembly presentations and programs.
    a. Supervising programs that have been direct outgrowth of classroom activities.
    b. Guiding children in originating and producing programs around special problems or topics.
    c. Directing children in presenting special day, week, and holiday programs.
2. Guiding children in planning and presenting pageants centered around geography, sacred and secular history, international relations, topics of civic interest—such as patriotism and safety first—and other fields of interest.
3. Directing children in planning, preparing for, and carrying out activities in connection with festivals—holiday and seasonal.
4. Assisting with exhibitions, contests, meets, and other extra-class activities staged by departments of the elementary school—music, art, language arts and dramatics, and physical education.

C. Serving in the capacity of directors, counselors, or advisers in a variety of children's in-school and out-of-school extra-class activities.
1. Directing and participating in children's organizations.
    a. Guiding children in club work—book and literary clubs, citizenship and safety-first clubs, stamp and other hobby clubs.
       (1) Serving as counselors to children's clubs.
       (2) Assisting, as need arises, in the organization of new groups.

      b. Assisting in the direction of children's orchestras, bands, glee clubs, operettas, and other individual and group musical activities.
2. Directing the children in various phases of physical education and recreational activities.
      a. Directing group and team games, dancing, posture work, and relaxation exercises.
      b. Supervising children during recess and other intermissions.
3. Guiding children in planning and taking part in general social functions.
      a. Counseling with children in planning room and school parties.
      b. Chaperoning children's school parties, picnics, and other social functions.
4. Assisting with children's school publications.
5. Supervising lunch rooms and cafeteria.

(III) *Activities Pertaining to the Development of Desirable Teaching Personality*

Modern education recognizes a broader responsibility than that of simply disseminating information. The accomplishment of its purpose in helping the children to meet successfully life situations involves the physical, emotional, social, and moral aspects of life as definitely as the intellectual. The responsibility of the teacher to the children for guidance, in relating such diversified aspects of life, renders the development of desirable teaching personality an issue of paramount importance in teacher-education. The influence of the teacher in determining the atmosphere of the teaching and learning environment becomes the more significant when due consideration is given his or her position, as evaluated by the child.

It is as much the function of the teachers college to promote personality development as to furnish adequate academic and professional backgrounds. Advantage should be taken of every instrumentality that will contribute to the development of well-integrated personality. The entire elementary curriculum should furnish a great variety of situations that will exercise and strengthen character, and that will help to develop superior personality traits; for it is only through activity that personality is made evident and provided opportunity for growth, and it is only through rich and full living that prospective teachers will develop the well-rounded personalities that are essential to successful teaching.

The effectiveness of teacher-preparation in fostering the development of the ideal teaching personality will be largely determined by the natural endowments and cultural backgrounds of the prospective teachers; the success with which diagnosis, remedial measures, and guidance are provided and adjusted to the needs of each student; and the intensity and intelligence with which each individual takes advantage of all opportunities for progress and improvement. The fundamentals of equipment with which students enter their teacher-preparatory work should comprise: high mentality, a sound body, strong character, personal integrity, and those interests and attitudes of mind that will permit the realization of their maximum possibilities. A very high level of personality development on the part of the teacher is necessary before there can be inculcated in the child habits of straight and substantial thinking, wholesome attitudes toward and constructive uses of leisure, and the fundamental principles for developing and safeguarding physical, mental, and social well-being. Such a stage of progress can be attained only through the associate and simultaneous development on the part of the teacher of vigorous health, broad and profound scholarship, intellectual curiosity, worthy professional principles and interests, skill in the art of teaching, desirable habits and traits, high ideals and standards, and wholesome attitudes. It is required of prospective teachers, who are to instruct and guide children, that they become well-integrated personalities and forceful characters—emotionally stable, mentally alert, physically fit, aware of their potentialities and limitations, and sufficiently acquainted with the work of the world and with a representative cross-section of humanity to secure the necessary perspective of their individual importance to society.

Although the development of a well-rounded and well-balanced personality should be an integral part of all other activities, the following are recommended as being particularly helpful in contributing to the development of personality:

A. Setting up objectives and goals to be attained in personality development.

B. Studying and analyzing personality traits.

    1. Interviewing faculty members and other interested people.

        a. Discussing personal problems with critic teachers and other faculty members.

        b. Developing a spirit of friendliness and good will between student-teachers and faculty members.

        c. Accepting constructive criticisms in the right spirit, and being receptive to suggestions.

2. Making personality studies.
   a. Approaching personality study through analysis of traits of others.
      (1) Studying biographies of some great teachers.
      (2) Studying and analyzing personality traits of successful teachers and of outstanding people in various fields.
      (3) Endeavoring to determine what qualities of character and personality helped to make these people successful.
   b. Making studies of their own personality traits.
      (1) Analyzing and diagnosing their own personalities in light of the principles and objectives of modern education.
      (2) Evaluating their own personality traits by use of rating devices.
         (a) Discovering strong and weak points in their own personalities by means of definite check lists.
         (b) Evaluating and rating their own personality traits with the aid of objective measurements, such as personality rating forms.
         (c) Utilizing standards and criteria for determining the progress made in personality development.

C. Attaining certain desirable goals in personality development by means of definite instruction or other effective media.
   1. Securing individual help and instruction.
   2. Applying any necessary corrective measures for overcoming deficiencies in physical equipment—motor co-ordination, carriage, posture, voice, hearing, sight, teeth, complexion, and general health.
   3. Making such adjustments as are recommended in the interest of increasing personal attractiveness.
      a. Exercising care in the details of grooming.
      b. Developing taste and judgment in the selection and wearing of clothes.

D. Building up personality and character of high order by living a full, rich, and well-balanced life.
   1. Living in wholesome, pleasant, and cultural environment.
   2. Setting up high standards of excellence in workmanship; endeavoring to achieve high quality of work—academic, professional, and vocational.
   3. Taking initiative and assuming responsibility in connection with a variety of in-school and out-of-school situations.
   4. Making contacts of a cultural nature.
      a. Associating with cultured people through reading, conferences, and personal contacts.
      b. Attending functions of intellectual, social, and aesthetic value, such as:
         (1) Lectures and chautauquas.
         (2) Fairs, exhibits, and expositions of local, national, and international scope.

    (3) Operas, concerts, and other musical programs.

    (4) Social functions and activities: luncheons, teas, dinners, banquets, receptions, dances, and parties.

    (5) Theaters, plays, and high grade moving pictures.

c. Participating in activities of a physical nature, such as:

    (1) Various athletic meets and contests.

    (2) Activities of athletic organizations.

    (3) Games and sports—archery, ball games, crew, golf, hiking, polo, riding, swimming, tennis, track, and games of various types.

d. Participating in the extra-class organizations and activities of the teachers college, such as:

    (1) Clubs, honor groups, sororities and fraternities.

    (2) Musical, artistic, and dramatic productions and activities.

    (3) Assembly programs.

    (4) Publications.

    (5) School social and recreational functions.

e. Making effective use of the press and the radio.

f. Traveling at home and abroad.

    (1) Taking journeys, excursions, and field trips.

    (2) Visiting places and structures of interest—civic, historic, geographic, scenic, and scientific.

5. Co-operating with and participating in the work of religious, civic, social, and philanthropic organizations of the community; exercising constructive leadership in some of the affairs of community life.

6. Securing, through frequent and sympathetic association—vicarious and actual—with as great a variety of personalities and in as great a variety of situations as possible, proper concept and perspective of individual endowments and personal importance.

7. Utilizing reading, cosmopolitan social and professional contacts, and thoughtful discussion with intelligent people from many walks of life as means for developing worthy social qualities and attitudes, such as altruism, co-operation, open-mindedness and tolerance, willingness to accept and discharge obligations and responsibilities, respect for properly constituted authority, and constructive criticism of political policies and economic conditions.

(IV) *Activities Involved in Making Contacts with the Staff-Personnel*

The establishing of proper relations with the staff-personnel of a school system is of fundamental importance to the success of the work of student-teachers as well as to that of teachers in the field. The need for fellowship on a professionally desirable basis becomes imperative especially in those teacher-preparing institutions where co-operative laboratory schools are used for responsible teaching and where the critic teachers in charge are not regular members of the college staff; but the necessity for maintaining relations acceptably in such schools gives rise to practical experiences that are invaluable in preparing prospective teachers to cope successfully with personnel problems that they will later meet in the field.

The following are suggested as effective means by which student-teachers could obtain contacts with the staff-personnel of any school system:

A. Developing habits of willing helpfulness and active co-operation by participating in all of those activities that provide opportunities for sharing the functions of the staff-personnel.

   1. Assisting staff members in the performance of routine and clerical duties.

      a. Assisting in caring for school property.
      b. Helping faculty members in the preparation of records and reports.

   2. Co-operating reciprocally with the personnel of the school in various types of extra-class activities.

      a. Working on various types of committees.
         (1) With the faculty members.
         (2) With the student-teachers.
      b. Participating in educational research work.
      c. Assisting in the revision of courses of study and syllabi.

   3. Working with faculty members in their general advisory capacities—personal, social, and professional—and as special advisers of school organizations.

B. Attending and participating in conferences and faculty meetings.

   1. Meeting in conferences between faculty members and student-teachers.

   2. Attending regular faculty meetings of the school in which the student-teaching is done.

   3. Taking active part in general conferences.

C. Contacting faculty members of the school system in a variety of social and recreational activities.

(V) *Activities Pertaining to the Administrative Phases of Elementary Schools*

The proper execution of the offices of an elementary teacher, involving as it does the performance of so many functions other than instructional, creates a necessity for gaining some familiarity with the various phases of school administration. The expanding movement toward centralization of schools adds impetus to this need, although the intelligence with which teachers administer their work and co-operate with their administrative superiors—in whatever type of organization—depends upon their comprehension of the fundamentals of the school set-up.

The following is a list of suggested activities of an administrative nature of which student-teachers should be made conscious and in which they should participate as fully as possible, in the interest of augmenting their usefulness and efficiency in the field.

A. Gaining acquaintance with such component parts and physical factors of the whole school system as the school plant, equipment, available educational facilities, school staff, and student body.

B. Gaining an acquaintance with the policies and practices of general school administration.

    1. Investigating such administrative phases of a school system as:
       a. Administrative plans and policies.
       b. Organization and management.
       c. Underlying principles and philosophy.

    2. Studying such factors essential to classroom administration as:
       a. Classroom conditions and needs.
       b. Size of classes.
       c. Basis for grouping of pupils.
       d. Availability of supplies.
       e. Recency of textbook adaptations and modernity of equipment.

    3. Studying the school laws concerning elementary education and child welfare.
       a. Gaining understanding of the qualifications, duties, and rights of teachers in the elementary field.
       b. Studying the relative rights of parents and children.
       c. Becoming familiar with the laws in connection with compulsory attendance, child welfare and health, and employment.

C. Developing an intelligent understanding of activities and problems involved in curriculum construction by means of analytical approach to curricular studies.

    1. Investigating and studying various phases of curriculum construction, such as:
       a. Basic and general principles underlying curriculum building.
       b. Objectives, both general and specific.
       c. Content materials, activities, and teaching techniques for elementary grades.
       d. Procedures that might be utilized; and factors that might influence the construction or revision of the curriculum.
         (1) Modern progressive practices in curriculum construction.
         (2) Significant educational points of view and their applications to curriculum-making.

(3) Contributions of recent curricular investigations and experimental studies.

e. Problems relating to the curriculum.

f. Social and psychological factors involved in curriculum making.

g. Recent changes made in the curriculum as a result of the complexity of modern life.

2. Evaluating the curriculum in light of its suitability and efficiency in the local administrative set-up.

D. Participating as far as possible in school administration.

1. Utilizing child-accounting techniques.

a. Grading papers, notebooks, and tests.

b. Keeping records of children's progress by means of charts, graphs, and tables; recording results of classwork and tests; and noting pertinent personal information about children.

c. Making out report cards.

2. Making reports and keeping records of an administrative nature.

a. Keeping daily, monthly, and annual attendance records.

b. Making general school reports.

c. Compiling and filing children's records in permanent form.

3. Preparing class schedules and daily programs.

4. Taking inventories of supplies and equipment; requisitioning materials; and purchasing and sending for essentials.

5. Co-operating with the school authorities in carrying out the policies of the school system.

(VI) *Contacts with Community Activities*

The activities and functions of the elementary school are so inextricably interwoven with community life that teachers who wish to render the most successful and satisfactory service must inevitably participate in at least a minimum of community affairs. It is right that those to whom are entrusted so largely the care and education of the children of the community should concern themselves with the processes and vicissitudes of community life. In fact, elementary education falls short of materializing its potentialities to that degree in which it fails to obtain an active interest in and an intelligent understanding of the needs, problems, activities, and ideals of the community.

The activities suggested below are representative of those of which student-teachers should be made conscious and in which they might participate. Their participation, however, should depend upon the suitability of the given activity in relation to the situation at hand

and in relation to the student-teacher in question. It is probable that no one community or teaching personality would admit of participation in all of these activities during student-teaching courses, but it is recommended that as wide a variety of experiences be obtained as is expedient.

A. Interrelating the school and other agencies in the community.
  1. Studying the relation of the teacher to the community.
  2. Surveying community resources and needs.
     a. Becoming acquainted with the community resources available for educative purposes.
     b. Obtaining information relative to service agencies in the community; contacting proper officials to know where to obtain medical aid and relief for needy children in the school.
     c. Studying the relation of social agencies of the community to the needs of the children in social life.
     d. Studying the interplay of home, school, and community in relation to social needs.
  3. Adapting the school work to the community needs and interests.
  4. Incorporating into the school program educational opportunities offered by other community educational agencies.
  5. Relating the activities of the school curriculum to activities outside the school.

B. Becoming an integral part of the life of the community.
  1. Making contacts with, participating in, or contributing to such community enterprises and leading centers of interest as:
     a. Religious organizations—church, Sunday School, young people's meetings.
     b. Cultural and social clubs and activities of the community—displaying special talents; speaking before community gatherings; or participating in enterprises of cultural and social values.
     c. Civic affairs—co-operating with local authorities in promoting safety education and law enforcement; participating in programs looking toward community betterment.
     d. Recreational programs and activities.
     e. Welfare organizations—Red Cross, social welfare, relief or benefit programs.
     f. Business clubs and organizations—projects and undertakings of industrial concerns.
     g. Local fairs and exhibitions.
     h. Adult education programs—teaching night school classes.
     i. Campaigns, drives, and public relations programs.
  2. Establishing cordial relations with parents of pupils in laboratory schools through such means as:

a. Attending mothers' meetings.
b. Participating in parent-teacher association meetings.
c. Assisting in preparing for and attending parents' meetings.
d. Visiting homes of the pupils in the laboratory schools under the guidance of critic teachers or other faculty members.

(VII) *Activities and Contacts Conducive to Professional Growth and Advance*

Student-teachers should be encouraged and provided opportunities to make such professional contacts as are required of successful elementary teachers in the field. Types of professional activities and contacts from which they could derive much benefit are:

A. Cultivating acquaintance with contemporary education.
   1. Becoming acquainted with current professional literature.
      a. Keeping informed on recent educational writings.
      b. Gaining acquaintance with recent professional books in the elementary field.
      c. Becoming familiar with current educational magazines.
      d. Subscribing to one or more educational magazines.
   2. Making studies of recent research investigations and experimentations in the elementary field.
   3. Visiting modern elementary schools.
   4. Making professional contacts with educators outside the teachers college.
   5. Maintaining active interest in and direct connections with established educational organizations.
      a. Attending, participating in, and giving reports on professional meetings, such as:
         (1) National Education Association meetings.
         (2) State meetings.
         (3) County, sectional, or regional educational meetings.
         (4) Local, city, or town teachers' meetings.
         (5) Other educational organizations.
      b. Joining professional organizations, such as national, state, county, or local teachers' associations.

B. Taking the steps necessary to the development of professional poise.
   1. Making the professional adjustments that are required of teachers in the field.
   2. Gaining a working acquaintance with general works in education.
      a. Learning where to find lists of books and materials pertinent to professional topics and problems.
      b. Gaining familiarity with source materials.

    c. Reading pertinent professional materials—books, magazines, bulletins, reports, articles, and research studies.

3. Studying problems of professional ethics; building up a high order of professional ethics.

4. Setting up high professional standards; developing strong professional spirit; establishing wholesome professional attitudes and worthy professional ideals; and building up a sound philosophy of education.

5. Accepting new theories and trends in education critically, and only after thoughtful consideration.

C. Contributing to the further advancement of education through available channels.

  1. Developing a spirit of inquiry and investigation toward problems of teaching.

  2. Contributing to professional programs.
    a. Appearing on the programs of professional meetings.
    b. Participating in committee meetings.
    c. Taking part in round-table discussions and conferences.
    d. Sharing in panel discussions.

  3. Making contributions to educational magazines.
    a. Writing up experiments in the form of reports or articles.
    b. Writing good book reviews.
    c. Preparing professional articles for publication.

BIBLIOGRAPHY

BOOKS AND PUBLISHED MONOGRAPHS

1. ALEXANDER, THOMAS. *Training of Elementary School Teachers in Germany*. International Institute Studies, No. 5. New York: Bureau of Publications, Teachers College, Columbia University, 1929. 340 p.
2. ALSTETTER, MICHAEL LOUIS. *The Elementary Training School Building*. Contribution to Education, No. 67. Nashville: George Peabody College for Teachers, 1930. 103 p.
3. ARMENTROUT, WINFIELD DOCKERY. *Conduct of Student-Teaching in State Teachers Colleges*. Educational Series, No. 2. Greeley: Colorado State Teachers College, 1928. 209 p.
4. BLACKHURST, JAMES H. *Directed Observation and Supervised Teaching*. New York: Ginn and Company, 1925. 420 p.
5. CHARTERS, W. W. *and* WAPLES, DOUGLAS. *The Commonwealth Teacher-Training Study*. Chicago: University of Chicago Press, 1929. 666 p.
6. DAVIS, FRANK G. *A Course in Supervised Teaching*. New York: Inor Publishing Company, 1933. 123 p.
7. FITCH, HARRY N. *An Analysis of Supervisory Activities and Techniques of the Elementary School Training Supervisor in State Normal Schools and Teachers Colleges*. Contributions to Education, No. 476. New York: Bureau of Publications, Teachers College, Columbia University, 1931. 130 p.
8. MARSHALL, EDNA M. *Evaluation of Types of Student-Teaching*. Contributions to Education, No. 488. New York: Bureau of Publications, Teachers College, Columbia University, 1932. 91 p.
9. MEAD, ARTHUR RAYMOND. *Supervised Student Teaching*. Richmond: Johnson Publishing Company, 1930. 891 p.
10. MORRIS, ELIZABETH H. *Personal Traits and Success in Teaching*. Contributions to Education, No. 342. New York: Bureau of Publications, Teachers College, Columbia University, 1929. 75 p.
11. MYERS, ALONZO F. *and* BEECHEL, E. E. *Manual of Observation and Participation*. New York: American Book Company, 1926. 263 p.
12. PRYOR, HUGH CLARK. *Graded Units in Student Teaching*. Contributions to Education, No. 202. New York: Bureau of Publications, Teachers College, Columbia University, 1926. 114 p.

PERIODICALS, BULLETINS, AND REPORTS

13. ALEXANDER, THOMAS. "A Wider Extension of the Content of Student-Teaching." *Educational Administration and Supervision*, 16:352–358, May 1930.

14. ALEXANDER, THOMAS. "A Plan for a Demonstration Teachers College." *Virginia Teacher*, 12:192–196, October 1931.

15. ALEXANDER, THOMAS. "What May Teacher-Training Institutions in the United States Learn from Similar Institutions in Other Countries?" In *National Education Association of the United States, Addresses and Proceedings*. 1932. p. 736–741.

16. ALEXANDER, THOMAS. "Significance of New College." In *National Education Association of the United States, Addresses and Proceedings*, 1933. p. 730–735.

17. ALEXANDER, THOMAS. "New College Program for the Education of Teachers of Social Science." *Educational Administration and Supervision*, 22:447–470, September 1936.

18. ALEXANDER, THOMAS. "Education of Teachers in New College." *Teachers College Record*, 38:1–73, October 1936.

19. ANTHONY, KATHERINE M. "The Harrisonburg Program." *Educational Administration and Supervision*, 17:351–356, May 1931.

20. AYER, ADELAIDE. "Learning Educational Principles through Experience." *Educational Administration and Supervision*, 17:357–362, May 1931.

21. BAGLEY, WILLIAM C. "The Selection and Training of the Teacher." *New York State Education*, 14:219–223, December 1926.

22. BAGLEY, WILLIAM C. "The Future of American Education." *School and Society*, 32:1–6, July 5, 1930.

23. BAGLEY, WILLIAM C. "The Place of Applied Philosophy in Judging Student-Teaching." *Educational Administration and Supervision*, 17:330–335, May 1931.

24. BAGLEY, WILLIAM C. "What Does the Dominant American Theory of Education Imply for the Redirection of the Professional Education of Teachers?" In *National Education Association of the United States, Addresses and Proceedings*, 1933. p. 763–765.

25. BAIN, WINIFRED. "Service Studies as a Technique in Guiding Students to Analyze Teaching." *Teachers College Record*, 32:147–163, November 1930.

26. BARR, A. S. *and* RUDISILL, M. "Inexperienced Teachers Who Fail, and Why." *Nation's Schools*, 5:30–34, February 1930.

27. BARR, A. S. *and* EMANS, LESTER M. "What Qualities Are Prerequisite to Success in Teaching?" *Nation's Schools*, 6:60–64, September 1930.

28. BARRON, C. "Observation School." *Child Welfare*, 25:600–601, June 1931.

29. BELL, HUGH M. "What Do Elementary School Administrators Consider

Important Factors When They Select New Teachers?" *California Journal of Elementary Education*, 2:39–41, August 1933.

30. BRIM, ORVILLE G. "Creative Supervision of Student Teaching." *Educational Administration and Supervision*, 18:333–346, May 1932.

31. BRINK, WILLIAM G. "Internship Teaching in the Professional Education of Teachers." *Educational Administration and Supervision*, 23:89–100, February 1937.

32. BROOM, M. EUSTACE. "The Predictive Value of Three Specified Factors for Success in Practice-Teaching." *Educational Administration and Supervision*, 15:25–29, January 1929.

33. BROWN, H. ALVIN. "Some Next Steps in the Preparation of Teachers." *Educational Administration and Supervision*, 17:161–182, March 1931.

34. BUCHANAN, VIRGINIA. "Training the Elementary Student-Teacher in Curriculum Construction." *Virginia Teacher*, 13:13–15, January 1932.

35. BUTLER, FRANK A. "Prediction of Success in Practice Teaching." *Educational Administration and Supervision*, 21:448–456, September 1935.

36. CALDWELL, FLOYD F. "Challenge to Teachers in the New Education." *California Journal of Elementary Education*, 5:43–50, August 1936.

37. CAMP, CORDELIA. "Some Practices Used in Student-Teaching." *Educational Administration and Supervision*, 23:12–20, January 1937.

38. CANINE, EDWIN N. "The Administration of Student-Teaching in Indiana State Teachers College." *Teachers College Journal*, 2:5–11, September 1930.

39. CHARTERS, W. W. "The Technique of Determining Content of Student-Teaching Courses." *Educational Administration and Supervision*, 15:343–349, May 1929.

40. CLARK, EUGENE A. "Miner Normal School Graded Practice-Teaching." *Educational Administration and Supervision*, 13:48–52, January 1927.

41. CLASS, EDWARD C. "A Plan for Integrating Theory and Practice in the Preparation of Elementary-School Teachers." *Educational Administration and Supervision*, 23:175–183, March 1937.

42. CLEM, ORLIE M. "What Do My Students Think About My Teaching?" *School and Society*, 31:96–100, January 18, 1930.

43. COLEBANK, GEORGE H. "Practice Teaching in the Colleges of the North Central Association." *North Central Association Quarterly*, 3:376–431, December 1928.

44. COLLINS, EARL A. "Value of Practice Teaching in the Training of Teachers." *Peabody Journal of Education*, 12:233–237, March 1935.

45. COOPER, HERMAN. "Education of Tomorrow's Teachers." *New York State Education*, 22:7–10; 74–76, October 1934.

46. COOPER, HERMAN. "Admission to Teaching." *New York State Education*, 23:232–262, December 1935.

47. COOPER, HERMAN. "The Teacher—Her Professional Education." *New York State Education*, 24:348–349; 411–412, February 1937.

48. Davis, Calvin O. "Assuring Adequate Preparation of Student Teachers in Subject-Matter." *Educational Administration and Supervision,* 16: 364–371, May 1930.

49. Davis, Helen C. "Some Practical Problems of the Training Teacher in the Elementary Training School." *Educational Administration and Supervision.* 13:332–338, May 1927.

50. Dawson, Mildred A. "Current Practices in Participation." *Educational Administration and Supervision,* 23:294–306, April 1937.

51. Dearborn, Frances. "A Tentative Plan for Integrating Theory and Practice." *Teachers College Journal,* 2:17–26, September 1930.

52. Devore, Emily. "Improvement of Practice-Teaching as Suggested by Graduates of One Year's Teaching Experience." *Educational Administration and Supervision,* 13:611–624, December 1927.

53. Devoe, George P. "Some Evaluations and Recommendations Pertinent to Certain Curriculum Trends in State Teachers Colleges." *Educational Administration and Supervision,* 22:438–445, September 1936.

54. Dickson, Belle L. "Suggestions for the Improvement of Student-Teaching." *Educational Administration and Supervision,* 17:14–20, January 1931.

55. Distad, H. W. "A Student-Teaching Unit on the Conference and Discussion." *Educational Administration and Supervision,* 23:284–287, April 1937.

56. Donovan, H. L. "Training Teachers for the New Age." *Educational Administration and Supervision,* 19:578–588, November 1933.

57. Eddins, A. W. "Why Teachers Fail." *Texas Outlook,* 14:16, August 1930.

58. Eggertsen, Claude. "Pupil Analysis in Student-Teaching." *Educational Administration and Supervision,* 23:263–279, April 1937.

59. Elsea, A. F. "A Study of Student Teaching." *Peabody Journal of Education,* 7:345–350, May 1930.

60. Elsea, A. F. "Teacher Training that Benefits Both Teacher and Schools." *Nation's Schools,* 8:49–52, October 1931.

61. Engleman, J. O. "Supervised Teaching in the Teacher Training Schools from the Viewpoint of the City Superintendent." *Educational Administration and Supervision,* 13:322–326, May 1927.

62. Evenden, E. S. "The Critic Teacher and the Professional Treatment of Subject Matter; a Challenge." *Educational Administration and Supervision,* 15:373–382, May 1929.

63. Evenden, E. S. "Making the Preparation of Teachers More Professional." *National Survey of the Education of Teachers,* Vol. VI, Ch. III, p. 72–190. U. S. Department of Interior, Office of Education, Bulletin 1933, No. 10. U. S. Government Printing Office, 1935.

64. Evenden, E. S. "Professional Elements in the Education of Teachers." *Teachers College Record,* 37:667–678, May 1936.

65. FITZELLE, A. E. "The Heart of the Teacher Training Institution." *New York State Education*, 20:202–206, December 1932.

66. FOSTER, FRANK. "The Training School in the Education of Teachers." *National Survey of the Education of Teachers*, Vol. III, Part IV, p. 367–401. U. S. Department of Interior, Office of Education, Bulletin 1933, No. 10. U. S. Government Printing Office, 1935.

67. FRASIER, CLARK M. "The Selection of the Student-Teacher." *Educational Administration and Supervision*, 18:673–676, December 1932.

68. GILLAND, THOMAS M. "The Contribution of a Campus Elementary School to a Program of Teacher Education." *Educational Administration and Supervision*, 19:481–495, October 1933.

69. GIST, ARTHUR S. "Important Points of View in Teacher Training." *Educational Administration and Supervision*, 17:269–278, April 1931.

70. GOETTING, M. L. "Orientation of the Teacher for Curriculum Building." *Educational Administration and Supervision*, 21:13–26, January 1935.

71. GRAY, WILLIAM S. "Academic and Professional Preparation of Elementary Teachers." *Elementary School Journal*, 33:33–45, September 1932.

72. GROVER, C. C. "Child Study as a Basis for Teaching." *California Journal of Elementary Education*, 2:80–87, August 1933.

73. HALL, CECILE B. "Studies in Student Observation of Teaching." *Educational Administration and Supervision*, 17:43–51, January 1931.

74. HARTSHORN, HUGH. "The Training of Teachers for the Work of Character Education." *Journal of Educational Sociology*, 4:199–205, December 1930.

75. HATCHER, MATTIE LOUISE. "How to Secure a Functional Relationship Between the Course in Methods of Teaching Reading and Supervised Student-Teaching." *Educational Administration and Supervision*, 20:45–48, January 1934.

76. HATCHER, MATTIE LOUISE. "Qualities of Personality Compared with Success in Practice-Teaching." *Peabody Journal of Education*, 11:246–253, May 1934.

77. HILL, L. B. "Teaching Qualities in Former Graduates as Guides in Improving Student-Teaching." *Educational Administration and Supervision*, 15:362–366, May 1929.

78. HILL, L. B. "A Plan of Directed Teaching." *Educational Administration and Supervision*, 15:448–452, September 1929.

79. HILL, MAY. "The Student Teacher and the Whole Child." *Journal of the National Education Association*, 18:7–8, January 1929.

80. HOLMES, HENRY W. "The Training of Teachers and the Making of a Nation." In *National Education Association of the United States, Addresses and Proceedings*, 1928. p. 897–906.

81. HUNT, CHARLES W. "Some Policies in Teacher Preparation." *New York State Education*, 21:193–194, December 1933.

82. Hunt, Charles W. "The Teachers of Tomorrow's Children." *New York State Education,* 22:608–609, May 1935.
83. Irwin, Forrest A. "The Work of the Teachers College in Preparation for Student Teaching." *Educational Administration and Supervision,* 18:223–228, March 1932.
84. Jackson, R. E. "Some Implications of the Modern Conception in Education for Teacher-Training Institutions." *School and Society,* 42:507–509, October 12, 1935.
85. Jarret, R. P. "How May Teachers Colleges Expand Their Training School Facilities?" *Texas Outlook,* 11:12–13, October 1927.
86. Johnson, Harry C. "An Analysis of Student-Teacher Activity Reports in the Field of Social Science." *Educational Administration and Supervision,* 20:123–132, February 1934.
87. Kennedy, Katherine M. *and* Shannon, J. R. "An Experiment in Directing Observation." *Educational Administration and Supervision,* 17:205–212, March 1931.
88. Klain, Zora. "Student Teaching." *Journal of Educational Research,* 21:394–401, May 1930.
89. Lancelot, W. H. "Developing the Student-Teachers in Traits of Personality." *Educational Administration and Supervision,* 15:356–361, May 1929.
90. Lang, Albert R. "Individual Conferences with Teachers." *California Journal of Elementary Education,* 2:222–225, May 1934.
91. Lawson, Douglas E. "Basic Principles Underlying the Administration of Student-Teaching." *Educational Administration and Supervision,* 23:235–237, March 1937.
92. Leamer, E. W. "La Crosse Launches an Experiment in Teacher Training." *Nation's Schools,* 3:35–41, May 1929.
93. Ludeman, W. W. "Flexible Requirements in Practice Teaching." *Peabody Journal of Education,* 5:18–21, June 1927.
94. Ludeman, W. W. "Project Method for Practice Teaching." *School Life,* 15:179, May 1930.
95. McAllister, Jane Ellen. "Educating the Exceptional Teacher at Miner Teachers College." *Educational Administration and Supervision,* 23:225–234, March 1937.
96. McConnell, Robert E. "Evaluating Student Teaching." *Educational Administration and Supervision,* 17:426–428, September 1931.
97. Mead, Arthur Raymond *and others.* "Advantages and Disadvantages of Campus and Off-Campus Laboratory Schools." *Educational Administration and Supervision,* 16:196–207, March 1930.
98. Mead, Arthur Raymond. "Progress in the Study of Laboratory School Work for the Preparation of Teachers, 1930." *Educational Administration and Supervision,* 17:370–375, May 1931.
99. Mead, Arthur Raymond. "Statistical Data Concerning Student Teach-

ing in Ohio." *Educational Research Bulletin,* 11:69–71, February 3, 1932.

100. MERSEREAU, EDWARD B. "Study of the Virtues and the Faults of Practice Teachers." *Educational Administration and Supervision,* 13:467–475, October 1927.

101. MITCHELL, LUCY SPRAGUE. "A Cooperative School for Student Teachers." *Progressive Education,* 8:252–255, March 1931.

102. MOODY, WILFRED H. "The Effect of Practice Teaching on Educational Progress." In *American Association of Teachers Colleges.* Eighth Yearbook, p. 116–121. Washington, D. C., American Association of Teachers Colleges, 1929.

103. MORRISON, J. CAYSE. "Factors Affecting Teacher Training." *New York State Education,* 19:299–300, December 1931.

104. MORRISON, ROBERT H. "Factors Causing Failure in Teaching." *Journal of Educational Research,* 16:98–105, September 1927.

105. MORRISON, ROBERT H. "The Demonstration School as a Factor in Integrating the Professional Education of Teachers." *Educational Administration and Supervision,* 20:115–121, February 1934.

106. MORRISON, ROBERT H. "The Demonstration School as a Factor in Integrating the Professional Education of Teachers." *Educational Administration and Supervision,* 23:225–235, March 1937.

107. MOSSMAN, LOIS COFFEY. "Induction into Teaching." *Educational Administration and Supervision,* 16:503–506, October 1930.

108. MURRA, WILBUR F. "Induction of Student-Teachers by Participation." *Educational Administration and Supervision,* 20:26–34, January 1934.

109. MYERS, ALONZO F. "The Course in Observation and Participation in Its Relationship to Courses in Principles of Teaching, Methods, School Management, etc." *Educational Administration and Supervision,* 14: 404–412, September 1928.

110. NELSON, ESTHER MARION. "Student Teaching in Maryland State Normal School at Salisbury." *Educational Administration and Supervision,* 15:457–467, September 1929.

111. NORTON, JOHN K. "Demonstration Teaching." *Research Bulletin of the National Education Association,* 7:332–338, November 1929.

112. NULTON, LUCY. "Analyzing and Criticizing Student Teaching in the Early Grades." *Peabody Journal of Education,* 6:15–23, July 1928.

113. ORR, MILTON LEE. "The Administration of the Training School and of Student Teaching." *Educational Administration and Supervision,* 16: 147–151, February 1930.

114. PAYNE, BRUCE R. "Ten Years of Progress in the Service Rendered by Normal Schools and Teachers Colleges." In *American Association of Teachers Colleges.* Yearbook, 1928. p. 82–86. Washington, D. C., American Association of Teachers Colleges.

115. REINHART, EMMA. "Distribution of Student-Teachers' Time." *Educa-*

tional Administration and Supervision, 19:696–700, December 1933.

116. REYNOLDS, H. M. "Demonstration School and the Administrative Staff." *School Executives Magazine,* 49:134–135, November 1929.

117. ROBERTS, H. D. "Practice Teaching in Chicago." *Chicago Schools Journal,* 12:10–16, September 1929.

118. ROCHEFORT, ANNE. "Functional Organization and Treatment of Student-Teaching Activities." *Educational Administration and Supervision,* 15: 383–384, May 1929.

119. RUSSELL, CHARLES. "A Laboratory Technique for Observation and Participation." *Teachers College Record,* 24:344–354, September 1933.

120. RYAN, CALVIN T. "Improving Teacher-Training Through More Efficient Selection and Assignment of Student-Teachers." *Educational Administration and Supervision,* 18:35–40, January 1932.

121. SCHWEGLER, RAYMOND A. "Training Teachers Tomorrow." *Educational Administration and Supervision,* 21:275–280, April 1935.

122. SEEDS, CORRINE A. "An Interpretation of the Integral Program in the Elementary School." *California Journal of Elementary Education,* 3:89–107, November 1934.

123. SHANNON, J. R. "A Comparison of Three Means for Measuring Efficiency in Teaching." *Journal of Educational Research,* 29:501–508, March 1936.

124. SHARP, LAURANCE A. "Use Made of the Demonstration School by the College Teachers of the North Texas State Teachers College." *Peabody Journal of Education,* 7:332–336, May 1930.

125. SHERROD, CHARLES C. "The Organization of Directed Teaching in the East Tennessee State Teachers College." *Educational Administration and Supervision,* 15:685–688, December 1929.

126. SMITH, E. L. "A Critical Analysis of Rating Sheets Now in Use for Rating Student-Teachers." *Educational Administration and Supervision,* 22:179–189, March 1936.

127. SMITH, NILA BANTON. "Student Reactions to the Helpfulness of Training Teachers." *Educational Administration and Supervision,* 20:313–317, April 1934.

128. SMITH, RUBERTA N. "Student Teaching in a Two-Year Curriculum for Primary Teachers." *Educational Administration and Supervision,* 18:47–63, January 1932.

129. SMITH, W. V. "Functions and the Value of a Demonstration School." *Elementary School Journal,* 29:267–272, December 1928.

130. SOUTHALL, MAYCIE K. "Demonstration Teaching as a Means of Helping Young Teachers." *Childhood Education,* 7:98–101, October 1930.

131. STRATEMEYER, FLORENCE B. "Guiding the Student-Teachers in the Development and Use of Principles." *Educational Administration and Supervision,* 17:346–350, May 1931.

132. STRATEMEYER, FLORENCE B. "A Proposed Experiment in Teacher-Training." *Educational Administration and Supervision*, 18:353–358, May 1932.

133. SUHRIE, AMBROSE L. "Standard Provisions for Equipping and Staffing of the Laboratory School Departments of Normal Schools and Teachers Colleges to Insure Adequate Laboratory Experience (in Teaching) on the Pre-Service Level in the Elementary Grades." *Educational Administration and Supervision*, 16:345–351, May 1930.

134. SUPERVISORS OF STUDENT TEACHING. (Report.) Thirteenth Annual Session, Minneapolis, Minn., 1933. 92 p. (E. I. F. Williams, sec'y-treas., Heidelberg College, Ohio.)

135. SUPERVISORS OF STUDENT TEACHING. (Report.) Fourteenth Annual Session, Tiffin, Ohio, 1934. 120 p. (E. I. F. Williams, sec'y-treas., Heidelberg College, Ohio.)

136. SUPERVISORS OF STUDENT TEACHING. (Report.) Fifteenth Annual Session, Atlantic City, N. J., 1935. 62 p. (John G. Flowers, sec'y-treas., Upper Montclair, N. J.)

137. TOWSON REPORT BY FACULTY. "A Plan for the Closer Coordination of Professionalized Subject-Matter and Student-Teaching in a Normal School." *Educational Administration and Supervision*, 16:257–286, April 1930.

138. VAN PATTER, V. E. "The Individual Conference as a Technique in the Conduct of Student-Teaching." *Educational Administration and Supervision*, 23:121–126, February 1937.

139. WADE, N. A. "Distribution of Student-Teachers' Time in Conducting Recitations." *Educational Administration and Supervision*, 17:692–704, December 1931.

140. WILLIAMS, E. I. F. "Certain Aspects of the Use of Laboratory Schools by State Normal Schools and Teachers Colleges, 1933–34." In *American Association of Teachers Colleges*. Fourteenth Yearbook, 1935. p. 126–134. (Charles W. Hunt, sec'y, State Normal School, Oneonta, New York.)

141. WOODY, CLIFFORD. "Implications for Teacher-Training of the Survey on Curriculum Development in Michigan." *Educational Administration and Supervision*, 23:213–221, March 1937.

PAMPHLETS AND UNPUBLISHED MATERIALS

142. ADE, LESTER KELLY. *Provisions in the State Teachers Colleges of Pennsylvania for Laboratory-School Experience in Teaching the Elementary Grades*. Doctor's thesis. New York, N. Y., New York University, 1931. 136 p. ms.

143. CHRYSOSTOM, SISTER M. *An Evaluation of the Current Plans for the Organization of Observation and Practice Teaching*. Master's thesis. Notre Dame, Ind., University of Notre Dame, 1929. 102 p.

144. Cox, Warren W. *and* Cornell, Ethel L. *The Prognosis of Teaching Ability of Students in New York State Normal Schools.* Albany: The University of the State of New York Press, 1934. 59 p.

145. Dickinson, Vera L. *An Evaluation of the Observation and Participation Course in the Teacher Training Program.* Master's thesis. Columbus, Ohio, Ohio State University, 1930. 113 p. ms.

146. Duane, Florence G. *An Evaluation of Practice Teaching from Data Gathered in the United States.* Doctor's thesis. New York, N. Y., Fordham University, 1930. 104 p. ms.

147. Fox, Ethel Katherine. *A Study of the Effectiveness of Participation for Student Teachers in a Specific Situation.* Master's thesis. New York, N. Y., New York University, 1931. 31 p. ms.

148. Garrison, Noble Lee. *Current Practices in Coordination of College and Training-School Work.* Ypsilanti, Mich., Michigan State Normal College, 1931. 26 p.

149. Glaeser, John Henry. *The Supervision of Student Teachers in Normal Schools and State Teachers Colleges.* Master's thesis. Chicago, Ill., University of Chicago, 1930.

150. Graves, Marion G. *Observation in Teacher Training Institutions.* Master's thesis. New York, N. Y., New York University, 1930. 119 p. ms.